ASTROLOGICAL BIOGRAPHIES
(Seventeen Examples of Predictive Insights)

Astrological Biographies

SEVENTEEN EXAMPLES OF PREDICTIVE INSIGHTS

BEPIN BEHARI

MOTILAL BANARSIDASS PUBLISHERS
PRIVATE LIMITED • DELHI

First Edition: Delhi, 1996

ISBN: 81-208-1322-7 (Cloth)
ISBN: 81-208-1431-2 (Paper)

Also available at:

MOTILAL BANARSIDASS
41 U.A. Bungalow Road, Jawahar Nagar, Delhi 110 007
8, Mahalaxmi Chamber, Warden Road, Mumbai 400 026
120 Royapettah High Road, Mylapore, Madras 600 004
Sanas Plaza, Subhash Nagar, Pune 411 002
16 St. Mark's Road, Bangalore 560 001
8 Camac Street, Calcutta 700 017
Ashok Rajpath, Patna 800 004
Chowk, Varanasi 221 001

PRINTED IN INDIA

BY JAINENDRA PRAKASH JAIN AT SHRI JAINENDRA PRESS,
A-45 NARAINA, PHASE I, NEW DELHI 110 028
AND PUBLISHED BY NARENDRA PRAKASH JAIN FOR
MOTILAL BANARSIDASS PUBLISHERS PRIVATE LIMITED,
BUNGALOW ROAD, DELHI 110 007

PREFACE

These biographical studies discuss the application of basic astrological principles in the case of seventeen eminent persons born in different climes and active in different walks of life. They have been selected to show the universality of these principles. The classical astrological texts including allied religious and mythological scriptures have given enough material to reveal the divine forces working at different levels of human individuals, their society and the physical world around them. But these basic principles must be rightly applied and in their inner import understood. They have enough potential to solve many mysteries of human existence and alleviate much of our sorrows and frustrations. These principles cannot be comprehended merely by their superficial studies. One has to penetrate deeper and take an integrated view on life and the process of human growth and unfoldment. That is why astrology is considered *Vedanga,* a limb of the *Veda* or the Divine Wisdom. The present study is a modest attempt to show how it can be done in a practical manner. The readers will find that the method of analysis adopted in these cases could be usefully applied for their self-analysis.

The astrological texts often indicate the same house-division or the planet affecting so many aspects of one's life and in so many ways that many a time they seem contradictory, unrelated and even nonsensical. It is possible to overcome such difficulties if one could transcend the superficial verbal descriptions and try to develop an insight in the root characteristics of various house-divisions and basic impulses radiated from the planets. An attempt has been made in these biographies to show how these characteristics manifest themselves differently under different planetary conjuncture.

These characteristics affect different individuals differently. It is due to variation in the constitution of man and stage of the ego on its evolutionary path. As a result of various deeds performed at different levels of one's existence, every individual continues to evolve and unfold himself towards his archetype. These results are inbuilt in the various components of human personality. The Law of Karma takes care of this at all stages. The difference between a common man and those who have acquired eminence lies in their basic constitution. The common individuals do not have very developed and specialised psycho-mental-spiritual faculties. Such developments are shown in the development of physical and astro-mental sheaths of the individuals along with their coordination with their higher trinity comprising Atma-Buddhi-Manas and their integration in the case of seers and very developed egos. These seers are capable to absorb finer planetary radiations and make use of them to produce super-physical impact. The same planets which affect the common-man in one way manifest their impact on development of seers in a radically different manner because their essential ideational energy is completely modified by the personal radiations of the seers.

But all eminent persons are not spiritually developed seers. They have their specific faculties developed which make them eminent in their special area of operation. It implies that some of their sheaths and energy-centres, *chakras* as they are known in yoga literature, are better energised than in the case of a common-man. It is very likely, and often it is so, that these eminent persons are very ordinary in other regards. These characteristics can be deciphered by a careful delineation of planetary positions in their natal chart. The readers will find that in the biographies presented here, only the chief characteristics of these persons have been examined. It has been deliberate because we aim here to understand the astrological basis for their uniqueness.

A study of this kind is expected to give a new insight in the working of human individuals and the magnitude of height one has to scale. If we approach astrological studies with a view to acquiring self-knowledge, we can find enough material in the present publication. But we should be aware that all our pettiness, sorrows and frustration, lack of insight in life's problems and our various limitations are all purposive. They help us to evolve and integrate our personality better as and when we acquire knowledge of ourselves and causes of their origin and advantages of their alleviation. Many intimate details of these eminent persons given here aim at serving as mirrors for reflecting our own inner conflicts, weaknesses and several hidden qualities which we could also develop provided we tried for the same.

I have been originally very reluctant to present this study to the general readers. But I had to change my mind. Many of my friends and those who saw these studies at their very preliminary stage several years ago suggested to me that they could be immensely helpful and would encourage many individuals to live a more confident life if they could come across these studies. Many of these biographies were even translated in foreign languages and appreciation from practitioners and general readers from all over the world was enormous. This even made the request for preparing in some details a large number of biographies more louder. This warmth encouraged me to consolidate my thoughts on some of the eminent persons who have been widely known. This study, in fact, resulted from interaction with a large number of persons. One can reasonably say that this present publication is the fruit of joint efforts of a large number of readers who have been commenting (and even criticising me severely at times) and goading me to present a consolidated version of my efforts, the editors of several international journals who assured me of the favourable response from their extensive readership, and of the publishers who ventured to publish the study despite rocketing production cost.

I would like to acknowledge my gratitude to Dr. B.V. Raman, the doyen of Indian astrologers and the editor of *The Astrological Magazine,* Bangalore who encouraged me in my studies for the last five decades or so. I am also thankful to R. Santhanam, editor of *The Times of Astrology,* New Delhi for providing valuable space in his extensively circulated journal. I would also like to record my appreciation for Robben Hixson of Passage Press, U.S.A. who extensively made my work known in different parts of the world and assisted in my studies prior to his getting entangled in personal problems and sorrowful experiences of various kinds. (I pray that his afflictions are over soon.)

These exposures have confirmed my view that the common man, all over the world is presently thirsting for practical application of astrological principles. He is still thirsting for Divine Wisdom in spite of technological and materialistic advancement. In this study, I have tried to eschew technical terms as far as possible. So I hope that the general readers as well as students of astrological science may find it interesting. The experienced practitioners of astrology may find much in it to ponder over. And above all, those who are clamouring for some aid to self-knowledge and encouragement for non-materialistic approach to life may find much useful material in this publication. The author would be very happy to interact with the readers.

C-505 Yojana Vihar,
New Delhi-110 092

BEPIN BEHARI

CONTENTS

HINTS AND SUGGESTIONS FOR ASTROLOGICAL PREDICTIONS

Astrological prediction is an onerous responsibility. It can be fulfilled effectively when the practitioner has great reverence for the sacred science. It was revealed by ancient seers to help mankind so that they could attain Liberation making each moment of their life an oblation to the all pervading Eternal Deity. Vedic astrology assumed that the man was made by God in his own image. The man has the unique Divine Spark lying deep within him, but it is covered by several layers of material sheaths. Sankaracharya spoke of these sheaths in great detail in his *Viveka Cudamani,* the Crest Jewel of Discrimination. Very few astrologers attempted to correlate these sheaths with the effects of different planets. The ancient seers who taught yogic practices to their chosen students knew the relationship between these planets and the various *chakras,* the force centres, situated at different parts of the human body. This knowledge is not extensively available in the present time; the astrologers have its basic knowledge scattered throughout the various classical texts. If the significance of this relationship is properly understood, it could reveal some of the hidden laws of life. On the basis of this knowledge, the astrologers could effectively lead their inquirers to a purposeful realization of their individual uniqueness, which is the special feature of the Divinity latent in them.

Each human being, howsoever ignorant and miserable he might be, has the Divine Spark in him. It is always trying to lead him to realize his real-self which is subjected to different births and varying conditions of his existence. Many physical and non-physical forces impinge upon him even if he is unaware of them. The individual's ignorance of these forces does not minimise the importance of these forces. It is the special privilege of astrologers to have a knowledge of some of these forces and understand their repercussions on everyday life. The knowledge of astrology gives to its practitioners an idea of the evolutionary course decided for each individual through which he is guided, many a time unknown to him, leading him towards the attainment of his goal. The life of every individual is very sacred, as it is the temple of God, and the forces impinging upon it are decided with greatest care. The astrologer has to understand the nature of man and his divine mission very seriously and interpret the forces operating on him almost with a sense of awe. When an inquirer approaches the astrologer, he should consider both, the inquirer and the knowledge of astrology as a trust of God, and the opportunity for counselling a special benediction to him.

Every successful prediction requires a good grasp of basic astrological principles. But more than this, the personal life of the astrologer must be absolutely pure. The latter would enable him to peep into the esoteric side of this sacred science and have a better understanding of the significance of various planetary impulses operating at different levels of existence. The astrological prediction is an exercise in perceiving the flow of events in the time-dimension with specific reference to the individual concerned. If the astrologer is himself entangled in his own personal and psychological problems and works under individual psychic, psychological and religious limitations, he will fail to intuit this flow of events. Even if he is not a trained yogi or seer, he has to abandon his personal bias, likes and dislikes, social and religious attachments, as well as his inner urges for self-glorification, which may enter his psyche in many insidious manners.

Many kinds of difficulties of subtle psychological nature arise before the practitioner. There may be pride which may enter his psyche as a result of his correct predictions. He may begin to have a sense of (false) importance based on the social status of various individuals who sought his counsel. Sometimes the astrologer even gets involved in love-hate relationship with his clients. The astrologer has to be very careful of such aberrations. He has to eschew them completely. The astrologer must be like a clear mirror reflecting the divine message for the individual; he has to be a mouthpiece of the super-physical forces guiding the individual to produce in him certain specific psychological orientation for some radical changes awaiting his life. The astrologer should clearly realize that all important events—pleasant or otherwise—are intended to guide the individual towards a *pre-determined* goal. The latter may not be clearly perceived by the individual concerned and it is the responsibility of the astrologer to unveil it for him. The astrologer's primary task is to relate this ultimate goal of the individual's life with the various episodes through which his life's drama is unfolding. In case the astrologer himself is bogged down in his personal problems, he cannot clearly reflect the divine message awaiting the individual concerned.

The astrologer can make effective and helpful predictions when he rightly understands the laws of natural course of human development, that is, he must understand the laws of life very deeply. The world, including human beings, is progressing in an orderly way to realize its archetype. The astrologer has to understand the nature of this archetype set before the individual; each event in the individual's life is intended to indicate and lead him towards this goal. The astrologer has to have an extensive view, almost an eagle's view of the distant past as well as of the ultimate destiny of the individual. The various religious scriptures reveal a little of this view. In this context, Vedic astrology known as *Vedanga* or a limb of the Vedas has special importance.

Vedic astrology reveals the secrets of human evolution and the story of his soul's journey through births and deaths. Its knowledge is essential before a student is initiated in divine wisdom. This knowledge throws light on numerous forces encountered on this path of soul's evolution. An astrologer is concerned with identifying the various trials and tribulations of the path and externalizing them to his clients indicating to them the significance of the events. He has therefore to delve deeper in the mysteries of life and study the process of one's psychological and psychic transformations. This task can be discharged satisfactorily if he has a clear perception of the significance of godhood of man, reincarnation of human beings, the Law of Karma, and the individual's relationship with occult hierarchy and spiritual brotherhood. Without this knowledge, the astrologer may succeed in making correct predictions but will fail to understand their true significance in the life of the person concerned.

Each human being is unique. Being a fragment of the Divine, the spark in him shows his innate divinity which on the surface as perceived on the physical plane is known as his individuality. It differentiates him from his fellow beings. It is for this reason that no one, in spite of the various sufferings he endures, likes to barter his life with any one else in its entirety. He may be willing to exchange a few of his conditions, not the whole of it. This feeling springs from his tremendous faith at the unconscious level in his own inner uniqueness, which is extremely precious to him. In order to deal with total man, the astrologer also has to apply the predictive astrological principles in their wholeness.

The astrological chart represents the total man; it shows the transient nature of man as he lives from day to day, it shows the various events likely to occur in one incarnation, and it also indicates the ultimate goal, the archetype, for the ego. The horoscope also describes the main characteristics and qualities of the individual's various sheaths besides the specific areas which needed special attention. The level of predictions made by the astrologer depends upon his understanding of these sheaths and his ability to pierce them to reach the 'inner ruler immortal' dwelling in his innermost recess. Only then can the astrologer relate the ripples and waves on the surface with the current of life underneath. In fact, this knowledge would enable the astrologer to understand that a large quantum of human miseries, sorrows and frustrations are expressions of the struggle of the inner spirit to overcome different limitations imposed upon it by the impurities of these sheaths.

The mechanism by which the individual ego is led on the path of unfoldment of his uniqueness is usually described as the Law of Karma. Every condition of the individual's life is produced under this law. Each individual weaves his own web within which he is ensnared, and he himself liberates his self from this web. Edgar Cassey, in recent years has shown on the basis of his clairvoyant investigations, the rules under which this law operates on ordinary individuals. Other esoteric literature on the subject deals with the subject in depth, and as the individuals are at different stages of self-unfoldment, the astrologer will require a profound knowledge of this law operating at different levels of human existence.

The planetary disposition in a chart results from the karmic forces operating on the individual. The disposition of Rahu-Ketu axis in a horoscope shows the karmic fulcrum around which all the forces generated by different planets revolve. The horoscope gives a clearer understanding of the individual's struggle at different levels of his existence. In this process, Saturn and Mars—the two *tamasic* planets play a special role. They are the main agents for energizing the impulses generated by the Rahu-Ketu axis. The remedial measures with which many astrologers as well as the inquirers are frequently interested aim at expediting and sometimes overcoming the operation of the karmic struggles of the ego. The astrologer is expected to understand the significance of gems and precious stones, Tantras, various propitiatory observances as well as of psychological orientation in aiding and abetting the egoic struggle.

The Law of Karma extends throughout the egoic pilgrimage till the final goal is attained. Its operation over a limited period is studied with the aid of planetary delineation in a natal chart. The soul is incarnated in each birth with a few of its karmic burden and with the limited task of overcoming some of the impediments already created by his past omissions and commissions. Each birth is only a bead in the long chain of incarnations before attaining final liberation, the realization of individual uniqueness in its full splendour. In this long chain of births and deaths, the individual is sometimes assigned special mission which also takes place within the general limitations of the karmic bondage. During this period, however, the conditions are arranged in such a manner that the completion of the task which is primarily for the growth of the humanity at large, becomes easier. Special patterns of planetary relationships emerging in certain horoscopes reflect this special feature. On successful completion of such special tasks, the ego receives special credit, which however does not necessarily imply a period of ease and comfort.

The astrologer trying to study any specific horoscope is advised to cast his glance to inquirer's karma very carefully. It is for this reason that much importance is given to fifth and ninth houses and to the Mystic Depth represented by second, sixth, eighth and twelfth houses. They show the spiritual urges of the individual as well as his material proclivities opposing the evolutionary forces. They also show the vast reserves of karmic potential which have to be worked out over the various incarnations. The astrologer has to take a comprehensive view of the problems of the individual in order to proffer any effective advice, but he can do so only when he understands the mechanism and miracles of human births, the various decisions taken before the ego appears on this earth and takes his place in a family and a group of persons.

Each individual birth is ordained after much careful deliberations on higher planes. There is much information on the subject in Indian occult literature, but one has to be careful in securing right key for unraveling the meaning of various mythological stories and parables mentioned in the context. It is the spiritual plane on which different divine beings of various degrees of divinity operate and decisions are taken. Many clairvoyant seers and psychic individuals have confirmed the validity of these operations and deciphered the true messages of the mystical occult scriptures. Before an individual is born, the individual soul is consulted and when it approves of the general sequence of events as proposed in its total wisdom, then only it is sent down to the physical plane; he acquires his various sheaths during the course of his downward journey, but before he sets out on his terrestrial sojourn, his memory of the celestial deliberations on the course of his pilgrimage is completely wiped out. The precise moment of his entry into the physical domain is decided according to the presence (availability) of appropriate planetary conjuncture which could assist in the proposed plan of self-unfoldment.

The planets do not cause different events. They merely show the super-physical forces operating on the individual for the fulfillment of the joint decisions taken by the spiritual brotherhood and the ego concerned. When the incarnating ego turns his gaze towards this super-physical realm of existence, it expedites its spiritual journey. The past karmic impediments are made to work themselves out more expeditiously. As a result, the physical life of the person becomes full of struggles and difficulties, while the inner spirit grows in its splendour. The planetary combinations in one's horoscope at this stage become more meaningful. One has to interpret their results very carefully. Sometimes these hardships arise to unveil the individual's spiritual consciousness, sometimes they arise to test the intensity and maturity of spirituality already acquired. Gradually, the individual gains insight and attains clarity of inner perception. Then, he is able to bear his cross more patiently.

The general astrological rules given out in exoteric astrological treatises do not become redundant while studying the planetary impact on evolved souls, but their significance has to be understood from an inner and deeper standpoint. The usual exoteric results should be considered on the basis of special planetary disposition, the special methods of their operation, their relationships with different sheaths of the human personality as well as with the chakras, the force centres, about which the yoga literature speaks a great deal. The planets radiate their impulses throughout the life-span of an individual but these are intensified during the periods of their rulerships. Their rulership is decided on the basis of the position of Moon in an asterism at birth. One has however to be pragmatic about this computation as there are many imponderables related with it. Many astrologers, specially with the availability of computerised horoscopes, very meticulously work out even precise periods of *sukshma dasas* lasting only for a few days or so. This method from practical standpoint is unrealistic. There is no unanimity on precise value of *Ayanamsa,* and even the precise moment of birth is difficult to locate and register. These cannot be established so accurately as to have very fine Dasa-calculations.

The rectification of the horoscope is therefore resorted to but authenticity of any method for the same cannot be vouched. Each astrologer follows his own special method for it, according to his personal knowledge and experience. It is therefore wise to consider these periods of planetary rulership as the rough boundary lines over which one should superimpose the effect of planetary transits. In this connection, special *vedha*-points that is, the special restrictions and obstructions on their effects along with *Ashtakvarga* calculations require to be taken into account. The precise occurrence of any result may differ slightly from the stipulated moment of its occurrence, and the astrologer need not be very apologetic about such marginal variations.

The disposition of a planet depends upon the zodiacal sign in which it is placed, the house-division or the *Bhava* it occupies, aspects it receives, combinations it forms, and its position in navamsa chart and other harmonics. The retrogression of planets and special patterns they form and the inter-planetary relationships they acquire as well as their exaltation and debilitation are important considerations for assessing the egoic maturity or otherwise. Ordinary individuals who still have many of their faculties to mature and to learn many kinds of lessons on the physical plane do not show any special pattern in their planetary relationships. Differences in the location of planets in natal and *navamsa* charts reveal the difference between the latent possibilities and the freedom (possibilities) to release them during the course of any life-span.

The nature of ascendant, its sign and its lord, and the relationship of different planets with it are very important in every horoscope. Unless the ascendant lord is strong, the individual cannot succeed in achieving his assigned goal. Presence of *vargottam* planets in a horoscope assures a high social status, but the strength of ascendant lord will indicate whether the individual has the capacity to bear the strain of an active life. Next, the astrologer should examine the disposition of the *spiritual triangle* comprising the first, fifth and ninth houses. It shows the special merit earned by the individual: his creativity as expressed by the fifth house portends the qualities already acquired and aspirations felt during earlier lives. The ninth house of righteousness refers to meritorious deeds, the planetary beneficence already secured for the individual. These houses provide necessary impetus for spirituality to flower. On the other hand, the *material triangle* comprising the seventh, eleventh and third houses leads the individual towards materialization. Wife and sex relations, material gains and income, and fraternal connections are bondages from which it is extremely difficult to extricate oneself.

The spiritual and material proclivities provide the basic foundation for the individual to operate, but what he will do in life would depend upon the nature of the tenth house. The tenth house is an externalization of the fourth house from which it is projected for a limited duration and for a specific purpose. The fourth house is the eternal womb or the universal womb, the *Hiranyagarbha,* where seeds of future growth incubate in the form of potential and are expressed as psyche in any specific birth from which all urges for activities in a specific birth arise. Unless the basic seeds of the future growth are well preserved and nurtured, the efforts of the individual will go in vain and his aspirations will remain unfulfilled. The astrologer must relate the fourth and tenth houses together in order to understand the purpose of the individual's birth and the possibility of its fulfillment.

Mention has already been made of the Rahu-Ketu axis. It is very important in every horoscope. Rahu represents the nucleus around which all major incidents of a life will revolve. These events will act very deeply on the psyche of the individual. From it will arise certain understanding, frustration, hopes and spirituality. They will operate deeply on the inner plane of the individual. All planets should be related to Rahu and Ketu nuclei; the former represents the area of affliction, deprivation, while the latter indicates the area of spiritualisation, the experiences resulting from Rahu's affliction. All planets should be related to this axis and the specific houses related with them. All events in individual's life become meaningful only in relationship with these two shadowy planets.

More important than the horoscopic interpretation by the astrologer is the guidance and enlightenment imparted by him to the inquirer. Each individual has to bear his own cross. Most of the persons seeking astrological consultations approach the astrologer only when they are baffled and are seriously afflicted with some or the other malady. The astrologer is hardly in a position to wipe out the trouble or even to minimise it; he can however minimise its sting by providing right guidance to the individual. What the inquirer needs is not precise nature of the forecast; he seeks the precise knowledge of the causes that generated the same, the message it has for him, how best he can endure the affliction and confront it in a meaningful manner. It is primarily a problem of psychological guidance from an inner standpoint. The inquirer needs strength and guidance, nourishment and light, which can be given only when the astrologer understands the problem at its root and establishes a rapport at psycho-mental level and allows his understanding and strength to flow to the inquirer. This task can be fulfilled successfully only when the astrologer assumes the role of a spiritual teacher in modern times. It is for such considerations that the Vedic astrology is said to be a limb of the Vedas, *Vedanga.* The astrologer with his understanding of the *Divine Wisdom* and knowledge of the science of planetary influences is presently in a very enviable position. If he understands his own responsibilities and is able to guide the inquirers in enabling them to discover their own uniqueness and bear the cross of their life confidently and with hope, he would have discharged his onerous responsibilities admirably well!

1

RUKMINI DEVI ARUNDALE

Ketu Jupiter Mars		Asc.	
Sun	*29th Feb. 1904* (Rasi)		Moon
Venus Saturn Mercury			
			Rahu

Sun		Asc. Venus	
Rahu	*Amsa*		Saturn
Moon			Ketu Mercury
			Mars Jupiter

The singular credit for declining the offer of Presidentship of the Indian Republic goes to Shrimati Rukmini Devi. It so happened when Morarjibhai Desai as Prime Minister of India requested her to accept the position as it seemed appropriate to him, considering the cultural heritage of the country and her contribution to it. But she declined the offer. She candidly felt that her field of activity was elsewhere, not the statecraft. So she excused herself from this prestigious honour. It showed how clear-headed and well determined she was about her mission in life and her responsibilities. At birth, hardly anyone without divine foresight could predict or anticipate such a future for her. She was born as the sixth child of an almost illiterate mother, though of a distinguished engineer father without any political leanings. Unexpectedly, during the course of more than eight decades of mortal existence, Rukmini Devi passed through several stormy phases of social calumny, public ostracism and even murderous threats. But she remained unscathed. Finally, she reached the pinnacle of glory when the Presidentship of the Indian Republic was offered to her which she found would detract her from her destined goal. An astrological study of such a personality, who having been born in a traditional south Indian Brahmin family did not only marry a foreigner—forty years of age while she herself was sixteen, but she also created a stormy scene by dancing on the public stage—which at that time was considered only meant for temple prostitutes which the ladies of respectable families were not even permitted to witness.

The history of a nation is written in the stars and deeper layers of astrological principles operated only when the recipient of these impulses were appropriately attuned to vibrate to such highly spiritualized currents of planetary forces. The exoteric repercussions of planetary radiations, primarily acting on physical sheaths of the individual and on their immediate outer environment are not obliterated even in the case of highly evolved individuals, but they produce their repercussions in a different manner. The response of the inner being to external conditions depends on many imponderables. It involves the question of inner choice and the determination of the inner being in resisting temptations, a necessary process in spiritual advancement, which depended upon occult attainments, understanding of divine wisdom and clarity of the mission in one's life. It is for this reason that Asita, the royal astrologer in the court of Suddodhan, on studying the birth stars of Prince Siddhartha could not decide whether the royal child would be a mighty ruler or a divine saviour. Even in the case of Rukmini Devi, nobody could be sure that the tiny shy girl would one day be invited to take over as the President of India especially when her career had been non-political, primarily devoted to dancing and composing dance-dramas, and arousing public opinion for animal welfare. But, according to planetary radiations, it is obvious that each movement of Rukmini Devi had been guided and strengthened by supra-physical forces.

Rukmini Devi was born on Monday, February 29, 1904 at Madurai in South India, a quarter of an hour before the midday when seven planets were hovering around the midheaven, only the Moon and the ascending node of the Moon were below the horizon. Obviously, the planetary deities were eagerly watching the arrival of a mighty power—an important messenger of the divinity to shower their benedictions on the person, so that the task assigned to it could be satisfactorily completed. The Sun at her birth had just crossed the midheaven. The Moon which was still trying to reach the nadir point was occupying the third house in its own sign Cancer and *Ashlesha* nakshatra, though in Capricorn navamsa ruled by Saturn. Moon occupies sixth house from the Sun sign. As Moon reflects the atmic radiance signified by Sun, this placement indicated at the very initial stage of her mortal pilgrimage that she had to experience much difficulties though she would receive sufficient support from the divine powers (Jupiter aspected Moon) and display much courage and initiative in overcoming these difficulties.

The disposition of Moon also showed that the tiny girl had much wisdom deeply rooted in her. The Moon at birth was in Ashlesha, symbolised by the serpent; the nakshatra lord is Mercury, but she was born in the second quarter owned by Saturn and the general attribute of the nakshatra is (in exoteric astrology) said to accentuate egotism, *Ahamkara*. Often astrologers predict that the individuals born under such situation would be materialistic and engrossed in mundane activities for one's personal advantages. They often overlook the esoteric aspect of the Nagas, the presiding deity over the asterism and base their conclusions only on the negative aspect of the serpent symbology. The Nagas, the lord of the serpents are the custodians of secret wisdom,

Initiation in spiritual mystic schools, and opening the doors of occult hierarchy; these possibilities are greatly increased if such a Moon received benevolent aspect of Jupiter and beneficence of Saturn. But in a large number of cases, Moon in a weak position aspected by Saturn specially situated in an unfavourable sign and placed in the eighth house is said to produce an immoral character leading the person to establish hidden immoral relationships. In the present case, Moon is supremely auspicious enabling the individual to attain dizzy heights in the realm of spirituality. Moon, Venus and Mars—all the three enigmatic planets which greatly affect one's inter-personal relationships are superbly located in the horoscope of Rukmini Devi to unfold an extreme degree of sensitivity, receptivity, devotion, discipleship, courage, leadership, and transformation of the old fossilised traditional outlook into a dynamic chalice for the downpour of divine benediction. It would be erroneous astrological perception to conclude the association of Saturn and Venus and the combined aspect on Moon, or the association of Mars with Ketu in eleventh house leading to sexual promiscuity or immoral dealings with men and the society. The planetary disposition at birth in the case of Rukmini Devi reveals many deeper principles of astrological prognostication; it would be very interesting to examine in depth some of the special factors influencing the nature of Saturn and Mars.

Mars, the lord of the lord of twelfth and seventh houses, is very importantly placed with Jupiter and Ketu in eleventh house aspecting the sixth house, the house of latent faculties, *siddhis* or occult attainments. It also aspects fifth house—the house of creativity which is owned by Mercury which occupies the ninth house along with Venus, the ascendant lord, and Saturn, the planet of liberation, occupying its own sign. Mars is placed in Uttara Bhadrapada owned by Saturn, the second *pada* (quarter) of which where Mars is located is owned by Mercury, the significator of intellect, writing, and speaking: the asterism itself is said to represent the primary impulse of unveiling the wisdom, leading to *Kaivalayam* or *Nirvāṇa,* Liberation; Uttara Bhadrapada represents the divine impulse under which the 'dewdrop mingles in the ocean and the individual flame irretrievably merges in the universal flame. Mars aspects the fifth house which is detrimental for progeny; it generally leads to abortion. Rahu is positioned in this house which further intensifies the absence of creativity in the physical sense by way of childbirth. Jupiter's aspect on it, specially when it occupies its own auspicious Pisces sign, however, is extremely helpful for the fructification of this house. The result of these contradictory impulses rightly comprehended should indicate that the individual would be creative in an extra-ordinary sense, though on the physical level it would show no result.

The disposition of Mercury—the planet which is often considered an infertile planet, specially its association with Venus and spiritualising planet Saturn would lead to intellectual creation relating to extreme degree of perceptivity and sensitivity which might be *Moksha-dayini*, leading to Liberation. In retrospect, we know that the creative pursuits of Rukmini Devi were upheld throughout the world as highly spiritual, not erotic but extremely ennobling and spiritualising, soothing to the heart and inspiring to the Spirit. One cannot therefore apply the general (exoteric) rules of astrology in every case.

In the present case, the crushing and restricting effect of Saturn under the surveillance of Jupiter, which also happens to be the lord of the zodiacal sign within which Mars is located, completely destroys the sense of I-ness, egotism or *Ahamkara*, and inspires the person to proceed towards that stage of Liberation, spoken of by Patanjali as *Kaivalyam*. Such an attainment is possible only by intense efforts, penetrating insight and tremendous determination, which alone could pierce the "veil of illusion" and dispel all attractions for material attachments. As the lord of the seventh house, Mars must lead to a marital situation with much intense determination, courage, perseverance and externalisation of latent capacities for achieving this goal. Mars brooks no opposition. The goal being clear in sight, whatever the obstacles, it would surmount them whatever may be the personal suffering. In the case of Rukmini Devi, it is well known that her marriage was a stormy affair, which is quite characteristic of Mars, and it led to the outbreak of much opposition, which one may compare with a kind of stormy social upheaval. The association of Mars with Ketu and Jupiter is also significant in this regard.

Jupiter, the teacher of Devas and angels, powerfully situated in Pisces, is in Uttara Bhadrapada—the asterism in many ways connected with important landmarks in the process of enlightenment of Lord Buddha; Jupiter aspects fully and beneficially the Moon which is capable of receiving such beneficial radiations effectively.

Further, it may be noted that Jupiter, the planet connected with religions, temples, divine wisdom and religious rituals is situated in a trine house in relation with Moon. Ketu which is similarly placed in the asterism, and almost conjunct with Jupiter, the distance between the two being less than 2°, reinforces the spiritualising effect of Jupiter.

Ketu, Jupiter and Mars occupy an area in the asterism so closely that they occupy a region about three degrees in longitude; this closeness greatly intensifies their combined effect. These three planets, though retaining their individual uniqueness do not remain or retain their separate identity. Together they become a unique divine impulse. Ketu, as it is, cannot allow any meaningless ritual, yet it will decipher the deeper meanings and significance of every outer religious act which aims at uniting with the inner core of religious practices; Ketu is averse to all shallow philosophies of life and all attachments with the superficial external behaviour. Under its impulse, one would however dwell at the deeper, sometimes subterranean chambers of esoterism. It often makes the individual a recluse. But Mars is different. It externalises the inner attitudes, inner feelings and beliefs which in association with Ketu makes the individual courageous in brave declaration of principles and faith in one's inner convictions about deeper realities of the higher world: it does not let Mars remain a materialistic planet associated with land, bloodshed, accidents, reckless activities, but combined together with Jupiter and Ketu, Mars becomes a philosopher like Giordano Bruno and a scientist like Galilei Galileo. In the company of these planets, Mars completely alters its character. It becomes a fearless planet, always eager to march forward for attaining its spiritual destiny and Moon representing the psyche of the person shows that while there could be no ruffled external behaviour howsoever difficult may be emotional storm, the subterranean dynamism, restless till the goal is achieved would always inspire the individual to proceed towards its destiny. One knows that Rukmini Devi, even as a small girl of fourteen years of age, when she did not know the tribulations awaiting her in life resulting from her bold and fierce decisions, never swerved for a moment from her strong determination.

Mars, the lord of the seventh house, is placed along with its friendly planets Jupiter and Ketu (which is also considered identical with its very nature) which intensify its basic nature. But Mars also gets full third aspect of Saturn which is situated in its own house, and being a *yoga-karaka,* auspicious planet, for Taurus ascendant is generally inclined to do good for the individual concerned. Saturn is otherwise also well located for this chart. It is in *Shravana* nakshatra, which is owned by Moon and as Saturn is in its fourth quarter ruled by Moon, Saturn becomes extremely capable of imbibing the basic impulses flowing through the asterism. The basic orientation of Shravana is towards the great silence on which background subsists the entire scheme of manifestation. The asterism leads one to deep meditation, to listening the cosmic music. The sound of silence can only be perceived by self-discipline in the practice of Yoga. The perception of the voice of silence resulting from the annihilation of personality is a result of Shravana, of listening, in the true sense of the term. Such a listening that Shravana induces leads to a radical transformation in one's personality which requires clear perception of one's true nature beyond the veil of ignorance.

Under Shravana, one begins to perceive the truth of the manifestation concealed in illusory appearances. This unveiling results in the tearing of the old crust of traditional thinking and behaviour and transcending the hard crust of primeval ignorance. It is always a trying experience. Saturn being placed in this asterism, synthesizes the nature of the asterism with its own basic nature and vitally affects Mars and Moon which imparts to them restraint, equipoise, fortitude and the spirit of martyrdom. The Saturn's influence on Mars expressed itself in an extraordinary manner by affecting the marriage of Rukmini Devi with a foreigner against which the entire south Indian Brahmin community revolted, even the life of Rukmini Devi and her family members was in jeopardy. Yet it was this Saturnian impulse radiating the special role of Shravana in cosmic evolution that transformed the shy girl into a fighting rebel which finally transformed the cultural and religious outlook not only of the orthodox traditional south Indian Brahmin community but of the entire country. It was Rukmini Devi's marriage with Dr. George Arundale that the Indian dance-drama and spiritualizing impact of traditional Indian dances and songs are presently recognised throughout the world and is considered a unique contribution of ancient India. It must be recalled that Vishnu is the deity presiding over Shravana indicating the protective and civilisation-oriented activities as a result of which many of the qualities of Saturn are metamorphosed into the sustaining nature of Jupiter, if one may say so; it has also imparted special Buddhic characteristic to Moon.

Saturn is a *yoga-karaka* planet for Taurus Lagna; seven planets gravitate around this planet, and it directly aspects the remaining Moon. And this planet is deeply entrenched in Shravana. The life of Rukmini Devi would therefore turn round this asterism. The deeper nature of this asterism is revealed by the symbol of ear assigned to it. It signifies that careful attention to the divine premonitions and the divine mission for the individual could lead to great revelations. The *Guna*, attribute, influencing this asterism is *Sattwa*, harmony, but with *Tamas*, inertia or sloth, as its secondary radiation wherefrom the harmonious influences of this situation could be channelised for concretisation of the divine impulses. It is Saturn in such a situation that makes the individual really qualified for "initiatory rites" in mystic schools. It is on record that Rukmini Devi was admitted to the *Occult Hierarchy of the World* though we have no means to check the authenticity of such pronouncements, though they have come to us from persons of great integrity and veracity.

Mercury and Venus are two best friends of Saturn and they are closely associated with this planet in the same sign: Venus however is in the second quarter of the Shravana nakshatra which is owned by Venus itself while Mercury is in Dhanistha owned by Mars, and is in its first quarter owned by Sun. This asterism is presided over by the Vedic deity Vasu and its symbol is *mridangam*, drum. This asterism is said to enable a person move towards Adeptship and liberation; when it is directed towards literary and artistic creations, it endows qualities of perfection. The three friendly planets, namely, Saturn (concretisation) Venus (sensitivity) and Mercury (artistic and literary activities), together in the strong and auspicious ninth house, the house of *poorva punya*, past attainments and religious deeds, strengthen Saturn in a very significant manner. Saturn is never considered in regard to such cases as the present one as anything mundane and materialistic. As a personification of Lord Mahadeva, Saturn should naturally release enormous force for occult understanding and attainments. When this kind of Saturn aspects Mars, the lord of the seventh house in a strong way, the marriage of the person is bound to be crucial, non-traditional, spiritually inspired with much artistic and literary sensibilities enabling tremendous courage and boldness in facing the orthodox society. These planets fully aspect the Moon in strength situated in the third house, the house of courage and determination, so it is no surprise that the psyche of the person as well as her action and literary attainments all fully reflect the qualities of Saturn in the ninth house. Saturn is the lord of the ninth and tenth houses, thus becoming *yoga-karaka,* which provides special significance for the success in all activities in harmony with its nature. These include concretisation of supreme ideas into objective images, whether in architecture, sculpture or dance-drama depicting cosmic evolutionary processes.

In the present context, it would be appropriate to consider the nature of the ascendant and the tenth house before we begin to examine how these factors have been affecting the person concerned. The ascendant is Taurus whose lord is Venus placed with *yoga-karaka* planet Saturn in the ninth house. The ascendant is *vargottam* in navamsa, while in the navamsa chart its Lord is placed in the ascendant itself. The ascendant is in Rohini nakshatra owned by Moon in its third quarter owned by Mercury. The deity presiding over this asterism is Brahma, a *prajapati*—the creator of this universe. The symbol of this lunar mansion is the chariot, the means by which the royalty is carried on their entourage and the warrior chiefs go to their battlefields. The *Gunas,* attributes, influencing this area of the ascendant are *Rajas,* activity, as its main impulse and *Sattwa,* harmony, as the subsidiary one. It is under these influences that dignified personages with royal characteristics are born with strong artistic talents. Their artistic creations would be intimately connected with psyche of the individual or reflections of cosmic creative principles. Almost every dance-drama created (composed) and produced by Rukmini Devi reveals enormous amount of originality, spirituality and intense emotion intended to arouse much spiritual aspiration and channellising of Divine downpour.

Rohini, the ascendant asterism is also associated with *Antahkarana*—the inner voice of the individual, and with *Maya*—the creative illusion. Rohini is one of the most misunderstood asterism. It has strong earthiness about it while remaining ever in the centre of spiritual influx. Rohini is said to lead the soul into mundane activities with all its pleasures, attachments, and drunkenness, yet under this asterism the mind principle in man is in its state of exaltation and is able to experience the newness of its ventures. It immerses the individual in worldly involvements but like Balarama, even while indulging in intoxicating situations and bending the world to his whims and fancies, he finally helps his younger brother, Lord Krishna, to unfold the divine mission. Rohini is an incubator of creative potential: it has the quality of the great deep, *Bythos,* where every seed, every idea, is preserved and nourished until the right time for its fruition. Rohini produces deep involvement in sexual relationships which transcend traditional and social boundaries, but these would generally be induced by strong impulses of attachment and a state of intoxication. In spiritual terms, Rohini imparts the ability to "engineer" divine power, while on the materialistic side its chief preoccupation is with social progress, wealth and sensual pleasures. The entire life of Rukmini Devi Arundale has been misunderstood due to the interplay of two diverse impulses of *Antahkarana* and *Maya,* strong involvement with sensual feelings and sensitivity and the inner urge deep down within oneself to be a vehicle of divine inspiration and downpour of spiritual influx.

The marriage of Rukmini Devi with George Arundale—with considerable difference in age, caste, nationality and social status was indeed a kind of infatuation, intoxication and almost a drunken determination which aroused so much opposition from her caste, society and family circles that any one not in the knowledge of spiritual inspiration and other divine factors in this alliance would naturally have considered this marriage an expression of material aspect of Rohini. Yet those who were nearer to her and the psychology behind this marriage knew the strong spiritual determination of the shy young girl in her teens, who was bent upon transcending the social and other barriers in order to harness the creative and artistic potential latent in her which would unlease much of the ancient Indian spirituality. It is easy to understand the working of Rohini in retrospect; at the time of its actual operation, every one was taking sides and only Rukmini Devi had to walk on fire keeping her mind cool and determination of her inner being strong. In retrospect, we also know that the founding of Kalakshetra with which almost every danseuse of modern India at some time or the other had been related with, was founded by Rukmini Devi and it could not have been possible for a long time unless Rukmini Devi went through fire.

Throughout her life, Rukmini Devi's greatest asset had been the voice of her soul (or individuality) and she is very intimately connected with *Maya* as well, as it is evident from the fact that she had been relentlessly working for mundane activities such as the establishment of institutions for training and propagation of dance-drama (Kalakshetra), world youth movement, international centres for the cultivation of spiritual activities as at St. Michael at Huizen in the Netherlands, animal welfare centres such as the Central Animal Welfare Board at Madras, membership of Parliament (she was a member of Rajya Sabha for about a decade) and organization of world vegetarian congress. What is of supreme importance is her concern for other persons without getting herself emotionally involved with them. I have personally talked to persons from the United States, the Netherlands, the United Kingdom, Spain and many belonging to Madras. I have seen Pandit Jawaharlal Nehru's regard for her. I have also known persons whom she asked to leave Kala Kshetra for their permissive behaviour. All of them held her in high esteem. They venerated her almost like a mother. Her compassion, sympathy and anxiety to help and to make others happier were so sincere that she did not need sacred ash around her body or the putting up of an ochre robe to announce her great sensitivity with every form of life around her (Venus) or to be completely unconcerned with her own comfort and possessions. I recall that her quarters in New Delhi was once burgled and she received the news with an expression that the thieves probably needed those things more than she. Such a detachment could come only from such position of Saturn. Saturn and Venus, indeed, played the pivotal role in her life.

The tenth house in her horoscope is represented by Aquarius, whose lord, Saturn, is in the ninth house—the house of spirituality: she is expected to discharge such religious activities with which she had been connected in her past lives. The M.C. falls in Satabhishak nakshatra which is owned by Rahu, the rising node of the Moon and is in its second quarter owned by Saturn—the lord of the ninth and tenth houses and friendly to the ascendant lord, Venus, which is associated with it in ninth house. Rahu is said to be of the nature of Saturn itself, so there is accentuation of Saturnian qualities to be radiated from the tenth house as well.

The field of activities of Rukmini Devi therefore should lie more overseas—in Western countries, and her linkages should be with Western way of thinking and influences. In this particular case, the native owned much to her foreign husband, and to Anna Pavlova, a foreign ballet dancer—most renowned ballerina of her times, who agreed to teach Rukmini Devi even at the latter's advanced age, for she found her body extraordinarily supple for the training. Satabhishak asterism is connected with the sage Valmiki, which happens to be the patronymic of Manu, signified that Rukmini Devi should in some way or the other be connected with the establishment of a certain spiritual dynasty of her own. The establishment of Kalakshetra and the revival of Bharat Natyam from the shackles of temple Devadasis to girls of respectable orthodox families really enabled her to establish a spiritual-artistic dynasty of her own which survived her glory even after her death.

Rukmini Devi was born in a very traditional Brahmin family of Tamil Nadu and any public life for a girl of such a family could naturally create terrible opposition—both for the individual concerned and for her family members. But the lord of the fourth house representing the eternal reservoir from which a portion works out in any one specific incarnation, being the Sun placed in the tenth house moulds the destiny of the individual for the specific birth, and the sign Aquarius which occupied the tenth house has the special characteristic of releasing the universal life in the individual. The *48 Lives of Alcyone* which is a clairvoyant reading of the past lives of J. Krishnamurti carried out by Annie Besant and C.W. Leadbeater reveals Rukmini Devi's past association with a group of spiritual persons, who have been taking their births together for the last several millions of years for disseminating the divine message and for preparing the ground for divine descent. Even in this life, she was born with a powerful ego for a definite task ahead though in a female body.

The purposefulness of her present birth and the strength of her ego are well indicated by her Sun and M.C. being within seven degrees of the celestial orb suggesting tenth house influence in her case to be a very powerful deterministic impulse which could not be transcended by ordinary means. As indicated earlier, Satabhishak in which both the Sun and the M.C. are placed is symbolized by 100 flowers. It suggests that the multidimensional genius latent in the individual must come to fruition.

Such being the strong forces of destiny, the traditional obscurantism could not conceal the latent faculties of Rukmini Devi for long. But, the birth being in *Ashlesha* nakshatra giving a balance of 12 years 2 months and 11 days of Mercury, the period during which she could remain in the family-fold without much sparkle (Mercury is also the lord of second house representing family relations), though the Martian aspect was making the child internally restless. Mars is aspecting both the houses of Mercury, so it is almost certain that the early childhood of Rukmini Devi could not have been all quiet without any upsurge of inner forces, but the channel for their expression was not identified. The moment Mercury main period ended and Ketu main-period started, the voice of rebellion began to brew in, and the shape of the destiny began to clear. Ketu is in the eleventh house, the second base of the material triangle, so the voice of inner determination, *Ahamkara,* was expressed on the mundane plane. Ketu is also associated with the lord of the seventh house, the *Kalatrasthanam,* which happened to be the fiery Mars always precipitating its results with great force, often with violence and much fury.

Ketu also is a planet of early fructification; it produces precocious mind and early flowering of the trees. In the case of Rukmini Devi, Ketu worked itself through her strong determination to marry a foreigner outside her cast at a tender age: she met Dr. George Arundale when she was only thirteen years of age and married him when she hardly crossed her sixteenth year. It was all a very stormy affair but with full support of the heavenly bodies. The eleventh house *inter alia* signified friendship and social life: when Ketu's main period started, the sociability of Rukmini Devi began to unfold and she began to meet persons outside her family circle circumscribed by caste restrictions.

During the sub-period of Venus and of the Sun, her friendship with Dr. George Arundale, who was born with Sun, Moon, Mars, and Mercury in Scorpio fully aspected by exalted Jupiter, enabled herto have a marriage partner for whom her soul could sacrifice much, and Arundale also found in her a perfect companion in spite of her tender age. At that period, Rukmini Devi was also undergoing the 7½ years period of Saturn, when it transits the three adjoining houses near the Moon: a period when almost everyone passes through a critical situation in life and many persons undergo the bondage of karmic marriages. Before this period was over, during the Ketu main-period in the sub-period of Rahu, Rukmini Devi married Dr. George Arundale despite the terrible commotion in her psyche and storm blowing over her family. At the time of marriage, Jupiter in Cancer was transiting over Rukmini Devi's Moon and therefrom aspecting her seventh house—the house of marriage.

Despite severe opposition, the marriage could not be avoided and most of her brothers (Moon in the house representing siblings) fully supported the marriage, though there were some dissenting voices. The marriage however, led to social upheaval, beginning of the process of fulfilment of Rukmini Devi's destiny. Her absence for sometime was thought to cool the atmosphere and social acceptability of the marriage could be more peaceful. When the Venus period started, which also was the period of her ascendant lord, Rukmini Devi's life on the international arena began to take shape. In 1924, she commenced her world tour when she was about 20 years of age.

The major turn of events occurred when Venus, the lord of ascendant's main period started. It began during the middle of 1923, and soon Rukmini Devi became the President of the All India Federation of Young Theosophists, and subsequently, the President of the World Federation of Theosophists. In Venus period, she began her international tours; it began in 1924 itself and within five years she travelled around the United States, Europe, and Australia several times. In 1927, during the Sun sub-period in Venus main-period, she met Anna Pavlova, the famous Russian ballet dancer. Her friendship and inspiration became her life-long mission: through Rukmini Devi it could be possible to blend a synthetic influence of Western ballet enlivened by Pavlova and Indian spirituality brought to it by Rukmini Devi. In many cases, Rukmini Devi imparted even more life and energy to the traditional scriptural and mythological themes. Sun is situated in the tenth house, flanked on both sides by three planets and itself it is the lord of the fourth house representing the Great Deep, the *Hiranyagarbha,* which contains seeds, the potential for their unfoldment in future. It occupies the mystic Aquarius sign owned by Saturn representing the western world, initiated the process of Rukmini Devi's future missionary activities in this birth.

In Venus-Rahu sub-period, Rukmini Devi saw Bharat natyam for the first time, since then her whole life was dedicated, in reviving the art and placing it at its rightful central place of the Indian cultural heritage. In Venus-Jupiter period, she started learning Bharat natyam from well-established masters of the tradition and danced for the first time, *The Light of Asia* representing the life of Buddha before thousands of delegates to the International Theosophical Convention in 1935—where she played the role of the Swan saved by young Buddha, and Yashodhara who in her *swayamvar* selected Buddha as her husband; but suffered immensely in her personal life as Siddhartha, the Gautam had the destiny of becoming Lord Buddha earmarked for him. Rukmini Devi enacted these two roles in an extraordinary manner which required superb sensitivity and poise.

With the beginning of Venus-Saturn sub-period in the early months of 1936, a new phase began in the life of Rukmini Devi. She founded the International Academy of Arts which later became the famous Kalakshetra. In 1936, Rukmini was participating in the second Theosophical World Congress held at Geneva. The Jupiter and Saturn sub-periods during the Venus main period were very momentous for her. The sub-period of Jupiter started on eleventh July 1933 and lasted upto eleventh March 1936 during which period Rukmini Devi lost Annie Besant—her mentor and Rev. C.W. Leadbeater, who greatly helped in her occult attainments. Saturn's aspect on Jupiter had to produce some kind of psychological sorrow, and Jupiter placed eighth from her fourth th house, resulted in some kind of emotional setback for her. Saturn however in the present case has almost become an auspicious planet, which helped Rukmini Devi in concretising many of her dreams, which is a special feature of Saturn. Apart from laying the foundation of the Academy, which later became Kalakshetra, she also contributed vitally to Huizen Centre of Theosophy in the Netherlands which had assumed great importance because of the activities of J. Krishnamurti at that place.

Rukmini Devi was by now, no longer merely concerned with resurgence of Indian cultural heritage, but began to take charge for shaping the spiritual life of a large number of individuals—both in India and abroad. Caste and nationality barriers no longer existed in her activities and programmes. Nonetheless the revival of ancient dance-drama remained her primary mission, which was an expression of her understanding of the universal life-process as revealed through Theosophical teachings. Mercury, the lord of her fifth house and related with educational programmes had its sub-period in Venus main period from the middle of 1939 which made her travel much. Before she left for her south Indian tour in 1939, she gave a dedicated dance performance at the Nataraja temple of Chidambaram, which created a tremendous commotion and public applause. Nataraja being a personification of Lord Shiva (Saturn) in its cosmic form was appropriately the commencement of her future work which began with Alarippu to which thousands of spectators gate-crashed. By 1940, she attained such reputation that her delineation of *Sringara Rasa*—the erotic emotions as spiritual expression of the aspirant soul became superbly sublime without the slighest trace of physical passion and carnal vulgarity. The art critic of the *Times of India* reported that "her dance bears the impression of deep study of the intricacies of Bharat natyam and is in striking contrast to cheap performances. Subtlety is the keynote of her expression."

It was indeed hard labour of the young orthodox danseuse hailing from traditional south Indian Brahmin family that the classical rendering of *Sringara Rasa* was no longer associated with provocative prostitutes, but a difficult and rare attainment even for religiously inclined respectable social elites of the country. The position of Venus with Saturn in Capricorn in the ninth house along with the lord of tenth house could not but give such a restraint, grace and reputation. It was during the Venus main period that the chrysalis could attain its perfect form: it was during this period that Rukmini Devi got her first taste of self-reliance and gained self-confidence. It was achieved however in a hard way: she lost Annie Besant before she embarked upon her artistic and cultural mission for which Mrs. Besant was grooming her.

The Sun main period began on eleventh May 1943 and six years later in 1949, it ended in making Rukmini Devi as a unique figure in the cultural firmament of India: it also made her so lonely as not to have anyone with whom she could share her most intimate reflections. She lost her husband during Rahu sub-period in Sun main-period. Thus the Sun, which was expected to destroy all her personal barriers and support made Rukmini Devi completely self-reliant with the passing away of her husband, Mrs. Annie Besant was already gone. Now she marched alone towards her goal—the resurgence of cultural heritage of India and propagation of the message of spirituality in every form of existence.

Her preoccupation with composing dance-dramas continued with unmitigated vigour and zeal. Several dance masters withdrew their support from her, yet her energy did not slump. Her pioneering performance of *Kutrala Kurvanji* in 1944 and *Kumara Sambhavam* in 1947 did not only show the intimate relationship between the theme of her composition and the planets influencing her at the time of their composition but also the timeliness of their performance. The Sun in the tenth house put Rukmini Devi on the path of glory and renown.

The period of Moon reflected fully the impact of Jupiter and other planets connected in bestowing their choicest honour, social status and royal recognition and enough creativity. In Moon-Rahu sub-period, she was nominated to the Rajya Sabha of the Indian Union and having been renominated, she remained in the Indian Parliament till the end of Moon main period. During her tenure in Rajya Sabha, she introduced a bill for the Prevention of Cruelty to Animals and at the assurance of the then Prime Minister Jawaharlal Nehru that the Government itself would introduce such a bill she withdrew it. The Government of India subsequently introduced and enacted the law pertaining to the animal welfare. Animal Welfare Board was thus constituted with which Rukmini Devi remained connected till her death. During Moon-Mercury sub-period, she was the recipient of *Padma Bhushan* from the Government of India in recognition of her various cultural and humanitarian activities. Moon-Ketu sub-period brought her Sangeet Natak Academy award as the foremost dancer, the Queen Victoria Medal for her work towards the Prevention of Cruelty to Animals; she also received several other awards during this period.

During Mars period of planetary rulership, specially because of Mars' intimate relationship with the universal life-principle represented by the Sun and its close connection with life expressed as blood circulating in all forms of life, Rukmini Devi began working with greater vigour and enthusiasm for animal welfare. She became the chairperson of the Animal Welfare Board during Mars-Saturn sub-period, and composed *Rukmini Kalyanam* and other dance-dramas during Mars-Ketu sub-period. Her dance-dramas always bore close relationship with the ruling planets. Among such planets which have significantly influenced her artistic compositions, one could identify Saturn, Rahu and Ketu as important ones. These planets act at deeper layers of spiritual radiation, and Rukmini Devi was very sensitive to these levels, so it seems to have happened that she imbibed these influences and expressed them through various classical mythological stories. During Mars main period, and Rahu sub-period, Rukmini Devi also received Doctorate in Humanities from the Wayne University in the United States.

The Rahu-Ketu axis played, as it does in everyone's case, the role of main fulcrum around which all major events of one's life revolve. Rahu is placed in fifth house—the house of creativity and in the sign of Virgo ruled by Mercury which is placed in the ninth house along with Saturn and Venus. As a result of this polarisation of Rahu in the house of creativity, Rukmini Devi's main karmic involvements and mission revolved round her artistic creativity—expressing the all pervading eternal spirituality (Saturn). As her Ketu is placed in eleventh house along with Mars and Jupiter, her trials and sociability as well as status in life will be in a major way the outcome of her strong emotional upsurges and adamantine determination (Mars) and religious observances and belief (Jupiter). From them arose her artistic creation bringing down to the mundane level—the cosmic process of manifestation (Moon), and the innumerable awards and recognitions (the major planets of her life namely Saturn, Venus and Mercury situated eleventh from Ketu's sign) which strengthened her experiences of the life-process (Ketu). Thus whenever Rahu and Ketu appeared in a major way in Rukmini Devi's life, it was full of momentous events.

During the main period of Rahu, Rukmini Devi experienced not only incessant flow of her creative urges, but she received abundant recognition of her merit. During this period, she produced *Shakuntalam* (Rahu-Rahu), *Kuchelopakhyanam* (Rahu-Saturn sub-period), *Matsya Avataram,* and *Kurma Avataram* during Rahu-Mercury sub-period, *Buddha Avataram,* and *Ajamilopakhyanam* during Rahu-Venus, and *Meera of Mewar* during Rahu-Mars sub-period. Among the awards received during this period, one may mention the Fellowship of Sangeet Natak Academy, Prani Mitra Award of the Animal Welfare Board, Doctorate from the Rabindra Bharati and Vishwa Bharati award for the outstanding achievement in the field of Arts from the Maharashtra Engineers, and Rabindranath Tagore plaque from the Asiatic Society. In 1977, in Rahu dasa and Ketu bhukti, she was invited by the then Prime Minister of India to become the President of India, which she declined—for her work in the field of arts and for Kalakshetra might suffer due to its acceptance. It was probably an unprecedented incident in any part of the world that such a high position in the country was declined for such a reason, but Rukmini Devi was having Venus as ascendant and Sun only in its inimical sign Aquarius. It was a glorious renunciation for the good of a more spiritual cause! When Rahu operates on a spiritual plane, it shows material attractions and achievements as of no consequences at the very outset, while the same result is produced after enormous suffering in ordinary individuals. During the later part of Rahu period, she contracted the cancer of the lungs.

The Jupiter main period started from May 1984; the physical illness made her feeble but her zeal for creative pursuits did not abate. Since the beginning of this period, she suffered from ailments which could react more to spiritual healing and planetary remedial measures than to conventional medicines. During this period, the public showering of awards and honours did not diminish: she was the recipient of prestigious *Kalidasa Samman* from Madhya Pradesh Government, Mankat award from the United States for her Service to Animals, and on the occasion of the Golden Jubilee of Kalakshetra even the Prime Minister Rajiv Gandhi paid his special homage to this woman of celebrity. Towards the end of her life, when the news of her illness became known to various people, J. Krishnamurti on his own volition went to see Rukmini Devi at her private residence and stayed with her alone for sometime. Physically her health was deteriorating due to ill-health, and she was apprehending death to descend on her any time, yet she was vitally concerned with producing some more of her dance-dramas and put the work of animal welfare at a more sound basis. About a fortnight before her death in February 1986, when I met her she was still contemplating to compose a dance-drama, depicting the forces which transform the phenomenal being in death into an eternal consciousness. At the very initial phase of Jupiter main-period Rukmini Devi, in February 1986 left for her celestial abode.

The astrological study of Rukmini Devi's chart shows very clearly that the malefics also radically modify their influences on the life of the individuals, if the individuals are open to their spiritual nature and purify the chalice for receiving their beneficence by operating their purified sheaths at higher levels of creativity. Saturn,

Rahu, Ketu and Mars which are ordinarily considered very materialistic planets have clearly demonstrated the possibility of their bestowing high order of spiritual and occult attainments. It is however true that spiritual eminence can be achieved only by completely eschewing material proclivities. One cannot have both the worlds. The combination of Venus and Saturn which bestowed so much of spiritual art capabilities also made her personal life devoid of any 'personal' pleasure generally associated with Venus.

The Moon, which is the significator of the peace of mind, because of the aspect of Saturn on it, though it gave superb emotional restraint, did not lend any 'personal' peace and family life. Rukmini Devi came from a family of four brothers and four sisters, yet her personal life was very lonely. She played mother to a large number of men and women, but she did not have a child of her own, she did not have such a mother (though her physical mother lived to a very ripe age and died only a few years before the death of Rukmini Devi) to whom she could completely surrender as a child. Even Annie Besant, whom she treated like a mother passed away before Rukmini Devi was even 30 years of age and her stormy phase was reaching a climax. Hundreds and thousands of her students have received eminence and settled down peacefully and happily in different avocations, but Rukmini Devi derived no physical sustenance from them. Her entire life had been an ongoing journey which knew no rest, no personal pleasures or pain; a few persons were jealous of her eminence and renown, but she had her path well chalked out and had no place for human pettiness. Truly, her life showed that only after destroying the personal life, planets bestow, even if they are exoterically considered malefics, universal consciousness and real spiritual bliss. Underneath the seeming outer storms, they create the subterranean stream of compassion, sensitivity and identification with the universal life-force which has no place for personal sorrow.

2

ALAMGIR GHAZI AURANGZEB

		Moon Saturn	
Asc. Jupiter	*3rd Nov. 1618* (Rasi)		Ketu
Rahu			Mars
Venus		Mercury Sun	

Rahu Mercury		Sun	Saturn
Asc. Moon	(Amsa)		
Jupiter	Mars		Ketu Venus

Aurangzeb was probably the most maligned Moghul emperor; he was considered the most vicious, bigoted and cruel. Historians have accused him to be the cause of the downfall of the mighty Moghul empire. An impersonal study of his character shows that he was not the "white serpent" that his father Shah Jehan called him, rather he was merely an empty vessel pouring forth whatever the unseen forces were putting in it. It is evident by what Nalini, the bizarre old woman told the Moghul emperor Jehangir on 23 October 1618 at Dohad, at the crossroad between Gujarat and Malwa, when the emperor was returning after a triumphal march to the south. Nalini was clad in colourful costume of an unusual pattern, something like the travelling gypsies of eastern Europe. She accosted the emperor and sought permission to read the lines on the eyebrow of Prince (Shah Jehan). On permission being granted, she studied the forehead of Shahzada Khurram, as Shah Jehan was known then, and revealed that the child in the womb of the prince's wife, who was at that time accompanying the procession would be supremely brave and fearless. The prince (Khurram) would have four sons, daughters would be of little consequence in the scheme of the royal dynasty. She said that the male progeny, it was written clear on the brow would engage itself in many pursuits of the sword. The *Khandan-i-Mughalia* was not likely to profit therefrom. The third son of the prince stood high in the plan of the destiny. She ended by saying, "We begin to die at birth. The end flows from the beginning". And soon afterwards, on 3rd November 1618, Ajmand Banu gave birth to Aurangzeb. This child was fairer in complexion than all her previous children, and the court astrologers declared that a child born in the course of a triumphal journey was considered a good omen for the future of the kingdom and its guardians. But who knows what the astrology meant by 'good omen'!

There are conflicting accounts about the date of birth of Aurangzeb. Stanley Lane-Pode recorded the date of his birth as November 4, 1618. Sir Jadunath Sarkar affirmed it to be October 24, 1618. Muni Lal, a biographer of Aurangzeb has been inclined to agree with Sir Jadunath. Pandit Srikant Sastry of Varanasi gave his birth time as Saturday, Samvat 1675 at ghati 18. 30 after sunrise which suggested that Sun occupied Libra at 23°25' at birth and it was associated with Mercury, while Rahu was in Capricorn and the ascendant corresponded with Jupiter in Aquarius. The details available with another Indian source namely Anup Sanskrit Library has agreed with the details given by Srikant Sastry. It is extremely difficult to vouch accuracy of these details at the present time about four hundred years after the event. It appears that the horoscope cast on the basis of Aurangzeb's birth on November 3, 1618 at about 1.45 p.m. or so local time with a balance of Sun's mahadasa for about 2 years 2 months—seems to provide fairly accurate basis for deciphering the planetary impulses guiding the life-events of this last of the mighty Moghul empire.

Aurangzeb was born with Vargottam Aquarius ascendant. Saturn, the ascendant lord plays an outstanding role in his case. Since Saturn is also the lord of the twelfth house, its maleficence accruing due to this rulership cannot be completely absolved. It shows the truth of Nalini's pronouncement, "We begin to die at birth. The end flows from the beginning". If the ascendant is the beginning, the twelfth house represents the end. In Aurangzeb's life, the seed of self-destruction was firmly embedded in his very birth.

Saturn's importance is further increased due to its association with exalted Moon, the lord of the sixth house placed in the house of emotion. Saturn's third aspect on the sixth house and the association of its lord with this restrictive planet completely destroyed all the softer feelings and emotion in one's relationship with others. Aurangzeb was insensate; he could never display any trace of the milk of human kindness. He always felt insecure; he never trusted the safety of his well-being in any situation. Saturn so much concealed his inner feelings and designs that his external behaviour and demeanour gave absolutely no indications of what was brewing in his mind. It enabled him to carry out his treacherous schemes without their slightest inkling being perceived by others. This feature of a serpent in Aurangzeb was perceived by Shah Jehan quite early in the baby prince which made the emperor call the fair-skinned prince as 'a white serpent'. Saturn in the fourth house often makes an individual torn in conflicts, unhappy and lacking in spirituality. Such persons do not listen to rational and helpful advice; they could be humiliated by their spouse, children and even by their employees. If Taurus occupies the fourth house, such persons become very cruel, greedy, miserly and burdened with family responsibilities. Such individuals try to be very clever and outdo others, who are living a conventional everyday life; their own personal life are materialistic and emotionally very disturbed.

Aurangzeb's Saturn occupies the fourth house as ascendant lord and it occupies the sign of Taurus, while Moon also occupies this sign. These planetary disposition very much destroyed his finer sensitivity; his aura showed much ugly hue and radiated self-destructive mental projectiles.

The importance of Saturn in this horoscope also increases due to its direct aspect on the sixth house (the house of enemies), the tenth house (the house of *karma* or profession), and the ascendant (which represents the essence of life contained in any life-span). The exaltation of Moon associated with Saturn produced symptoms of megalomania. The desire for supernal eminence was so great in Aurangzeb that he wanted to be known as the most noble and divine, he wanted to be extremely rigid about his religious discipline and austerities, he aspired to have the biggest possible empire, and he even hoped to be the next prophet of Islam. Saturn's association with Moon, however, completely distorted his thinking, created a sense of illusion which he believed to be a reality, he precipitated the most heinous crime, while imagining that to be an act of retributive justice. Saturn occupies *Rohini* asterism, which provides an impulse of mission; there is a feeling that one's action is highly important. "Rohini is that attraction which compels the divinity in man to lose its pristine memory and become immersed in worldly gratification"[1]. Such a Saturn associated with Moon so much veiled the real nature of Aurangzeb, the human individual, that he lost touch with reality, it made him insatiably ambitious, camouflaged the true impulsions of his emotions and stunted his real spiritual growth.

Aurangzeb's life was greatly influenced by Saturn, specially because it was his ascendant lord. His ascendant is Aquarius which is extremely mysterious, enigmatic, full of energy of an unusual kind and ever ready to align itself with divine power and divine schemes of human unfoldment. The sign is so intensely misunderstood that astrologers generally miss its deeper repercussions and individuals born under it fail to recognise their basic impulsions. Consciously or unconsciously, rightly or otherwise, they always, almost invariably, believe themselves to be specially chosen individuals with a divine mission and cast in an exceptional mould. In a way, everyone is a divine child during birth with a special mission to be completed, but Aquarius individuals are different from them in the sense that they

---

1. *Myths and Symbols of Vedic Astrology*, Bepin Behari, Passage Press, U.S.A., p. 182.

think they are different from others, they are specially chosen while others are not. Thus, depending upon the level of their spiritual development and clarity of their self-knowledge their personal psychology and pattern of personality are moulded.

Whatever the level of his inner growth, an individual born under Aquarius will inevitably experience radical transformation in his life, and from the longer standpoint of his soul's growth he will necessarily be confronted in his present birth with such situations which would show the futility of material and personal acquisitions thereby giving him a new spiritual direction in his life. The historians have recorded the personal exasperations of Aurangzeb to his queen, his wailings in night, long prayers and personal 'communications with his God' towards the last phase of his life which showed how disappointed and disillusioned he was with his material success. Aquarius necessarily destroys the material base of the individual.

In the case of Aurangzeb, the ascendant is Vargottam. Jupiter occupies the ascendant. It occupies its own navamsa being located in Sagittarius. Such a situation produces great transforming potential. But Jupiter being slightly below the ascending arc remains merely a potential imparting a religious aura without fructifying the basic humanitarianism or philanthropy of the Jovian nature. The ascendant also receives concentrated aspect of Saturn, the former being less than 5° away from its central point. The restrictive impulse of Saturn further weakens the Jovian humanitarian impulse. The ascendant and Jupiter, both occupy *Satabhishak* nakshatra. It produces ultimate harmony, though there are trials and tribulations in the process which make the individual's life extremely miserable. "Satabhishak people are rarely happy within themselves. Life to them is a duty, not an experience of personal satisfaction. A flower is meant for the enjoyment and pleasure of others. It does not enjoy its own beauty, fragrance and freedom. The individual attaining spiritual knowledge may not be happy in his personal life, but having acquired spiritual knowledge, he has a sense of impersonal joy"[1].

Rahu is the ruler of this asterism which turns the individual consciousness to materiality. Under inner spiritual pressure and external material attractions, the individual is torn between antagonistic forces impinging upon him, he cannot share his inner turmoil with others, so he becomes intensely lonely and often suffers from

1. *Ibid*, p. 242.

psychological depression. Satabhishak people are rarely happy within themselves. Life to them is a duty, not an experience of personal fulfilment and gratification. It is for such impulsions that various biographers of Aurangzeb tried to speculate about his motives; an autobiography by Aurangzeb would have revealed his psychological turmoil and whirlwind raging in his psyche.

The ascendant is also powerfully aspected by Mars. Mars is situated in the seventh house, aspecting tenth and second houses besides the ascendant. It occupies Leo ruled by Sun which is posited in the ninth house in its debilitation sign. Mars occupies Purva Phalguni nakshatra which is ruled by Venus; it has the primary impulse of *Kama*, and its basic attribute, *guna*, is that of *Tamasic* sloth or inertia; *Rajasic* activity expresses itself only at its secondary level. The asterism is presided over by the Vedic deity Bhaga who bestows bliss. Purva Phalguni consolidates the divine impulse for its materialising activities which prepares the individual to await the final marching orders. The growth under Purva Phalguni is necessarily the result of *Trishna*, the thirst for experience. At this stage, the soul is let loose to wander forth and gain knowledge of the world. Purva Phalguni makes the individual ambitious. He usually gets mixed-up with dreams of life and existing mundane opportunities. He often rationalizes the necessity of involving himself in the world of matter. The impelling force of *kama*—passion makes the individual enthusiastic about all that he undertakes so that he could present his inner strength and vitality into every act. But, he is purposive, acquisitive and calculative of the advantages and disadvantages of the outcome. There is often a streak of selfishness in his approach to life and relationships.

When Mars is placed in such a relationship with Sun, the centre of the universe as the ruler of the sign in which it is placed, one could imagine the ferocity with which the individual would interact with the world around him. It would result in shedding blood and cutting into pieces the most pious individual and throwing the bits of his flesh and bones for the feast of vultures in order to create an impression on the commonfolk so that they did not fall into the same footsteps. These are intensely revolting acts when motivated by seemingly religious fanaticism or assumed divine impulsion. Self-centredness of Mars could often become devastatingly atrocious; it being placed in Scorpio in navamsa makes it very callous, mobilising the energy imparted for self-aggrandisment.

Such a strong impulsion for committing the most heinous crime, atleast from the ordinary human standpoint is greatly accentuated by the tenth aspect of Saturn on the ascendant, which also greatly ruined the nature of Jupiter placed there in its inimical sign. The treacherous action, not to reveal one's innermost motives even to one's most near and dear ones, and ruthlessness in executing one's nefarious designs can easily be inferred from such a Saturn. Jupiter in the ascendant under the existing constraints can only be a matter of personal solace to the individual. Surrounded by cruel deeds, the individual would suffer from a feeling of remorse, from a streak of remorse for his compulsive actions. One could say that such an individual is crucified on his emotional plane and none would comprehend his emotional suffering; the world would accuse such an individual, he himself may feel completely dissociated from his own physical actions; but there would be none to worship the martyrdom of the inner-man for his outer self-assumed (many a times false) responsibilities. So there is no surprise if Aurangzeb suffered from self-pity inwardly, while the world considered him a cruel tyrant. In the case of Aurangzeb, people compared him with Chengiz Khan and Timurlane—both rolled into one. Yet while decreeing the severest punishment to his son for rebellion, he would often bewail in private before his wife at the pains suffered by the father in him.

Under such stellar conjuncture, Aurangzeb had to traverse through the most incredible path: whatever happened to him and whenever it so happened were already contained in the cosmic plan otherwise Nalini, about whom mention has already been made earlier could not have succeeded in revealing the end of *Khandan-i-Mughalia* with the birth of the child which was then in the womb of the prince's wife. The treachery of "the white serpent" was not a cultivated behavioural trait, but it was an innate attribute of Aurangzeb's temperament.

Aurangzeb precipitated many cruel deeds over which the precipitator or the victim seemed to have any control. Everyone in the drama seemed to be under a mighty sweep, as if they were all "possessed" by some unknown force. Aurangzeb had all the visible expressions of a devout and a pious person (Jupiter in the ascendant), but inwardly he was tortured by aspiration, ambition, and ruthless cruelty (Saturn in fourth with exalted Moon; Saturn and Mars, both aspected the ascendant which happened to be Aquarius).

Aurangzeb ate simple food, regularly prayed five times a day even on the battlefields amidst the fighting soldiers and his enemies surrounding him. He is said to spend on his personal needs the money earned from copying and selling the Holy Koran or from stitching robes! He was certainly very austere in his personal life, but once his passion was aroused, his ambition inflamed and his religious fanaticism stirred, his courage knew no bounds and his ruthlessness was unprecedented. He was certainly uncompromising in matters which he considered as belonging to the State (the royal Moghul court): he generally shunned luxury in all its forms, he was averse to music, eschewed wine and inebriating herbal concoctions, but when he was elated on account of his megalomaniac achievements he could let himself go to the most glamorous and ostentatious festivities: he would even order the most outrageous beauty-queens from the south for the royal dancing parties. On entourage, he took only a few wives, mistresses and concubines, but never brook any denial if he felt attracted to a Muslim maiden or others. Yet, he would generally like to confine to the number of wives enjoined under Islam. He fasted on all days of the month of Ramajan, when Muslims are expected, while doing so he did not show any laxity in royal responsibilities: he continued attending to official duties, meeting chieftains and *sardars,* received diplomats, and issued firmans to distant officers.

Aurangzeb cherished his Islamic injunctions to such an extent that he did not put any pearls, jewels or robes of silk. He continued his religious observances even during the periods of his illness. He distributed alms to the poor with his own hands on holy days, and slept at night on hard ground when in camp. Historians have depicted him as living the life of an ascetic while playing the role of an emperor; he practised in word and deed, according to his own understanding, the teachings of the Holy Koran and the preachings of the Holy Prophet. Such a contradiction in his life, austere living with ruthless crimes resulted from Jovian occupation of Aquarius, giving him extreme religiosity, and malefic aspects of Saturn and Mars on it.

The emotional strain through which Aurangzeb passed since his childhood was evident in many ways. The epithet "the white serpent" though bestowed on him as an affectionate appellation was based on certain traits of character noticeable in a marked way even during his infancy and early childhood. Aurangzeb always suspected others;

proved treacherous in his dealings, heartless in executing his nefarious deeds and heinous crimes. These were evidently expressions of Saturnian disposition. He was so ruthless with his father, brothers and sisters that he never hesitated in inflicting murderous pain on them. He not only imprisoned Shah Jehan, his father and made him suffer innumerable tortures, but eliminated his brothers Dara Shikoh, Shuja and Murad in order to capture the throne to which he was not righteously entitled. He suspected that they would have done what he did to them if he failed to do what he did. He had so much affection for his sister Roshanara that he "looked upon her as an angel who had come to earth to rescue him from his follies", and for whom he prayed that "her beauty be as indestructable as her goodness", yet on suspicion of her having some affectionate (romantic) relationship with a junior palace officer, got her poisoned to slow death.

Aurangzeb's religious fanaticism was so much ingrained that he could stoop to the most heinous cruelties. Bhai Mati Dass, according to Sikh tradition was sawed alive into two. Bhai Dayal was set ablaze. Shambhuji and Kavi Kailash, who were his political adversaries are said to have been captured, hacked to bits, and scattered limb by limb on the banks of river Bhine, 15 miles east of Pune, their flesh and bones provided as feast to vultures hovering overhead. Sometimes, he acted heinously under astro-mental compulsions when he was possessed by religious fanaticism or wrong sense of divine justice or faulty understanding of an emperor's responsibilities. Aurangzeb imprisoned his eldest son Muhammad Sultan for his alleged subversive role in the war of succession. He (Sultan) died in prison itself. His eldest daughter Zai-un-Nissa languished in state prison at Delhi. Shah Alam was a captive in the fort of Daulatabad. His favourite son whom he tried several times to trap and subdue, managed to escape to Persia where he died as a fugitive.

On feeling envious of Dara Shikoh, his eldest brother and rightful heir to the throne, a scholar with liberal views, who was respectful to saints and priests of different religions and faiths, Aurangzeb managed to send royal army—captured, chained and dragged him on the streets of Delhi and finally got him executed. Not satisfied with these, he got his head separated from torso, put in a nice presentation box and made a special gift to his father Shah Jehan, while the latter was languishing in the Agra fort, pining for a morsel of food and water to quench his thirst. On seeing it, the erstwhile emperor of the Moghul Sultanate wailed till he became mentally deranged. Later, the head was put on a spear and fixed in front of the fort, lest someone rebelled against Alamgir Ghazi Aurangzeb—the emerging Moghul emperor, the third son of Shah Jehan about whom Nalini had stated that he "stood high on the planes of destiny". The lord of the ascendant with an exalted planet aspecting the tenth house while ascendant was Vargottam had made Aurangzeb an extraordinary person. Yet, Saturn associated with Moon in exaltation aspecting the ascendant which is also aspected by malefic Mars made him a cold-blooded murderer.

Vengeance is a reaction to the hurt—real or imaginary, felt inflicted on one's ego. Egotism in Aurangzeb is evident from the disposition of Saturn, the ascendant lord. It aspects the ascendant which happens to be its own house, which is suitably strengthened by the placement of Jupiter therein. It could easily inculcate the feeling of self-righteousness. The aspect of Mars on it from the sign of Sun, which happened to be debilitated with the lord of the eighth house, an inauspicious house intensified the feeling of revenge especially when the innate selfish urge to capture the centre of power, the throne of Delhi (Sun) was challenged and attempts were made to thwart his design. The serpent is well recognised for its self-consciousness and revengefulness. This trait is greatly pronounced in the planetary disposition in Aurangzeb's natal chart.

The liquidation of the Bohra divine Qutb-ud-Din and his two followers is said to be basically the result of the Emperor's wrath caused by the rumour that the Bohra divine had lent his blessings to Dara Shikoh, when the latter fled to Multan after his defeat in the battle of succession at Samugal. The disturbances between Shi'ite and Sunni factions of the Bohra community were only an excuse to still another voice, known to have spoken in favour of one whom Aurangzeb regarded as his deadliest foe. Execution of Muhammad Said, a Persian Jew who had embraced Islam in Sind and was highly devoted to Sufism as a mystic of very high order, on the pretext of his seeming profanity and nudity was actually motivated by his (Said's) closeness and respect for Dara Shikoh, who had introduced the Sufi to Shah Jehan during his reign.

In 1672, Aurangzeb ordered the execution of Shah Muhammad Tahir, a poet-philosopher who became a legend of his life-time. He equated love with universal spirit and everything else as wrekage of ignorance, ego and pride. The poet was summoned to the court, reprimanded for feeding the people on heresies under which laid hidden a revolt against the holy prophet and his enunciations about the good and evil, the real and the unreal. Shah Muhammad denied the charge saying that "my respect for the prophet is great, but my veneration is greater for the values that made him greater." Aurangzeb considered the reply in consultation with the Ulemas, but this catholicity of view did not blend with the Emperor's obscurantism. When the poet was publicly executed, he did not protest against the sentence, but it showed how resistant to any openness was the Emperor; his *Ghazi* did not allow him to bear with the propagation of such a philosophy of universal love and immanence of universal spirit. The worst example of vengeance is seen in the Aurangzeb's treatment of his elder brother Dara Shikoh from whom he usurped the kingdom which rightly belonged to Dara. The impact of Saturn in materialising his egotism was so intense that he felt himself as the ultimate law.

One's remorse at the cruel episodes in human history is greatly minimised on an understanding of the inner cosmic drama in which the kings and the queens are mere pawns: the wide chessboard enables diverse players to act their role during which process the individual, nation and the humanity at large work out their *karmas* at different levels. Astrology throws much light on this aspect of human history and religious metaphysics, but we are not much concerned with this subject presently. Here we are content merely by suggesting that the planetary dispositions reveal predestined inner forces working through Aurangzeb: whatever his action and howsoever heinous his response to external conditions, he was unconscious of the same, which probably was being led by higher forces towards a specific direction. This is evident from what Allima Mooltani told Dara, when he approached her this time as a fugitive while on previous occasions he had been to her as a prince with Shah Jehan.

Allima Mooltani was a saintly woman living midway between Sirhind and Lahore. Her dwelling was a mud-and-straw hut in the middle of mango grove. She lived there alone with God and her never expressed sorrows. A woman of few words, she spoke only when she thought that the great prompter wanted her to say something. It is said that Shah Jehan had made it a point to spend some time with her—whenever he went either to Lahore or Kashmir. Jehangir had even offered her a better place near Delhi or Agra to live, but she politely declined the offer. When Dara Shikoh approached her, being chased by the royal army of Aurangzeb, Dara, his wife, his family members, and his loyal soldiers experienced immense hardship in running away from one place to another, this turn of fortune for Dara made no difference to Allima Mooltani. On Dara's prayers for divine intercession towards the restoration of his safety, she replied after a long pause:

> All of us are subject to the dictates of fate. To argue with her is to deny the existence of the Super-Power that controls the affairs of men. Sorrow can mend no bones. Neither can a spell of pleasures reserve for one a place in heaven. Both joy and grief are diseases of the mind. These ailments can be cured through upliftment of the soul to a point, where duality ends and unity takes centre. O Prince of princes, you are well-read in the mathematics of the spirit. There is no place in it for doubt and speculation. Faith is the key to unmixed bliss. At all the lower stages of development, man remains a prison of his ego, his doubts, his fears and his aspirations.
>
> It is no secret that you differ from Aurangzeb in mental disposition, chiefly in your greater tenderness and less selfishness. His toughness is the product of many lusts, not of beliefs and convictions. On the other hand, your comparative gentleness arises from your scholarship, your study of man and its Maker, your pre-occupation with the spirit and its manifestation. *Aurangzeb and you are created by nature for different purposes.* He will die with his death. You may live for ever. He may wear the crown. That headgear will not, however, give him a place among the immortals of history. O Prince, you may be slain by your enemies but, heed my words, they will have no power to rub your name out of the annals of the Mughals. Carry on. Nobody has the power to alter one's destiny. The lines on the palm of the hand can neither be changed nor erased. The realization of the inevitability of fate diffuses greed; it also makes pleasure less pleasant.
>
> Just as a lewd woman never forgets her sex, a soldier never forgets that his profession is to kill; Aurangzeb is at best a soldier and, at worst a pretender. Beware of him. He belongs to the freak species who rise by sin. To kill for him is nothing but the final argument. The throne is his end. *He is one of those*

who will try even to eliminate God, if He stands in his way to the high seat.

I have said all that the Lord prompted me to say. Prayers and acceptance of the pre-ordained go ill together. My good wishes are, however, with you. The road before you is long and full of traps and pitfalls. May the great God protect you. To accept His will is to be saved.

Dara Shikoh left Allima Mooltani a changed person; he accepted his preordained destiny, while Aurangzeb suffered mental torture of his own inner compulsions through long life of eighty-nine years. That is what happens when Saturn aspects lagna: one suffers for a life-long period.

Aurangzeb had been lonely throughout his life, psychologically marooned, and wrapt in self-made cocoon, wherein he tried to derive security and satisfaction with his self-assumed titles of *Padshah* (Emperor), *Alamgir* (conqueror of the world), and *Ghazi* (the Holy Warrior). He thought that his life's work was "the demolition of all the citadels of infidelity". The general policy of Aurangzeb's regime was "to demolish the schools and temples of the infidels and put down their teachings and religious practices with the object of spreading Islam and overthrowing of infidel practices". In order to carry out the promptings of his inner voice, he was prepared to proceed alone with the martyr's zeal, courage and devotion. He was prepared to bear immense deprivations and hardships for his missionary goal. This was his *karma*—his destiny, for which his soul had taken physical garments. It is obvious from a study of his *karmasthana,* the disposition of the tenth house in the natal chart.

The tremendous power latent in him, ready to explode and come forth on the surface—for physical manifestation becomes apparent from the disposition of Scorpio, the sign occupying the tenth house, and that of Mars, which rules the house, placed tenth from the tenth house. Scorpio is fortified by Venus on the one side and Sun and Mercury on its other side. Its lord Mars, as we have already indicated attracts the predictive principle of *Bhavat bhava* that is, the significance of a house is deciphered by the disposition of the same house relative to it. Consequently, Mars assumes greater significance for Aurangzeb's career and his mission. The dispositor of the tenth lord in the present case would be the Sun, the lord of the house where Mars is posited. But, the Sun is debilitated in the ninth house though aspected by Jupiter from ascendant and it (Sun) is associated with Mercury, the lord of the fifth house and the eighth house. The tenth house is also aspected by Saturn with exalted Moon, and by Mars whose sign-lord is situated in the sign of its debilitation. Such conjuncture of planets greatly vitiate the disposition of seventh, ninth and tenth houses. As a result, Aurangzeb's personal relationships with close associates (seventh house), religious proclivities (ninth house) and interaction with the world, his karma or profession (tenth house) would be so much skewed and crooked that there would not be harmonious blending of various aspects of his life. He was bound to have troublesome life, insecure within himself and discordant between what he ought to do and what he actually did; he was distrustful—unable to coordinate his various loyalties and always disturbed to understand the right intonation of his inner voice (Sun).

With regard to tenth house, Rahu assumes its position in third from tenth house, fourth from it is occupied by Jupiter, tenth by Mars and twelfth by Sun and Mercury. Saturn—a malefic planet associated with an exalted planet aspects the tenth house. At the same time, it should also be recognised that the tenth house is aspected by the lord of fourth house from itself as well as by the lord of the ninth house from tenth house. Such considerations make it clear that the impact of different planets will be powerful but of a mixed character: there is nothing untainted in the life of Aurangzeb. He attains rulership of the most extensive Moghul empire but its foundation was based on much cruelty; he was a very pious Muslim, but his religiosity was practised with heinous murders; he lived for ripe old age of about nine decades—not a single day of which passed without some intrigue and conflict of mind.

The various planets in the natal chart of Aurangzeb constitute a special pattern. All the planets occupy either third or fifth from their own signs except Moon. Jupiter as lord of Sagittarius is third from it (while situated in Aquarius, it is twelfth from its sign Pisces). Saturn, the lord of Capricorn is situated in the fifth house from this sign (as in the case of Jupiter, it also occupies a different relationship with its sign Aquarius, thus like Jupiter it is capable of producing different kinds of impulses as well). Mars as lord of Aries is placed in Leo, which happens to be fifth from this sign (though as the lord of Scorpio, it occupies a different relationship). The Sun in debilitation in third house from its sign Leo, while Mercury is in fifth from

Gemini (though from Virgo it occupies second place). Moon is the only planet which occupies eleventh position from its own sign, an exception from the general pattern. The psychological study of Aurangzeb confirmed the abnormality of his mind, its constant pre-occupation with self-seeking endeavours. The fifth house influence induced Aurangzeb to be engaged always in achieving some results (creativity), the third house results provided him immense courage and initiative, but the inter-relationship between the benefics were so mixed up that his courage, initiative and creativity went in a wrong direction with extraordinary vigour. These planets made him appear as if he was possessed with some super-physical power making him assume the role of a special messiah for the destruction of temples (twelfth from Pisces), desecration of idols of worship, convert the 'infidels' to Islam, build mosques and establish the Muslim rule over the vast landmass of 'Hindustan' thus leading him to concentrate all his energies and strength for the fulfilment of his pre-ordained mission despite serious hardships and deprivations he had to undergo in the process. (We are not concerned here with metaphysical judgement over the ethicality of the action ordained and their implications.)

Scorpio is a mystic sign. It has the potential for producing the most materialistic, deeply selfish or self-centred individuals, as well as it may make the persons born under its influence highly spiritual, working in harmony with the secret universal divine energy. According to Yavanacharya, Scorpio represented the house of death, and a deep opening in the earth corresponding to the middle portion of the human body consisting of its generative and excretive organs. The sign is, in fact, a cavity, a hiding place, a hole, in which resides Vasuki, the serpent Naga used in the churning of the ocean whereby was enacted the stupendous drama of cosmic and human creation. It is under Scorpio that the potency in Libra can fructify and attain its fullness so that it is effectively enabled to produce the necessary spirituality in the individual. The serpent Nagas were the 'Initiators' into Divine Mystery to which was granted entry to those who had overcome their personal predilections and psychological (astro-mental) obscurities. It was done so for the sake of universal advancement and unfoldment of the divine plan of human evolution. Such 'initiations' were often imparted at secret places, away from the din and bustle of human inhabitation, free from the malignant influence of materialism at places, which have been spiritually surcharged with meditation of saints and seers and absorption of divine vibrations at highly magnetic centres. Often these centres are identified as secret places, caves and forests, or high snowclad mountains or even wilderness of deserts. These are the places associated with Scorpio, but the reference is more to the mystic unfoldment of human consciousness rather than on the physical location of these barren, inhabited places. After the immersion of life-force in deepest layers of materialism, represented by Libra, the individual now looks toward his primeval dwelling place. This change in one's direction often results from deep contemplation, introspection, in the loneliness of one's innermost cavity of heart. Either sorrow or enlightenment can lead the individual to this stage of loneliness of the being. This is the main function of Scorpio in the scheme of egoic evolution.

In the life of Aurangzeb, his biographers have recorded that after his long life of 89 years—most of which was spent in hectic bloodshed, warfare, persecution and executions—in which process he was alienated from his brothers, father, and sons; he found his life-experiences turning to dust: there was no attainment which brought him unsoiled happiness or emotional pleasure. He often wept bitterly at his emotional voidness. True to the nature of Scorpio, he destroyed all those who had any soft relationship with him, but in the end, his own life was unbearable to him. Like the scorpion, he behaved in his professional career represented by the tenth house occupied by Scorpio; he never trusted nor confided in anyone and had always been playing a treacherous game. Such loneliness must have been intensified to such an extent that his after-death experiences would have given him much material for contemplation so that a radical transformation was possible in his future egoic life. The Scorpio-born sorrow and loneliness paved the way for spiritual awakening for which time is no barrier: that is why Scorpio representing the eighth bhava of *kala purusha* is said to be a hidden aspect of life.

The extraordinary nature of Aurangzeb as the suspicious lonely emperor is signified by the importance of his tenth house occupied by Scorpio. In fact, the tenth house is the centre-piece and other aspects of his life exist in an important manner in relation to this. In case, we look at this house as the lagna, we would find that the planets align themselves in relation to it in a special manner. The tenth house is flanked on either sides by inner planets: Sun and Mercury in its twelfth house and Venus on its second; Jupiter and Mars in its fourth and tenth respectively. Moon and Saturn are situated in seventh house from itself. The shadowy planets are in third and ninth from it. This pattern of planets emphasises the basic goodness of Aurangzeb completely veiled by malefics. Jupiter occupies an inimical sign, Venus is the lord of its twelfth house and Mercury acquires the disposition of eighth house ownership. The lord of its tenth house occupies twelfth house. It shows that the karmic forces were so ordained that "he will try even to eliminate God if He stands in his way to the high seat", as Allima Mooltani had described Aurangzeb.

Aurangzeb was born under the Sun's main period, which lasted for about the first two years of his life. During this period, the prince, as the grandson of the ruling Mughalai-Azam was brought up in all luxury and care. Jupiter aspected the Sun which also gets debilitation cancelled as the lord of Aries, where it gets exalted, Mars is in a cardinal house in relation with ascendant as well as the Moon sign. Moreover, Sun occupies *Vishakha* asterism ruled by Jupiter and presided by two Vedic deities namely, Indra and Agni, and it (Libra) being the exaltation sign of the ascendant lord Saturn are very significant features for the pleasantly powerful situation in which the infant Aurangzeb found himself during his early years. The birth during the triumphal march of Jehangir considered auspicious, but accompanied by cruelties of warfare reflected the basic trait of Aurangzeb. As an infant, who lost his mother soon after his birth, the only effect of the Sun's main period was observed in frequent travel along with the royal entourage and vibrations of ruthless military manoeuvres. The only perceptive hint of Sun's disposition that the future historians observed during this period was that Aurangzeb had the seed of ruin even at that tender age sown in his psyche. He was destructive in his every act in order to achieve what *he thought* was constructive and righteous objectives.

The Moon's main period extended from the age of two years to twelve years. Birth of Aurangzeb was extremely painful for his mother: Ajmad Banu never before had suffered so much during her delivery. As a child, Aurangzeb witnessed the war of succession in which royal intrigues, murders and rebellions played important part. Even the royal harem was not a silent spectator of this turbulent drama. Aurangzeb's father had fought with Jehangir and fearing the worst he rebelled, surrendered, fled to the south and experienced much humiliation. Yet, it was during this main period that Aurangzeb's father ascended the throne of Delhi after much bloody fights. It was during this main period that Aurangzeb knew of his grandfather's arrest and Nur Jehan's manipulation and management of his release. He showed least interest in the subjects taught, but his teachers realised that he possessed "a spirit without a blemish and a heart without fear". It was during this period that Aurangzeb had realized that the success of one's achievements even by unfair means would ultimately be overlooked by the society, specially if the winner happens to be a powerful person. His contact with various Sufis and other religious teachers and Ulemas whom his father and grandfather had patronised instilled in him religious fanaticism, which was radically different from the catholicity of his elder brother Dara Shikoh. It may be recalled that Moon lies in the asterism of Krittika owned by Sun, presided over by Agni, and is symbolised by a razor.

The relationship between Kartikeya and this asterism well explained Aurangzeb's exposure to war of succession, and ferocious blood-letting around him. It also reveals the basic impulses which steeled Aurangzeb's heart so as to participate in heartless cruelties in which his later life was grossly enmeshed. Moon as the lord of the sixth house and associated with Saturn as the lord of the twelfth house, very strongly laid "the beginning of the end" which finally led to his total collapse and the ruin of the Moghul empire. Nalini had described it by saying that "the end flows from the beginning": the Sun and the Moon, indeed, began the flow to the end.

The main period of Mars began almost towards the last days of 1630, when Khan Jahan Lodi in the south rebelled against the Moghul rule, but was ruthlessly suppressed and finally executed. Mars was very important for Aurangzeb: it was posited tenth from the tenth house, it was also the lord of the tenth house. The Sun was its dispositor being the ruler of the sign in which Mars was placed. Mars was aspected by the greatest benefic of the planetary system namely Jupiter, it also established a relationship between tenth and eleventh house lord as a result of Mars-Jupiter mutual aspect. These planetary dispositions made the Mars mahadasa very propitious specially for enhancement of status (tenth house), augmentation of income (eleventh house), general growth of personality (ascendant) and cooperation with others (seventh house). On his fifteenth birth anniversary, he was weighed against gold mohurs, and 6,500 pieces were set apart for charity in his name. It took place during Saturn sub-period during Mars main-period. Mars as the lord of tenth house and Saturn as the lord of ascendant gave Aurangzeb, the first taste of personal importance as a royal child. During this period, a radical transformation took place in the psyche of Aurangzeb. Associated with Moon, placed in fourth—the house of emotion and aspecting Jupiter as well as the ascendant and having relationship with twelfth house due to ownership to the sign, Saturn made Aurangzeb feel the same kind of detachment with material affluence, which all spiritually advanced people feel. (One is reminded in this connection the planetary combination in the horoscope of Lord Buddha, where Saturn was associated with Sun, Mars, tenth house and had aspected the Moon, though the comparison has several serious limitations.) In 1634, along with the royal entourage, Aurangzeb went to Kashmir. The general poverty of the people there greatly disturbed him. His tutor Muhammad Hakim said, "Beauty amidst poverty is more enchanting than beauty amidst affluence. This is one of God's ways of pronouncing that material riches and spiritual beauty go ill together". From that day, it was reported that Aurangzeb discarded wearing silk and pearl. He wanted to enter paradise through the gates of indigence. This is a rare and spectacular result of powerful Saturn and Moon situated as they are in Aurangzeb's horoscope.

In 1634, when Mercury sub-period in Mars main period was running, Aurangzeb received his first military rank when he was made in-charge of 10,000 horsemen which heralded a long career on battlefield. It uncovered not only his genius in warfare but also his infinite faith in the protective hand of God. (Mercury in ninth house aspected by Jupiter) He began regarding himself as an instrument in the hand of God to execute Divine Will (Mercury, the messenger). Mercury in the chart of Aurangzeb occupies a special position: it is the ruler of fifth and eighth houses associated with Sun in the ninth house. It is well known that fifth is the house of creativity but the rulership of eighth house, enabled Mercury to link itself with untapped divine will so as to develop his hidden faculties. The overlordship of Mars directed this faculty and the process of its growth and unfoldment through Martian impulse generally evident on the battlefield. Mercury's placement in navamsa chart in the sign of Jupiter but in association with Rahu had defiled the nature of Mercury. It was during this period that iconoclastic tendency in Aurangzeb became much intensified. Under his orders "ancient temples of Orcha and other places were converted into mosques, the families of the nobility were given the option of conversion or death, ladies of the royal palace of Hauhar Singh were distributed among officers and men of the imperial army, idols of goddess Vindhya and other deities were broken up and thrown unceremoniously into the river Behat."

During Mars-Venus sub-period, Aurangzeb experienced glory and disenchantment simultaneously. He was made the Viceroy of the Deccan, a coveted position with much power and great many conveniences, but inwardly he experienced an intense feeling of discontent. He did not feel happy with what he possessed. Venus is the lord of fourth house as well as of the ninth; Saturn in fourth house and debilitated Sun in ninth house led to the feeling of discontent. The period of over-lordship assigned to Mars provided much upsurge of physical and sensual power—thus the contradiction in emotional life became pronounced. Mars has been so powerful in producing emotional upsurge as well as valour besides military skill as can very well be gauged by the fact that soon after the death of his mother, he was much emotionally moved that he even composed poems of six verses on the subject though he was not so accomplished in versification. The Martian impulse was also evident by the fact that during Mars-Saturn sub-period, he subdued a mad elephant by piercing his sword in its jaw and thus killing it; during Mars-Venus sub-period, in the presence of his father he shot from the back of his trotting horse—five pigeons flying at heights ranging from one to five hundred metres for which feat he was specially rewarded by the emperor. Sun sub-period provided Aurangzeb a wife: he married Dilraj Begum, a Persian princess: Sun was the ruler of the seventh house while it is posited in the sign of Venus and is aspected by Jupiter, which occupies the sign belonging to foreigners.

The main period of Rahu, which began towards the end of 1637 A.D. created much upheavals for Aurangzeb: Rahu and Ketu invariably leave deep imprint on the egoic life of the individual. In the present case, Rahu is posited in *Shravana* asterism owned by Moon; the asterism leads to serious meditation among those who are spiritually inclined while in others it instils the quality of obedience and servitude. It was under the impulse of Rahu that Aurangzeb fell in disgrace, he was stripped of his status of viceroyship and in a bout of depression felt that the prospect of his ascension to throne was very bleak, he even retired to a quiet corner of the western ghat mountains. His distrust and suspicion of Dara Shikoh was much accentuated. Most of these occurred during Rahu main period and Saturn sub-period. Mercury sub-period in Rahu gave him some relief, but Rahu-Ketu sub-period again brought loss of status and mental anguish. There occurred much trouble from the Emperor and failure in various assignments entrusted to him. Many of the difficult tasks which he was required to fulfil were given to him as a sort of punishment. During this period, Aurangzeb was psychologically much disturbed, he contacted several marriages, got involved in royal disgrace, and had troubles with Dara Shikoh. He also got his first male child from his favourite wife Dilraj Begum. The smoulderings of the war of succession began during this period and Aurangzeb began planning his game of deceit and intrigues. All these were characteristic results of Rahu in the twelfth house in the sign of Capricorn ruled by Saturn.

The main period of Jupiter started at the age of 37 years towards the end of 1655. Aurangzeb had married Aurangabadi Mahal in 1654 but soon after the beginning of Jupiter main-period, married Hira Bai, a Christian lady of Hindu origin: Jupiter a Brahmin planet and Saturn a *malechha*, both aspect the seventh house. Hira Bai was later named Zainabadi Mahal. During this period, Shah Jehan fell ill and war of succession began. As soon as the sub-period of Saturn began, Aurangzeb's intrigues and manipulations started fructifying. Jupiter is aspected by war-loving Mars and Jupiter itself aspects the debilitated Sun, the *Pitrukaraka* planet located in ninth house which is concerned with the welfare of father. There was much manoeuvre for getting to the throne after eliminating Dara Shikoh and others before Aurangzeb could succeed in his nefarious design. No one could outdo "the white serpent" in surreptitiously usurping the throne. Dara Shikoh was mercilessly captured, chained, humiliated, executed and his head presented to his (Dara's as well as Aurangzeb's) father, Shah Jehan, who was already imprisoned. That was the limit of heartless display of venomous spilling. He crowned himself twice, first on tenth July 1658 and later on 13th May 1659 with great ostentation and fanfare including a special dance performance by girls brought for the occasion from south with the peacock throne displayed on the occasion.

But during Jupiter-Mercury sub-period, the situation changed. There was a peasants' revolt which was however ruthlessly suppressed. Brother Murad, a likely danger subsequently was liquidated. Shivaji began to display his great prowess against the Mughalaisultanate and became a great menace for Aurangzeb. Mercury being the ruler of the eighth house and a *Bhratru karaka* situated in proximity with debilitated Sun showed its destructive nature during this period with marked virulence. Mercury also made Aurangzeb ill during this period from which he could recover only 'miraculously', but for recuperation, he had to depend upon the support lent by Ketu situated in sixth house and aspected by the ascendant lord Saturn.

During Ketu sub-period Aurangzeb went to Kashmir. Ketu is also a *Moksha-karaka* planet, which enabled Aurangzeb at Kashmir to meet a *Qualandar,* a divine person, who came to meet him and both had much talk together at which none else was permitted to be present. During Jupiter-Rahu sub-period, Aurangzeb was beset with much worry. In 1669, there was Jat rebellion, which had to be suppressed powerfully. Aurangzeb was also disturbed on account of the death of his daughter Badr-un-Nissa who passed away at an early age of 22 years; his beloved sister Roshanara Begum who had nursed him so devotedly also died of slow poisoning in September 1671. Yet, the main period of Jupiter with diverse and cross currents finally established him well entrenched as the head of the Mughal empire. However, when the following planetary rulership of Saturn began to take away over the events in Aurangzeb's life, once more he was put under storms and whirlwinds: his mind was greatly distressed and his actions displayed much criminality. The period characterised much bloodshed and extensive religious persecution. Saturn occupies a central position in Aurangzeb's horoscope so during the main period of its mahadasa, the innermost nature of Aurangzeb had to come to the fore. Saturn's main period began in December 1671, and the following year, in 1672, Aurangzeb ordered execution of Shah Muhammad Tahir, a poet-philosopher, who had become a legend of his life-time. Tahir equated love with the universal spirit and everything else to the wreckages of ignorance, ego and pride.

During the summer of 1671, when Jupiter-Rahu was running, Aurangzeb had summoned Tahir and reprimanded him for "feeding the people on heresies" under which was hidden a revolt against the holy Prophet and his enunciation of good and evil as well as about the real and the unreal. This controversy between the emperor and the poet-philosopher took a strange turn when the main period of Saturn began. Muhammad Shah denied the charge levied against him. He submitted by stating that: "My respect for the Prophet is great but my veneration is greater for the values that made him great". This created a storm in the mind of Aurangzeb. He himself was great follower of the Prophet, his approach to the Prophet and his teachings was almost blind. What the philosopher said showed the difference between the religious approach aroused under the Jovian impulse and that created by Saturn's fanaticism.

Both the spirits were latent in Aurangzeb which he found difficult to reconcile (which was also the problem of his life) between the two, yet he felt that there was some kernel of truth in what Shah Muhammad Tahir was saying. So he pondered over the reply and finding it difficult to come to any conclusion (which was also the case relating to the impact of Jupiter and Saturn throughout his life which made his life full of contradictions and conflicts), he asked a panel of orthodox Ulemas to pronounce judgement on the poet's formulation. For three days, seven interpreters of the Holy Koran debated in private the different aspects of Tahir's pronouncements. In the end, they gave the verdict that no principle, precept or transcendental value could be classed above the Prophet, who was the quintessence of all virtues, truth and forms of excellence. It expressed extreme degree of fidelity to a person and refusal to face abstraction of virtue instead of worshipping the individual who represented the virtue. The pronouncements of the Ulemas did not resolve the conflict between the openness of philosophy and freedom of thought and expression on the one side, and blind faith in the greatness of a person or validity of a thought whether based on rationality or obscurantism on the other.

The Ulemas, having given their findings left to the emperor the punishment that should be met to the poet. It was however recommended that on Tahir's penitence and acceptance of not to make such expressions in future, the guilty person could be treated leniently. But Tahir was genuinely convinced of his approach to life which led Aurangzeb to tilt towards his Saturnian impulse. He decided on public execution of Shah Muhammad Tahir. This incident epitomized the basic effect of Saturn in the case of Aurangzeb, which dogged him generally throughout his life, especially during the main period of Saturn and in a concentrated intensity during Saturn-Saturn sub-period. During this period, Aurangzeb also engaged himself in Afghan war which in his strategy of intrigues and arousal of inter-group rivalry led to huge expenditure of money and men, yet the outcome was dismal. Saturn's aspect on tenth house inevitably lead to frustration in one's undertakings.

Mercury produced devastating results in the garb of mischievous righteousness. It is placed in a very difficult situation. It is associated with a debilitated Sun. It is combust due to proximity with Sun, the distance between them being less than four degrees. It has the rulership of eighth house and in navamsa chart, it is in its own debilitation sign along with Rahu. Furthermore, it is sixth from the major planetary ruler during the period. These have completely spoilt the disposition of Mercury and made it very inauspicious for Aurangzeb. During Saturn-Mercury sub-period, there occurred the execution of the ninth Guru of the Sikhs, Guru Tegh Bahadur who was in the habit of undertaking extensive tours in the Punjab. Wherever he went, he attracted large crowds and was given handsome donations by his admirers. He gradually built a very large following. His exhortations to the people to stand firm were often considered as a call for rebellion against the Moghuls. Even Islamic expansion seemed in jeopardy as a result of his injunctions.

Aurangzeb's self-imposed divine mission did not harmonise with the teachings of Guru Tegh Bahadur. Consequently, the Guru was summoned to Delhi. Moghul officers who carried the summons to Anandpur, the Guru's main seat, returned to report him missing. The Guru was declared an absconder and a warrant was issued for his arrest. He was apprehended along with a band of his devotees at Agra, was brought to Delhi, arraigned before the court of the Qazi and was sentenced to death. The tortures to which the Guru and his followers were subjected revealed how inglorious Mercurial impact could be under adverse conditions. The historians have recorded that the barbaric tortures inflicted on the Guru's followers, in particular Bhai Mati Dass, Bhai Dayal and Bhai Sati Dass were such as to make one wonder if the milk of human kindness in the heart of Aurangzeb had dried out completely. (Saturn veiled Moon; Jupiter occupied Aquarius aspected by Mars from Leo, while Sun was debilitated). The mystery also deepens because the body of the Guru before it could be quartered and exposed to public view was stolen under the cover of darkness by one of the devotees of the Guru. The mental conflict of Aurangzeb began to manifest during Saturn-Ketu sub-period. He began to feel that his apparent righteousness in the pursuit of God's mission for establishing the Islamic dominance did not absolve him from his personal sorrow and difficulties. His eldest son Muhammad Sultan from his second wife Nawab Bai—a Kashmiri princess died at the age of only 38 years. It marked a new phase in Aurangzeb's personal sorrow.

Saturn-Venus sub-period began in October 1678. His youngest son prince Akbar, whom Nur Jahan once wanted to marry her daughter from her first husband and had harboured the hope that he could succeed one day the Moghul throne, was becoming restive that the emperor even though more than sixty years of age was not showing any sign of decrepitude. He proclaimed himself the emperor but gave up the illusion of usurping the throne; He began fleeing from one place to another and taking refuge in (Aurangzeb's) enemy's quarters. Aurangzeb was not dispossessed of the throne, as Venus, the ruler of the ninth and the fourth houses was placed in eleventh house which constitutes *Dhana Yoga,* a combination of affluence, but the disposition of Jupiter which was the dispositor of Venus being the ruler of the sign in which Venus was placed did not leave Aurangzeb free from troubles and anxieties about his personal and financial well-being. Venus in navamsa is situated in the eighth house along with Ketu in the sign of Mercury which itself is afflicted, so as soon as Venus sub-period started Aurangzeb was for some time engaged in military action against the Rajput rulers of Ajmer, Marwar and other kingdoms after which he had to tackle his son Prince Akbar and defeat him. He could not capture Akbar, but imprisoned his eldest daughter Zaib-un-Nissa in Gwalior for her alleged abetment of revolt by prince Akbar. He was also disturbed by deteriorating conditions in the Deccan. One of his comfortable feeling during this period was aroused by the news of the death of Shivaji which took a major thorn out of the mind of Aurangzeb. During this period of Venus under Saturn main period, there was no significant damage to his kingdom or his supremacy, but Aurangzeb was psychologically very much disturbed.

During his operations against the Marathas in general and Prince Akbar in particular, he was so much upset that he ordered all divisions under operation against them to return to Aurangabad where he was staying at that time and rumours gained ground that he had lost his mental balance. He had arrived at Aurangabad during Saturn-Sun sub-period, but during Saturn-Moon, according to the court physician Manucci, the emperor lost almost one-third of his weight. A slide downward caused alarm and generated gloom in the palace.

During July 1683, the emperor shut himself in seclusion for

sixteen days and remained confined in the first floor of his royal apartment without meeting any visitor. It was said that the fear of future haunted him. The strain of ugly thoughts could not but affect his health and outlook. Many times, he was heard raving in incoherent lamentations at night in which he seemed to invoke God for more light. Moon in the chart though exalted was greatly afflicted by Saturn; its association with Saturn in the natal chart and in the sign of Saturn in navamsa could not lead to serenity of composure. During Saturn-Rahu sub-period, the emperor further heard of his son Akbar's escape to Persia, annexation of Golconda fort to his empire but also of rebellion by his son Prince Muazzam who had to be imprisoned.

During Saturn-Jupiter sub-period, Aurangzeb felt the greatest satisfaction of his life but it was during this period that he precipitated the greatest cruelty. He conquered the Maratha empire which occurred with the defeat and capture of Shambaji and Kavi Kailash, his adviser. The news of Shambaji's capture was sent through a farm-Qanungo in the court of Bijapur, Sikandar Ali Khan. He was a man of high learning, who won the respect of the emperor by his piety and unfailing concern for the needy. Aurangzeb loaded him with honours at "the happiest tiding of my life" and as was his custom, sent in thanks giving large gifts of money to the shrines of Muslim saints in the Deccan. The occasion was truly great for him: he exclaimed, "the whole of Hindustan was now under his commandment", and what was perhaps more to him, "all the citadels of infidelity have finally been demolished".

The empire that Babar built, he reckoned was now safe for Islam. His life's mission was done. Orders were issued peremptorily for the demolition of remaining temples in the Maratha territories. The treatment met to Shambaji reflected the disposition of Saturn: "Shambaji soon after his capture was blinded in both eyes. Kavi Kailash's tongue was cut into twelve pieces, salted and thrown out as snacks for dogs. For the next two weeks, Shambaji and Kavi Kailash were subjected to barbaric tortures in an attempt to seek information about the hidden wealth. Neither broke the silence even when they were put on wheels over a blaze of fire. They were more dead than alive when the Mufti gave them the death sentence on charges of infidelity. On 11th March 1689, they were hacked to bits, limb by limb, on the banks of the river Bhine, 15 miles east of Pune. Their flesh and bones provided a feast for vultures hovering overhead.

Their heads were stuffed with straw and paraded on poles in all major cities of the Deccan. Thousands of men and women watched these grim processions with tears in their eyes".

This event greatly affected even the emotions of Aurangzeb; he became much more reflective than before. There was a radical change in his philosophy of life, yet the thought that a king should always be at war and discharge his royal duties which never left him till his very end. By now, he was past 70 years of age, but he never rested upon his oars.

During the following Mercury main period, Aurangzeb kept his royal schedule busy in waging wars, suppressing rebellions, invading new territories and annexing them, issuing firmans personally everyday and meeting visitors and diplomats. He never interrupted his offer of *Namaz* five-times everyday. Yet deep down within, a great disenchantment was growing importantly. The entire period of Mercury mahadasa, Aurangzeb spent camping out pursuing his enemies and extending his empire. From the day of his return from Rajputana in 1682 or so, until the day of his death in 1707, a period of 25 years, Aurangzeb never returned to Delhi. He was intensely apprehensive that a fate similar to that of his father Shah Jehan awaited him, if he returned to Delhi and lived amidst the palace intrigues. This period was not only for expansion of his empire but also of immense psychological turmoil and intense introspection. Even during the last years of Saturn-Jupiter sub-period, Aurangzeb often cried aloud before his senior Begum Aurangabadi in the name of justice and said that the Fate had been very cruel to him in forcing on him the decisions as a king which he could never have taken as a father. His heart was greatly disturbed with anguish and he thought that four of his children had come to grief, because of his obligations to himself and to the empire. This streak of introspection became acute during the Mercury main period.

From 1690 till his death in 1707, during the entire Mercury major period Aurangzeb experienced many situations which could have given him some happiness and relief yet his restfulness did not return to him. He was reconciled with prince Muazzam who was restored to honour in 1695, when Mercury-Venus sub-period was running, and he captured the fort of Satara during Mercury-Mars sub-period. One of his daughters died during Mercury-Rahu sub-period. During the same period, when Aurangzeb was camping at Khwaspur, there was torrential rain for over sixty hours. On this occasion, while going from one camp to another in hip-deep swirling waters in order to supervise the conditions of soldiers and others and to offer his daily prayers he met with an accident. While returning after his Namaz—seeking mercy for redressal from the rains, nearing the site of the royal tent, he stumbled against the roots of a fallen tree, fell heavily and dislocated his right knee. Despite the best efforts of the court surgeons, he remained lame for the rest of seven years of his life. It left a deep scar on his psyche.

During the rest of his life Aurangzeb continued his royal duties, waged wars against the enemies, and attended to the daily chorus of the court, but increasingly he was becoming introspective. His protracted wars had resulted in his protracted woes. More than once, he was heard beseeching death to take possession of his body and soul. The capture of the fort of Wagingera, situated midway between Bijapur and Golconda on 27th April 1705, which marked the beginning of Mercury-Saturn sub-period, brought to Aurangzeb the greatest joy of the years, but it also brought to him the lamentations of longevity. His old age was particularly sad, as it meant the end of all hopes. During the same period, a communication from Guru Gobind Singh brought him the final lesson of life. The Guru was a scholar of Persian and Sanskrit; he used to write hair-raising *shlokas* in praise of courage, freedom and generosity. His denunciation of the sins of aggression and treachery was equally soul-stirring. "The Lord will abhor both the blood thirsty and the deceitful men", he wrote in his letter known as *Zaffar Nama* to Aurangzeb. In his high spirited communication, the Guru told the emperor point blank about the sins he had committed against men and God. He also spelt out fearlessly the fate that inevitably falls upon those "who prayed with their lips and dissembled in their double-heart". This was a soul-search warning from a man of the spirit to a monarch, who ignored what the Guru called the fundamentals of life and death.

The tone and contents of this letter stirred Aurangzeb's conscience. Sad at heart, he called a halt to operations against the Guru. It is said that he was never the earlier religious megalomaniac again. Eighteen months later on February 20, 1707 he passed away perhaps as a penitent but more likely than not—a man dismayed at the failure of his mission. High fever struck him on February 15th. Ignoring the pleas of his physicians, he continued to pray and perform his religious and administrative duties till the 18th day, when semi-consciousness seized him. Though his tongue could utter no word, his lips continued to move up and down in prayers for the next 48 hours. During Mercury-Saturn sub-period itself, Aurangzeb passed to the other plane.

Aurangzeb's grave is bereft of beauty—either of stone or marble and only flowers grow in wilderness. Simplicity with him was an obsession. Before the obsequies ended, there fell a light shower of rain that led the faithful to believe that the heaven itself was in tears. This ended the long unfoldment which was contained in the very beginning. Nalini was right that we begin to die at birth, and the end flows from the beginning. In that case, our judgement about the human individual who acts his part on the stage largely in ignorance of the central motivating energy need not be considered decisive unless one could decipher the coded message in the stellar constellations for him and for the humanity at large.

3

CHANDRASHEKHAR AZAD

			Jupiter
Saturn (R)	*23rd July 1906* (Rasi)		Moon Rahu Sun, Mars
Ketu			Mercury Venus
	Asc.		

Moon	Saturn Mercury		Ketu
	(Amsa)		Mars
			Sun Venus
Rahu	Jupiter		Asc.

Chandrashekhar Azad was a unique personality of pre-independent India. He was born in a little known village Bhawra in Jhabua tehsil of Madhya Pradesh on 23rd July 1906 in the early afternoon. He belonged to an ordinary purohit family of Tewari Brahmins, whose main profession was to perform religious and social rites for the villagers. Chandrashekhar's parents Pandit Sitaram Tewari and Smt Jagarani Devi were simple devout, religious minded persons. Chandrashekhar was their fifth and the last child who died before completing his 25th year of age. His impact was so great on the political history of the country that it shook the very foundation of British imperialism in India which collapsed in about a decade and half after his death.

Chandrashekhar was born with a mission which unconsciously led him to a path which aroused tremendous upsurge of nationalism among the young generation who began to feel proud of being Indians and demand self-rule for the country. He represented the fiery enthusiasm of Mars and the cold perseverence and determination of Saturn. Kartikeya presided over the planet Mars and Hindu scriptures described him prior to his role as god, who vanquished Tarakasura made invincible by the blessings of Lord Shiva, as born of the radiance of Lord Shiva but preserved in his form of a horse by the Ganges and nurtured by the six Krittikas, the fiery asterism. Saturn is presided over by Yama, and officiates for Shiva in his aspect as one who dissolves everything into their ultimate essence; he has the tremendous perseverence of Time and has the vision of Eternity before him; he works to impart karmic retribution in order to reestablish natural harmony and equipoise. The combined impulse of Mars and Saturn representing Kartikeya and Yama was deeply ingrained in Chandrashekhar from his very infancy. The disposition of these two planets in his natal horoscope showed their enormous control over his life and activities.

As a child, one could find Chandrashekhar Tewari not much interested in educational activities but was much interested in physical culture such as wrestling in which he was very good. He was also considered an *enfant terrible.* It was this indomitable courage combined with his unsurpassable patriotism that made him shoot himself on 27th February 1931 when 80 soldiers surrounded him under the command of two British officers. Chandrashekhar died a martyr and his death was considered so glorious that the Indian people collected the bloodstained earth as memento so that they could tell their children that such a selfless patriot lived on the Indian soil. The British Government had put a reward of Rs 500 on his head but they could not capture him even after surrounding him for more than 32 hours on all sides. It is said that the police shot at him several times even after he had killed himself when only one bullet was left with him. His funeral was attended by many stalwarts of Indian resurgence movement like Purushottamdas Tandon, Kamala Nehru and others. People even started worshipping him after his funeral in spite of the Government's much resistance to the public doing so.

Chandrashekhar Tewari was born in Scorpio lagna with debilitated Mars in the ninth house obtaining *Neecha Bhanga Raja Yoga* as Saturn the lord of its exaltation sign, Capricorn, though in retrogression occupied its own sign Aquarious and is located in fourth house. Along with Mars were placed Sun and Moon, the latter occupying its own sign thus making Chandrashekhar a cool and determined patriotic self-sacrificing idealist. Venus and Mercury were in the tenth House while Jupiter was placed in eighth, and Ketu occupied the third house. Seven of these planets were located within a distance of 75° longitude clustering around Rahu, five of these planets namely Mars, Sun, Rahu, Moon and Mercury were within only 25° form one another. Even the distance between Saturn and Ketu the other end of the polarised planets was only 32°. The distance between Mars and Sun, which are friendly to each other is only about 4° but Rahu was 12° away from Sun while from Mars it is a little over 15° away. Mars the ascendant lord and Venus, a planet which occupies the tenth house were Vargottam.

Such a planetary disposition indicated very clearly that he was evidently born with that divine power which descends on earth only on special occasions for generating special evolutionary impulses even if it entailed considerable sacrifice and hardships to him personally. He was born in order to effectively exert special influence to produce new turns and twists in God's plan. Persons like him may remain unperceived, unknown and even unsung, but their contribution to human history is outstanding. Chandrashekhar Azad, who was the storehouse of tremendous energy, courage and complete dedication (Mars) to the cause of Indian independence contained within him that ruthless cruelty which under ordinary conditions might be considered heinous (Saturn), but combined with patriotic dedication and self-effacing personality, it becomes a mighty instrument for removing unsurmountable difficulties in the evolutionary course of a nation.

Events unfolded themselves in the life of Chandrashekhar in such a way, as if they were well-integrated episodes in a modern thriller. As a young boy, Chandrashekhar was a student of a Sanskrit Pathshala which was an elementary and very unorganised primary school teaching Sanskrit. As a student, he did not make much mark, but he subdued a notorious rogue of the region which earned him a name for being tough and it made him some kind of a hero. It happened before he joined the non-cooperation movement in 1921 when he was hardly 15 years of age. His chivalry and courage so much impressed Acharya Narendra Deo, the great socialist leader that he took Chandrashekhar away from the non-descript Sanskrit teaching institution and got him admitted in the Kashi Vidyapith at Varanasi which prepared students on nationalistic lines.

It was a turning point in Chandrashekhar's career. There he came across famous personalities who were fired with Indian nationalism and were chafing to dedicate their life to fight the British government for the sake of Indian independence. At this institution, Chandrashekhar met famous Manmathanath Gupta and Pranawesh Kumar Chatterjee. They did not believe in non-violent struggle: they later became famous revolutionaries of India. In this company, Chandrashekhar was fired with intense patriotism and absolute dedication to the cause of motherland. He was renowned for his tremendous urge for self-sacrifice, rather self-immolation for the nation but was never considered cruel, insolent, impertinent, insensitive or rigid.

Azad was always cool and composed with goodness at his heart. He was determined and uncompromising as far as national glory and Indian independence were concerned. When he was produced before an I.C.S. magistrate at Khareghat court in 1921 in connection with his non-cooperation activities, in reply to a question as to what was his name, he replied, *Azad* (meaning independent), his father's name was 'Swadhin' (independent) and his address was *Jail-khana* (prison house). It was after this incident that he became known as Chandrashekhar Azad. During the same period, in Central Jail at Shivapuri, he was given punishment of 15 times caning for shouting the slogan *Bharat Mata ki Jai* and *Mahatma Gandhi ki Jai*. It was however his last imprisonment; he could never be arrested again in spite of his active militant revolutionary activities for about a decade.

At the end of it, when he realized that he could no longer elude police, he shot himself dead with his own bullet. He died before he attained his 25th year of age.

During the decade 1921-1931, Chandrashekhar Azad had an active involvement with independence movement which however was of the most unconventional kind. After his association with non-cooperation movement in 1921 and his imprisonment on this accord, his *modus operandi* changed. He felt the need for money in order to organise militancy and to sustain the active workers engaged in the movement. In order to raise resources for this purpose, he felt no compunctions in organizing dacoity and robbing the rich industrialists. In December 1924, he is supposed to have raided an owner of a sugar factory in village Bamarauli in Pilibhit district. In March 1925, he carried out such a raid at the house of a rich merchant in Bichpuri village, as well as at the house of such a rich money-lender in Dwarkapur village in Pratapgarh district. In order to acquire money for his organization, he even volunteered to be a disciple of Mahant of Udasi Akhara in Gazipur district hoping that the property could be inherited by him after the death of the Mahant. But realizing that the Mahant was in a good state of health and there was no possibility of his early death, so the prospect of inheriting property this way seemed remote. He ran away from the place in about a couple of months.

By now, the anti-establishment proclivities of Azad were well known and the government was on his trail to nab him whenever an opportunity was available. Meanwhile, his involvement in Kakori murder conspiracy which surfaced in August 1925 made him extremely careful. This case was so important that Motilal Nehru and Jawaharlal Nehru along with others appeared on behalf of the accused. Azad absconded and went underground. For some time, he remained very quiet and only after 1928 he began to actively involve himself in the revolutionary movement. During the period of his underground life, he assumed for sometime the name of Hari Shankar Brahmachari and lived at the banks of a river in village Dimarpore near Jhansi and began to recite and explain Ramayana to the villagers and sustained himself on the offerings made thereat. This however was a cover for reorganising the terrorists group after the Kakori incident and to teach shooting and other acts of terrorism.

The danger in living for long at one place in the same guise made him change his place. He then moved to the Nai Basti mohalla of Jhansi and began working as a motor driver. Thus for several years after the Kakori murder case, Chandrashekhar Azad spent a variegated life, sometimes assuming the garb of a religious mendicant, teaching and preaching Ramayana and other scriptures while on other occasions, he functioned as a motor mechanic and a driver. But all through his primary involvement was with the organization of the revolutionary movement in the country. It needed an organisation and also a leader to command the activists. In 1928, Chandrashekhar Azad functioned both as the Chairman of the Hindustan Secret Republican Association which in fact was the Indian Revolutionary Party as well as its Commander-in-Chief, "Senapati". At that time, he was known in the Revolutionary Party as Senapati Azad.

The Revolutionary Party entered an active phase in 1930. Its organisation became more streamlined. It had a programme of action. Ad-hocism seemed to be replaced by a well-thought out programme of action. In July 1930, Azad organised a Gadodiya Store in Delhi and subsequently Himalaya Toilet Factory, but the real purpose of these was not to manufacture soap or to vend certain articles of daily use. It was an explosive manufacturing unit of the party and a centre of dacoity to raise resources for the national programmes. These were closed down after a few months, towards the end of 1930 itself. The same year, the Delhi conspiracy case surfaced. In fact, after Chandrashekhar Azad became the Senapati of the Revolutionary party, the organisation entered in a very active phase which was evident from the Viceroy train explosion in 1929. Then came the explosive manufacturing unit at Qutub Road in Delhi, followed by Delhi conspiracy which revealed the non-peaceful intentions of the party.

Now the police were after Azad and wanted to nab him, and he remained absconding. The leaders of the Indian National Congress were divided about the role of the Revolutionary party: some wanted it to continue in its militancy, whereas Motilal Nehru and Abul Kalam Azad thought differently. As a result of the intercession of Purushottamdas Tandon, a meeting was arranged between Chandrashekhar Azad and the moderates in the Congress but nothing emerged from the meeting. The Congress however failed to lend any support for the Revolutionary Party.

Meanwhile, the fiery zeal of the revolutionaries began to flag.

Many inspired leaders were already arrested and the discipline among the remaining members began to decline markedly. Such a situation produced much anguish in the mind of Azad. He began contemplating infusing new energy in the party and to introduce modern techniques of revolutionary movement. He wanted to incorporate the lessons of Russian revolution for which purpose he began to arrange for sending some volunteers to Russia for securing appropriate training. One batch was to leave on 1st March 1931. Plans were being finalised so that a group could leave for U.S.S.R. via Burma and Afghanistan. For this purpose, Azad had called Sukhdeo Raj, the great revolutionary who was later hanged, for consultation at 9 a.m. at Alfred park in Allahabad. But a person of his own community is supposed to have informed the Police and the Alfred park was accordingly surrounded by not less than 80 soldiers. There was a pitched battle and several rounds of shots were fired and many officers claimed Azad to have fallen from their shot, but Azad finding that his fire power was ending, shot himself with his last bullet and died. The following day when Lt. Col. Townsend, the civil surgeon at Allahabad carried the post-mortem, he confirmed his death to have occurred from his own bullet. Thus ended the 25 years aged glorious revolutionary, who became an apostle of freedom struggle with his courageous deeds for a decade in the service of his motherland.

This short profile of Chandrashekhar Azad shows how divine power (as that of Kartikeya for the annihilation of Tarakasura) is sent at an appropriate time to produce certain results. The planetary disposition at birth does not produce a result, but only reveals the divine dispensation. Heavy concentration of seven planets in eighth, ninth and tenth houses with Saturn in the fourth house forming Sasa, one of the *Panch Maha Purush Yogas,* evidently show that a mighty soul had descended to induce an impulse which could inspire the new generation to die valiantly for the independence for one's motherland. Such an impulse needed placidity of a tranquil lake which could reflect the moon-beam without any distortion, purity of spirit which contained no dross of egotism, self-surrender of a disciple which never questioned the command of his teacher, and the absolute detachment of Death-God Yama, who is never swerved by emotional cries.

The horoscope of Chandrashekhar Azad reveals much of these qualities otherwise a boy of 15 years of age could not shake the foundation of the mighty British Imperialism. The Rahu-Ketu axis in the chart indicates the fulcrum around which his whole life revolved. Ketu is placed in third house in Capricorn in Satabhishak asterism occupying Gemini navamsa, while Rahu is associated with Mars the lord of ascendant as well as Sun and Moon in the ninth house. The third-ninth house axis relates the ego with his punya karmas, his past meritorious deeds on the one side and his valour, and initiative on the other. We have seen above that the life of Azad flowed almost in a natural manner in a particular direction effortlessly; he did not have to take any conscious decision to regulate the course of his life: he was drawn by Narendra Deo to Kashi Vidyapitha without any effort on his part, there he met the revolutionaries and the subsequent events followed in the most natural manner.

Azad's courage was inborn: a small child does not ordinarily challenge a notorious rogue and subdue him. A boy in his early teens does not hurl explosives at the Viceroy's train. Before an individual attains the voting age, he hardly thinks of joining a political party, leave aside nationalist movement with plans to send volunteers abroad to obtain military training. In spite of such courageous activities and involvements, Chandrashekhar never showed any sign of 'emotionalism', he was always inspired by nationalism and his behaviour and actions were always grounded in ethics and righteousness (ninth house result). The Karmic axis has Rahu in ninth house and Ketu in the third house: his courage and initiative would arouse a deep sense of understanding and fulfilment of the purpose of life (the effect of Ketu), but these would be the result of his involvement in righteous deeds (Rahu in ninth house). The clubbing of planets around the ninth house shows that the karmic forces in his life were concentrated around a single goal. The ninth house and the planets related with this house held the key to his innate nature and the goal of his life.

The ninth house has the sign Cancer and its lord Moon occupies it. Cancer is a watery sign representing life-essence. But it is more than that: it is ruled by Moon which reflected the radiance of Sun. Water reflects the Moon-beam and carries the illusion of manifestation in the realm of matter. Often, Cancer is compared with Noah's ark in which the seeds of future regeneration were preserved in safety during the period of dissolution for their safe transportation to the desired land for their future growth and evolution. In a sense, Cancer is considered as the Hiranyagarbha, the Cosmic womb, which contains all that is yet to reveal. This fathomless treasure in the ninth house is a unique feature of this horoscope. The ninth house shows the divine benediction; its deeper significance lies in its relationship with the world beyond the perception of the physical sense perception. As a result of this house, the individual tends to unite with his higher self a result of the eight *siddhis*. Since Rahu is placed in this house, the entire past is churned and the 'self' in the individual is greatly minimised; he comes closer to his inner nature.

In the case of Azad as it would appear from the above, he had transcended his family and caste limitations, he was unconcerned with his own sustenance and betterment. His higher nature identified with good of the nation and freedom for the teeming millions so much overwhelmed him that he became almost oblivious of his personal needs and basic requirements. The power of Rahu in this position is so much increased also because of its occupation of Ashlesha asterism, which is presided by the Nagas, the custodians of esoteric wisdom as well as an instrument for the 'churning of the ocean'.

From the very beginning of his life, Chandrashekhar had been restless, dissatisfied with the external inequities and always pining to establish harmony in the society and among the people. This basic impulse of his life was greatly accentuated by Rahu's association with Sun, Moon and Mars. Mars and Sun are close to each other within a distance of 3°, but others are distinctly away without any combustion. The superficial surmise about the combustibility of Mars due to its proximity with Sun does not hold good in the present case on deeper considerations. Both the planets are of the same element; they are fiery in nature; both are engaged in sustaining life on earth, Sun does it on the inner plane while Mars provides energy for the maintenance of physical energy. Both of these planets occupy Pushya asterism, which contains within itself contradictory impulses. The Vedic God Brihaspati who is identified with the planet Jupiter presides over it while Saturn, which is associated with dissolution, eternity, concretisation and death rules over the asterism. Brihaspati provides sustenance, impels growth and expansion, arouses devotion and admiration for idealism. The concentration of these two opposing impulses in Pushya makes it unique in many ways. It is at this stage of cosmic evolution that divinity concretises, assumes material robe, expresses itself in efflorescence of floral beauty. Jupiter aids expansion, it protects and nourishes its beneficiary, while Saturn concretises, condenses and crystallizes nebulous matter. The combined effect of these two planets helps to stabilize materializing energy, and then enables it to fructify in an entirely new form. At this stage, the subjective aspect of cosmic evolution becomes objective archetype. This asterism links the subjective idea with the objective archetype. We therefore find that the combined effect of Sun and Mars in this asterism in the present case greatly accentuates the spirit of idealism (Sun) in manifesting itself in selfless devotion to nationalism, organising revolutionary parties to make the spirit of nationalism a reality in the life of Indian millions (Mars).

Chandrashekhar Azad was neither a lotus-eater nor a visionary philosopher; he believed in action (Mars), he wanted to do things. So his idealism (Sun) was also an impulse for action (Mars). The close proximity of Sun and Mars has not resulted in the combustion of Martian influence, rather it has reinforced the concretising influence of the latter. It is worth noting that Mars though debilitated both in rasi and navamsa chart becomes Vargottam, while Sun occupies its own sign in navamsa. Moreover, during the course of their movement, these two planets continue to increase their distance which makes Mars more powerful to exert itself; it becomes extraordinarily strong and effective in expressing the solar idealism in his everyday life, in his mundane sphere of action. The importance of Mars in this horoscope is increased also on account of other factors, which cannot be overlooked in delineating the influence of the ninth house, which we would be examining shortly.

Meanwhile, it may be noted that the impending movement of Sun towards Rahu and the tendency to associate itself with Rahu, while extricating itself from Mars will make Azad extremely elusive, secretive, deeply active and often acting in a non-conventional manner. Rahu is described as immensely powerful, born of a lioness, having a huge body like a mountain of lamp-black colour, snake-shaped, terrible mouthed and a devourer of the Moon and the Sun. The special power is enjoined to Rahu, because it is a messenger of the Cosmic Law under which the entire universe operates. When Rahu begins to produce changes and externalize the karmic forces, its impact is not necessarily on the surface: it is a great turbulence, however, on the psychic plane. The revolutionary nature of Chandrashekhar Azad was an expression of this turbulence which received marked thrust from solar and martian impulsion. When

Rahu is likely to be covered by solar rays, and both are in their positive disposition, the individual under their influence becomes a mighty force for pulverization of well-established social mores. They are willing to stand against the millions and adhere to what they think right whether in action or in words. In the present case, Sun is sufficiently far away from Rahu to get afflicted by its dark shadows, but immediately behind it so as to throw its energizing radiance to Rahu in order to make it powerful enough to go against the existing thought current; Azad was fired by nationalism but he did not tow the line of the moderates like Motilal Nehru, Abul Kalam Azad and others. Chandrashekhar Azad was a tender hearted (Cancer with Moon) indomitable (Sun) terror (Rahu) who carried out his plans ruthlessly (Mars).

The ninth house in the present chart contains so many planetary impulses with such intricate relationships that the psychic constitution of Azad becomes difficult to decipher. The association of Rahu with Moon and Sun in the same sign does not enable these luminaries to function in their normal manner. The combination of Sun and Moon in the ninth house produces a powerful Raja yoga: Moon is the lord of a trine and Sun the ruler of a cardinal house. A similar Yoga is formed by the combination of ascendant lord Mars and the lord of a trine house Moon. The placement of the lord of ascendant in the ninth house also produces an auspicious result and is said to be productive of much wealth. The effect of these planets cannot be considered nullified by the presence of Rahu as the latter itself in Cancer is said to produce beneficial effect. In the present case, the presence of these combinations cannot be considered operating on physical plane.

Chandrashekhar Azad had often to obtain his livelihood from *Madhukari vritti*, almost the life of a mendicant. However, the ninth house being a house related with past meritorious deeds, these planets almost overflooded him with such impulses which were earned and woven into one's *sanskaras*, psychological make-up which very smoothly enabled him to achieve the mission of his life. Rahu being one of the planets in this house enabled him to mobilize these impulses for the life's task ahead of him. The inspiration and the innate urge to dedicate oneself for Indian independence, the idealism of nationalism, did not arise in him as a result of intellectual understanding of the significance of independence, or the family background of politicians, or even as a reaction to atrocities committed by the alien government: his patriotism and adherence to revolutionary philosophy, armed rebellion even if it meant fighting single-handedly arose as a result of his past karmas. His urges and inspirations were genuine and innate.

Mars which also happens to be the ascendant lord is debilitated but obtains *Neech Bhanga,* cancellation of its debilitation due to Saturn's occupation of a cardinal house in relation with ascendant in its own sign. Saturn in retrogression becomes significantly powerful. As a result of Saturn's occupation of a cardinal house in its own sign, *Sasa Yoga,* which is a *Panch Maha Purush Yoga,* is formed. In exoteric astrology, this situation of Saturn produces a person who is courageous, middle stature in height with muscular thigh, slender waist and able to perceive weakness of others. He is wise and erudite, a commander and leader of armies, wanderer of forests and other inaccessible regions, knowledgeable in metallurgy and chemicals. He is agile, fond of sexual pleasures and attracted to other person's wives, capable of appropriating other's wealth and greatly devoted to his mother. Many of these features were applicable in the case of Chandrashekhar Azad, but they do not reveal the greatness for which this yoga stands. The combination also lays down that the person lives for about 70 years, but Azad died before he was 25 years of age.

The contradiction can be resolved if we refer to esoteric implications of *sasa yoga.* It qualifies for extraordinary greatness because, *swagrihi** Saturn in a cardinal house either with respect to ascendant or the Moon sign suggests activation of *Muladhar* force-centre located at the base of one's spine. When this force-centre is energized, it arouses serpent fire, *Kundalini,* which releases much latent power. As a result of this activation, the individual obtains much physical energy whose expression however depends upon other planetary disposition in a chart. In an ordinary person, still functioning on physical plane devoid of emotional refinement and absence of aspirational fire, the kundalini arouses almost uncontrollable sexual power which is capable of making the person wayward and even make him a sexual wreck. But if the latent energy is well regulated and properly directed, it could lead the individual to spiritual development enabling him to receive 'Initiation' in (esoteric) mysticism which is often imparted in secluded places like

* Residing in one's own house.

forests inaccessible to ordinary human beings or in mountain caves, which are often difficult for the general public to discover. Those who are religiously inclined and fired with the spirit of selfless social action and pursuit for higher objectives in life with righteous living will find this energy of immense help in their mission. In the case of Chandrashekhar Azad, Saturn is aspected by Mars and Jupiter which is the lord of the second and fifth houses. Mars is the ascendant lord as well as the lord of the sixth house; the sixth house is also aspected by Saturn. This relationship makes Saturn extremely significant.

Such a planetary situation produced tremendous difficulties and uncomfortable life for Azad. Throughout his life, he was beset with physical difficulties of different kinds (the lord of sixth house in ninth house), but these were accentuated due to his own decision regarding his mission in life (the sixth house lord which happens to be Ascendant lord in ninth house). The Saturn's aspect on sixth house completely destroyed the impact of these difficulties. The direction of Saturn's energy (Kundalini activated due to arousal of *muladhar chakra*) was towards philanthropic activities (Jupiter's aspect) and the movement of this energy was under control of the individual (Ascendant lord which also happened to be Mars aspects Saturn). Thus we find that the relationship between Saturn and Mars and the concentration of a large number of planets around the ninth house provided the clue to the life of Azad.

The planetary rulership also unfolded the life of Chandrashekhar in such a manner that the right planets took control of his affairs for which he lived. He was born with about two years balance of Mercury main period. It was the period of his infancy about which nothing much can be said. The following seven years of Ketu made him a precocious child more inclined to physical culture. Only when Venus main period began in his life that remarkable events began to unfold. The Sun sub-period in Venus main period began towards the end of 1918 which brought him in close relationship with eminent persons like Narendra Deo and others. Sun is the lord of his tenth house and Venus is posited in that house. Sun being twelfth from Venus, nothing spectacular could be expected. During the Moon sub-period which extended from 1918 end to the third quarter of 1921, he began to undertake his political activities. He was still non-violent and working on Gandhian lines. Moon is in Ashlesha asterism and in the navamsa of Jupiter. Eighth from it is Saturn. It was twelfth from Venus—the ruling planet. As a result, he was jailed for a noble cause and punished, while expressing his dedication to nationalism. He was caned while he shouted *Bharat Mata Ki Jai* and *Mahatma Gandhi Ki Jai*. But he came in his real element, when Venus-Mars period prevailed. During this period he made much preparations for his revolutionary programme and was not traced.

It was only during Venus-Rahu sub-period that much of his dacoity, political murder and use of explosives became pronounced. The Kakori murder case occurred during this period: Rahu sub-period in Venus main extended from October 1922 to October 1925. During this period, Chandrashekhar Azad had even to reap the consequences of deeds performed during the sub-period of Mars, which initiated him in militancy. Jupiter sub-period extended upto June 1928 and for about six years from 1925, Azad was absconding and eluding arrest. Jupiter occupies the eighth house and his existence during its rulership became secret, but as it aspected Saturn with its ninth aspect, it encouraged the activities under the domain of Saturn. Yet, it led him primarily to organizational work.

As soon as the Saturn sub-period under the Venus main rulership began, there was a marked change in his life. Azad became the *Senapati*, the Commander-in-Chief, and Head of the Revolutionary Party. He opened an explosive factory in Delhi, and became involved in Delhi conspiracy case. He was organising to send trainees to U.S.S.R. and other countries so as to get training in militancy. The *Sasa Yoga* was fully operative during this period. But Saturn is placed eighth from Moon and the ascendant lord, so treachery could not be ruled out. At the same time, Venus, in spite of its being placed in tenth house, is the lord of seventh and twelfth house connected with death. Even Mercury with which it is associated is the ruler of the eighth house. And above all, the period of Venus-Saturn is generally fraught with misfortune and calamities. Saturn plays the most crucial role in the life of Azad, and during its rulership within inauspicious Venus occupying its enemy's house, Azad killed himself with his own bullet though several police officers and government detectives also fired at him till he was thought completely dead. Saturn aspected the ascendant and Rahu was associated with Moon, so it was under the planetary impulse that Azad thought in accordance with cosmic law to end his life.

Thus, under the planetary propulsion of Mars, Rahu and Saturn, one of the brightest sons of Mother India rose like a meteor in the firmament and disappeared within a decade of its rise!

4

KIRAN BEDI

	Rahu	Mars Mercury(R) Sun	Venus
	9th June 1949 (Rasi)		
Jupiter (R)			Saturn
	Moon	Ketu	Asc.

Jupiter	Rahu	Mercury	Asc. Saturn
Mars	*(Amsa)*		
			Sun Moon
Venus		Ketu	

The sixth sign of the zodiac namely, Virgo, is symbolised by a woman standing in a boat carrying with her corn and fire. This description of Virgo given by Yavanacharya is full of mystic allusions, which reveal the basic impulse flowing through it for the evolution of mankind. It is a symbol of primordial feminine creative power and for the inner quietitude and tranquillity of any individual the grace of the virgin is essential. Yet in everyday life one finds that Virgo ascendants are generally dissatisfied with their existing conditions and are miserable. Their misery however is of unusual kind. It results from the difference between the actual and the aspired for conditions. "Their idealism, their martyrdom, their dreams are more envigorating than their crippled, restricted and materialistic life. Virgo-born are dissatisfied with their present environment and pine for that which is not present. If they are spiritualistic, they are martyrs for an ideal for spiritual regeneration of the society or for producing a supra-mental level of consciousness. As materialists, they would strive for more extensive power, higher status in life and a larger number of human conquest. Whatever the outer expression, the Virgo-born are always dissatisfied with existing circumstances."[1]

Indicating the various esoteric relationships of this constellation, Blavatsky even quotes one French scientist, who equated the sign with Durga, the most ancient goddess of India. Endorsing the views of Swami T. Subba Rao, she mentioned that Virgo represented *Shakti* (power) personified by *Mahamaya* who represented the six primary forces in Nature[(+)]. The various characteristics of this sign indicated by the seers are very well expressed by the symbol of the sign in which boat represents the mainstream of the flow of life represented allegorically by *Kshirasagar* on which Vishnu reclines during the Manavantric evolution; Fire represents the *Fohat,* the Creative Energy, which vibrates in every form of manifestation as the life principle; and the bundle of stalks of corn stands for that which sustains Life. In this way, Virgo ascendant stands for the tremendous

---

1. *Introduction of Esoteric Astrology*, Bepin Behari and Madhuri Behari, Sagar Publication, New Delhi, p. 97.

(+) *Parashakti* (the supreme power generating light and heat), *Jnanashakti* (the power of knowledge and wisdom), *Ichhashakti* (will power), *Kriyashakti* (the power of thought and volition), *Kundalini* (the Serpent Power) and *Mantrashakti* (the power of mantras).

power that preserves and impels life to evolve towards its ultimate destiny. Idealism, responsibility, perseverence, dauntless courage and complete transcendence of personal consideration are some of the important features of those, who are evolving under the impulsion of the sixth sign of the zodiac. And Kiran Bedi is one of those persons, who was born under this constellation.

Kiran Bedi was born on June 9, 1949 at Amritsar in Punjab in the afternoon at about 2.10 p.m. when Virgo almost in the middle of Hastha asterism was rising on the eastern sky. The ascendant lord Mercury which was Vargottam and retrograde in Taurus was going to have its direct motion in a few days' time. Though situated in between the Sun and Mars, the two very dynamic planets of the sky, it was not combust and exchanged signs with Venus, which was posited in the tenth house. Mercury also received full fifth aspect of restrograde Jupiter and of debilitated Moon which enjoyed *Neecha bhanga Raja Yoga* due to the situation of Mars in a cardinal house from Moon and the lord of its exaltation sign in a cardinal house, the tenth house, from ascendant. It (Mercury) also received full tenth aspect of Saturn from twelfth house which was situated in the sign of Sun, Leo and in Gemini navamsa. Thus, the ascendant becomes very powerful giving much strength to the horoscope.

In this conjuncture of stars, the direction comes from the impulsion of Hastha asterism supported by Mercurial planetary disposition. This asterism is ruled by Moon, the receptacle of cosmic energy, whereas Mercury, which rules over Virgo within which this asterism completely lies, establishes a link between the human and the divine. Mercury which rules over mind, intelligence, is exalted in this constellation. Its primary motivation is *Moksha*—Liberation, while its basic attribute—*guna* is Tamas, inertia at both primary and secondary level with Rajas activity at the tertiary level. The deity presiding over Hastha is Savitar, the Sun-god, particularly as the reservoir of all generative energy in the universe. The symbol of the asterism is the palm of the hand, through which the entire individuality of the person can be read. About the influence of this asterism, it is stated that:

> Hastha gives self-reliance and control over the outgoing cosmic energy that is always ready to proceed further. Various impediments arise in this enterprise as natural reactions to it. Whenever any kind of energy moves over static matter, there

> is resistance to it. Such an individualistic approach to life as is natural under this asterism must bear this kind of confrontation. The inner faculties can develop only through such an exercise.
>
> The hand stands for prowess or the capacity which enables the individual to withstand confrontation. The hand also refers to full confidence in the soul's capabilities to march ahead. This self-reliance springs from the fact that the individual is aware of his own faculties through an understanding of his real nature and the laws of the universe. This is the basic and most important characteristic of Hastha.[1]

Kiran Bedi's life for more than four decades shows that the ascendant lord is very powerful: it does not matter what specific task she is assigned, she does that with full vigour and dedication. Her application is total and its result extraordinary. Truly like a Durga she plays her role and succeeds in directing the cosmic energy for effectively completing the task in hand. Her strongest forte is her total application with complete dedication and herself concerned only with coolness of her composure, boldness of approach, complete impersonality in her application and full trust and confidence in her own self. Such an attitude however has not made her without human feelings, without any milk of human kindness.

Her relationship with family members—husband, friends, daughter, colleagues as well as with her superiors and subordinates are very warm and very well balanced. Yet, there is complete identification as well as total detachment in all she does: this contradictory, verging even on enigmatic quality, springs primarily from her Virgo ascendant. She is intellectual, full of passion and warmth, yet completely detached always concerned with what she should do rather than enjoying the fruits of her past successes or licking the wounds of her past failures and frustrations. It is for such characteristics that Kiran Bedi cannot be fitted in a stereotyped pattern. Sabina Sehgal Saikia very well described the Kiran Bedi effect as follows:

> There is a touch of drama in whatever she does. And her long list of 'firsts' has ensured her two decade long presence at the

1. *Myths and Symbols of Vedic Astrology*, p. 208.

centre of media attention. But there can be no denying that the quintessential supercop—Kiran Bedi—has come a long way from the early firebrand days when she was catapulted to fame for being the first woman to enter the IPS. Gone are the abrasive edges, the controversial quips that for instance, marked her battle with the Delhi lawyers or underlined her vehment defence of her daughter's controversial admission into a medical college in Mizoram.

The energy 'Crane' Bedi is now a creature of the distant past. Today, a sensitive Bedi offers a humane insight into the travails of the most celebrated of Indian prisons—the capital's Tihar jail. As Inspector General (Prisons), a position she was assigned last May (1993) after nine months of no work, she has laboured relentlessly to provide dignity to the prisoners and jail staffers alike.

"My endeavour as IG (Prisons) has been to move ahead from the primary function of ensuring security to the equally important role of creating a human atmosphere within the prison", says Bedi. She has been able to win over most of the prisoners who regard her with a mixture of awe and admiration. Even the high-security inmates, who have not been able to participate in the activities introduced by her were moved by her gesture to allow them to watch the World Cup and Wimbledon tournaments on television.[1]

Saikia has very well indicated the transformation seen over a number of years in the temperament of Kiran Bedi. The change from firebrand (fire in the hand of Virgo) to civilising influence on Tihar inmates (a handful stalk of grain in Virgo's hand) is only a difference in the expression of the essential cosmic energy radiating from Virgo. The disposition of ascendant lord in association with fiery Sun and Mars fully aspected by Moon and Saturn made Kiran Bedi versatile in many ways, but it is displayed in an extraordinary manner by making her absolutely fearless completely trusting herself to destiny, fate or God, whatever one may like to call this nameless absolute power.

Kiran Bedi does not seem to concern herself with naming this universal cosmic energy—energising and protecting every form of

1. *The Times of India,* (Delhi Edition) dated 26th June 1994.

manifestation. It is this absolute trust in the supreme power and complete confidence in her own self that put her 'first' among her peers; it also provided her with tremendous courage to confront difficult situations without any trace of nervousness. As a woman police officer—she had been the first woman officer of the Indian Police Service, when almost no such high ranking woman officer existed even in advanced western countries like the United Kingdom and the United States. She braved sword wielding mobs with nothing more than a baton in her hand. Her enthusiasm or rather the abundance of it, often put her on the uncomfortable side of the powers that be, but she took it all her stride. Astrologically, it would be unnatural for Kiran Bedi to be anything other than what she is—her own real self.

She was born as the second daughter of Prakashlal Peshawaria and Premlata Devi among the four daughters her parents had. Usually in an Indian family, when the first child of a couple is a female, their natural expectation and desire is to have male issue; the female second child has often to satisfy the psychological, emotional and social expectations (and sometimes disappointments of the parents) but Prakashlal was different. He brought her, as well as his other daughters, not as a girl or a boy, but as human beings which did not discourage them to have the humane consideration and compassion associated with *Jagadamba*, the world mother whom the Virgo sign represented, but it also gave her the freedom, boldness and assertiveness of a man which comes by a full integration of one's internal self and external conditions.

This unique balance which is evident in her planetary disposition and is confirmed by her responses to various situations, through which she had passed was greatly fostered by her father (Sun) who drilled to her that she would have to keep asserting herself to get to her goals. This assertiveness made Kiran Bedi to leave Mizoram state for Delhi to enjoy her right that the medical seat earned by her daughter would not be usurped under sectarian governmental pressure, for which action she remained without posting and salary for about nine months. It was not gender specific but an expression of her inner strength, sense of righteousness, and boldness to stand against the world for one's right. This assertion is identified as 'empowerment for any of the men or women, holding firm against societal status-quoists'. Kiran Bedi is not considered overtly aggressive, saying, 'I'm a woman, I'm at a disadvantage, so I have to push'.

Instead, what strikes one about her is her equipoise, a rare attribute in both sexes. More important, defiance does not seem to have anything to do with it. In fact, what Kiran Bedi has displayed is on-rush of creative force which impeded by anti-evolutionary inertia, the result of status quoists erupts as defiance, aggression or even ruthless high-handedness. Virgo produces such an outflow of evolutionary impetus, which is founded on compassion, responsibility for the preservation, nourishment and growth of humanity, and total disregard for one's manipulativeness. Idealism, sympathy, courage, and tremendous responsibility to one's inner self are basic features of this nature.

During the course of her existence for the last four and a half decades, whatever the situation in which she was placed she has shown complete involvement as a result of which she succeeded in producing the most spectacular results. As a student, she secured first class honours in English during her graduation, in her post-graduation she opted for political science; she again got a first class topping in her college. During the course of her service, she even received a doctoral degree for her research in narcotics. She had been an excellent photographer, skilled dramatist, and an eminent sportsperson. In 1972, she was the Asian champion in lawn tennis, in 1970 and 1973, she represented India abroad and in 1974 she was the national champion. It was on the tennis court that she met Brij Bedi and during the course of their friendship, the courtship lasted for about a year and then they decided to get married in presence of their parents in a temple. So Kiran Peshawaria became Kiran Bedi. Her husband is an engineer and a businessman living at Amritsar, where her parents lived. They have a very intelligent daughter doing medical course and the family is very well-knit and loving to one another. Her relationship with her parents as well as with her in-laws is extremely sweet. The couple have to live separately due to professional consideration, but because of self-confidence and trust in each other, the family is extremely attached to one another. Kiran Bedi has sufficient quota of femininity. Yet her outflow of energy in areas of male domain is no less powerful.

In 1972, she entered the Indian Police Service through allied services examination and was the first female officer in India (and as a matter of fact, first even in the world for a comparative status appointments). In 1975, she was given the prize for being the best female cadet. In 1976, she was put on duty for Indira Gandhi's security. As Deputy Commissioner for Delhi's West and North districts, she earned the gratitude of thousands of beggars for whom she arranged loans and assistance so that they could set up legitimate business of their own. In 1978, she confronted Akali-Nirankari agitation with exemplary show of courage and presence of mind that she received the President's Bravery (Police) medal for the same. She was also put on duty for the security of Charan Singh. During 1982, she managed the Delhi traffic so well that she almost became known to every household in Delhi. Whatever she did, she achieved spectacular results and for her contribution, the people gave her several appellations which have stuck to her. For her control of traffic congestion in Delhi, she was known as 'Crane' Bedi. For regulating three-wheelers in the metropolis, she was called 'Danda' Bedi. But in all these appellations, there is enough of affection, and admiration for her dedication and efficiency. The usual talk among the Delhi grapevine had been that everyone has a price but not Kiran Bedi. This in fact, has been the most rewarding contribution and acknowledgement for her integrity.

But the Delhi lawyers would not have discipline through the hands of a lady police officer. The trouble began when she showed courage by handcuffing a lawyer, who was accused of some criminal act and the whole crowd became unruly and began asking for her 'blood', for her resignation, transfer, disciplinary action, and what not. This was during the Ketu main period and Kiran Bedi had to bear some mental anguish. The government and the Supreme Court were both seized with the complicated nature of the problem. Kiran Bedi was found very unwelcome in Delhi by certain bureaucratic group, and she was transferred to unpopular posting. The agitation in Mizoram against her personal rights specially when it concerned the future of her daughter which the daughter had earned on merit made her stand against the unjustified demand of the State Government and the people. She came abruptly to Delhi, defying the normal practice and remained without any posting for nine months.

When in 1993, she was given the charge of Tihar Jail, it was felt that the end of Kiran Bedi had come. Her fire will be extinguished and she would lapse into humdrum of regular police routine. But the fire in Kiran Bedi was the cosmic fire which would burn everywhere either for the destruction of maleficence or for providing nourishment for evolutionary seedlings. It was her role as Inspector General (Prisons) that she received Ramon Magsaysay award for community service for which Prime Minister P.V. Narasimha Rao congratulated her. The Home Minister, S.B. Chavan congratulating her said that the honour bestowed on Kiran Bedi had brought glory to the entire security forces of which she is a member. This prestigious award was given to her—not as a concession and consideration for her being a female officer; it was the foundation's community service award in the whole of Asia. She was the second Indian to receive it; the first was the award in 1959 to Sir Chintaman D. Deshmukh.

Kiran Bedi was awarded the 1994 Ramon Magsaysay award for government service, which carried a prize of $ 50,000 and is among Asia's most prestigious awards. Shortly before this award was announced, Kiran Bedi was invited by the United States President Bill Clinton for a breakfast meeting, which she was not permitted to accept.* But the Magsaysay award was different and was hailed by the highest authorities in the country. The foundation cited that "No social relationship in Asia is more fraught with ambiguity than that between the police and the people. For too many people, the police are not a positive good, only a necessary evil." The citation also referred to Kiran Bedi's contribution in establishing the drug rehabilitation centres that were expanded when she became Deputy Director of the Narcotics Control Bureau. As Inspector General (Prisons) in the Delhi area, where 8,000 inmates were housed, 90 per cent of whom were simply awaiting trials, she made their life so humane that most of these undertrials followed a positive regimen of work, study and play. Illiterate prisoners learnt to read and write. In prison workshops, prisoners kept their skills tuned and earned wages to save at Tihar's new bank.

Kiran Bedi, who earlier had been accused of becoming ruthless in executing justice or extending the long hand of police authority specially with regard to the Delhi lawyers, created a new history in the relationship between the police and a portion of condemned section of humanity. Navjyoti, Delhi Police foundation for correction, de-addiction and rehabilitation owes a great deal to the new dimension of creative initiative taken by Kiran Bedi. It was established during the peak period of career-wise most troubled period of Kiran Bedi, in 1987. During the first seven year period, it detoxified 7,000 drug addicts, who came not only from Delhi but

(*) On a later occasion, she was permitted to do so.

from far-flung areas of Rajasthan, Uttar Pradesh, Jammu and Kashmir, Haryana, Shillong and Assam. Since its inception at Delhi, such centres are now opened in Uttar Pradesh, Maharashtra, Kerala and Haryana. At the foundation, vocational training was also imparted to women and street children in Yamuna Pushta slums and Jehangirpuri resettlement colony. Evidently, it was the expression of feminine caring attitude rather than the aggressive exercise of police authority.

At Tihar jail, which is the largest prison in the Asia-Pacific region, Kiran Bedi brought in a new impetus of life-force. She inspired the inmates so much that there has been popular slogan in the jail: *Ham Jayenge To Wapas Nahin Ayenge* (After we leave the prison, we shall never return), yet more touching has been the experience of an inmate crying at leaving the sympathetic and creative *milieu* that 'Danda Bedi' created for them. It has been a centre of social activity, which probably is much better than the inmates expected outside the jail.

Kiran Bedi considered the premises of jail, the staff working for the prison and the inmates of the jail as problems of human relationships: none of these needed to be neglected, because they were concerned with those human beings, who were either suspected of criminal behaviour or whose guilt had been proved. They are also human beings who have committed a crime and needed the same kind of sympathy and understanding as those who were outside the prison. Kiran Bedi was struck by the overcrowding of the jail. There were more than 8,700 inmates, 300 women posing special problems, and all of them housed in near sub-human conditions. The premises was built in 1956 —originally designed to house only 2,200 prisoners but now the number has increased four-fold. So she tried to have some more floor area available for the inmates, and attempts were made to have some new buildings for the purpose in Mandavali, Narela and Rohini. About 80 per cent of the convicts were mere undertrials—which implied that their crimes have neither been so far identified nor proved, and many of them have been waiting for their trials for several years.

Kiran Bedi thought that the police should have been more 'circumspect' before arresting them. Her responsibility in this capacity was to look after their welfare, so she tried to clear the general pollution in the premises. For this purpose she made Tihar- a non-smoking zone which greatly reduced the incidence of such diseases as coughing, spitting and bronchial ailments. Nearly one-fourth of the inmates were suffering from respiratory diseases over which the government had to spend substantial amount of money, and the inmates were suffering from ailments which were avoidable. The government spent Rs 108 per prisoner a day for providing medicines, food, water and electricity. Converting the jail into non-smoking premises was helpful to the inmates as well as for the State.

Kiran Bedi also introduced special provisions for imparting vocational training, besides the teaching of basic education; she arranged for the inmates to work and receive payments for their productive activities, which could be deposited in special accounts owned by them. As there were a large number of female prisoners who gave birth to children while in prison, she made arrangements for those kids to be around their mothers upto the age of five years. Creches and nurseries were organised for them. She was also concerned about their physical and mental health. On January 26, 1994, the inmates of Tihar jail celebrated Republic Day as the 'Health-care Day'. A team of medical experts provided them complete medical check-up and advice. All prison inmates were given health cards giving details of their health, blood pressure, weight, and other details of their physical well-being. All those who needed specialised care were given pink card, while others were given white card. The official interest in the physical health of persons supposedly held for some act of criminality, radically altered their attitude to the state authorities. This change even harmonised their behaviour and integrated their personality better. They seemed to take a positive attitude towards life in general.

But another programme initiated by Kiran Bedi was extraordinary about which she herself stated that if officials of a foreign jail witnessed such large gathering inside a prison, they would have suffered a heart attack. It was in connection with a ten day 'vipasana' (meditation) course conducted inside the prison in which 200 inmates participated. Kiran Bedi attached considerable importance to cosmic energy and believes that properly channelised could bring a radical transformation in one's life. She therefore introduced this line of experience in December 1993, to see whether the inmates were sensitive to such influences. She invited Swamy Anand Swabhav of Osho Commune International—a disciple of godman Rajneesh at the Tihar jail to conduct a meditation camp on December 27, 1993. It was a first camp of its kind in which any Sanyasi undertook a mission in jail. Herself being a skilled dramatist, Kiran Bedi knew the advantages of interest in fine arts. She organised theatre group inside Tihar jail in which the inmates themselves participated. On some occasions, even special programmes were organised by school children in colourful costumes. The high-security prisoners, unable to participate in the activities introduced by her, were arranged television sets to watch World Cup and Wimbledon tournaments.

In these programmes, she has been clear about her task. "My endeavour as Inspector General (Prisons) has been to move ahead from the primary function of ensuring security to the equally important role of creating a humane atmosphere within the prison", she said. Kiran Bedi enjoyed great satisfaction from her relationship with the prison inmates who regarded her with a mix of awe and admiration. Most of the inmates use simple expressions to describe this metamorphosis: one of them stated, "*Yeh Swarg Jaisa Lagta Hai*" (This place feels like the heaven). The jail itself is rechristened. It is now known as *Sudhar Griha*—the House for Reform.

The change has been so spectacular that the prisoners are losing their hostility and non-cooperative attitude and becoming more amenable to discipline and regulations. Joseph Obi—an African national who has been an undertrial at Tihar since 1991 expressed that 'it was like a Nazi concentration camp earlier, but now it is like a school". Arif—a Pakistani national, after fumbling many times before he could get the words to describe what he felt says, "I had plenty of hate for India till I landed in Tihar". As a member of the theatre group inside the Tihar, he says, he thought he would never be accepted so well by Indian prisoners. Now, with his feelings transformed, he said, "What is happening between India and Pakistan is political warfare. There is no malice in the heart". Greater satisfaction comes to Kiran Bedi when an inmate is released, and he or she begins to shed tears at the parting.

T.N. Seshan who had offered her a job of Deputy Chief Election Commissioner when she was without any salary or posting for months, called her a "baton-wielding Florence Nightingale". K.J. Alphons, Land Commissioner, Delhi Development Authority, said that she had "infused hope and humanity" in the heart of the prisoners of Tihar jail by transforming it into an *Ashram*. He called her "the greatest government officer in Asia, who has set a remarkable example for the country". But Kiran Bedi herself considered to be an ordinary person. "I am a very ordinary person. I just do my duty everyday to uphold the rule of law", she said. About the Ramon Magsaysay Award, she stated, "It recognises the power of government service to correct, to spread a message of hope". But to many persons, the change in Kiran Bedi from baton wielding 'Crane' or 'Danda' Bedi to a docile and meek social reformer whirling round the prayer wheel and organising meditation classes among the convicts is a transformation in her own psyche. Abhinav Aima, reacting on the Magsaysay Award to Kiran Bedi very rightly exclaimed, "who would guess that a police officer who led a lathi charge against Delhi's lawyers with the war-cry, *Maro Salon Ko* (Kill the anti-social), would earn the Ramon Magsaysay award for community service? Who would believe that Danda-Bedi who once sent shivers down the spines of errant drivers would organise meditation classes for hardened convicts? Has Kiran Bedi really transformed into a peacenit? Or, is she, like always, just doing her duty?" And he himself answers when he states that "she has been criticised and idolized, but it goes to her credit that so far little has changed in her outlook. The woman just cannot be moved from her resolve and her beliefs. A bundle of energy she moves around the Tihar compound,—determined to put her plans for day into action". Describing her own quality, Kiran Bedi has stated that he has tremendous perseverence and the urge to tackle every problem that confronts her and not to slide back. In fact, astrologically speaking, Virgo ascendants have these qualities in abundance, but in the case of Kiran Bedi her ascendant lord was Vargottam and special relationship with all the planets in sky has given her a special role to play in the world.

The horoscope of Kiran Bedi is heavily concentrated towards her ninth house, the house of Purva Punya. It shows that much of the impulsions as well as power for executing her programmes came from the merits earned in her past lives. Except Moon and Jupiter—both debilitated in the horoscope and also yielding to *Neecha Bhanga Raja Yoga*, cancellation for their debilitation—all other planets are connected with the *Mysterious Depth*[+], which relate them with primordial potentials of the manifestative principles. Jupiter is also retrograde. These planets have the function of reflecting the archetypal goal (Moon) and nourishing the individual to attain the same

(+) The second, sixth, eighth and twelfth houses in a natal chart represent the *Mysterious Depth*.

(Jupiter), while the planets posited in the *Mysterious Depth* channelise the forces radiated from the universal cosmic consciousness.

In Kiran Bedi's horoscope, Rahu and Ketu occupy the second and the eighth houses and the special life force related with these houses provide the fulcrum around which all major events in her life revolved. The eighth house represents the enemy's fortress and unexpected sudden events in life while the second house stands for creativity—the positive attitude to life and its various relationships. Mercury which is the lord of Kiran Bedi's ascendant is retrograde in the ninth house which suggests its great affinity with the eighth house. Though placed in the ninth house for producing certain special impact in the life of the person concerned, yet would be inclined to give the results of its placement in the eighth house towards which it is moving. Mars owns the eighth house, Sun is the ruler of the twelfth house. Venus which occupies the tenth house and exchanges house with Mercury, is the lord of the second house. Saturn which rules over the sixth house is even placed in the twelfth house.

As a result of these placements, Kiran Bedi will be in the midst of such important events which would be sudden, unexpected, arising from hidden centres—and provide her enough opportunities to show her creativity. Two of the most crucial confrontations in her career had been her tough stand against the Delhi lawyers and her bold stand against personal discrimination in Mizoram, pressurizing her to surrender the seat in medical college earned on merit by her daughter, but these events gave such twists in her career that she was without any posting for about nine months receiving no salary during the period. As a punishment, without reducing her rank, she was posted as Inspector General (Prisons) where her creativity (second house) earned her the most prestigious award for Asian government officers. It was a coveted award for any Indian during the last 35 years—the first Indian to receive it was Sir Chintaman Deshmukh in 1959. The *Mysterious Depth* and the planets related with it always produced extraordinary results in her life.

The ascendant in the horoscope is hemmed by two malefics namely Saturn and Ketu. The general effect of such a conjunction is imprisonment, limitations, and unmerited difficulties. These physical level difficulties cannot be denied in her life. It is important to understand that the planets act at all levels of one's existence, therefore what they are expected to produce on the physical level cannot be undone by other impulsions in the horoscope or by any planet itself. The good as well as bad results of planets could be experienced by an individual provided he had the requisite capacity to imbibe them. The finer forces generated by Saturn and Ketu produce tremendous objectivity in Kiran Bedi's approach to various problems in life. Ketu is very finely situated: it does not impinge on the ascendant nor afflict the Moon. Situated in the second house with full third aspect from Saturn, it has acquired the capacity to concretise its abstractions.

Kiran Bedi is a visionary working for an ideal situation under the tremendous impetus from Saturn. The lord of the sixth house, Saturn represents store-house of various perfections—*siddhis,* placed in twelfth makes her personal and bodily injuries unimportant for achieving the goal she sets for herself. She hopes to achieve under the constricting and difficult conditions the expected results. She attains personal satisfaction, liberation, by accepting her limitations and working in that situation impersonally. When she received the Magsaysay award, she felt that the credit for the same should go to those in Tihar and outside, who helped her in realising her dream of reform in the jail. Similarly, her Police service and odd postings arrested her stay with her family members. She could not devote as much time to her daughter as she desired to do. She was unable to care for her husband, nonetheless, she accepted the limitations and working in a detached manner, she has succeeded in making them—her family members—daughter and her husband—happy with her caring nature for them. Such is the result of two malefics—Saturn and Ketu, flanking her ascendant.

The fourth house, which stands for emotional nature of the individual also reveals the status of family life, mother, immediate environment and the storehouse of all the past karmas. It is only in exoteric astrology that the fourth house stands for home, private life, transport facilities, landed property, mother, diseases of the chest and peace of mind. Kiran Bedi has two benefics flanking this house, and Jupiter by the virtue of its being retrograde tends to give the result of its occupation of this house, so all the auspicious features prognosticated by this combination can naturally be expected in her case. In fact, she does possess abundance of these. But in deeper or esoteric astrology, the fourth house signifies many other conditions of one's inner life. The esoteric astrology indicates the close relationship between the fourth and the tenth houses. While the tenth house signifies aspirations, ambitions, public standing and all matters outside the home such as career, profession, and social status, the fourth is the source from which all these spring. The tenth house draws the individual to the future, while the fourth reveals the past—the environment into which one was born, the family support one receives, the landed property, vehicles, clothes and ornaments one receives as well as the emotional nature one has inherited.

All these things reveal the type of karma—the individual has already generated. The karmic past is called *Sanchita Karma,* the primeval seed from which the evolutionary pattern flowers. In this sense, this house is related with Hiranyagarbha, the Golden Egg, which is one of the names of Brahma himself. It is the inner creative principle—the "seed" or the potential which forms the basis of one's psycho-spiritual nature. The planets flanking this house in the case of Kiran Bedi make her highly evolved, but she does not have the nature or the mettle of which seers and saints are made. Moon and Jupiter are both debilitated which makes them material minded; Venus is also a planet of sociability. Mars aspects this house (fourth) which also increases her concern for physical life—the life here and in the present tense. As a result of her concern for the present, she enjoys life to the brim without transgressing moral laws, she is extrovert but is not impractical, she applies all her moral values (arising from Moon and Jupiter) for the betterment of one's existing conditions and discharging of the given responsibilities, but not the assumed ones. It is for this reason that everyone in contact with her has the admiration for right behaviour though nobody could take any liberty with her. It is indeed an extraordinary achievement in Indian society to keep mother, father, mother-in-law and father-in-law as well as one's husband happy by a working woman. But in spite of her being a police officer and having a very busy schedule, she keeps everyone of these relations very satisfied.

Moon and Jupiter, both yield to Neechabhanga Raja Yoga, which enhances her financial status. The relationship between the lords of second house (Venus), the ascendant lord (Mercury) with ninth and tenth houses leads to affluence. Kiran Bedi has Venus in the tenth and Mercury in the ninth. So one does not have to worry about her financial stability, even if she were not paid her salaries for long period. The planetary disposition in her horoscope reveals at the very outset that an extraordinary person with a mission to bring some kind of social transformation is born. She is born with much innate energy for creating social transformation than for her own spiritual development in the sense of devoting oneself to yogic practices and disseminating scriptural teachings. One should note the position of Ketu in the house related with speech: she would rather use foul language and do virtuous deeds rather than intone sonorous Sanskrit *strotras* and indulge in nefarious and shady deals.

The planetary rulership also occurred in such a sequence in her case that the various qualities and situations, which were useful for the externalization of her innate qualities could get the best opportunities. She had Saturn balance of 17 years 1 month and 20 days. This was the formative period for Kiran Bedi. Her future psychological attitudes were formed during this period. Saturn in the twelfth house brings to the surface those intimations from the eternal past which urge the individual onto the path of spiritual unfoldment. The native is persistent in getting whatever he wants; his opinions are very important to him. Sometimes, there may be deep-rooted spiritual intonations in those ideas, but the native is primarily activated by the fact that these are his own ideas, and for that alone he will work. Saturn in the twelfth house is primarily a spiritualising planet, but it leads the individual through a difficult path so that the lessons learnt on it are enduring. The usual expression of it on a growing child is that he or she becomes determined, not ready to yield to others and there is always the innate desire to get what one wants.

In the present case, Saturn is in the asterism of Makha symbolized by a palanquin or a house which stand for inner drive. At this stage, the soul in its fullness as a representative of the supreme embarks upon its material journey, the outer journey ordained for it. At this stage, the soul is informed of its divine mission and is stationed at the place wherefrom it can make its onward journey. But under this impulse one experiences conflict. One part of the being urges the soul to swift action, while the other part puts on a brake to bring the movement to a halt. Generally speaking, Makha leads to substantial psychological tension and frustration. Saturn under this asterism placed in the twelfth house produced a vibrant child, full of energy, very determined but not feeling satisfied with the given conditions of life. The very fact that Kiran was a second female child in an Indian family with the following two as female issues could not provide her a natural milieu for upbringing howsoever understanding and reconciled the parents might have been. They never showed any unnatural feeling towards her, but the very fact that she was extremely dynamic and had a female body created an extraordinary situation. She learnt what a boy could have, but she had the natural emotional make-up of a loved female child. So she could have a disciplined and harmonised personality development, capable of adjusting and making her mark in any kind of society.

The Mercury period started in the middle of 1966, which emphasised the importance of educational achievements in her career. Mercury is related with intelligence. Its main period occurred at a time when the native was deeply engrossed in her educational activities. Mercury contains within itself all the qualities of Venus which imparts to it the qualities of sensitivity, easy rapport with the world around oneself, and intuitive understanding of ideas, feelings and expectations of others. But additionally, it also receives the sparkle, the intuitive flashes radiating from the Sun, which gives special importance to Mercury. It is the reception of the solar ray that makes Mercury creative, intelligent, capable of penetrative insight into the most difficult problems or adaptable to the most difficult situations. Mercury is placed in the asterism of Rohini, which provides a kind of impulse—which was displayed in the career of Kiran Bedi for the entire period when the planet was ruling her life. The period extending from 1966-83 from the age of 17 to 34 years was the one in which Kiran Bedi showed so much of her inner capabilities and achieved such a remarkable status in India and abroad that her subsequent experiences during Ketu and Venus periods could be borne with equipoise and dignity. It is stated that "astrologically, the symbol of Rohini is a chariot which is a means of transportation for royalty, especially to the battlefield. Swift and dignified movement is its special feature. It is led by horses which stand for virility and divine kinetic energy. Rohini functions to transport the universal life-force, which is essentially regal and dignified in nature, protecting at its initial stages until it reaches the time, when it is strong enough to meet its adversaries. These are the various allurements of the outer existence." But in the present case, Mercury is greatly strengthened in its influence by its association with Sun and Mars—the former making its actions very dignified and the latter by providing its tremendous kinetic energy in externalizing the inner potential. The Sun and Mars are result-oriented planets. Jupiter also aspects it and so does Moon and Saturn. As a result of these planetary aspects, Mercury has succeeded in externalising the inner cosmic energy with dignity (Jupiter), intelligence (Moon) and restraint (Saturn).

It has been during the Mercury main period of planetary rulership that Kiran obtained first class in B.A. (Hons.) in English and obtained her post-graduate degree in political science securing first class, standing first in her college. She became an extraordinary tennis player (Mars) and represented India abroad in 1970 and 1973, she became the Asian champion in 1972 and was the national champion in 1974. It was on the tennis court that she met her fiance, whom she married after a year's courtship. The marriage was not solemnized in the traditional style. They were married in a temple (Saturnian sign Capricorn is occupied by Jupiter which owns the seventh, the house of marriage) but it was with the consent of the parents and their presence (Jupiter owns the seventh house). In 1976, she was associated with the security of Indira Gandhi. In 1978, she boldly confronted the Nirankari-Akalis with only a baton in her hand and for exemplary bravery was awarded the President's Bravery (Police) medal. She was also put on the security duty with Prime Minister Charan Singh. As incharge of Delhi traffic, she earned the wrath and admiration of errant drivers, was also called the 'Crane' Bedi. As in-charge of traffic control during the Asian Games, Kiran Bedi achieved the greatest glory of her professional career. Her reputation as an efficient organiser and the director of the most difficult human problem soared very high. Her contribution to the organisation of India's most stupendous international undertaking since independence was so spectacular that she almost became a symbol of efficiency and orderliness. That happened during Mercury-Saturn sub-period; their relationship represented *Kendra* (cardinal house) and *Trikona* (Trine) combination producing a kind of *Raja Yoga*. Moreover, Mercury is very auspicious but Saturn is also no less helpful. Saturn becomes auspicious by occupying twelfth house as a ruler of sixth house; as a ruler of fifth aspecting tenth lord and ascendant lord, it bestowed much organisational capacity leading to glorious achievements. It was a period of much personal and professional satisfaction to Kiran Bedi.

Ketu main period began from the middle of 1983. At that time, Saturn began flanking the Moon, which is usually known as the period of *Sade-Sati*—7½ years of inauspicious influence. During the same time, Rahu occupied her tenth house, and the eighth position from Moon. These heralded the advent of the most trying phase of her career. The popularity earned during the earlier period had aroused much animosity against her and many persons were disturbed by her upright behaviour. She would not tolerate any compromise with law and order regulations. But the society was not ready to accept such a correct posture. So friction seems to seethe at various levels, which erupted in different forms, with the Delhi Lawyers' strike when Ketu main period began.

It is alleged that a lawyer supposed to belong to a respectful profession was accused of indulging in some unlawful act and Kiran Bedi ordered him hand-cuffed. The lawyers agitated over the issue and wanted punishment of Kiran Bedi. It drew adverse attention of the authorities and the case was dragged to law-courts. It was a very distasteful and even humiliating experience for Kiran Bedi, who had so far received only kudos for brilliance in the performance of her official duties howsoever difficult that had been. The Lawyers' strike and similar experiences gained during this period brought a radical psychological change in Kiran Bedi. It was an inner churning; she realized that the individual should not only be true to one's profession, but also devoted, ethical, upright and uncorrupt and holding the rule of law to the best of one's ability, he has to be harmonised with his inner or higher self. There should be no compromise on what is right even if it meant one's greatest sacrifice. One's profession was merely an extension of one's inner creative unfoldment.

Ketu's main period began a phase of spiritual humiliation, mysterious illumination and psychological regeneration. She realised that her anchor in life should not be a professional career, but the latter was just a means of her own creative unfoldment. So under the transformation produced by Ketu, the outer conditions remained the same, but there was a radical change in her inner self. Now, she did not wish to work for approbation, but her profession became a means for inner growth and discharge of personal responsibilities at all levels and to be willing to undertake every hardship that may occur for the same. So an indirect, covert punishment posting to Mizoram was a different kind of test presented to her. Will she accept the political pressure to save her profession and disregard responsibilities to fight for the right of her daughter? She opted for the latter. There was a great risk involved. The action gave strange signals at various levels. Kiran Bedi who once sent shivers down the spines of errant drivers in Delhi and boldly defended her act in handcuffing an alleged criminal even if he belonged to an honourable profession (thinking that a criminal act was a criminal act, which was an individual's act, and not that of his profession, so he should be treated according to his act and not according to the coat he wore) was now subjected to a similar psychological strain. Will she break down under the strain? Could she survive, if she were given no posting and no salary for a long duration? She was not made of wool: she could stand any professional, political, and covert pressures.

Finally, she was given the posting, where there was no authority of the police force; she was no more to exercise any power over the individuals. She was made the Inspector General (Prisons) of Delhi Tihar Jail—a posting which was among the criminals and under-trials, a responsibility, which to a common police officer, who once confronted sword wielding Akalis with nothing more than a baton in her hand should have been demoralizing but it was not so for Kiran Bedi. She was by now sufficiently evolved spiritually under the churning operation of Ketu. She had become sufficiently open to the onrush of the cosmic power and was much more attuned to universal life-force rather than to her professional status and the glory resulting from the star strips on one's uniform. She took her new assignment as a spiritual responsibility, not merely a professional task. By this time, Kiran Bedi had started her Venus main period, which began in the middle of 1990.

Venus stands in a special relationship with Kiran Bedi. It exchanges place with the tenth lord, unaspected by any malefic. It is placed in Ardra asterism. It presides over the second house related with creativity as well as with one's affluence. It is placed ninth from its sign in the second house. Tenth from tenth house is ruled by Jupiter which is very auspiciously placed in this horoscope. These have been extremely favourable indications and one could have expected extraordinary results during this period, but there seemed not much opportunity for Mrs. Bedi. She was devoting herself to the welfare of the inmates of the jail and there seemed nothing much to show one's initiative and creative faculties. She was concerned about the welfare of the inmates and was not worried about their criminality. She thought of them as human-beings and was trying to establish rapport with them just on that level. With Venus as the lord of ninth placed in the tenth house, it was inevitable that in her relationship with thousands of inmates, there would be some kind of humane consideration and what form it could take no one could comprehend. Venus is sociability, arousal of sensitivity and higher emotions in one's relationship. Venus encouraged relationships both at horizontal and vertical levels. Being related with ninth and tenth houses, Kiran Bedi began to treat them like human beings providing them freedom of expression and living within the limitations imposed by the rules regulating the prison life.

The Tihar jail was one of the most crowded prison in the country. It was built in 1956 for only 2,200 prisoners, but presently there are more than 8,700 inmates. It included 300 women prisoners. To give them relief from overcrowding, she began finding ways and means for making them enjoy the open air life within the precincts of the jail. She began organising sports and cultural activities. She began to arrange for their educational programmes, acquisition of professional skills in different trades. She arranged for the prices to be paid for their products and money deposited in their personal account with which they could rehabilitate themselves when they go out. For the babies born in the jail, special creches and nurseries were opened. Specially qualified doctors began to attend to their physical ailments: special health cards were issued to them indicating what special attention do they need. The jail was made a non-smoking zone, which reduced their susceptibility to breathing, bronchial and heart (tuberculosis) diseases. She organized for de-addiction of drug addicts. She invited many 'swamis' to conduct meditation classes for the inmates. As more than 80 per cent of the inmates were mere undertrials waiting for charges to be framed against them, which was not the responsibilities of Inspector General (Prisons), Kiran Bedi began treating them as human beings with enough scope for living a fuller life while in the prison—which could very well be an opportunity for them to adapt themselves well in the society when they go out. She was continuing with this kind of programme in her usual manner—unconcerned with the consequences—a lesson which she learnt during her Ketu major period.

But as soon Sun's sub-period began, auspicious events began to take place. It started from December 1993 and on July 11, 1994 Ramon Magsaysay Foundation announced that the award for government service for the year 1994 was being awarded to Ms. Kiran Bedi, the Inspector General (Prisons), Delhi. It acknowledged that "no social relationship in Asia is more fraught with ambiguity than that between the police and the people. For too many people, the police are not a positive good, but only a necessary evil." The citation recalled that "Today its (Tihar Jail's) inmates follow a positive regimen of work, study and play. Illiterate prisoners learn how to read and write. In prison workshops, prisoners keep their skills tuned and earn wages to save at Tihar's new bank." As a result of such contribution to community welfare, Kiran Bedi became eligible for the prize which carried $ 50,000, which is one of the most prestigious award in Asia. She was the second Indian to receive it after a gap of 35 years. Overnight, Kiran Bedi became the highly prized first Indian Police woman officer. The Home Minister S.B. Chavan considered that the honour bestowed to Mrs. Bedi "has brought glory to the entire security forces of which she is a member"

The lady who had been charged several times for the contempt of court and the officer whose dismissal was sought by Delhi lawyers, and whose career itself was in jeopardise for her fight for her daughter's medical seat earned on merit was now given a word of appreciation even by the Supreme Court judges, who were trying her for the contempt of the court. Kiran Bedi said that the award "recognises the power of government service to correct, to spread a message of hope" and underlined the importance of the service in ensuring public welfare. Such results follow from Venus occupying Gemini in the tenth house. Venus in the tenth house enables "the individual to establish an immediate rapport with others. He can have an intuitive perception of the special requirements of people coming into his sphere. At the same time, he will have knowledge of nature's harmonising effects. Together, these two faculties will produce captivating actors, political leaders, and practical scientists, as well as great reformers who may change the world. The native will have hypnotic power over people".[1] When it happens in Gemini, "coveted social status comes unexpectedly and money flows to the individual without any impediment. He is much respected and obeyed and his sociability and diplomacy are both of an extraordinary nature![2]

The future of Kiran Bedi is still unexplored. It is just the beginning of Venus main period and various political parties have begun inviting (and luring) her to join them. Janata Dal, the Congress and the Bharatiya Janata Party have all approached her, but her family is against it. She herself does not "have a gut feeling for joining politics"

---

1. *Planets in the Signs and Houses,* Bepin Behari, Passage Press, Utah, U.S.A., p. 198
2. *Ibid.*, p. 203.

but she has not closed her options. She may do so, if the system is cleansed. That is a big question mark, but astrologically, one certainly feels that she has a long way to go before she settles down to any humdrum routine life. The days of her turmoil and difficulties are not yet over. Moon, Jupiter and the ascendant lord Mercury are in adverse relationship with Venus which have still a long-period to go.

5

THE 14th DALAI LAMA

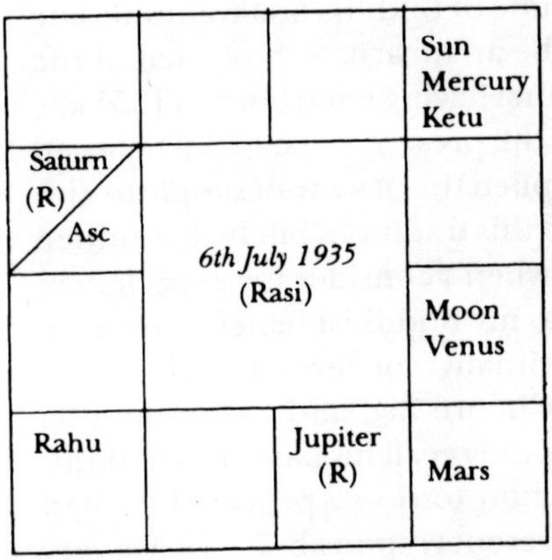

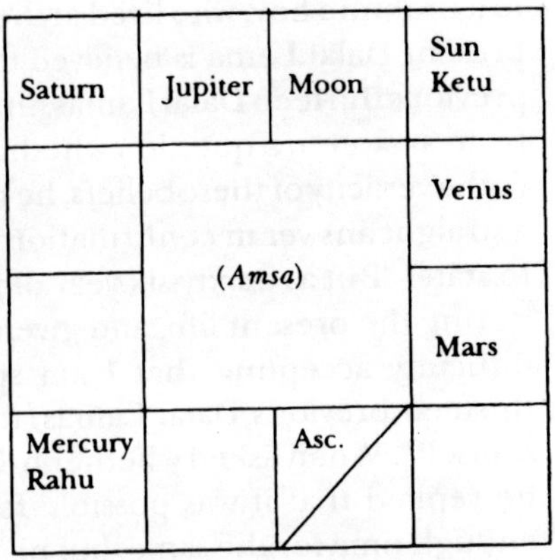

Dalai Lama is the most outstanding political leader of the twentieth century—zealously struggling to save the perishing ancient Tibetan spiritual culture under the Chinese repression. He exudes Buddha-like love, compassion and friendliness. He has tremendous insight in laws of human manifestation. He is capable of delving deep into the inner realities of life. However, on the physical plane in the discharge of his temporal duties, he has failed so far to achieve his goal. His personal life is very lonely, full of pain, suffering and deprivations. These extraordinary features of his life present a very unusual example of stellar disposition. Much mystery surrounds his personal life, and there are powerful planetary influences affecting his life. The common rules of physical (exoteric) astrology does not very appropriately explain the relationship between the planets and the inner struggles and developments of the man.

The legends suggest that the Dalai Lama is a manifestation of Chenre Zig, the seventy-fourth at a lineage that could be traced back to a Brahmin boy, who lived at the time of Buddha Shakyamuni. The present Dalai Lama is believed to be an incarnation of each of the previous thirteen Dalai Lamas, the first having been born in 1351 A.D. In an answer to a question whether the present Dalai Lama believed in the veracity of these beliefs, he replied that it was not simple to give a straight answer in confirmation to this tradition, but he continued to state: "But as a sixty-six year old, when I consider my experiences during the present life, and given to my Buddhist beliefs, I have no difficulty accepting that I am spiritually concerned both to the thirteen previous Dalai Lamas, to Chenre Zig, and to the Buddha himself". When asked whether he could recall his past incarnations, he replied that it was possible for him to do so provided he had enough time for the same, but his present responsibilities leave very little time for such exercises.

The consciousness working within the present Dalai Lama is aware of its glorious lineage, tremendous responsibilities in the present birth, but his present experiences have not been very pleasant. Does he know the future awaiting for his mission? Nobody can answer it, and Dalai Lama himself is silent about it. He is relentlessly progressing towards his goal; his journey so far has been very arduous. He is subjected to tremendous physical hardships, emotionally he is unduly humiliated and has often seemingly very hopeless task to accomplish, but he continues with a placid mind in his mission. Dalai Lama was awarded Noble Peace prize and invited to address prestigious fora, but his basic task remains unfulfilled. His present life has been full of setbacks, much frustration and several threats even to his physical life. On many occasions, even his requests for interviews with several dignitaries were turned down. He was bullied and ill-treated by Pandit Jawaharlal Nehru. The Chinese Premier Chou En-lai threatened him of dire consequences, if he did not tow his line of advice. Dalai Lama was accorded during the early phase of Tibetan occupation even red-carpet treatment, was made a Vice-President of the Steering Committee of the People's Republic of China and was invited to China where he was provided with all sorts of luxurious conveniences. In spite of such adulations, when the Chinese illusion about him was dispelled, the level of humiliation gradually increased so much so that at one stage Mao Tse Tung cajoled him and the Chinese military began contriving opportunities to arrest, torture and even (possibly) annihilate him. The psychological pain many a time was accompanied with physical deprivations, health hazards and failures in his well-meaning endeavours.

The enigma of the inner greatness, the inner consciousness stretching upto the period of Lord Buddha and his spirituality being the same as that of the first Dalai Lama born in 1351 A.D., is difficult to be resolved. It is not easy to reconcile past legendary claims with his experiences during the present birth. Apart from metaphysical questions involved in it, to us there is another basic question. Does the stellar disposition at the time of his birth reveal the inner greatness and the spiritual heritage or is astrology merely concerned with physical events?

Astrology in the ordinary sense which one studies in exoteric books reveals the physical evolutionary course, the trials and tribulations the individual encounters and the manner in which he ends his life. There is however another problem very vital for spiritually inclined persons. Can astrology reveal the process by which each individual (given his uniqueness) in the process of consciously integrating outer consciousness with inner placidity comes to gradually identify himself with his eternal nature and finally attains *Nirvana*, the final redemption?

Exoteric astrology is related with outer events, outer or physical experiences and responses, and as the individual has various sheaths covering the inner spark, it is possible to understand the nature of these sheaths and their evolutionary process. Esoteric astrology could however indicate the state of the inner consciousness, the critical mission assigned to the incarnating ego, the level of inner realization of the ego and such other problems with which very few persons are interested. In order to get a feel of esoteric principles, one has to step out of the usual planetary disposition and relate the chart and the planets with their deities, elements, and the cosmic forces they represent. These are difficult studies, but one cannot overlook them if one desires to know the deeper possibilities as in the case of spiritual persons like Dalai Lama, Ramana Maharshi, Sri Aurobindo and others. Only such a study could reveal the nature of egoic pilgrimage of such advanced souls.

The immensity of spiritual connections and vast expansion of consciousness of Dalai Lama stretching over millenia accompanied him in this birth with enormous physical impediments and psychological limitations arising from several restrictions imposed by karmic factors of the physical sheaths through which the ego had to function and carry forth the divine mission. The astrological studies relating to such seers must distinguish between the consciousness within and the outer sheaths; the stellar forces on these two must be analysed appropriately. The rules of esoteric astrology will apply to the inner man and the exoteric results of the planets will affect the physical garments with which the seer carries his everyday responsibilities. It would be apparent from the study that Dalai Lama does not bring into operation occult attainments, while discharging his mundane duties. In fact, in scriptures also we have stories when great ones behaved like common individuals and suffered the consequences like any other mortal. The rules of occult world do not allow the divine emissary to invoke his higher powers for every mundane undertaking. (We shall have more of it when we discuss the life and work of J. Krishnamurti subsequently.)

An important feature of Dalai Lama's inner impulsion is the complete abandonment of his occult forces while working for controlling and guiding the evolutionary course of humanity. Nonetheless, several biographical studies of Dalai Lama have shown that the inner forces and motivations are more important to him than the logic of outer events: Dalai Lama depends on superconsciousness in times of emergency than the 'rational' and logical inferences based on known facts of the situation, but his non-conformism with the mental reasoning does not make him an eccentric. The proclivities of the past, his *purva samskaras* align him much in harmony with hidden forces of nature and constantly move him towards his ultimate mission. Under this impulsion of superconsciousness, he is ever willing to risk his life, his security and all his material position and status. In obedience to the superphysical command received, he is prepared to sacrifice the security of his mundane counsellors. Recalling the intensity of such intonations from early childhood, which he received quite frequently, Dalai Lama has himself recorded that "One of the favourite occupations of mine as an infant was to pack things in a bag, as if I was about to go on a long journey. 'I am going to Lhasa, I am going to Lhasa' I would say". He also recorded that he would insist that he be allowed always to sit at the head of the table. He never allowed anyone excepting one of his sisters to handle his bowl. He never showed any fear in meeting strangers. These personality traits which found expressions much before any one else had any inkling that he was going to be the fourteenth Dalai Lama, were his inner being peeping through the outer self. These intonations from the past would have been considered meaningless aberrations, if the heavy mantle did not fall on him. His psychological make-up and inner (unconscious) promptings revealed the powerful and highly evolved status of the being that ensouled the weaker outer sheaths, as these could not have been the reflex of one born in humble farmer's family among whom he was born and who were making a precarious living.

When Dalai Lama grew older to carry out innumerable responsibilities of political governance of a religious state faced with difficult situations, he sought the guidance of the unknown sources, his personal super-physical guardians as well as the deities controlling and supervising the destiny of Tibet. He had special methods for doing so. He was often forewarned of impending dangers by them in many special ways. On such occasions, when he experienced serious tremblings of the land and occurrences of 30 or 40 explosions, which were some sort of natural phenomena and the people saw strange blood-like red glow in the sky, the explanations given to him by seismological experts did not satisfy him. In this case, Dalai Lama recorded: "I find it much easier to accept that what I witnessed was metaphysical. At any rate, warning from a high is mere rumblings from below, the situation in Tibet deteriorated rapidly thereafter".

This is one of the many examples showing that the external events and the omens were very real to Dalai Lama. He was more in communion with the unseen powers when he needed specific guidance for action. For example, it was at the instance of Dorje Drakden, the deity guarding Tibetan affairs that he was given full temporal powers two years before his time; he abandoned the idea of seeking some sort of refuge in India when Chou En-lai threatened him with dire consequences. It was also at the advice of the unseen that Dalai Lama stayed in Tibet even when he and his advisers apprehended threat to his life. When he fled to India, at the bidding of the unseen, his personal feelings were that the advice was very strange, unpractical and inopportune. Dalai Lama has recorded that prior to his acting on such an advice he decided "to lay prostrate and pay his reverence and devotion to the shrine dedicated to Mahakala, his "personal protector divinity". When he did so, he was advised to "develop confidence and courage". The journey that followed and the ordeals through which he passed, and the Chinese air-borne surveillance that tried to shadow him and his party are well known. Dalai Lama had surrendered himself completely to the control and direction of the superphysical guide as soon as he was convinced that proper safeguard has been taken against "the gods lying when they too became desperate". In his mind, he is ever convinced that the power from the beyond is more knowledgeable than the superficial intellect of the physical self; once the message was clear, he did not hedge against the risks in obeying the voice. Apparently in his mundane behaviour and responses, Dalai Lama uses his common sense and intelligence, but always believed in the sagacity of the higher voice when important action-decisions were involved and uncompromisingly he obeyed such commands. He completely trusts the wisdom of the unseen.

Many strange intonations from the superphysical planes have been recorded by Dalai Lama. He does not claim any clairvoyance or extraordinary psychic faculty, yet he does not deny his communion with higher sources of intelligence and power. Even in such cases, he does not abandon his intelligence. He often experienced unusual phenemena communicating to him messages from the unknown. For example, on his journey to the Chinese capital in early 1954 at the invitation of the Communist government with a view to rapprochement between the two countries, Dalai Lama perceived an unusual occurrence, which he recorded himself as follows: "At Ganden, when I left Tibet's third greatest university monasteries to continue my journey to China, I noticed something very strange. A statue of one of the protector divinities of Tibet, which is represented as having a buffalo's head had clearly moved. When I had first seen it, it was looking down with rather subdued look on its face. Now, it was facing East with a very ferocious expression. (Similarly, I heard that at the time of my escape into exile, the walls of one chapel at Ganden ran with blood)".

Once enquired about the relationship between the present Dalai Lama and the memory of his past lives, he indicated that "he does not have the memory of these past lives, but if he had the time required for the task, he could work them out". He does not have only the continuity of consciousness, but the perception of the super-physical existence and the protection and guidance from the Unseen to which he is completely dedicated and is in total obedience to it is also not absent. He believed in the possibility of reincarnation and the theory of Karma. These dimensions of life have made him very uncommon with his inner life, outer responsibilities, his unswerving application towards the attainment of his assigned task—yet, he is not 'unduly' perturbed by non-fulfilment of his present political goal. His immensity and innocence at the inner plane of existence while at the mundane level his involvements with preoccupations and innumerable limitations make his life unique.

In the life of a person like Dalai Lama who lives a fuller life on inner planes of existence, the four houses namely, the twelfth, eighth, sixth and second which represent the *Mysterious Depths* of manifestation are very important; one should add to them the fourth house which is the cosmic womb or Hiranyagarbha where every potential in seed form is preserved, and the tenth house which represents the ultimate destiny of Manifestation expressing in a natal chart the realm of individual's interactions with the external world. In the case of Dalai Lama, these houses have assumed extraordinary importance: no planet except Mars which occupies Virgo in his eighth house is placed in any of these six houses. The flanking of Mars by three benefics, viz., Moon, and Venus placed in twelfth house and retrograde Jupiter in second from it shows as if they are going to converge on Mars. These four planets present the most intriguing feature of the horoscope which reveals to a great extent, the planetary support to Dalai Lama's rapport with the superphysical plane.

The dispositor of Jupiter, that is the lord of the sign in which Jupiter is placed namely Venus occupies Leo ruled by the highly spiritual Sun and it (Venus) is associated with the Moon which owns the sixth house—one of the four houses representing the mysterious depths. Mars in the eighth house which stand for initiation in mystic schools and involvement with the unseen world rules over his third and tenth houses. Mars is the planet known for courage, idealism, and tremendous spirit of devotion, it owns the third house representing courage, prowess and siblings (and is one of the houses of materiality), and also the tenth house which indicates the ultimate destiny of the person. Mars therefore has the great inner force in arousing the most extraordinary dependence on the unseen for the discharge of his mundane responsibilities. It is also worth noting that Scorpio as the tenth house and its lord in the eighth house which happens to be Mars whose primary function is to externalise the inner would lead Dalai Lama as a part of his goal in this birth to externalize the hidden realities (Scorpio) of the unseen realm.

Venus is yoga-karaka for Aquarius ascendant, as it owns fourth, a cardinal, and ninth, a trine house. The fourth house, as we have mentioned earlier, represents the cosmic womb and ninth represents *purva punya* or the past (meritorious) deeds. As a result of this situation, Jupiter as well as Venus have very special role in boosting up the externalizing energy of Mars the only planet located in the *Mysterious Depth.* Moon as the ruler of the house of *siddhis,* accomplishments in the powers latent in the man and nature supports Venus by its association. These planets are uniquely related with Saturn which is the lord of the ascendant, but rules over twelfth house as well which is one of the Mystic Depths, the world beyond the limitations of physical existence—the plane of the dead, where human beings go after their death, where dwell the deities concerned with immediate protection and guidance of the physical world, and which is also the plane wherefrom messages of the unseen (as in the case of dreams) are communicated to the individual. Saturn is retrograde in ascendant, that is, it is more inclined to give the effect of the twelfth house. But the houses in which Saturn is inclined to exist namely Capricorn and the house where it is actually posited namely Aquarius are its own signs; it indicates a high degree of integration between the physical and super-physical life of Dalai Lama.

Another feature of Saturn is that it aspects fourth house as a result of its hindsight attained due to retrogression. It produces extraordinary stillness in Dalai Lama's astral body. It makes his emotions completely placid (life-less?) so as to reflect effectively the messages from the high. The tranquility of emotional vibrations enables him to register these messages without any distortion. The disposition of Saturn is greatly modified by the fifth aspect of Jupiter from the ninth house as well as by the direct aspect of Moon and Venus being highly auspicious due to its rulership of fourth and ninth houses. Moon's placement in second house from its sign qualifies it to manifest the results of its ownership of the sixth house. Dalai Lama's high degree of psychism is intensified due to this position of Moon as it is a planet connected with psychic faculties and so is the sixth house. Moon's association with Venus which is yoga-karaka, relates Moon as well as Saturn with the characteristics of the fourth house, the house owned by Venus. These influences greatly transform the common malefic nature of Saturn into a high degree of beneficence. On its own Saturn leads to renunciation, detachment and total annihilation of materialism, thus Dalai Lama becomes a very active man of the world with much emotional detachment, but ever in rapport with the unseen mystic realm of manifestation. The aspect of Jupiter on Saturn keeps Dalai Lama close to his deities and the rituals. The relationship between these two along with Mars in the eighth house qualified Dalai Lama to perform the most difficult ritual of Kala chakra.

Mars in the eighth house provided courage and perseverence due to its ownership of the third house, which it aspects also, but more importantly, it arouses initiative in exploring, hidden aspects of life (eighth house) and externalises the hidden force. The nature of Mars is not soiled by the aspect of any other planet, rather its auspicious disposition is greatly strengthened by the location of benefics on its either side. The effect of Mars is well demonstrated in Dalai Lama's special meditational practice. The characteristic nature of Mars is not so much to draw down upon the earth the divine downpour as it is to raise the individual to higher realms of divine beneficence and be an active cooperator in the divine plan. Mars produced devotion but this devotion is not of servile nature; it is like the devotion of Hanuman, ever willing and eager to work for the Lord. The difference between Hanuman and a common human being lies in the scale of cooperation. Hanuman, moreover, had all the eight *siddhis* to their highest degree of perfection which could make him an effective co-worker with the Lord to carry out his will, while to a common man Mars bestows boldness, initiative, perseverence, and originality to struggle and acquire the faculties needed for a task.

Dalai Lama does the same during the course of his meditational practices. His meditation aims at delving deep in higher consciousness, penetrate the same effectively so as to comprehend the reality of the higher realm, and with his consciousness thus enriched he carries the Divine Will at lower levels of existence. He practices what is known as *Lam Rein* meditations, which is based on a text which expounds a stage by stage path to enlightenment through mental training. Such meditational practices require the disposition of Mars and Mercury both; in the chart of Dalai Lama, the dispositor of Mars, which is placed in the Mercurial sign Virgo is Mercury. Virgo is the exaltation sign of Mercury, while Mercury itself is situated in Gemini, which also is its own sign, and furthermore, it is associated in this sign with Ketu and Sun which are highly supportive of such meditational practices. All these three planets are located in fifth house which is helpful for the purpose in an extraordinary manner. Dalai Lama himself described the nature of this meditation as follows which very clearly brings out the special influence of Mars, Mercury and Sun:

> The rationale behind this practice is quite simple. During the first part of it when I make prostrations, I am taking refuge in the Buddha, the *Dharma* and the *Sangha*. The next stage is to develop *Bodhichitta* or a Good heart. This is done firstly by recognising the impermanence of all things and secondly by realising the true nature of being which is suffering. On the basis of these two considerations, it is possible to generate altruism.
>
> To engender altruism, or compassion in myself, I practice certain mental exercise which promotes love towards all sentient beings, especially my so-called enemies. For example, I remind myself that it is the action of human beings rather than human beings themselves that make them my enemies. Given a change of behaviour, that same person could easily become a good friend.
>
> The remainder of my meditation is connected with *sunya* or emptiness, during which I concentrate on the most subtle meaning of interdependence. Part of this practice involves what is termed 'deity yogi', *l bai nal jor*, during which I use different *mandalas* to visualise myself as a succession of differ-

> ent deities. (This should not, however, be taken to imply belief in independent external beings). In so doing, I focus my mind to the point where it is no longer pre-occupied with the data produced by the senses. This is not a trance produced by the senses, as my mind remains fully alert: rather it is an exercise in pure consciousness. What exactly I mean by this is hard to explain, just as it is difficult for a scientist to explain in words what is meant by the term 'space-time'. Neither language, nor everyday experience can really communicate the experience of 'pure mind'. Suffice to say that it is not an easy practice. It takes many years to master.

One of the special qualities of Mars is to break materiality and impel the individual to aspire towards the Unknown Supreme. If such an impulse is accompanied by *Budha-Aditya Yoga* formed by association of uncombust Mercury with Sun, specially in the fifth house, it leads to tremendous psychological unfoldment. In whatever Dalai Lama does, he cannot escape the imprint of his Ascendant Lord Saturn which is characterised by Void, *Sunyata,* as well as detachment of Death God, *Yama.* His meditational practices reveal the influence of Saturn on them. This feature of his meditational practice is evident from the following excerpt:

> One important aspect of my daily practice is its concern with the idea of death. To my mind, there are two things that in life, you can do about death. Either you can choose to ignore it, in which case you may have some success in making the idea of it go away for a limited period of time, or you can confront the prospect of your own death and try to analyse it and in so doing, try to minimise some of the inevitable suffering it causes. Neither way can you actually overcome it. However, as a Buddhist, I view death as a normal process of life. I accept it as a reality that will occur whilst I am in *samsara.* Knowing that I cannot escape it, I see no point in worrying about it. I hold the view that death is rather like changing one's clothes when they are torn and old. It is not an end in itself. Yet death is unpredictable—you do not know when and how it will take place. So it is only sensible to take certain precautions before it actually happens.

Death has special significance for Dalai Lama. Saturn is his ascendant lord and the lord of the twelfth house connected with the realm of death; by retrogression, Saturn is inclined to occupy this house. Jupiter which is the lord of the second house which is also related with death, aspects Saturn. Mars situated in the house of hidden aspects of one's life (death being one of the aspects of the second house) directly aspects this house thus accentuating the importance and reality of death in Dalai Lama's life. It is therefore natural to expect that he would have special experiences of death. He has himself confirmed that:

> As a Buddhist, I further believe that the actual experience of death is very important. It is then that the most profound and beneficial experiences can come about. For this reason, many of the great spiritual masters take release from earthly existence that is, they die—whilst meditating. When this happens, it is often the case that their bodies do not begin to decay until long after they are clinically dead.

Dalai Lama was born with a special purpose. Three trends were operating on him from his very beginning. Firstly, the consciousness of the ancient being which ensouled him was highly evolved and it was expressing through the young body of Dalai Lama in many ways even while it was not yet conscious of its ancient heritage. Secondly, the karmic limitations of Dalai Lama could not be wished away; the vehicle that carried through the ancient spirit had its own limitations, expressed themselves in various ways which Dalai Lama could not avoid. Thirdly, the special mission which the Dalai Lama had volunteered to undertake on behalf of the occult hierarchy entailed (as is the case with all missionary births) much psycho-physical pain and hardships which the super-physical powers knew though the Dalai Lama did not carry the conscious memory of having accepted to undergo these hardships willingly for the mission.

The timing of his birth, the family, social as well as the administrative set-up of the region were all planned in consonance with this mission. The consciousness of Dalai Lama is attuned with that of the mighty beings at the super-physical plane which do not *always* as a matter of course impinge on his physical mind and brain; the Mighty Beings having set the birth time of the volunteering body did not later interrupt the planetary forces to coordinate their impulses with events at the physical plane which in fact occurred due to the momentum generated by the inter-relationships of various planetary impulses themselves.

Dalai Lama was born on 6th July 1935 in a small village named Taktser situated in far north-eastern part of Tibet in the province of Amdo to the north-west of which lies the Chaglang, an area of frozen desert. At birth, Dalai Lama was named Lhamo Thondup meaning a *wish-fulfillng goddess,* many people thought the word meant *Wish-Fulfilling Jewel.* Whatever the meaning one takes to characterise the future Dalai Lama, the result is the same: a goddess is also a vehicle for the expression of the will of the god whom she consorts, while a jewel also reflects some special stellar light without which its radiance would be absent and its special significance greatly minimised. The accidental naming of the young child from the very beginning suggested his being merely a vehicle to carry forth the impulse of some other consciousness than his own, his personality being not of much significance.

But this reflecting medium was a part of the *Roaring Tiger,* Taktser, which could, if need arose, roar like a tiger, pounce upon its prey with suddenness and with all ferocity and determination. Had these characteristics not been ingrained in Dalai Lama, he would have been killed by the Chinese, or the Muslim warlord of Amdo, Ma Bufeng (who had succeeded in establishing a regional government in the district loyal to the Chinese Republic) would have annihilated his spiritual possibilities at the very birth. (It often happens with such missionary births.)

Strange things happened at the very time of Dalai Lama's birth. When Lhamo Thondup, the Dalai Lama as known during his infancy, was identified as the fourteenth Dalai Lama, it was opposed in many ways by Mo Bufeng, but eventually the infant could be taken by his parents to Kumbom monastery, where he was installed in a ceremony that took place at dawn. [The Puranic stories describe similar difficulties in the case of Lord Krishna in whose horoscope Saturn is said to have aspected his ascendant which was its friendly sign, Taurus, whereas in the case of Dalai Lama, Saturn posited in its own sign in ascendant aspected the tenth house and that also Scorpio, a sign owned by Mars, which occupied the eighth house: it created difficulties for him throughout his career specially in relation with his temporal position.]

At the time of his birth, almost like a miracle his beneficence began to affect the persons around him. According to Dalai Lama himself, "an interesting story was told about Father about the time of my birth. He had been ill for a number of weeks and was confined to his bed. No one knew what was wrong with him and people started to fear for his life. But on the day I was born, he suddenly began to recover for no obvious reason. It cannot have been excitement at becoming a father since my mother had already given birth to eight children, although only four had survived." In the birth chart of Dalai Lama, his ninth house (Libra with retrograde Jupiter) as well as the disposition of Sun (the lord of a cardinal house in a trine aspected by the benefic Jupiter) both are very favourable. After the birth of Dalai Lama, the status of his parents improved. During his early childhood, his family was making a precarious living from land in the village, but on his being proclaimed as the Dalai Lama, they acquired the status of the highest nobility.

The Dalai Lama has a unique planetary disposition which revealed not only his favourable influence on his parents and other family relations, but he was generally a benefic influence around the locality. The position of Sun, Moon, ninth, fourth and the third houses were all highly auspicious: the planetary disposition also revealed his own greatness. Apart from Rahu being in the eleventh house, the rest of the planets occupied only five houses which constituted *Pasha Yoga*, a combination for eminence and involvement in righteous activities; all the eight planets occupied two trine houses and the two important cardinal houses signifying their ever readiness to support him in his life's mission. These planets occupied all the three houses of the *Spiritual Triangle*, that is, the first, fifth and the ninth houses, and the two cardinal houses representing *kshetrajna*, the self, and *kshetra*, the field on which the self expresses itself, that is the first and the seventh houses. Mars, the planet for generating electrical fluid or the vital energy essential for physical existence is posited in the eighth house—the house of hidden possibilities. This placement of planets enabled Dalai Lama to play a very important role both for his own personal evolution as well as for the society in which he was born.

The planets in the spiritual triangle impel the individual to perform meritorious deeds which in the long pilgrimage of the soul qualify it for enduring reward, especially in the future life. Powerful Mercury in the fifth house, an important base of the spiritual triangle, along with Sun and Ketu and receiving auspicious aspect of retrograde Jupiter from the ninth house, another base of the spiritual triangle enabled Dalai Lama to unfold successfully his spirituality.

In the case of Dalai Lama, Rahu-Ketu axis joins a base of the spiritual triangle with another base of the material triangle. The fifth house as a base of the spiritual triangle is concerned with accumulated merit, profundity of experience and enormous spiritual urge, while the base of the material triangle represented by the eleventh house in which Rahu is placed which necessarily happens to be the seventh house from the fifth house—base of the spiritual triangle represents the area or the sphere where Dalai Lama's intelligence, past spiritual experiences and his present education can be effectively utilised. Sagittarius with Rahu in this material house while Ketu and Sun are associated with Mercury in Gemini in the spiritual house indicate that the spirituality of Dalai Lama will be directed towards spiritual regeneration (Sagittarius) of the material world (Rahu); it is the material world and the materialistic social and personal relationships (eleventh house Rahu), where his spiritual qualities have the suitable field for its fruition.

Political attainments (Sun, Jupiter, and tenth house) are not so pronounced as to suggest Dalai Lama's success in his liberating mission of Tibet as for his own soul's growth and for spiritualizing the modern society in which he lives, especially as a result of his own personal life-style, creativity, intelligence and communications. Saturn at the apex of the spiritual triangle (first house) shows his tremendous objectivity and detachment with all that he does, especially for his siblings and colleagues (third house), personal relationships (seventh house) and for the society in which he lives (tenth house).

Mercury has made Dalai Lama very thoughtful of whatever he does. There is no casualness in his approach to any person or an event. On one occasion, he stated that "in one sense a supposed enemy is more valuable than a friend, for an enemy teaches you things such as forbearance, that a friend generally does not". This is precisely what Mercury does. The role of Mercury is two-fold. It enables the messages of the higher personality, or the higher triad, which consists of Atma-Buddhi-Manas represented by Sun-Moon-Mercury, to be passed to lower personality, or the *lower quaternary*, viz., physical body, Pranic vehicle, emotional vehicle and the vehicle arousing altruistic aspirations represented by Saturn, Jupiter, Mars and Venus. Mercury ponders over one's various experiences, chews the cud so to say, and derives lessons from them for the benefit of the permanent ego, and transfers the experiences to one's higher personality. The two-way traffic regulated by Mercury associates it with *vishuddhi chakra*—the throat chakra, of the yogis.

In the case of Dalai Lama, Mercury's association with Ketu and Sun enables it to transform worldly experiences (due to Ketu's association) to the individual's inner being (Sun) and to carry the messages of Atma (Sun) for the welfare of the humanity (Budha-Aditya-Yoga in the fifth house and the aspect of Jupiter on the combination from the ninth house). Mercury is placed in Ardra asterism, which provides it the necessary strength in its role as the bridge. Ardra refers to the power to comprehend in a general way rather than to acquire knowledge of anything in particular. It is connected with the freshness of recognising one's real self, seeing the working of one's mind, and thereby acquiring self-knowledge. This recognition comes through the mind. Such a comprehension—the direct perception of reality, whether within oneself or without is always new.

Mercury in the present case becomes vitally energized to establish relationship with the universal mind, *Mahat*. The Sun which is associated with Mercury is in Punarvasu asterism which manifests the powers which materialises ideas at a higher plane and transfers them to the lower ones. The asterism concretises abstract ideas. At the stage of Punarvasu, the creative agents are imparted fresh impetus for the performance of their arduous work on the mental level. It provides a resting place for the downward flow of Divine energy with a view to enabling it to function with the increased intensity later on. Punarvasu is not so much concerned with results as with the provision of essential conditions for the onward journey of the soul. Both Sun and Ketu occupy this asterism. They provide to Dalai Lama much concretised divine thought and prepare him to conserve enough strength to carry further his mission of spiritualizing the materialistic world. Mercury being a link makes Dalai Lama, a suitable agent for disseminating the spiritual ideas in the present materialistic world (something which Lord Buddha did a little over 2,500 years ago).

The occupation of the first house, the apex of the spiritual triangle, by Saturn and of the seventh house by Moon and Venus reveals the relationship between the Dalai Lama and his mundane responsibilities. The first house represents the positive or the active aspect of the same phenomenon of which the seventh house is the negative or the passive aspect. Saturn posited in Aquarius becomes the main actor of the drama. The primary function of Saturn is to direct the evolving soul back to its source. Saturn has immense patience in order to attain the desired result. It has tremendous perseverence and in spite of various hurdles on the way, it is always successful in arriving at the desired goal. Its action is decisive. By casting a deep shadow on the radiance of the life-force, Saturn produces a psychological change under which the individual begins to recognize the inevitable influence of the supreme power and begins his backward journey—the path of return. Such planet in ascendant intensifies its results and makes the person very spiritually oriented, almost one with the universal life, the all pervading divine beneficence in which there is complete absence of materialistic desire and proclivities.

A person born under the Aquarius ascendant shows these features to a great extent. A person under this sign is carried by a gale of the past karma—let loose by the *Lipikas* so that the human child could acquire a new outlook, a new direction in his life, and in his relationships with his fellow beings. In Aquarius, there is the undercurrent of all the three planets which are greatly connected with all spiritual pursuits. The very nature of the ownership of the sign by Saturn suggests that the person would be intimately connected with his past lives. Aquarius has been universally acclaimed as the pitcher from which water flows out, and water stands for cosmic life-force, the one universal solvent which quenches the thirst of all and transmutes the base, craving individual into a satisfied and placid soul with all desires for worldly individual possessions completely obliterated. It absolves the individual from all sins and purifies his heart. Under Aquarius, the evolving ego hopes to be a conscious cooperator with the universal creative power.

In predictive astrology, the sign is considered unfortunate, because it exerts a grinding influence on the separated personal will. Under its influence, the individual is gradually prepared to realize his ultimate mission in life, whereby he begins to transcend his individual considerations and surrender himself to the Supreme; he gradually becomes a slave to his duty to the Inner Government of the world and wants to share the heavy karma of the orphan humanity. All his personal predilections, preferences and considerations are gradually subordinated to his love for the human race. Dalai Lama, with his consciousness stretching back to the hoary past, now works for the humanity. Seventh house, the field for his activities and application of his inherent powers and impulses is the world at large, not his narrow family circle or even his country or the specific religion in which he is installed as its leader. He has a very wider horizon to work which is obvious, because Moon and Venus occupy the seventh house in the sign of Leo ruled by Sun, which occupies the fifth house along with Mercury—the ruler of the eighth house.

Moon represents the cosmic creative power which nourishes every living entity on this earth. Moon has the great quality of tending everything on this earth like a mother, though functioning within the ambit of divine law. Dalai Lama has that great quality of a mother though with complete detachment as to what it would bring to him. Venus is the divine socialising impulse; it attracts the being to others, it enables a person to love, to sacrifice, to care and to merge in the other being. It is for this quality of Venus that it is associated with marriage, social relationships and amiability of disposition. Dalai Lama's heart winning rapport with the fourth estate and forging amicable relationship even with political heads (who had once turned him away) which has enabled Dalai Lama to be awarded the Nobel Peace prize (in spite of his being at the root in the present incarnation, a political agitator) indicate the importance of Venus in its socializing aspect. Moon and Venus are both in the sign of the Sun which occupies the house of creativity: this situation indicates that Dalai Lama must apply his energy to the regeneration of a new humanity, he should devote himself to the birth of a new altruistic, humanistic, creative way of living.

His speeches at various international fora, his personal example of life-style and above all, the way he is trying to tackle the Tibetan problems— show the impact of these characteristics. His direction of efforts is intensely practical, seemingly material as it aims at concretising the spiritual ideals: but the relationship between the apex of the spiritual triangle and that of the material triangle will necessarily impel the individuals under this influence to act in this way. The predominance of the spiritual triangle and the relationship between the two special angles of the spiritual and the material triangles have given a new and special direction in the life of fourteenth Dalai Lama, and these astrological features transcend several other combinations present in the horoscope of which the classical texts speak.

Apart from *Sasa Yoga* which is one of the *Panch Maha Purusha Yogas* qualifying an individual to be considered a great man, and *Pasha Yoga* enabling him to righteous activities, there are many important planetary combinations which strike significantly in Dalai Lama's horoscope. Dalai Lama is certainly a sovereign even in the temporal sense. He enjoys the prestige and position of a sovereign, but this special position does not give him a very comfortable life. His biography indicates that when he was born his eyes were not properly open and his sister who was acting as a midwife had to put her thumb to force open the eye-lid. His family was not very well off and there were frequent deaths of his people in it: his mother had borne sixteen children of which only seven lived. He was identified as the future Dalai Lama in 1937, aged 2½ years or so after the death of the thirteenth Dalai Lama.

Thupten Gyatso had died in 1933 when he was only 57 years of age. The new Dalai Lama experienced considerable difficulties in moving to Lhasa. The local governor of Amdo—a Muslim warlord Ma Bufeng with loyalty to the Chinese Republic was refusing him to move to Lhasa without ransom payment. It delayed his departure for about 18 months. Identification as the Dalai Lama and the period of his installation in a ceremony at the Kumbun monastery which generally thrills a general reader who reads these descriptions did create much unhappiness to the baby Dalai. He himself noted that "there began a somewhat unhappy period of my life. My parents did not stay long and soon I was alone amongst these new and unfamiliar surroundings. It is very hard for a small child to be separated from its parents". It was during the same period that he was slapped by his paternal uncle which made him very terrified. It made such a deep impression on the young child that "for years afterwards I was haunted by his very dark, pock-marked face and fierce moustache. Thereafter, whenever I caught sight of him, I became very frightened", Dalai Lama recalled.

After he was finally installed at Lhasa in July 1939, when he assumed greater responsibilities he had to undergo serious discipline and at the same time take many unpleasant decisions. Though his temporal duties required him to establish diplomatic relations with several governments, send congratulatory messages to the British government's representative —the Viceroy of India, Lord Wavell, yet he could not escape the task of arresting Reting Rinpoche, one time his teacher and guardian, when after retirement he returned and began creating problems for the State by claiming Regency back. Reting Rinpoche had to be arrested and a considerable number of his followers had to be put to death. It was a kind of suppression of a rebellion. At the age of 12 years, Dalai Lama's father died making him very sad. From about the same time, the Chinese began creating problems for Tibet: attempts were made to convert him to communism, for which he was cajoled, seduced, brainwashed, and ultimately abducted and would have been probably liquidated. These induced him to flee the country and be in exile. In this condition also, his difficulties were in no way less apart from the problems of settling the refugees, trying for internationalising the problem and retrieving the country. He even suffered from serious illness. In 1966, he was afflicted by Hepatitis which seriously affected his health and impaired his working efficiency. These are only some of the examples of situations in which external conditions of power, prestige and responsibilities do not always go in the same direction as the internal state of psyche. The impulses generated by Saturn are very much like that.

A powerful Saturn invariably works on a very big canvas, but internally it completely denudes the individual of his individual emotional pleasures, conveniences and any feeling of elation. Humility and compassion that radiate from Dalai Lama are expressions of Saturnian influence. It has enabled him to work on a very big scale: the whole world is his field of activity — he is endeavouring to build a society which transcends the life and conditions in Tibet, but with its basic values of life, with compassion, friendliness and righteousness. He is intensely practical, concretising the ideals in reality, yet within himself his life is lonely, void of anything which he can call his own. Saturn placed in the special situation in the case of Dalai Lama plays the role of the lord of the burial ground reducing everything to their ultimate constituent, void, nothingness. That is the centre on which Dalai Lama meditates everyday and that is the reality which gives him all the dynamism in his life.

The powerful *Sasa Yoga* formed by Saturn either in exaltation or its own sign occupying a cardinal house produces greatness in the realm of occultism and spiritualism in which field the individual has acquired greatness during his past lives. It is only when the planet is associated with unethical vibrations that this yoga shows undesirable results as well. In the present case, Saturn's position in ascendant in retrogression while situated in Aquarius (A sign which radiates intensely spiritual impulses) and aspected by Jupiter from the ninth house makes it greatly qualified to impart highly spiritual influences.

There are several Raja Yogas which show that there would be several changes improving his material conditions. He rose from the position of an ordinary farmer to that of temporal and religious head of a country and finally to the most venerated apostle of Buddhism and leader working for peace and happiness of the whole of the humanity. One may mention here, as an example of these Raja Yogas, the combination of trikona lord (Mercury) and the kendra lord (Sun) placed in a trikona house. Another example is that of the lord of the second and eleventh houses (Jupiter) placed in ninth house which also additionally aspects the ascendant and the ascendant lord. But the most important feature of his horoscope is not so much the existence of such Raja Yogas, but the special configuration of the planets at the time of his birth. The planetary placements have assumed a pattern showing purposefulness of the native's present birth. The ascendant lord is second from its sign Capricorn, and so is Moon. The luminary which itself is the stream of cosmic creative energy, and the ascendant lord which represents the vehicle through which all activities have to be implemented are placed second from their own signs which shows their readiness to be creative. Sun is in eleventh house from its own sign, Mercury is tenth from its sign (Virgo), Mars is also in eleventh from its sign (Scorpio), and even Jupiter is reinforcing these planets in their activities by itself occupying the eleventh house from its sign (Sagittarius); and even Venus is in eleventh house from its own sign (Libra) in which the greatest benefic of the planetary system Jupiter is placed.

The eleventh impulse of the Cosmic Man, the Kalá Purusha, leads to the unification of the individual stream of consciousness with the universal consciousness making it a vehicle of the divine will. Most of the planets are supportive of this impulse in the chart of Dalai Lama making his life from the very time of his birth one-pointed, with a view to preparing him to be a fit vassal of the Nature's supreme energy.

Thus transcending all the common conditions of affluence caused by Raja Yogas, troubles and misfortunes arising in his political status (due to the aspect of Saturn on the tenth house) and various hardships of emotional isolation, religious austerities and hardships of tantric training and practices, Dalai Lama is immensely satisfied with his destiny. He had willed a life like that, the Lords of Karma had approved of his desire, and the planets aligned themselves to assist him in his task. The special emerging pattern from the planetary alignment reveals the maturity of his soul and his position on the evolutionay scale.

Dalai Lama was born in Venus mahadasa and Saturn bhukti lasting for a few months. It was not a very auspicious period: he was born in an ordinary farmer's family. In fact, the first few years of his life was full of physical discomfort and hardships. The following few months of Mercury and Ketu sub-periods could not make the child very happy, specially because of Mercury's lordship over the eighth house and its association with Ketu. But it was during this period that a successor of Thupten Gyatso was being searched for. During this period, strange things were happening in the mystic land of Tibet. While Thupten Gyatso, the 13th Dalai Lama remained sitting in state since 1933, during this period his 'head was discovered to have turned from facing south to north-east' and the Regent, who was himself a senior Lama, had a vision. Looking into the waters of the sacred lake, Chamoi Lhatso in south Tibet, he clearly saw the Tibetan letters Ab, Ka and Ma flow into view. These were indications of the direction in which the present Dalai Lama was born and the search party should move towards Kumbun monastery to locate the new Dalai Lama. The new born babe was also showing its natural impulse towards this position during the Venus main and Mercury sub-period. He often thought during this period to travel; he would take his belongings and say that he was going to Lhasa.

During Venus-Ketu, the latent purpose of his incarnation, the spiritual mission (Ketu) for which he was given this birth, became identified. The 'wish-fulfilling jewel', Lhamo Thondup was now identified as the future Dalai Lama. With his identification as the 'tulku' of the thirteenth Dalai Lama, his personal hardships and emotional isolation increased. Ketu deeply affects the psychological make up of a person, and makes the emotional life of a person very barren and his life very lonely, thoughtful and precocious. For the nation in which he was born, it was a period of great jubilation, the period of uncertainty was over, and the people got their temporal and religious ruler, but for the young 'tulku', it was a very unhappy period. He had to experience the parting from his family members, familiar environment and begin a new life radically different from that of a care-free child.

With the beginning of the Sun main period in October, 1939, the new Dalai Lama began to adapt to his new environment with new responsibilities. His inner grace began to show itself in his behaviour. It was during this period that he occupied his new office, his parents acquired new status of nobility. He began to receive deputations from foreign missions and receive royal presents. For a boy of seven, these were extremely significant experiences. When at the age of eight years, his brother Lobsag Sante who was staying with him was sent to a private school, it saddended him very much, because it made him completely on his own without any visual link with his family members. The sun shines alone in the firmament: it makes the individual sparkling, graceful, independent but he cannot have any mutually interdependent relations with any one.

The period of Sun is often characterised by spiritual glory, temporal power and extremely dynamic life, but emotionally it is a period of loneliness, self-introspection and intuitive understanding of spiritual truths. It was during this period that Dalai Lama began his studies of monastic subjects and tantric teachings which also involved greater conformity with traditional religious austerities; the urge to have power as well as maintain discipline probably induced the child Dalai Lama to be fond of military drill. He also became greatly interested in mechanical toys such as meccano, singing birds, and watches and clocks, many of which he would undo and often succeed in reassembling them.

During the Sun main period, his psychological conditions markedly improved. Given his new status, he began to live among respectful surroundings and several servants were also assigned to him. Even his parents were permitted to live closer to him. In winter 1940, during Sun-Rahu, he moved to Potala and was officially installed as the spiritual leader of Tibet. Rahu is in Sagittarius, the sign owned by Jupiter which is placed in the ninth house aspecting the ascendant and the fifth house Sun whose mahadasa Dalai Lama was running. Rahu was placed in Uttaraashadha asterism, which is primarily a spiritual asterism whose presiding deity is Vishwadeva, universal collectivity of the divine powers. Vishwadevas are "fosterers or increasers of man and upholders of his labour and effort in the work, the sacrifice". Rahu is eleventh from ascendant thus capable of producing gains to the individual; it is fifth from the Moon sign thus enabling Moon to radiate spiritual impulses; and it is seventh from Sun whose main dasa Dalai Lama was running, and this position enabled the Sun to effectively work through the special impulses of Rahu, which is to immortalise material gains, implying that it would help in the perpetuation of divine powers. The installation of new Dalai Lama was certainly one of such activities. The influence was sufficient to bestow spiritual status to a child of five years of age. His spiritual as well as monastic and tantric studies with training started during Sun-Saturn period.

These monastic studies and lessons in nature's hidden powers as reflected in tantrism indicate the nature of influence Saturn is imparting. By retrogression in Aquarius, Saturn is inclined to give the results of its occupancy of the twelfth house in Capricorn sign which implies efforts to merge one's action organs and sense organs with cosmic creative impulses and to retrieve these occult powers for assisting the divine evolutionary impulses. Rahu also occupies Satabhishak, the asterism is symbolised by a thousand petalled flower. Its presiding deity is Varuna, the Vedic deity who bestows wisdom. The acquisition of higher knowledge and comprehension of universal principles which Varuna bestows, destroy the hold of material sheaths and enable a new awakening. Such a process which results in an expansion of consciousness entails the abundant austerity and sacrifice on the part of the individual for the good of others. The training that Dalai Lama began during this period was intended to expand his consciousness and prepare him for his serviceability to his society. During the same period the second world war ended and the child Dalai Lama began receiving royal delegations and send missions abroad. The main period of the Sun established the child as a competent and wise, temporal and religious sovereign of the state.

When the Moon main period began in October 1945, Dalai Lama faced the most trying period in his career. As a young boy of 12 years of age, he had to deal with the internal rebellion and to punish the guilty even when they were personally close to him. The lordship of the sixth house can never be peaceful. Moreover, Moon in this case is aspected by a malefic. It was during this period that he had to arrest Reting Rinpoche, who was his one time teaher and Regent. Rahu's affliction to Sun was one of the contributory factor which resulted during Moon-Rahu for his father's death.

In 1949, during Moon-Jupiter period, the Chinese mission in Tibet had to be ordered closed which in a way was the beginning of the Sino-Tibetan conflict. Jupiter is the lord of eighth house from Moon, but that does not sufficiently justify this incident. The fact remains that the independence of Communist China as the People's Republic of China was determined to annex Tibet sooner or later, while the great moral right Tibet was feeling for its sovereignty could not permit the two to live together: the coexistence of communism and spiritual state with the religion as its foundation was an impossibility. The beginning of such a relationship which ultimately led to the subjugation of Tibet could not be explained astrologically: probably in the divine scheme of things, there was some deeper reason for the start of the conflict at this time.

In summer of 1950, when Dalai Lama was having Moon-Saturn sub-period, there was the severe earth tremor of which we have spoken before; it eluded every scientific explanations and Dalai Lama had the premonition that this natural disturbance was a bad omen for the country. Almost simultaneously with it the Chinese began infilteration, invasion and their programme of "peaceful liberation of Tibet". The Government of Dalai Lama appealed to the United Nations for the violation of human rights, protection of Tibet's sovereignty and restrain on the communist China from invading their country. But the international organisation took a different stand; as Tibet had remained outside the organisation to preserve its special status, neutrality and uniqueness of its life-style, the United Nations did not come to its rescue. This intensified the trouble in Tibet and increased the personal problems for Dalai Lama.

So far the new Dalai Lama had not completed his religious training; he was not ordained for the full status of the religious head. Even for the full temporal power, he was short by a couple of years when the same could be conferred on him. The Moon-Saturn produced the full quota of their impact. The lord of sixth house and the lord of the twelfth house in mutual aspect, and Saturn as the lord of the twelfth house aspecting the tenth house were powerful in creating troubles for Dalai Lama at different levels. Yet, the voice from the other world (the twelfth house) and the aspect of Jupiter, the greatest benefic from the ninth house, and the powerful ascendant lord could not remain unprotected and left to sink. It was during this very period that Dorje Drakden, the protector deity of Tibet spoke when the oracle declared the wish by revealing that "His time has come". The Moon-Saturn sub-period saw Dalai Lama being enthroned two years before his normal majority: the astrologers fixed the date of enthronement to be 17th November 1950. On the advice of the astrologers, a green cloth was tied round his waist as this colour was deemed auspicious for him. It shows the special importance of Mercury, forming a Raja Yoga by combining a lord of trikona (the fifth house lord Mercury) with the lord of a cardinal house (Sun the lord of the seventh house). The astrologers' appreciation of the green colour for Dalai Lama reminds of the relationship between Mercury and its power to confer a royal status.

But the Chinese military pressure continued during this period. In January 1951, he had to take refuge in south Tibet (Dromo) and remain *in cognito,* lest he was arrested and tortured by the Chinese. He managed to seek official delegations to Nepal, Great Britain and the United States soliciting their help against the Chinese incursions. But nothing tangible came out of it. Most of the Chamdo region was by now under the Chinese occupation and Dalai Lama thought it better to come to terms with the Chinese government. Negotiations began between the two countries and a 17-point agreement for the peaceful liberation of Tibet was forged between the communist Chinese government and Tibet.

When Moon-Mercury sub-period started, Dalai Lama was back in Lhasa. But Mercury and Moon both are troublesome planets for Dalai Lama: the former as the lord of the eighth house and the latter that of the sixth house. During Moon-Mercury sub-period, in spite of their being helpful in several ways, they created much difficulties for him on the physical plane: more than 3,000 troops of the Chinese 18th Army entered Lhasa and all the expectations of peaceful settlement were dashed to pieces. Yet, the auspicious nature of Mercury was not completely absent. Mercury showed its impact on the mental plane. Dalai Lama continued his spiritual studies with greater enthusiasm, completing his final examination without much difficulties.

It was also during this period that Dalai Lama began *Lam Rein* meditation, which was intended to gradually expand consciousness, stage by stage path to enlightenment through mental training. This effort to establish direct contact with one's higher being was completely in consonance with Mercury's radiation resulting from its association with Sun and Ketu, placed strongly in the house of intelligence and creativity (the fifth house) and the general period of planetary rulership being that of Moon— the planet related with *Buddhi,* higher intelligence. Even the damage expected from the Chinese military manoeuvres was greatly contained and some sort of (uneasy) truce was worked out between the two countries.

During the period of *moksha-karaka* planet Ketu, Dalai Lama received one of the most difficult initiations in *kalachakra* ritual. Describing the importance of this initiation, Dalai Lama mentioned that, "it is one of the most important initiations in the tantric tradition with special significance for world peace. And, unlike other tantric rites, it is given before large public audiences." Ketu is very rightly called the mysterious splendour, and Ketu is placed admirably well for bestowing its results in this case.

Venus is very deceptive in many ways; it is capable of using godly (Daivic) techniques for serving demonic purposes: one should remember the Puranic stories wherein it is shown how Shukracharya performed severe austerities to obtain *Mrityasanjeevani* so that the *Danavas*— the demons could never be vanquished by the Devas— the gods. He once even impersonated himself as Brihaspati in order to delude the gods and to serve the purpose of the demons. This role of Venus is overlooked, but its bestowal of pleasures of senses, and material gifts are primarily intended to delude the individuals from turning their gaze to their real nature, the Supreme's reflection in the fragmented selves. This role of Venus is evident in the case of Dalai Lama, when he was passing Moon-Venus sub-period. During this period, there appeared on the superficial level, some rapprochement with the Chinese government. In early 1954, he was invited to go to China and was made the vice-president of the Steering Committee of the People's Republic of China. During this period, even Dalai Lama was playing his diplomatic game: the seeming harmonious relationship established between the two states, he wanted to utilise for his religious studies and disseminate the spiritual influence.

During the Tibetan festival of Moulam in 1954, Dalai Lama received full ordination as a Buddhist *bhikshu* in front of the statue of Chenrezig in the Jokhang temple. During the year at the request of a group of lay women, he performed the Kalachakra initiation ceremony for the first time "during this life time". Venus being lord of fourth and ninth houses, occupying the sign of the Sun in association with Moon enabled Dalai Lama during this period of Moon-Venus sub-period to concentrate on his religious duties and give regular teaching to both small and large groups. But the Venusian disposition of duplicity that Dalai Lama was experiencing during this period in the Chinese government and other official communications and relationships, made him also to learn the technique. He stated that "I too had to learn a similar form of communication: how to put on false appearances when dealing with the Chinese under different circumstances."

On being invited to China, though Dalai Lama was advised by his counsellors otherwise, he decided to go there; "no matter what anyone told me", he said. People apprehended that Dalai Lama might during this visit be arrested, imprisoned or even liquidated, but Dalai Lama showed a will of his own. The super-sensory power of perception which Dalai Lama was already developing during this time (specially due to the association of Venus with the sensitive Moon as the lord of the house of latent faculties, the sixth house, and the aspect of the lord of the twelfth house on it) enabled him to see a strange sight at Ganden, the Tibet's great university monastery. A statue of one of the protecting divinities of Tibet, which is represented as having a 'buffalo's head had clearly moved." When Dalai Lama had first seen it, "it was looking down with a rather subdued look on its face, Now, it was facing east, with a very ferocious expression". It was a clear indication that a meek and submissive Dalai Lama had to be different: he had to show his firmness (ferocity) when he went to China (East) in defending the Tibetan values.

When Dalai Lama went to China with about 500 retinues, he was accorded very dignified reception, efforts were made to woo, brainwash, show him all the material achievements of communism in China, even given prestigious status, but everything was done to seduce Dalai Lama to abandon his religious mission and be one with the communists. Towards the end of this period, he returned from a conducted extensive tour of communist China in time for the preparation for the celebration of Losai, the Tibetan New Year.

With the start of Moon-Sun sub-period, when Dalai Lama met with Mao Tse Tung, his eyes were opened: while he was so far feeling dazzled by the communist achievements in securing welfare measures and technological advancement in China, he got the shock of his life. Mao told Dalai Lama: "Your attitude is good, you know. Religion is poison. Firstly, it reduces the population because monks and nuns must stay celibate, and secondly, it neglects material prosperity". Dalai Lama felt a violent sensation all over his face when he heard this statement from Mao. He said, "I was suddenly very afraid. So, I thought, 'you are the destroyer of the *Dharma* after all".

With this realization when he returned to Lhasa in June 1955 he realized that he should complete his studies soon and meanwhile establish some sort of co-existence between the Chinese authorities and the Tibetan administration. Sun gave him this matured realisation of hard realities which resulted from turmoil and stress experienced under powerful planets. It was also during the same period that Dalai Lama became "conscious that outside Tibet, the world had turned its back on Tibet. Worse, India, our nearest neighbour and spiritual mentor had tacitly accepted Peking's claim to Tibet." He became disillusioned with Nehru signing in April 1954 a new Sino-Indian treaty, which included a memorandum known as Panchsheel, whereby it was agreed that India and China would under no circumstances, interfere with one another's internal affairs. According to this treaty, Tibet was a part of China. Such incidents occurring during the Moon main period made Dalai Lama realise (during Moon-Sun sub-period) that in diplomacy and matters of the state, it was necessary and judicious to be practical.

The main period of Mars extended from October 1955 to October 1962. It was the most troublesome period in the life of Dalai Lama. It brought his downfall. He fled his country into exile. The country was mauled by the communist government of China; the sanctity of religious purity was destroyed. Dalai Lama was no longer the sovereign of Tibet, whether in the realm of temporal or religious matters. It was the destruction of a way of life and a civilisation which existed nowhere else in the world. It was also a period of greatest challenge for Dalai Lama: whether he could universalise the spirituality hidden and preserved in the mysterious mountainous country, or he could fight with all the might of a small peaceful state to save its physical identity. As far as the role of Mars in preserving the status of tenth house, which it ruled was concerned, it was a failure because its occupancy of the eighth house did not help in the matter. But as far as externalization of Tibetan mysticism and the way of life was concerned, Dalai Lama with courage (third house ruled by Mars) and perseverence succeeded to a great extent. Mars enabled Dalai Lama to tap his hidden spiritual resources in disseminating the message of Buddhism, its compassion, understanding, and deeper mysticism (tantricism) throughout the world, which was ultimately recognized and (during the main period of Jupiter) he was awarded the Nobel Peace prize.

During the Mars main period, he had to work hard in order to save the way of life of the Tibetan people which faced the possibility of its extinction. Because of the special situation of Mars and the period following it of Rahu, Dalai Lama achieved the outstanding feat of universalising the Tibetan way of life not only to save it from extinction, but to make it much more expansive. In this drama, Mars played the crucial role of creating personal downfall for Dalai Lama, subjugation of Tibet by the (irreligious) communist government, exile of the religious head along with a large number of Tibetan refugees and carrying dexterously the cause of Tibet to different countries and peoples, thus arousing their interest and sympathy for the way of life that seemed on the verge of anihilation. In this sense, Mars marks the end of one phase of Dalai Lama's life and the beginning of another for which his present incarnation was given to him. (The following period of Rahu had to discharge the special responsibility entrusted by virtue of Rahu-Ketu operating as the fulcrum of one's life's mission.) It is also noted that Mars is inimical with the ascendant lord Saturn, and its period on the physical plane could never be pleasant for Dalai Lama.

It was at the very beginning of Mars main period that the Nechung oracle announced that the 'Light of the Wish-Fulfilling Jewel', which was a name of the Dalai Lama, will shine in the west. Initially, it seemed that Dalai Lama would travel to India and have a successful trip. In fact, the oracle had much deeper implications which became clear only after several decades: at the moment, it seems, it was intended to encourage Dalai Lama as not to lose heart, because the coming few years were going to be quite trying for him.

During Mars-Rahu sub-period, Dalai Lama was exposed to numerous delegations and dignitaries. Rahu-Ketu axis being important in every one's life, situations during the Rahu sub-period that occurred to Dalai Lama were of much deeper significance. Marshal Chen Yi, deputy prime minister and foreign minister of the People's Republic of China arrived with his wife and a large delegation from Peking to represent chairman Mao. During the same period Maharaj Kumar of Sikkim —the crown prince also came to Tibet carrying an invitation for Dalai Lama to attend the 2,500 birth anniversary of Lord Buddha: the invitation was from the Indian Mahabodhi Society of which the Maharaj Kumar was the President.

The Chinese initially disallowed permission for Dalai Lama to travel to the celebration, but later at the intervention of India, he was permitted to do so. It was indeed of immense importance that Dalai Lama could visit India during this period and come to experience many things at first hand. In November 1956, he left Lhasa and at Lha Gyal Lo, (which meant Victory to the gods!) 'for the first time in their present life, all the five brothers of Dalai Lama were together'. On his arrival in India he even met the President of India Dr Rajendra Prasad, whom he found to be very humble. He also met the Prime Minister Nehru on several occasions. Dalai Lama thought that Pandit Jawaharlal Nehru "was a tall, good looking man whose Nordic features were emphasized by his small Gandhi cap. Compared with Mao, he appeared to have less self-assurance, but there was nothing dictatorial about him. He was honest, which was why he was later deceived by Chou En-lai." On one of these occasions, he spoke to Nehru about his desire to seek exile in India but Nehru, naive as he was in international diplomacy retorted by saying that he would speak to the Chinese Prime Minister who was expected in Delhi during the course of the next few days, and that he would even arrange a meeting between the two. Probably, Nehru had revealed to Chou En-lai Dalai Lama's intentions of seeking exile in India— as it was evident from the conversation between Chou and Dalai Lama. Chou En-lai told Dalai Lama that he had heard a rumour that the latter was considering staying in India which he warned would be a mistake.

No sooner Dalai Lama went on a pilgrimage to Bodh Gaya, he received a message that Chou En-lai would like to see him immediately. When Dalai Lama reached Bodh Gaya, a telegram awaited him from General Chiang Chin-Wa suggesting Dalai Lama to return to Lhasa forthwith. Dalai Lama consulted the oracle, and two of them advised him to return. During this period, Dalai Lama even tried to contact the United States Central Intelligence Agency which were perfunctory in assuring assistance except some sort of help in guerilla warfare. Thus he felt disappointed from all sides.

At the outset of Mars-Jupiter sub-period, Dalai Lama with a heavy heart decided to return to Lhasa. On reaching his capital on April 1, 1957, he realised that the situation throughout Tibet was rapidly slipping not only from the Chinese control but also from his own. Astrologically, Jupiter has great protective power, but it has very limited control over the grant of any tangible material reward. Mars and Jupiter are friendly planets, so one could only expect that actual hostility during this period could be avoided. Dalai Lama by this time had realized that external political or military assistance would not be forthcoming to him. The Chinese were concentrating to assert their military strength. His own monastic preparations were so far not complete. Realizing that disaster was in the offing, Dalai Lama announced that he would present himself for his final monastic examination during the *Moulam* festival of 1959. It was about eighteen months from that time. During the Jupiter sub-period, Dalai Lama spent much of his time preparing for this examination.

With the beginning of Mars-Saturn sub-period, disturbing activities began to surface. Keeping with the Tibetan tradition (Jupiter's aspect on Saturn), Dalai Lama moved into a new palace at Norbulingke; each successive Dalai Lama was to found his own building within the Jewel Palace. Meanwhile, the people were feeling restive. They wanted to revolt against the Chinese occupancy. The members of the freedom fighers' alliance, the *Chusi Gangdruk* wanted to precipitate the inevitable crisis: they wanted to besiege a major Chinese garrison at Tsethang, hardly more than two days' travel from the gates of Lhasa itself. Further advance would have led to immense bloodshed without any commensurate outcome.

The crisis was averted but it alerted the Chinese Administration. They realized that Tibet could not be kept captive under peaceful obedience as long as Dalai Lama was present. They began to work out some strategy to remove him from the scene. Dalai Lama had the premonitions of Chinese manoeuvres. But as long as his monastic examination was not over, his wings were not fully grown. His first priority was to stave off direct confrontation with the Chinese military and in the meanwhile, to complete his final examination. Towards the end of summer in 1958, Dalai Lama went to Dreping, and then to Sera monastery for the initial part of his final monastic examination. It involved several days of debates with the most outstanding scholars of the two centres of Tibetan learning. Early in 1959, he left the Norbulingke to take up his residence for the Moulam festival after which came his final examination.

The examination occurred during Mars-Mercury sub-period, and Mercury in his chart was very strongly placed. The final examination involved discussions for several days on diverse subjects without any break. The strong intellect and deeper understanding of scriptures and metaphysics, logic and tantrism resulting from the special placement of this planet enabled Dalai Lama to emerge successful from this intellectual struggle. He has himself recorded the final outcome showing the seriousness of the examination and its impact on him as follows: "At last, at around seven o'clock in the evening it was all over. I felt exhausted, but relieved and delighted that the panel of judges had unanimously agreed that I was worthy to receive my degree and with it the title of *Geshe,* or Doctor of Buddhist Studies." It was a happy termination of a serious obstacle in his religious eminence. With this he left Jokhang where the examination had taken place on March 5, 1959, on his triumphal return to the Norbulingke in a splendid procession.

But Mercury was not only the ruler of the fifth house, it also ruled the eighth house, which is important for its inauspicious disposition. Soon after his return to Lhasa on March 8, 1959 the Chinese design to entrap him began to be unveiled. A Chinese dance troupe arrived for a function. Two days before the date of performance, Dalai Lama was invited, but the conditions stipulated were very suspicious. Dalai Lama's refusal to the invitation could be construed as a sign of rebellion against the Chinese administration, but its acceptance required him neither to take any security personnel nor any firearms, his attendance to the function was to be kept a complete secret. These were forebodings of the coming calamity. The advisers of Dalai Lama were averse to acceptance of the invitation and did not like him to participate. The common people were also opposed to it. The crowd leaders announced to the government that they would post guard outside the cabinet office, which was situated within the outer wall of the Norbulingke. Dalai Lama was in such a fix that he was unable to decide his course of action. He was not even sure whether he should remain in Lhasa or flee the country. Mercury has the unique nature of producing mental conflicts and presenting justifications for both sides of the line of every action.

In such a state of conflict, Dalai Lama invoked Nechung oracle which advised him to stay in Lhasa, but to keep open the dialogue with the Chinese. Still Dalai Lama was not very sure about the advice received. He wanted to check with his own form of divination, so he spent the afternoon performing *Mo,* a form of personal divination but got an identical advice. Meanwhile, violent encounters had begun between the crowd and the Chinese, who were determined to ruthlessly suppress the Tibetan people and affirm the military supremacy.

On 16th March 1959, five days after the Nechung Oracle asking Dalai Lama to remain in Lhasa, the situation came to a flash-point. Any further stay of Dalai Lama in Lhasa could prove vulnerable to his life. In that condition of indetermination, on 17th March 1959, he once again sought the counsel of the Oracle. To his great astonishment, the Oracle shouted just the opposite message given six days earlier: it said, 'Go, Go, Tonight'. The medium still in his trance struggled forward and grasping up some paper and pen, wrote down quite clearly and explicitly, the route that Dalai Lama should take out of the Norbulingke, down to the last Tibetan town on the Indian border. His directions were not what might have ordinarily been expected. To his bewilderment, Dalai Lama found himself in a quandary. So he wanted its confirmation through his own form of divination and the counsel was identical. The answer agreed with the Oracle, though the odds against making a successful break seemed terrifyingly high.

Now the die was cast. Dalai Lama had to leave Tibet come what may. Such is the decision of Saturn; it does not compromise in its decision and its course is always set resolutely. Now for the last time Dalai Lama went to the shrine of Mahakala—the very personification of Saturn, and his personal protector divinity and paying his obeisance for the last time he received the advice with such words as "Develop Confidence and Courage". Now, on that very night, a few minutes before ten o'clock, Dalai Lama put on unfamiliar trousers and a long, black coat and began the pilgrimage of a religious mendicant or the travail of the fugitive. Near the Tibetan border, still within the boundaries of his 'kingdom' Dalai Lama repudiated publicly the 17-points agreement between the Chinese administration and the Tibetan government made in 1951 for the "peaceful liberation of Tibet" between the two countries, and at Lhuntse Dzong, he also announced the formation of his own government to be the legally constituted authority in the land. Dalai Lama entered India in April 1959 during Mars-Mercury sub-period suffering dysentery.

During Mars-Mercury sub-period, Dalai Lama experienced one of his greatest disappointments in life which was very latent. He had hoped that India—his neighbour, a religious country believing in truth and non-violence could sympathise with the Tibetan cause and provide some political support in its struggle for independence from the Chinese domination. But the hope was soon dashed to pieces in less than a fortnight of his arrival in India; he was asked by its Prime Minister to eschew political activities and abandon hopes of gaining Tibetan independence by non-violent means without any bloodshed. It was on 24th April 1959, still during Mars-Mercury sub-period itself that Dalai Lama was temporarily stationed at Mussoorie where Pandit Jawaharlal Nehru himself arrived to see him. They talked for about four hours. Reporting the conversation with Pandit Nehru, Dalai Lama stated:

> I then explained that I had not originally intended to seek India's hospitality, but that I had wanted to establish my Government at Lhuntse Dzong. Only the news from Lhasa changed my mind. At this point, he became rather irritated. "The Indian Government could not have recognized it even if you had", he said. I began to get the impression that Nehru thought of me as a young person who needed to be scolded from time to time.
>
> During other parts of our conversation, he banged the table. "How can this be?", he asked indignantly once or twice. However, I went on in spite of the growing evidence that he could be a bit of a bully. Finally, I told him very firmly that my main concern was two-fold: "I am determined to win independence for Tibet, but the immediate requirement is to put stop to the bloodshed." At this, he could restrain himself no longer. "That is not possible!", he said in a voice charged with emotion. "You say you want independence and in the same breath you say you do not want bloodshed". His lower lip quivered with anger as he spoke.

The Government of India debated over the Tibetan issue in its Parliament and Nehru also spoke of Sino-Indian relationship and his commitment to Panchsheel. All these things were coming to the knowledge of Dalai Lama and they were not what he had anticipated to be the attitude of the friendly Indian Government. These made a very deep impression on him. He became very introspective. Commenting upon his own state of the mind, he wrote:

> I began to realize that my future and that of my people was far less certain than I had imagined. Our meeting ended cordially enough, but as the Prime Minister left, I experienced a profound feeling of disappointment.

Mars being the lord of the tenth house posited in the eighth house could not let Mercury though conferring Raja Yoga by associating itself with Sun, do anything positively helpful for the attainment of

Tibetan independence. Mercury is a very weak planet to produce any concrete action: it is very good in issuing statements, amiable conversation and adaptation with any kind of external situation. So even when inimical Mars ruled the main period, Mercury during its sub-period gave much travels and press conferences. It enabled Dalai Lama to spend some time in visiting some places, undertaking pilgrimages, and meeting eminent persons. During the period, even the United Nations passed some sympathetic resolution in favour of Tibet. He met Dr. Rajendra Prasad who seemed to Dalai Lama 'a true Bodhisattwa'. The only tangible thing that Dalai Lama could achieve during this period was the organisation of Tibetan refugee programmes.

Only during Mars-Ketu sub-period, he succeeded in making some sort of internationalisation of the Tibetan problem. During this period, he met some members of the International Commission of Jurists. They invited him to give evidence before them and he did so. The results of their Legal Inquiry Committee was published in Geneva in August 1960. It vindicated the Tibetan viewpoint. This was also a kind of dissemination of information on what happened in Tibet; it was not any concrete step towards the settlement of the Sino-Tibetan conflict. In fact, Mars was so strongly entrenched in the eighth house that it was almost impossible to hope anything better. During its seven year period, Mars led to the loss of his kingdom, his temporal power, made him an exile seeking refuge in a foreign land, and face humiliation and disappointments from a friendly Prime Minister.

The Rahu mahadasa which started towards the end of 1962 was very fruitful for Dalai Lama. During this period, he succeeded in internationalising the Tibetan cause and the Tibetan approach to life. It was during this period that he travelled to a large number of European countries and the United States and made them register the cause of the Tibetan people. So far Tibet had remained a place on the map of the world, not a country of people throbbing life and philosophy. Rahu destroyed the isolation of the Tibetan people and opened the country and its people to the world view. Dalai Lama succeeded in publishing and even translating some of the Tibetan scriptures in English and other international languages.

As soon as Rahu main period began, India had to encounter the Chinese attacks, and the war between India and China was nerve breaking and very disillusioning. Many people thought that this was a direct result of India offering hospitality to Dalai Lama and the Tibetan people. The breakdown in the health of Pandit Nehru which ultimately led to his death was to a great extent the direct consequence of the loss of the great trust and allegiance he had put in the leadership of the Communist China. For Dalai Lama, it was a period of almost no action. It was however accompanied by some setback in his personal circle, and there were some deaths also. Even the death of Nehru was a personal loss to him, as he had established a kind of rapport with him which was unique in many ways.

The Jupiter sub-period brought some activity in his camp. When Lal Bahadur Shastri became the Prime Minister of India, the earlier tilt towards China was absent. It seemed that Shastri's government would recognize the Tibetan government in exile. But there came the Indo-Pakistan war. It attracted full attention of the Indian Government. Soon after the cessation of the Indo-Pakistan war, Lal Bahadur died. Mrs Indira Gandhi was a different person. The question of Tibet was once more discussed at the United Nations without any outcome. Dalai Lama himself suffered from the hepatitis and was much troubled by it. He met a large number of people from different walks of life including J. Krishnamurti, the renowned mystic philosopher of the twentieth century. But nothing helped him in securing his ultimate objective. A unique feature of Jovian influence is its hopefulness, eminence, protection from danger, but bestowing substantial material attainments is not possible for it. For such results, it has to seek some other planet's support, but in the present case it is neither associated nor aspected by any other planet. During Rahu-Jupiter sub-period, Dalai Lama gained prominence, but his political problem was no where near solution. It however gave him his first journey outside India. He went to Japan and Thailand—the two important Buddhist countries.

During Saturn sub-period, the only noteworthy event, if at all that could be called so was Dalai Lama's meeting with Father Thomas Merton, who was an important American Benedictine monk belonging to the order of black monks, who put black robes (not belonging to any ethnic group). The meeting opened a channel of communication with the American people.

During Mercury sub-period, Dalai Lama could not obtain visa to visit the United States and thus his meeting with President Eisenhower who had expressed his willingness to meet him could not materialise. It greatly disappointed Dalai Lama. With the advent of Ketu sub-period, Dalai Lama experienced overpowering desire to withdraw from the mundane existence and go for a retreat for about three years or so. It was quite in keeping with the results of Ketu's disposition which received ninth aspect of Jupiter from the ninth house. Ketu enabled Dalai Lama to achieve some lasting results in advocating the Tibetan case before the international fora. In 1973, Dalai Lama made his first trip to Europe and Scandinavia. During this trip, he covered eleven countries and succeeded in carrying his message to the most powerful people. Ketu gave him a sense of fulfilment, renown and helped him to establish useful contact for his impersonal Tibetan cause.

During Rahu-Venus sub-period, the greatest adversary of Tibet, the Chinese President Mao Tse-Tung died in September 1976. It slightly improved the Tibetan situation. But the Chinese authorities were however not yet willing to do anything substantial for it. After the death of Mao, Dalai Lama realised that the communist leaders who at first seemed to have a single mind inhabiting their different bodies were in reality not so: all of them were at each other's throat in matters of their personal interests. It greatly helped him in dealing with different Chinese leaders. As Sun was helpful to Dalai Lama, its sub-period brought some thaw in Sino-Tibetan relationship. The Chinese leadership seemed moving towards reconciliation. Dalai Lama seemed hopeful. In April 1977, Ngabo Ngawang Zigme, a high ranking officer of Beijing administration publicly announced that China would welcome the return of Dalai Lama and his followers in India. In February 1978, the Panchen Lama was suddenly released almost after a decade of imprisonment.

At the beginning of Rahu-Moon sub-period, Dalai Lama called the Chinese authorities to allow unrestricted access of foreigners to Tibet. He suggested that the Chinese should permit Tibetans in occupied regions to visit their families in exile and vice versa. Deng Xiao-ping as the head of the Chinese Government showed signs of improvement in the Sino-Tibetan relationships. In April 1978, 34 persons who were mostly elderly members of the Tibetan administration were publicly released with great ceremony in Lhasa. In February 1979, the Chinese administration assured that Dalai Lama need not have any doubt about the happiness and welfare of the Tibetan people, if he was actually interested in the same. A week later, invitation to Dalai Lama was even repeated by Radio Lhasa and it announced the formation of a special committee to welcome and receive the Tibetans living abroad. The Chinese Government also accepted the suggestion of organizing a fact finding mission to visit the occupied Tibet. Early in June 1979, Dalai Lama left for a visit to Moscow, Mongolia, several European countries and the United States; in August 1979, a delegation comprising a few members of the Tibetan government in exile left New Delhi enroute Tibet via Beijing. These were certainly very encouraging features which occurred during Moon sub-period in Rahu mahadasa. Moon in association with Yoga-karaka Venus and placed in a cardinal house could yield a good feeling of fulfilment specially because Moon was placed ninth from Rahu which was well placed in eleventh house.

The following sub-period of Mars merely continued the trend though nothing spectacular came out of it.

As Jupiter has the extraordinary quality of making a person feel hopeful of his achievements and grant of prestigious awards and social eminence, but producing no material gains unless it is supported by other planets, its impact on Dalai Lama could not be different. By the time Jupiter began to rule the life of Dalai Lama, he had already established himself as one of the most outstanding statesman of the world and a very respected and pious religious leader. In October 1979, he completed his another round of world tour covering Russia, Mongolia, Greece, Switzerland, and finally the United States of America and at all these places he made a deep impression of the genuineness of his cause. Jupiter helped him to make his task with regard to Tibetan autonomy, well received at different world fora, he made them realize the seriousness of the problem. The world governments recognized the need for doing something about the same and to support the cause of Tibet. Jupiter in the ninth house brings forth goodwill from unexpected sources for the cause of the individual.

With the beginning of Jupiter main period, the Chinese Government changed their attitude and seemed ready to settle the Tibet's dispute. In April 1982, a three-member team of negotiators from Dharmashala, where Dalai Lama lived went to Beijing for discussions, but nothing came out of it. In fact, the Chinese repression of Tibet was intensified. Executions were reported in Lhasa, Shigarze and Gyantse; further arrests were made in Chando and Karze and at other places. It was contrary to what the Chinese had proposed; it greatly upset Dalai Lama. The sub-period of Saturn which aspected the tenth house produced this disappointment. In

May 1984, Dalai Lama realized that the Chinese had not basically changed; they aimed at complete absorption of Tibet and destruction of its uniqueness. They were settling many military personnel and others in the Tibetan region in order to completely exterminate the original Tibetan population in their own country. At the same period Mrs. Indira Gandhi was assassinated and Dalai Lama lost in her an understanding friend.

Under the influence of Mercury in the main period of Jupiter, Dalai Lama was able to raise his voice against the Chinese repression. He was invited to address the Human Rights Commission of the U.S. Congress in Washington D.C. and on 21st September 1987, during Jupiter-Ketu sub-period, he enunciated his Five-Point Puace Plan for the settlement of the Tibet problem. There was much popular acceptance of this proposal. (Ketu in fifth house with Sun and Mercury was capable of proving intellectual superiority of Dalai Lama and his creative genius in seeking out a solution, though Ketu by nature does not produce material satisfaction.) The Chinese authorities denounced the proposal. They wanted to placate the local Tibetans by instructing the monks to celebrate their *Moulam* prayers, festivals and usual celebrations. The monks were averse to the suggestion; a large number of their people were still in prison and the new education was indoctrinating the Tibetan children against their cultural background. The refusal was met with greater repression; it was not till March 1988 that some kind of peace prevailed in Tibet, even though it was very fragile. At the end of a prayer meeting when the Tibetan people were expressing unhappiness at their subordination, the security forces could not tolerate the same. The Tibetans were severely charged with clubs, electric cattle prod and such other instruments. The incident produced much sorrow to Dalai Lama.

In June 1988, at the European parliament at Stratsbourg, he urged the European nations to support the Tibetan cause by trying to convert it as a zone of peace. During Jupiter-Venus sub-period, the Chinese Government wanted to discuss not only the status of Dalai Lama but all matters relating to Tibet if Dalai Lama could agree to meet them immediately in early 1989 at Geneva. As soon as Dalai Lama agreed to the proposal, the Chinese began to wriggle out of it. (The aspect of Saturn on Venus could not produce any satisfactory temporal result to Dalai Lama.) During this period, Panchen Lama, who had been a close associate of Dalai Lama, and since the Sino-

Tibet trouble began, was taken to Beijing—died on a rare visit to Tibet. The Tibetan people by this time were becoming very restive under the Chinese rule. Demonstrations and repressions had become normal features of Tibet without any seeming end of the tunnel. The Chinese atrocities continued, while the western nations such as the United States, France and the European parliament condemned the atrocities. But there was no lessening of the strain.

During the same period, however, in Autumn of 1989, Dalai Lama on a visit to the United States learnt that he was awarded the Nobel prize for peace, which was the effect of yogakaraka Venus with full aspect of ascendant lord on it. Personally it was a glorious period for him (Venus was placed eleventh from the main ruling planet of the period). The world at large recognised the great restrain Dalai Lama was showing in tackling the Tibetan problem, while helping the humanity by his messages of peace, harmony and compassion. It was a period of profound triumph for him; the lord of the fourth and ninth houses placed in a cardinal house aspected by a powerful ascendant lord bestowed upon him the rarest status, and that also in the western countries (Saturn rules over the western countries) but his own home country remained embroiled in conflict, bloodshed and groaning repression under the martial law. This is an extraordinary situation in cases like that of Dalai Lama that powerful planets work differently at different levels and it is often difficult to decipher their effects in advance on any specific aspect of his life.

Generally, those planets which produce material deprivations are much effective in arousing spiritual impulses. In such cases, it is necessary to view the situation with much care in applying the rules of esoteric astrology, while keeping a watch on the exoteric repercussions of these planets: the seer may suffer physically under the physical repercussions of the planets while on spiritual or higher levels of existence he may gain much auspicious spiritual progress. In the present case, Saturn is powerful and it has auspicious disposition as the ascendant lord, while it is extremely adverse in mundane matters as the lord of the twelfth house. Its aspect could sometime help and sometime create devastation.

There lies the enigma of astrological prognostication which can be resolved only by the experience and insight of the astrologer. Such difficulties in the case of Dalai Lama arise, both with regard to Saturn as well as Venus; even about Mars one cannot be very sure of its repercussions. Jupiter-Mars sub-period caused difficulties with local (Indian) population and Dalai Lama was much upset about the same. Jupiter-Rahu sub-period made Dalai Lama somewhat depressed and lose heart. He began talking about the impatience of the Tibetan people with the non-violent struggle. He was apprehending that they might even refuse his leadership and abandon their peaceful compaign. In such a situation, Dalai Lama was himself contemplating to disassociate with the Tibetan struggle for independence. If that happens there would be bloodbath of an unprecendent kind and nobody knows what would be the shape of things at that time. When the rulership of Saturn starts towards the end of 1996, Dalai Lama begins an extraordinary period of his own spiritual growth, but will that period be helpful for the Tibetan independence? May be towards the turn of the century, during Saturn-Mercury sub-period, some solution is reached between Tibet and the Chinese Government, but who can predict the nature of enigmatic Saturn?

6

MORARJIBHAI DESAI

			Asc.
Sun Rahu	*29th February 1896* (Rasi)		Jupiter (R)
Mercury Venus Mars			Ketu Moon
		Saturn (R)	

Sun		Venus	Saturn
Mars	*(Amsa)*		Mercury Ketu
Rahu Asc.			
	Moon		Jupiter

The unique feature of Morarji's personality was its magnetic nature but there were many questions about him, which have remained unanswered by those who wished to understand the central motivating force of his life. Astrologers have wondered whether he was a captive of the stars or was a freak in nature. The psychologists have pondered over his eccentricity and they wanted to speculate on his schizophrenic aberrations: but could not be sure about the tremendous strength of his individuality. The politicians were not sure whether Morarjibhai was motivated purely by philanthropy and idealism or was a very crafty and elusive politician trying ever to draw the attention of the public to secure their adulation. People in general however have wanted to know whether Morarjibhai was merely a heartless creature behaving as if he has no emotion, or was a successful hypocrite. No conclusive answer to these questions could be adduced to the divergent speculations about the real, basic character of Morarjibhai Desai. Only his autobiography could dispel the various misgivings about him. There was great suspicion that even his pronouncements about his own self might not be taken at their face value. A careful analysis of his planetary disposition to a great extent could perhaps help in revealing his innate nature as well as the various reactions of the people to his behaviour and attitude.

Morarjibhai was Gemini ascendant with heavy concentration of planets around the lunar nodes thus making their axis extremely important in his life. The retrogression of two major planets, namely Saturn and Jupiter in his natal chart makes the horoscope extremely enigmatic: their impact on all the rest reveals many extraordinary stellar characteristics. Gemini being his ascendant, he was bound to be elusive. It was a dual sign and as such he had the potentiality of acting in the most aggressive manner—as well as of being extremely receptive or passive to external forces. The ascendant lord occupied the eighth house which was a house related with hidden aspects of one's life so, by nature he cannot be strictly identified in any stereotype pattern. It was natural for him to be Mercurial, difficult to be put to any fixed shape. Gemini divides his personality in two distinct parts. Mercury was the harbinger of divine messages but was also a traveller between the gods and men. Gemini was a couple—a male and a female. The ascendant lord Mercury aspected by Jupiter expands however the seen, the objective world and the parameter of the visual stage on which one plays one's role in the world. Saturn in retrogression became extraordinarily powerful and when such a tamasic planet aspects, specially because of its hind sight due to its retrogression, its restrictive impact on the ascendant was exceptional. Such a situation occurs in the case of Morarji Desai, so it was quite clear astrologically that he might blow hot and cold simultaneously. Contradictions in his life would be its basic characteristic. The life of Morarji Desai was therefore often compared as that of Dr Jekyll and Mr. Hyde. Sometimes, he was observed as holier than the holy, and on other occasions, he functioned like a heartless brute. In spite of such apparent contradictions and inconsistencies, there was unity in his life; such an integration of personality between the inner man and his outer expression was rarely found. In fact, he was a unity between gods and men, he was a synthesis between the male and the female principles in one's self.

Morarji Desai was a self composed individual, who acted on his inner propulsion whose motivation sprang not from outer personal considerations but from certain moral principles. He was as emotional and compassionate as a mother, whilst on the exterior side he behaved like a judge who had to impartially adjudicate between the guilty and the innocent, or to function like a surgeon who had to extricate the diseased limb in order to save the whole body. He dissociated himself completely from what he did while himself remained identified with his inner conscience and the sense of righteousness. This was the cause of his enigmatic personality. If various traits of Morarjibhai Desai were analysed astrologically, it would appear that he was merely a pawn in the hands of planetary design and a captive of the stars; believing in this fundamental truth about life and its unfoldment, Morarji tried to be as objective about his psycho-physical dimensions of life as it was humanly possible, while maintaining his freedom of will to his inner conscience.

Morarji Desai was born on February 29, 1896 at Bhadeli, a small village, three miles from Bulsar—the southernmost district of Gujarat at approximately 1 p.m. local time. At the time of his birth, Sun was with Rahu placed in Saturnian sign of Aquarius, which happened to be the ninth house. Saturn itself in retrogression and in exaltation occupied the fifth house. These planetary dispositions from the very beginning showed that the child was going to have tough time with the authorities; his ego from the very beginning asserted its strength, as there were three planets in exaltation and two in retrogression. No planet attained vargottam navamsa to indicate smooth progress towards higher status in life.

But the pattern of planetary positions revealed a configuration which suggested an eventful life. All the planets had moved from their signs in such a way that they occupied auspicious relationships with their own signs as well as with signs of their exaltation. Sun was in a cardinal house in relationship with its own sign Leo and eleventh from its exaltation sign. Moon was second from its own sign and fourth from its exaltation sign, Taurus. Mars was placed in tenth from Aries and occupied its own exaltation sign, Capricorn, and its occupation in third from Scorpio gave it much courage to take initiative. Jupiter was in fifth position from Pisces, occupied its own exaltation sign, but it was in eighth house from Sagittarius which showed much efforts for developing his latent faculties but inability to gain occult insight. Saturn was exceptionally powerful as it was placed tenth from Capricorn and was in ninth from Aquarius and it occupied its own exaltation sign. Venus occupied ninth position from Taurus, fourth from Libra and eleventh from its exaltation sign Pisces. Mercury, the ascendant lord, however, does not possess unmitigated auspicious nature: it was situated fifth from the sign of its rulership and exaltation, namely Virgo but it was eighth from its own sign Gemini which showed much responsibility, tremendous original creativity and efforts to understand his personal inner nature. It also gave a life beset with much difficulties. Thus we find that all the planets in Morarji's natal chart were prepared to bestow their choicest beneficence to him. It also showed that there was a higher purpose—a mission distinctly different from his mere personal growth. He was so to say, born with some special purpose—some important functions in the natural scheme of personal (and social) evolution.

Sun and Moon aspected each other showing that there was a very close link between the deepest urges of his life and the receiving channels in his consciousness. The Sun indicated the inner urges, while the Moon represented his consciousness. The five planets namely, Sun, Rahu, Mercury, Venus and Mars which at the time of his birth were importantly above the visible horizon of the sky were preparing to set below it, which indicated that they would be radiating more unearthly, something ethereal than those impulses which bestowed worldly comforts and affluence. The most important planet and the most powerful in Morarji's chart was Saturn, which was moving (because of its retrogression) towards the nadir point, the fourth house, which characterized undue check on his creative power and inability to receive much support from his inner depth. He could feel the presence of inner power, but was unable to tap its beneficence for the discharge of his worldly responsibilities. The inner forces in the life of such individuals produce much unsettling results. These planets were determined to *boulevarse* his life at every stage of his unfoldment. Rahu's disposition with Sun and Ketu's with Moon aggravated the result. The association of Rahu-Ketu axis with the luminaries characterised the karmic significance of their influence. Desai could be helpless in counteracting their results and directing them in any other manner.

Another disquieting feature was the placement of three planets namely Mars, Mercury and Venus in twelfth house from that of the Sun, and of Jupiter—the most powerful benefic from Moon. Evidently, all these planets excepting Saturn were involved in the churning operation, trying to externalise the forces aroused earlier (in previous births), which created psychological storms in order to completely re-orient his inner life and its attitudes. Saturn maintains equidistance from these disturbing planets: it is fourth from Jupiter, and the trio of Mercury, Venus and Mars were fourth from it. It aspects Jupiter with its tenth sight, thus minimising the beneficience of Jupiter to a great extent, while the trio were placed in Capricorn making them greatly under the surveillance of Saturn. These were the portents to show that the life of Morarjibhai would be full of troubles and conflicts at all stages of his life. Saturn will always be drawing out retributing forces from the mysterious depths—the eternal reservoir, where the karmic results were stored, and it would externalise them to be churned by various planetary impulses so that the past karmic debts were counterbalanced and his life becomes free to undertake fresh divine mission. The churning of his physical and psychic life could make him completely isolated without any support in meeting the storms in his life. The Saturnian impulse produced this kind of karmic churning and physico-psychological seclusion. This impulse was very powerful in the case of Morarjibhai Desai. Only when the ego had gained some strength that such impulses were released so that the individual could withstand their impact and Morarji certainly was born with a very powerful ego.

Saturn was very important in the life of Morarjibhai Desai. He was born on a Saturday, his ascendant lord Mercury was in Saturn's sign Capricorn; Saturn was exalted in his horoscope and it was retrograde acquiring special strength. Five planets were in fourth and fifth from it and Jupiter was in tenth house in relation with it. It made all the planets except Moon in trine and cardinal houses from its placement. These planets would be inclined to support Saturnian impulses, but Saturn itself owned the eighth and ninth houses in the chart. These houses were significant in every horoscope—the former represented the secret or the hidden aspects of one's life, whereas the latter was concerned with results of the past meritorious deeds. Saturn's restrictive control over these houses generally distorts the normal growth of one's personality. Morarjibhai therefore had immense difficulties and impediments almost in every sphere of his life. His life became austere, his beliefs rigid and in his consciousness an awareness of purposefulness of the unknown power impinged which affected his everyday life.

The tremendous power exerted by Saturn, which completely nullifies the effect of human endeavours, and moulds them in its own manner, made Morarjibhai accept that the best any individual can do was to surrender oneself to higher forces and adapt oneself to the mighty current of events trusting God's hand in everything. The psychic development of Morarjibhai Desai since his childhood and the way he braved the ups and downs of events at every important step showed the importance of Saturn in his life. His whole life had been an exercise in self-discipline and spiritual development, following the lead of *his own* intellect and understanding both of which were controlled by Saturn and Mercury in his life in an important manner.

In the life of Morarjibhai Desai, the luminaries were associated with the nodes and the Rahu-Ketu axis joins the third and the ninth houses. Jupiter in exaltation, occupies the second house and has natural direct motion towards Moon with which it has natural affinity but, because of its retrogression possibly due to the location of Ketu with it, Jupiter recoiled from joining it: it remained poised in its exaltation sign aspecting tenth house but inclined (due to its retrograde motion) to associate with ascendant, thus imparting to it the deep urge towards righteousness. With its inclination to associate with ascendant and its aspect on the tenth house, Jupiter acquires great protective force, and it saved Morarji from many severe misfortunes in life.

The trio consisting of Mercury, the ascendant lord, Venus the lord of the fifth house and Mars the lord of eleventh house, all in their forward motion, were eagerly approaching the Rahu side of the Rahu-Ketu axis, where lies the Sun in the ninth auspicious house though represented by Aquarius ruled by Saturn. The eighth house in this chart becomes important, because of the occupation of the trio indicating that the inner life of Morarji would accentuate the karmic forces and the events arising from the past would have much importance in unfolding his personality. The association of exalted Mars among the planets moving towards the ninth house shows that the spirit of Morarji, his urge to uncover his latent faculties never flags in spite of great difficulties experienced in the effort. These three planets were also connected with Saturn due to Saturn's tenth hind-sight on them (which takes place due to the retrogression of the planet) and impairs their smooth operation.

Due to similar hindsight third aspect on Moon and Ketu-side pole of Karmic axis, Saturn so much affects the clarity of lunar perception of the solar message that the thinking process of Morarji was often stilted and jarred the common man's viewpoint, which made him unpopular, rigid, and even pompous and pedantic. Morarji's sociability, specially due to the disposition of Venus, which interchanges signs with Saturn and owns the twelfth house and was placed in the eighth and was aspected by Saturn due to its hind tenth aspect had been one of his worst features in the chart, which explained much of his unsavoury relationship with his colleagues and others. As these planets were attracted in an important manner with Rahu and Ketu poles and no planets escaped this attractive influence, no part of Morarji's life remains outside the purview of karmic forces. Naturally, therefore life for Morarji Desai became a responsibility, a burden, a bondage, which had to be carried out whether one likes it or not; it was not a pleasant process of one's divine unfoldment.

The shadowy planets, specially Rahu, associated with the luminaries, created much frustration in the life of Morarji Desai. Ketu with Moon made his experiences unreal to his perceptive mind, and Rahu with Sun aroused so much expectations (or could it be called ambition?) that any level of achievement was unsatisfying to him; his expectations always exceeded the achievement which aroused considerable restlessness and frustration goading him towards more vigorous pursuit. Such a life cannot but be full of sorrow, frustration and anguish, though all these may not be apparent from his facial expressions. The shadowy planets leave their imprint on the psychic life of the individual.

Morarji's father was suspected to have committed suicide a few days before Morarji's marriage. Morarji Desai was not allowed to take his matriculation examination when he was due for it because he was underage. When he joined the government service as a civil servant, he functioned with efficiency, intelligence and with impartiality but he was always found on the wrong side of the authorities, he was charge-sheeted for working in a communally biassed manner; though the charges did not stick to him and he was honourably exonerated, yet he found it more convenient, specially due to his own inner compulsions, to resign from the service. He worked whole-heartedly with great devotion and integrity for the Congress party, but he was finally ousted or moved out of it and made to form a different party. Even this political party did not stick with him for long and he became politically isolated.

He was once invited from Maharashtra by Jawaharlal Nehru to join the central cabinet, but soon after his arrival in Delhi, Panditji became unusually cold towards him. Indira Gandhi made him Deputy Prime Minister, but shortly afterwards he was removed unceremoniously by sending him an open letter to this effect. He forged unity among the opposition parties and piloted them to the seat of power, and became the Prime Minister of India, but soon after there was disaffection in the party forcing him to step down, but soon afterwards the party and his Government both paled into insignificance and ultimately went into oblivion. At one stage, the Pakistan Government awarded him the highest decoration it could to any foreigner for friendship and goodwill, which however was soon withdrawn. Such difficulties and turn of events which had been the recurrent story of Morarji's life resulted from the impact of Rahu-Ketu axis. More than their physical effect, the shadowy planets influenced the psyche of Morarji more than any other aspect of his life.

Morarjibhai Desai was born in an ordinary village in the community of ordinary Anvil Brahmin community—reputed for plain speaking, hot temperament and independent behaviour, but the position of Sun in his chart raised him to the highest status in the country, and was held in high esteem all over the world. Almost every statesman of the world thought him to be a man of integrity, power and candid behaviour which were rare for a politician. It all happened so, because the Sun brought to him from his past lives the quality of identifying oneself with the one universal life-essence pervading entire manifestation which expressed itself with resolute determination to follow ethical principle of righteousness at all cost and even at his own peril.

Sun's association with Rahu occupying the ninth house in the sign of Aquarius reveals this innate characteristic of his psyche. The power that in his past lives went to his head and involved him in atrocious behaviour returned to him, as *nemesis* to teach him a lesson that human consideration in life was much more important than rigid following of the law; power does not last for long and the only enduring feeling was the trust in Nature's suprěmacy (which in other words implies candid surrender to the Supreme Lord,—the God). This experience gained in one of his past lives seems to have been imprinted on Morarji's psyche very deeply, because of his continuous failure in life and everlasting personal suffering, specially connected with his relationship with authority. Misuse of power in the past came back to the individual to arouse the feelings of dispassion in respect of power. This detachment, impersonal approach to authority, planted the seeds of spirituality.

Such karmic *nemesis* which leads to psychological reorientation became clearer by an examination of the disposition of the Sun. Rahu's association with Sun always heralded karmic nature of the solar power and one's unhappy relationship with authority. The spiritual tendencies of Sun were evident in the present case by its association with Rahu as well as its position in Aquarius which makes one's life generally very impersonal. Sun's occupation of the Saturnian sign Aquarius showed that the individual could attain satisfaction only by working as an agent of the Supreme, making all his words and deeds as expressions of the will of God.

In the present case, the Sun in Jupiter's navamsa, being in the sign of Pisces indicated that satisfaction to the individual would be experienced only when he uses his authority for the sake of some moral purpose.

Sun occupies Satabhishak asterism which fell within the zodiacal sign owned by Saturn, a planet leading to renunciation and authority, but the asterism itself represents the culmination of manifestative function of Saturn—its essential characteristic being symbolised by 100 petalled flower. The symbol was related with *Brahmarandhra,* or the crown chakra, whose blossoming heralds the complete activation of Kundalini, the serpent fire, which enables an individual to transcend the necessity of birth-death cycle. Sun in this asterism signifies powerful downpour of divine power. In householders' life, it shows the arousal of spiritualistic tendencies and belief in the immanence of God. In fact, in the life of Morarjibhai Desai from his very childhood, the various conditions in which he was placed arose not casuall}, but as a result of karmic impulses to teach him some moral lesson, to arouse some special latent faculties, or to enable him to pay back some of his old karmic debts as subsequent events showed them to be extremely important in influencing his life's direction and psychological evolution.

The asterism however revealed several other characteristics, which affected his life deeply. The asterism was related with Manus, Daksha Prajapatis and Valmikis. These were great seers and sages, who transformed their own life, put in abeyance their personal development, and dedicated themselves for the furtherance of evolutionary plan of the Supreme. They did it at immense personal sacrifice; they did so to be helpers in the process of cosmic ideation. The *100 flowers* assigned as the symbol for the asterism represents the culmination of the divine will, the end result of any effort, the ultimate achievement of any process of growth: in human individuals, it stands for psychological transformation—a kind of mutation which brings into the being a kind of radical change, it stands for cleansing of the chalice for the downpour of divine impulses, observance of strict discipline and self-imposed austerities so that the personality does not intervene in the discharge of one's spiritual responsibilities.

The asterism was presided over by the shadowy planet Rahu, which in the present case happens to be associated with Sun. In the life of Morarjibhai, these planetary dispositions affected and spiritualised his psyche so much and made his life so impersonal and idealistic that he began to be greatly misunderstood by his political colleagues, who could never accept such to be the genuine feelings and qualities of a political leader. Morarji was a dedicated, idealistic and self-sacrificing political worker, not a politician playing the game of duplicity, and it made him much misunderstood.

Satabhishak's relationship with Manus, Daksha Prajapati, and such other seers produced several responsibilities to Morarjibhai, which he had to bear from very early stage in his life. Sun in Satabhishak along with Rahu occupying the ninth house made Morarji not only austere, but also completely dedicated to the spiritual impulses in life accepting everything that happened to him as a part of God's plan for him and the world. He had to shoulder onerous family responsibilities, and later on tremendous responsibilities for national affairs. But the Vedic deities presiding over this asterism were vested with unlimited knowledge and tremendous insight in the growth and evolution of the universe which were necessary for carrying out their various responsibilities.

In the present case, Sun soaked with the influence of associated planets bestowed much knowledge, wisdom and indomitable will to Morarji Desai which made him fearless and confident without any feeling of inferiority vis-a-vis seers like Sri Aurobindo, Ramana Maharishi, or in respect of politicians like Mahatma Gandhi and Jawaharlal Nehru; he treated equally with ease eminent social workers like Vinoba Bhave, whom many politicians held in great awe and spiritual terror; Morarji was equally natural with international statesmen of different shades of political opinion like Bulganin, Kruschev, John F. Kennedy and others. Sun in the natal chart of Morarji Desai bestowed upon him the immense willpower and self-confidence as well as unfathomable courage (Mars in exaltation in eighth house), which were essential for the discharge of diverse responsibilities devolved on him from his *purva janma*, past incarnations. The responsibilities, the capacity to weather them as well as praise and blame for the results thereof were all carefully packed in his present life by the Lords of Karma.

Moon in the present chart occupies fourth quarter of *Poorva Phalguni.* It was placed in a fiery sign Leo, owned by Sun and directly aspected by the sign lord. Such a situation of Moon was capable of destroying emotionalism from the individual's nature, making him function in a completely detached manner, as if he were an agent of the Law—an unbiased authority. Yet *Poorva Phalguni* was an asterism owned by Venus—the planet of sensitivity, sociability and personal rapport with others. The fourth quarter of the asterism was owned by Mars, which was capable of arousing the deepest emotion, infatuation in love, martyrdom in devotion. The basic impulse of *Kama*, passion, surrounds the asterism; it was symbolised by a couch, a fire-place, or a platform, all of which indicate the readiness to involve oneself in worldly, social or family activities.

It was said that Lord Mahadeva started for his marriage under this asterism. The basic urge of *Poorva Phalguni* was thirst, *trishna*, which involves the ego in materialism. It arouses the urge to enquire, to dominate and to achieve. But on higher planes, it makes the individual surrender himself to the will of God, realizing the universality of the Supreme. Often, Morarji stated that the Supreme was absolute, having the power to transcend his own edicts. On material plane, he however felt that no attainment was impossible unless the ultimate was opposed to it.

Morarji's belief in the absolute nature of the Supreme and the desirability of the surrender of oneself to the will of God was accentuated by several other planetary combinations. For example, the three malefics namely, Saturn, Mars and Sun in Vishakha, Uttara Ashadha and Satabhishak respectively also lead to similar results. Vishakha was symbolised by the potter's wheel, presided over by the celestial architect Tvastra and the zodiacal sign in which the asterism lies was Libra ruled by Venus. The exalted Saturn in this sign has made it inclined to fashion the individual in harmony with his destiny. Under this situation, Saturn operates as an instrument in the hands of the celestial architect to remove the superficial clay, so that the destiny of the individual was attained and the will of the God could mould him in the desired manner. It was a difficult process, yet it makes the individual at all levels of his existence, in conformity with the divine will. To Morarji, such a Saturn produced much suffering, much restriction (often he went to gaol under the influence of this planet) and penance (he undertook several times, fasts unto death in order to pressurise his opponents to get his viewpoint accepted). The celibacy, dietary regulations, renunciation of special privileges accorded to him, and denial of financial gains accruing to him under special circumstances were some of the restrictive effects produced by Saturn.

Mars aspecting Moon from the Saturnian sign Capricorn, posited in the eighth house or the house of death has the quality of making the mind impulsive, selfish and exploiting (acquisitive). But these were not the basic martian impulses, they only appear at superficial level in many ordinary individuals. Intrinsically, Mars was concerned with externalising the inner qualities and nature of the individual, which can be deciphered to a great extent by the asterism in which the planet was posited. In the present case, Mars was placed in Uttara Ashadha, which was owned by Sun, a planet with much occult potential. Sun was not much concerned with superficialities of everyday existence: it acts at the inner-most, Atmic level, which arouses the latent divinity in man. Mars made Morarji Desai very 'unworldly'. The deity concerned with this asterism was Vishwadeva, who inspires the ego to view the world itself as God, there being no difference between the Supreme and his manifestation. Under this influence, one would realise the cosmic unity, and in evolved egos it will arouse the feeling of humility, whilst on the lower planes it may produce self-centredness. The aspect of Mars on Moon produces tremendous outflow of energy, dauntless courage in the display of external activities arising from the realization of cosmic unity. Philanthropic activities under such impulses were genuine expressions of the inner feelings of universal unity. For this reason, Morarji Desai functioned from an entirely different centre of operations, which the common man often failed to appreciate.

Morarjibhai Desai greatly fascinated by the unknown, sought to discover the reality that lies beyond the ken of ordinary human mind. He was basically an occult inquirer. This mental characteristic was well represented by the disposition of his ascendant lord. In fact, *Shravana,* the asterism in which his ascendant lord was placed, played an important role in his life. Mercury, the ascendant lord and Venus, the lord of the fifth house were both placed together in Shravana asterism. The distance between these two planets was less than 7°, showing close affinity between the two. But in navamsa, Venus occupies its own sign Taurus. The closeness between these two planets especially because of their association with Mars in the same sign, where the latter attains its exaltation has assumed an extraordinary disposition: Venus has lost its usual sensuous cravings and even made Morarjibhai Desai to take the vow of celibacy. The unique combination in the eighth house—the house of secrecy and hidden aspects of life aroused great initiative and determination in him to explore the hidden aspects of life and his own inner nature.

Shravana leads to meditative attitude, desire to listen to the intonations from the unknown realm, and strong urge to obey and accept with full faith the higher truths. Planets under its influence were tuned towards spirituality. When Mercury and Venus were thus influenced, they impart tremendous sensitivity to spiritual forces and induce the individual to carry to the everyday world the extra-ordinary messages of the unseen world. For this very reason, due to the other-worldliness of Morarji Desai, many persons not acclamatised to such finer occult forces felt extremely uncomfortable in the company of Morarji. Pandit Jawaharlal Nehru was radically different from Morarjibhai and therefore, in spite of his personal greatness and great attraction towards Morarji was often ill-at-ease with him, many people felt even afraid of some unknown fear from Morarji. Morarji Desai often deciphered many unusual radiations in the aura of different persons. When Morarjibhai Desai visited Ramana Maharshi, he perceived an aura of light around him. Even in relation with daily occurrences, he felt the presence of divine hand in creating many happy as well as unhappy events in his life and he accepted them as such with equanimity. These were some of the effects of Mercury-Venus combination in Shravana, specially when they were placed in the eighth house, which was the house that reveals the possibility of unfolding one's latent faculties and hidden qualities.

Mercury—the ascendant lord received full Jovian aspect which ruled over the seventh and tenth houses. These houses were important for a politician as well as for a civil servant. Jupiter was exalted and in retrogression. The tenth lord in the second house becomes very auspicious and it produces combinations for much fortune and royal status. Jupiter was also aspecting the lord of the eleventh house. These were important yogas for worldly persons, but in the present case, its being in *Pushya* nakshatra shows full fructification of higher Jovian influences. It was due to this planetary disposition that Morarjibhai succeeded so well in bringing to a dirty game of political activities, the ethical values and behaviour worthy of only evolved spiritual persons, specially when it called for personal sacrifice. In navamsa, Jupiter attains Virgo, which caused hardships to Morarji in following the voice of his inner conscience represented by Jovian influences in discharging his worldly obligations.

In discharging his everyday responsibilities, Morarji acquitted himself with clarity of understanding expressed as Mercurian influence obtained by deeper insight in the interaction of basic forces on higher planes (Venusian intuition). His indomitable courage in carrying out the dictates of his inner voice was the result of the Martian impact. His entire life revolved round his *Atma-Buddhi axis* indicated by Sun-Moon opposition joining the ninth and third houses. Gemini—the ascendant sign, many a time, made him play the role of Dr. Jekyll and sometimes of Mr. Hyde under planetary compulsions. Morarji had been honest on both these occasions, and in his mind there had been no intention of duplicity though in ordinary human society it often seemed so.

It was true that Morarji Desai was often considered holier than the holy and on other occasions, a heartless brute. These were because of the intensity of carrying out the inner conviction that Morarji seemed to put his heart in everything that he did *at that very time of action* without carrying sediments of the act in his psyche subsequently. The unique feature of Morarji's personality was its magnetic attraction. Gemini being his ascendant sign, it was dual in character. It divides Morarji in two distinct parts. Mercury was the harbinger of divine messages and it was a traveller between the gods and men. Gemini was symbolised as a couple—a male and a female simultaneously. The ascendant lord Mercury was aspected by Jupiter which expands the seen, the objective, and the parameter of the visual stage on which the individual plays his terrestrial drama. But Saturn in retrogression also aspected this planet by its hind tenth aspect. Consequently, it exerted restricting influence on the ascendant Lord and made the individual very much introspective and self-centred.

As a result of these contradictory impulses, expansive impulses radiated from Jupiter, and restrictive ones from Saturn, while both of them were almost of equal strength and were without any nullification due to their mutual interaction, Morarji Desai presents a unique feature of duality in unity. He unites in him gods and men, he synthesises in his personality the qualities of a male and a female. Resulting from such an integration, Morarjibhai within him had the emotional nature of a mother while externally, he behaved like a judge. He tried to live as detached as it was humanly possible a psycho-physical life in which his inner determination born out of Saturn's enduring hold on spirit was not destabilized by the changing storms of everyday life. He succeeded to a great extent in synthesizing the two parts of his personality by his personal insight in the working of his psycho-physical personality.

Morarji started his life in Venus mahadasha with a balance of approximately 2 years and 4 months. Venus, the lord of twelfth house occupying eighth house produces an auspicious *Viparita Raja Yoga.* It was also the lord of a trine (the fifth house) which was the house of creativity and it was associated with Mercury, the ruler of angles, thus there was the union between *Vishnusthanam* and *Lakshmisthanam,* which produces a powerful Raja Yoga. The rulership of such a planet at the very beginning of one's life was not very spectacular except by way of producing an easy and comfortable infancy. One does not know whether the infancy of Morarji was more self-conscious, observing the various impulses impinging upon his tender psycho-physical constitution, or he was in the habit of demanding satisfaction for his own basic needs and pleasures. Indications were that his infancy was more concerned with the former.

The Sun main-period began in July 1898. During this period, Morarji devoted much of his time in open air, bullock cart driving, wrestling, and enjoying open air and sunshine outside his house. Sun's association with Rahu made his physical life very ordinary: its sparkling brilliance was tarnished by the shadowy planet Rahu. The main-period of Sun was quite uneventful, but his schooling began during Jupiter sub-period. He also moved outside his rural setting and visited Ahmedabad, which was important for the child as at this stage, Morarji Desai was exposed to the sophistication of urban life and of the world at large.

The main period of Moon's planetary ownership began towards the second half of 1904, which marked the period of his psychic unfoldment. Moon is afflicted by Ketu, aspected by the third hindsight of Saturn, and eighth aspect of Mars. All these were important planets in the present case, which required great attention. Their aspects on physical plane produce inauspicious results.

The Moon mahadasa was an unhappy period of the child Morarji. It was financially an uncomfortable period: the lord of eleventh house (income) and the lord of the sixth house (difficulties, enemies) located in the eighth house aspected Moon, the lord of the second house (financial resources). Ketu's affliction of Moon further intensified Morarji's mental anguish. During Moon-Saturn period, Morarji experienced difficulties in his educational career: Saturn was placed in fifth house, which was connected with education. Morarji was due to appear for his Matriculation examination during this period, but he was declared underage so was disqualified to take the examination. It was a karmic misfortune (Saturn). During Mercury sub-period, Morarji's father died, probably as a result of suicide (Mercury twelfth from Sun representing father, sixth from Moon producing mental anguish, and eighth from its own sign—Gemini produced some death).

His result at the Matriculation examination, however was outstanding. He was declared one of the fifty toppers at the university. Mercury associated with Venus and Mars receiving direct aspect of Jupiter—the lord of the tenth house gave Morarji a brilliant academic result. He was married during this period: Mercury was aspected by Jupiter—the lord of the seventh house, the house of marriage, while Mercury itself was associated with Venus, the karaka of marriages. But the placement of Mercury, an eunuch planet, in the eighth house, its association with Mars which was a planet very much averse to marital relationship, and the hind-sight of Saturn on Mercury as well as its direct aspect on the seventh house were all detrimental to the consummation of marriage during this period.

During Ketu sub-period, Morarji's sister accidently died, she got burnt on a Deepavali day (Ketu in third house with Moon opposing Sun which (Moon) also happened to be the main planetary ruler of the period): Ketu and Moon were aspected by the fiery Mars from the eighth house having enough potential for causing accidents from fire. The accident made a deep imprint on Morarji's psyche (Moon), as he was deeply attached to his sister.

The main planetary period of Mars started in 1914. Soon afterwards, he joined the college. Keeping to its basic nature, Mars imparted much courage, boldness, ability to stand against every kind of injustice. The planet influenced Morarji's physical and emotional life. At the beginning of this period, Morarji began to pay greater attention to physical culture. He began to attend gymnasium regularly; he could even defeat elderly persons in wrestling and his early timidity began to vanish. His inner boldness and individuality began to externalize. He joined the University Training Corps and began to take a leading part in demanding legitimate rights for the trainees.

Rahu was karmically related with Morarjibhai in an important way. It was during Mars-Rahu that the seeds of Morarji's future political activities were sown and took deep roots. Rahu was associated with Sun in ninth house representing *Dharma*—the basic destiny of the individual. Rahu under appropriate conjuncture arouses deep spiritual urges and in the present case, it was associated with Sun which represents *Atma*—the innermost core of one's being. Both these planets situated together brought Morarji Desai in close relationship with many eminent persons and highly spiritual seers. Many of them left deep imprint on his psyche. It was during this period, in 1915, that he for the first time saw Mahatma Gandhi at the annual session of the Indian National Congress; he attended a lecture delivered by Dr Annie Besant—the great theosophical leader, which greatly inspired him to work for Indian nationalism.

During Saturn's sub-period, the martian discipline and austerities were intensified but it also made him sexuality effective. He consumated his married life, which to him was a kind of personal bondage. Saturn was related with Venus by its location in Libra Saturn aspected the seventh house of marriage but because of its retrogression, it was not effective in destroying completely the seventh house results; by its hind-sight it aspected Venus: all these conditions produced a very unusual result on Morarji's married life. Saturn's exaltation mitigated much of its destructive nature, yet it could not completely absolve itself of its restrictive nature. As a result of all the various adjoining factors, Saturn did not deny marriage, but it did not let him have the full expression of a married life. It produced material (physical) marriage but did not enable him to enjoy it psychologically.

Mars-Mercury period was a training period in Morarji's career. Mercury was the ascendant lord and it received the aspect of tenth house lord Jupiter, which was basically a teacher connected with education, learning, and Mercury also received the benefit of the association of Mars which was a self-reliant planet. During Mars-Mercury sub-period, unassisted and unsupported by any unfair influence, without any outside pressure for securing the government service, which at that time was quite rare, Morarji Desai appeared for the Provincial Civil Service examination and was offered a position. He was appointed a Deputy Collector in Ahmedabad in May 1919 on probation. During Ketu sub-period, the young officer was promoted as Sub-Divisional Officer. Soon afterwards, during Mars-Sun sub-period, Morarji began to practise *Tapas*—penance of several sorts; he became interested in studying *Gita* seriously which deeply affected his mind and behaviour. He decided to give up every kind of anger as he considered it 'no good being swayed by it'.

The seed sown during the sub-period of Rahu in the main planetary period of Mars began to sprout and flower during its own main period. Rahu played a very significant role in Morarji's life. Associated with Sun, it partook much of its characteristics and added to it the spirit of independence and religious fervour. During the main period of Rahu, Morarji got promoted in his service career, but was also involved in a disciplinary inquiry, resigned his job, joined the Congress party, was jailed, and one of his children died, he became interested in religious literature and began practising many kinds of austerities. Finally, during this main period itself, he became a Minister in the Bombay Government.

The Jupiter sub-period gave him transfer, promotion and enabled him to make an intensive study of *Ramakrishna Kathamrita,* a religious scripture, which intensified his religious sentiments and made his belief in God much stronger. He also read a great deal about Ramakrishna Paramhamsa—a very powerful spiritual contemporary saint. His interest in *Gita* intensified much deeper. He also decided to give up oil, condiments, and salt but later on, gave up the idea of abstaining from salt. Jupiter also gave him his second daughter. During Saturn sub-period, he gave up salt again on experimental basis. Jupiter's aspect on the sixth house producing much hostility against the native created such a situation in Morarji's career that he was charge-sheeted by the Government and an enquiry was constituted against him to find out whether he had acted on bias of communal nature in discharge of his official duties.

During Mercury sub-period, he was exonerated from the allegation, but he had already decided to resign from the service and awaiting the decision of the enquiry, lest some stigma was attached to his name. Thus ended his service career and he began to take active interest in political activities. During the same period, he became actively involved in political activities and was gaoled as well. The Rahu-Mercury sub-period stands as a watershed in the career of Morarji Desai: he left the Government, which he had served for about 14 years and embarked upon a new career fighting the government, agitating for national independence in which cause he began frequenting Indian prison houses.

Rahu-Venus sub-period, revealed another aspect of his life. During this period, his religious susceptibilities became intense and Raja Yogas in his horoscope began to fructify. Venus in *Shravana* nakshatra enabled him to be receptive to the finer vibrations from the spiritual world. This tendency was accentuated by the Jovian direct aspect from the second house, while Venus itself was the lord of the seventh and tenth houses which were important quadrants. During this period, Morarji went to Pondicherry Ashram of Sri Aurobindo and had discussions with Mother; he exchanged views by letter on certain personal, religious and spiritual matters with Sri Aurobindo. He went to Ramana Ashram and had closer contacts with the sage. He also discussed with Mahatma Gandhi matters of spiritual and political importance. Venus in the horoscope of Morarji operated to a great extent on spiritual and intuitive plane rather than at physical level of consciousness. Apart from being in the eighth house in Saturn's sign and Shravana nakshatra, it was situated in twelfth house from Rahu and was aspected by Jupiter in the natal chart. It was also in its own Taurus navamsa. These factors created a genuine thirst for spiritual perception and understanding. With the beginning of Rahu-Moon sub-period, the regal status specially produced by full aspect of Sun on Moon began to be devolved upon him. During this period, he joined the Bombay Government as a Minister and functioned almost like the Number One.

Jupiter was usually very deceptive and its effects were often misunderstood. It was so even in the case of Morarjibhai's chart. In this case, Jupiter was the lord of tenth house and was placed in second house forming a kind of Raja Yoga, but during this period he spent much time in jail. Even when he was in the Government, during this planet's planetary rulerships under different planets, he worked very hard and had very little recognition for the services rendered. As a matter of fact, he used to assume blame and discredit for unpopular measures taken by the Chief Minister and others while he was working on behalf of the Chief Minister. During the main period of Jupiter, he suffered from several complicated physical ailments like lumbago and even in 1952 general election, he lost the election which indicated that there was some general resentment against him. But the greatest contribution of Jupiter had been that it protected his public image and brought him in close relationship with great ones, political and otherwise, of the world. Even when he was defeated in election, he was not permitted to resign from the Government. These were some of the typical effects of Jupiter.

Jovian effect was primarily to protect rather than to bestow some new status and material affluence, but what Morarji received during this period was prestige and relationships of a satisfactory nature. Details of events and their occurrences in different spheres, disturbing or otherwise took place due to the effects of sub-period lords. With the advent of Jupiter main period of planetary rulership, the general resignation from the Government as a result of the second world war and the public resentment against the British declaration of Indian participation with the allies to which the Congress party resented led to the resignation of the popular Ministries in various Congress States. Consequently, Morarji Desai also had to quit.

The loss of status and subsequent imprisonment which lasted from August 1942 to the middle of 1945 was important in many ways. During this period, the effect of Jupiter by itself could not have been so trying; but due to the direct aspect of three planets located in eighth house and some sort of adverse relationship with Saturn, Jupiter lost much of its beneficence. The disposition of Jupiter in the present case was quite uncommon and such was the effect endured by Morarji during this period. During Mercury sub-period, the earlier status of Morarjibhai Desai was restored; he became an important minister in Kher ministry, where he was operating as second-in-command; but was not given the title of Deputy Chief Minister. Mercury after all having the various fetters imposed on it could not make Morarji Desai what he should have ordinarily become.

Gandhiji was assassinated when Morarji was running Jupiter-Venus. The relationship between Mahatma Gandhi and Morarji Desai was not only political, but there was a kind of religious and spiritual bond between them. Venus was connected with the twelfth house which was associated with life-beyond the physical plane and it was also related with Saturn, which was the planet connected with death. Some death during this period which could seriously affect Morarji Desai could not be avoided. It was also during this period that Morarji was defeated in the general election.

Mars was the lord of the sixth house besides being the lord of eleventh house, and its being in the eighth house in spite of its being capable of bestowing certain social prestige brought to him some stigma and loss of face. Despite Jupiter and Mars both being exalted and in intimate relationship with each other, Mars produced the effect of sixth house, though the adverse effect in any other situation could have been much more exaggerated. Morarji lost election, it created some mental pain to him, some unpopularity was also there but the Jovian aspect and inherent strength of the two planets saved the personal status of Morarji though Pandit Jawaharlal Nehru had to intervene to save the upsetting. Such disturbances during Martian effect could be expected.

During Rahu sub-period, Morarji was brought in very close relationship with foreigners like Marshal Tito of Yugoslavia, and St. Laurence of Canada. He also had some deep-level discussions with Vinoba Bhave on spiritual matters. Thus ended the main period of Jupiter in the life of Morarjibhai Desai.

The following Saturn main period was quite in keeping with its natural traits; the period was full of rise and fall for Morarji. Saturn in his chart was to teach some lasting lessons of life and with its very outset of planetary rulership, it began to make its impact felt. At Chawpatty meeting during this period, Morarji was hit by a stone; he welcomed Bulganin and Krushchev befittingly without any difficulty in spite of the apprehension about their safety in Bombay. He fasted on account of violence in Maharashtra-Gujarat movement. He was shown black flag, had food poisoning and he was invited to the Centre to become the right-hand man of Pandit Jawaharlal Nehru. When Morarji was 60 years of age, in spite of his resistance to the proposal, the public collected for him a purse of rupees one lakh which he donated to charitable institutions.

Saturn-Mercury sub-period took him to a world tour, meeting statesmen and financiers of the world, and the tour also exposed him to international political and financial magnates. Wherever he went, he carried his individuality. With every person he met, he could put forth his views in a forthright manner with clarity and in a convincing manner. Mercury was in its best form at that time. But with the beginning of Ketu sub-period, Morarji began to feel change in Pandit Nehru's attitude to him which made Desai feel let down—a characteristic trait of Ketu with Moon.

Saturn-Venus sub-period was very difficult and trying. He was subjected to many hidden intrigues and humiliating experiences. The allegations relating to his son Kantibhai suggesting that the latter took undue advantage of the official position of Morarji was revived. The introduction of Gold Control Bill and the Compulsory Deposit Scheme created further difficulties for him; his popularity sank to a dismal depth. Meanwhile, Pandit Nehru died but Morarji's hope to step in his footstep and become the next Prime Minister was dashed to dust. In any natural circumstances that should have been the natural sequence of events, but Morarji's planets were not favourable. He was so much feared by his colleagues that they made Lal Bahadur Shastri the Prime Minister of India and he did not even find a place in his cabinet. But the self-respect of Morarji could not swallow such humiliating manoeuvres. Yet it was during this period that Morarji directed his gaze towards spiritual influences more earnestly: he visited famous Amarnath shrine in the Himalayas in search for peace and enlightenment. Venus denied the material welfare and socio-political status (its inherent weakness for doing so has already been discussed above) but produced result at higher planes as a consequence Morarji's sensitivity to finer forces and his union with his higher-self became more intensive.

During Saturn-Sun sub-period, Morarji was invited to become the chairman of the Administrative Reforms Commission which gave him some official status but not commensurate with his earlier ones. Lal Bahadur Shastri did not live for long, and the tussle for succession again became acute. It was hoped that this time Morarji Desai would be compensated for waiting in the wings, but he was once more overlooked. He did not obtain support of his political colleagues, who thought that he would be too powerful for them, whilst they wanted a "Dumb Doll" so that they could pull strings and make it dance the way they liked. Morarji was not made for such a situation. Saturn and Sun, both were powerfully entrenched in his horoscope to destroy all his material hopes and cravings.

During Saturn-Moon sub-period, Indira Gandhi included Morarji in her cabinet and made him Deputy Prime Minister, which was expected to rehabilitate him somewhat and minimise his bitterness against her. But the arrangement did not endure for long: the rapport between the two was not harmonious. He however had another international tour, meeting world leaders, but deep down in himself it did not provide any personal psychological satisfaction to him. His dissatisfaction with the existing state of affairs gradually increased.

Saturn-Mars sub-period further aggravated his trouble. The previous allegations about his son Kantibhai was again revived. (Saturn in the fifth house throughout its period frequently aroused such humiliating situations related with his offspring. The association of Mars with Venus, the lord of the fifth house also could easily aggravate such difficulties). Rahu associated with Sun during Saturn's main period brought out one of the most humiliating experiences for Morarji Desai. Indira Gandhi relieved Morarji Desai from his Finance portfolio without even asking him to resign from the Government, which made him greatly hurt. Its deeper implication was that Morarji's self-respect (Sun) was greatly hurt (Rahu) and became greatly disillusioned (Saturn) from the Congress party. Saturn-Jupiter sub-period was devoted mostly in constructive social work which was quite natural during Jovian rulership.

During the main period of Mercury realise, which began in the middle of 1974, Morarji Desai began to realize his life's ambition. He began to get an inner understanding of the purpose of his present birth. His understanding of Atmic supremacy and dedication of one's life for the fulfilment of Divine Will began to give a radically different and fulfilling psychological interaction. At the very outset of Mercury period, Morarji staked his life unto death for resolving certain problems with regard to Gujarat Assembly, which in the beginning was being resisted by the Congress party. With determination unique to Morarji Desai when he embarked on his fast, Indira Gandhi bowed down to his wishes, though she felt greatly mortified due to her submission (to her long-term adversary). It was considered throughout the country a spiritual victory of Morarji over materialist and manoeuvring politics. Morarji felt that this was what happened due to his meditational practices and complete surrender to God's will in working for a social cause selflessly. It showed that Mercury was not a weak planet; its categorization as eunuch was merely an esoteric veil. One should not always consider that it always officiates for the planet with which it was associated. It has some positive functions of its own. It brings celestial messages for the human world. It can even sustain much hardships for carrying out its own plans and ideas. It heralds a new psychological beginning, which has its repercussions and reflections on one's physical conditions. Mercury was described as very young, because it was capable of original way of thinking and living which at times gives the appearance of extra-ordinary pliability. The beginning of Mercury main period provided to Morarji Desai great opportunities in concretising his concept of a good government. The great success in this field was however realized during Ketu sub-period.

Ketu is an intellectual planet; it does create much hardship on physical plane but often there were deaths of near and dear ones, breakdown of nervous system, and even accidents may take place. It makes the person intellectually very active. Under Ketu's influence, one thinks much ahead of his time, which explains why a child under Ketu's influence becomes precocious. Ketu was symbolised by a flag—a standard, which suggests success but that is in the realm of ideas, something which is more permanent and enduring than physical relations, achievements and events. In achieving such a result, Ketu inflicts death-like sufferings.

In the present case, Ketu was in Makha nakshatra, which is symbolised by a palanquin suggesting victory, regal status, proclamation of one's supremacy. Ketu was in the sign of Sun being located in Leo, thereby it obtained the capability of discharging to a great extent, the effect of Sun which was very important in this horoscope, even for bestowal of material status. Ketu was also associated with Moon, in whose house Jupiter was very favorably posited. It was quite natural therefore to expect that Morarji under its impact could attain the status of his dream. (Ketu gives material attainments to arouse disenchantment with them). Morarjibhai

Desai had every reason to feel emotionally satisfied by becoming the Prime Minister of India, a position which he had missed several times. However, there were reasons to believe that he suffered much psychological conflict and turmoil during Ketu sub-period.

Two years later, when Venus sub-period was ruling, there was destruction of his political edifice (Venus was the lord of his twelfth house with Saturn's hind-sight on it destroying his mundane achievements) and a sense of righteous indignation upsurge in him. This was the beginning of a new life for Morarji Desai. He attained what he aspired for, but ultimately found that the fruit was not so sweet. Subsequent planetary periods did not arouse interest in Morarji for material achievements or for restoration of his political supremacy. His path of renunciation and search for Truth began a new career for Morarjibhai Desai.

During Mercury-Jupiter sub-period, deep meditation and reflection on basic religious tenets occupied Morarji: he began to chew the cud of his past experiences of several decades. Morarji entered into a deeply personal phase of life of which knowledge on the external plane was difficult to obtain. Mercury-Saturn sub-period was important for the attainment spiritual goal. Saturn in tenth position from Mercury, while the latter was posited in Saturn's sign when Saturn itself was fifth from ascendant, which happens to be a sign of Mercury made Morarji extremely introspective, often reaching higher realms of spiritual perception. It would certainly have been a period of intense spiritual (occult) experiences devoid of material glamour. He lived during the remaining period of Mercury major almost detached from physical affiliations, dwelling on larger problems of human welfare. Physically weak but mentally matured and alert, this period must have produced some extremely personal spiritual experience revealing hidden mysteries of life, attained by death-like experiences but not exactly death yet completely rejuvenating him psychically. Mercury could not produce death to Morarji as it was greatly fortified by Jovian aspect.

Ketu main period began towards the middle of 1991. After this, Morarji took retirement from political world, but the leaders of various political parties approached him to seek his blessings. Even after living for full nine decades and going strong in the tenth, Morarji did not show any sign of senility. He was able to penetrate very deeply in the political forces in the country. He was neutral in his opinions but had no desire to impose the same on others. Ketu brought him glory at the fag end of his life. *Bharat Ratna* is the highest award the country could bestow on any of its citizen. It was awarded to him: even when he was unable to attend the official investiture, a special emissary of the President decorated him with the lotus insignia of the award at his residence. Ketu rewards when the physical charm for it was over; it makes a deep imprint on psyche which was more enduring than anything physical. During Ketu-Rahu sub-period, Morarjibhai breathed his last at 1.45 p.m. on 10th April 1995 after a brief illness at Jaslok Hospital, Bombay when the nation was preparing to celebrate his birth centenary. Thus ended the most enigmatic stalwart of the recent political history of India.

7

AN EUROPEAN DIPLOMAT

Jupiter (R)	Saturn (R) Ketu		Moon Asc
	6th October 1939 (Rasi)		
Mars			
		Rahu	Sun Mercury Venus

Asc	Mars	Moon Saturn	Ketu
	(Amsa)		Sun
Mercury			
Rahu			Jupiter Venus

Diplomacy is a fascinating assignment. It involves challenging manoeuvres. It requires skill in managing international relations, negotiating trade transactions and tackling of high state matters. These functions often involve uncandid and deceitful acts, but with such shrewdness that the other party does not get any inkling in the duplicity of the game. Nowadays, a diplomatic mission is even concerned with espionage and intrigues. It is difficult to find out whether a diplomat is an honest person or not, whether he means what he says, but as a person the diplomat has to have high degree of skill in several directions along with acute intelligence and clarity of vision and purpose. He has to understand the language of expressed as well as hidden or unexpressed communication. The personal life of such a person is very much detached with whatever he does: whatever his private life, his personal sorrows and pleasures, his personal likes and preferences, these should not be ordinarily reflected in his public behaviour, utterances and dealings. In many ways, a successful diplomat has his life and its reactions so well regulated (and concealed under the sophisticated facade) that he may even seem as austere and detached as highly evolved and disciplined yogis. In many ways, a diplomat is an enigma. Nonetheless, the success or the failure of many state operations depends upon his skill and managerial acumen. It is extremely difficult to identify the special features which make an individual successful as a diplomat, yet astrologically it is possible to have some understanding of the stellar disposition, which could make an individual adept in his profession.

A successful diplomat must be suave, sociable and self-effacing, but not necessarily a colourless personality. Many successful diplomats-both in the East and in the West, who had been very much uncouth, crude, blunt and unpolished had proved extremely successful in conveying the messages of his country furthering their objectives. Sociability is a greatly desired trait for a good diplomat, but not an essential base of diplomatic functions. Often the diplomats express their pleasures or displeasures in such ways that to an outsider it may not seem very peculiar though in the diplomatic parlance its meaning and significance are well comprehended. For example, once the head of the mission of a foreign country had to be conveyed the un-happiness of the host country concerning some matter. For this purpose, a special communication method was used; in fact, all diplomatic communications are through subtle suggestions. The head of the mission of the foreign country was "invited" for discussions/meetings and the appointment was fixed for it with a very high official of the host country, whose responsibility was to convey the displeasure without giving any offence. When the visiting dignitary came for the appointment, he was asked to wait in the visiting room unduly long and later on was met only by a junior official with "profuse" apologies on behalf of the senior officer and the ambassador was told that the senior was "unexpectedly" held up with certain "unavoidable" work. In this way, after receiving him, he was informed very casually and told of the matter which had aroused the displeasure of the host country in "diplomatically correct language". He was served no tea or drink. The dignitary, after the meeting was seen-off by the personal assistant of the junior officer and not by the officer himself. This is one of the ways of expressing the state of displeasure, which every diplomat understands, but he cannot take objections to the same. It is so because, every act has been correctly performed in outward appearance.

The diplomats—both representing the host country as well as the foreign states have to function more or less like actors in a well managed dramatic act without bringing one's personal emotions in the relationship. There is difference in the code of behaviour between diplomats, but this difference does not lie in spoken language or the expressed behaviour, the diplomatic language is the language of unspoken suggestions and implications. The diplomatic language is the language of non-verbal communication. Diplomatic behaviour need not be necessarily polished and civil. Yet, the important point to note is that the diplomat has to be extremely clear-headed about his objective, method of articulating the emotion without making it too obvious and he has to be extremely skilful in handling people of diverse nature.

This kind of psychological make-up does not come only by the disposition of Mercury, though the contribution of this planet cannot be minimized. The stellar support of Venus and Sun is necessary for success in diplomatic mission. Venus could give instantaneous empathy with the other person; Venus could bestow the gift of sociability and good rapport with others. Yet, these planets are liable to make the traits so genuine that the individual could not achieve the objectivity needed for a diplomat. So Saturn's association is also needed; the individual also should have the support and confidence of his own head of the State.

It is also significant to note that a diplomat is not necessarily a statesman, but a statesman has to be necessarily diplomatic. The diplomat carries the wishes of the statesman, he is a communication channel, whereas the statesman has to communicate his message directly by himself. The diplomat's efficiency lies in his mastery over the communicating medium like a dancer, who expresses the various emotions by his or her expressions; the diplomat has to be a linguist, an erudite scholar, a psychologist, while maintaining perfect control over his personal predilections. He has to act on behalf of the statesman (Sun) but in playing the role he has to use his own resources, intellectual, emotional and physical, in completing the task assigned to him by the statesman and as such he is necessarily to combine in himself the role of two persons, of his own self and of the other, he has no right to interfere with the other personality functioning on behalf of the statesman. The important task before the diplomat is to completely isolate these two personalities, functioning within himself, whereas the statesman neither has this compulsion, nor does he function on behalf of anyone else.

As diplomatic assignment in each country depends upon special characteristics of the country concerned, so no general criteria can be laid down of the diplomats as such. Yet, on the basis of essential requirements for a successful diplomat and the individual characteristics of different countries, the planetary impulses for making an accomplished diplomat can be worked out. The astrological biography of an European diplomat brings out some of the salient features of stellar support essential for success in this profession. The biography belongs to a very colourful and effective diplomat of an European country, namely Belgium which in recent years has become the hub of international relations in many ways. The person made a mark in the diplomatic circle in a very short period. His selection and rise as a diplomat had been so spectacular that many of his contemporaries considered his rise dependent upon his 'manoeuvreability' or on his 'craftiness', but astrologically it could be observed that this person was very suitable for this kind of difficult assignments. It is indeed a matter of great luck that any country could have a personality of this kind, so that its purpose could be effectively and appropriately achieved. If an astrological basis for the selection of this kind of posting would have been there, this person would have easily scored high position in the merit list of the selection.

The person was born in October 1939 (other details are suppressed purposefully) in Belgium and that was the time when conditions were very unsettled, when the country was still having the impact of the second world war. Like most of the second world war and post-war generation, he had a very unsettled life and his education was very much interrupted. He had been a student of European history. He had been exceptionally well versed in economics. He had to supplement his income by exercising his musical skill in conducting orchestras. He had joined several business establishments and reached top position therein. He had a very interesting assignment with the World Bank. Feeling at one point of time in his life, the need for a more secure and respectful national posting, he entered the national diplomatic service and represented his country on several occasions to African state capitals. His performance at his foreign office was so exemplary that at a very young age he was chosen for a critically very sensitive post in the foreign minister's cabinet, from where he soon afterwards moved to an important South American country where a difficult bilateral relationship required to be straightened.

It is also significant that the person concerned is not a painter himself, but is a great art connoisseur and had been connected with organisation of several important painting institutions and exhibitions; he had been instrumental in the setting up of several art museums and in the revival of many others. He had been very much interested in astrology and as a result of this interest, he was able to attract persons very easily to himself and was able to strike instantaneous friendship with them. He had the knack of maintaining personal friendship and in this regard he was very candid and straightforward. His married life had been unstable and he was a divorcee. He had been desirous to marry again (when I knew him last), but his expectations from his wife were very 'idealistic' and to some extent unrealistic. Looking at his chart, we can see how the planetary impulses have shaped him.

The most important feature that strikes as the key-note astrological base of the horoscope is the ascendant and the placement of its lord itself. The ascendant is Gemini in Meena (Pisces) navamsa. The Moon is in Gemini and in Taurus navamsa, the sign of its exaltation. Retrogression of Jupiter and its placement in Pisces, which occupies the tenth house is significant, but it is additionally in a cardinal position with regard to the Moon sign as well as with ascendant. It produces *Gaja-Keshari Yoga.* In navamsa also, Jupiter is in Virgo (with Venus), the sign ruled by Mercury as well as the sign where it (Mercury) attains its exaltation. Mercury itself is exalted in the natal chart and is in Saturn's navamsa. In the natal chart, Mercury—the ascendant lord is in the fourth house—the house of learning and emotion; Mercury is associated with Sun and Venus, while Venus is the lord of the fifth house which happens to be the house of intellect and creativity; it is also the lord of twelfth house—the house connected with foreign countries. These astrological combinations are very propitious for making an individual successful in diplomatic assignments. They very much accentuate the Mercurial character of the native.

Gemini is primarily the sign of polarity—the polarity between spirit and matter, the subject and the object, the male and the female principles of life, the power and the harmony—and individuals under its influence are capable of functioning at different levels very efficiently. In diplomatic assignments, one has to completely subjugate and often conceal one's personal and private feelings, and express entirely and radically different emotion often completely at variance with that which lies within him. It is the same skill and talent which make an individual a good dramatist. Such dissociation of inner feelings and outer expressions is easily possible under the sign. As in this chart, the Moon is in the ascendant and that also in a well-fortified position with immense capacity to control and regulate one's emotions (Saturn in the eleventh house aspects Moon and is placed with exalted Moon in Navamsa), the individual is capable of playing well his role of a diplomat.

It is said that conflict and instability are important characteristics of Gemini. Contentment, satisfaction, stability, and tranquillity are not found in Gemini ascendants and it is very true in the present case also. As given in the introductory life-sketch of the person concerned, he is never restful, he is always changing, he is always moving, he is always working on several planes of existence, he is always different, sometimes working on the subjective level of existence and sometimes on the objective. He is always restless and whatever his achievements in life, he has always been pining for that which is non-existent for him at that time. As a diplomat, it is necessary for the person to move from one activity to another, from one country to another, and to always adapt himself under differing circumstances. Without this degree of flexibility and adaptability, the efficiency in high diplomatic missions could be jeopardised. This person's capacity for dissociation and adaptability has to a great extent been responsible for his remarkable success, though they put great strain on his personal life.

The next point to note in this chart is the special characteristics of Mercury and its ability to influence the person. The winged planet is the messenger of gods, carrying messages between the gods and the men; he is the intellect which can soar very high and give energy to every human effort. Conversational skill of Mercury is of very high order. Mercury is also capable of interpreting facts to the best possible advantage to the speaker; it is a good advocate, a good speaker, capable of accumulating and presenting vast amount of data in a very meaningful way. Mercury is also a planet which gives swift movement from one place to another as well as from one subject to another. It bestows an appearance of youth so as to enable the person always to radiate from him a freshness of tender grass or a newly sprouting plant. These qualities are of special importance for a diplomat.

The success of the native has been greatly enhanced due to Mercury's association with Sun and Venus. The Sun bestowed dignity, sharpness, royal favours, and deep sense of purpose on all the activities and talks of the person. The individual's interest in astrology and occult subjects as well as his knowledge of royal intrigues and manipulations with which the European history is replete are also to a great extent due to this combination. Venus is the ruler of the fifth house, the house of creativity which has given to this person, the disposition to operate on the mental plane; this aspect of Venus is further accentuated due to its occupation of a Mercury's sign and close association with Sun. To some extent, the instability in the individual's marital life and his sexual habits can be attributed to the placement of Venus with Sun and Mercury—both do not ordinarily produce effective and harmonious sexual partners. Pleasantness of the person and his affable temperament are also the result of the same combination.

A singular factor which has given the individual accelerated rise and special favours from the heads of the government is connected with Jupiter in the tenth house. Jupiter is retrograde here in Pisces. Jupiter would have some connection with Aquarius ruled by Saturn, because of its tendency to associate in retrogression. Saturn in the radical chart is also retrograde, thereby it is inclined to relinquish some of the qualities occurring due to its debilitation in Aries and acquire the qualities of Jupiterian sign Pisces. Saturn is also placed with Ketu. Such a planetary situation and relationship between different planets occupying Aquarius, Pisces and Aries, and exalted Mars aspecting Saturn make the psychological composition of the person so intriguing that nobody would be able to decipher his inner motives. Such a deceptive look is often admirable virtue for a diplomat. These placements occur near the tenth house which make the individual extraordinary in his diplomatic profession.

Personal discipline of the individual has arisen from retrograde Saturn with Ketu, but the aspect of exalted Mars from the hidden (and mysterious) eighth house on Saturn placed in a Martian sign of Aries bestows tremendous self-imposed discipline on the person and at the same time provides great enthusiasm from unknown quarters for some enigmatic purpose. Saturn aspects the Moon placed in ascendant, which also makes the person, greatly controlled and self-disciplined. Consequently, not a word, or even a single expression can be displayed by the person, unless he wanted the same to be shown on his face. The exchange between Mars and Saturn and the direct aspect of Saturn on Moon, which is bereft of its malefic nature in this connection due to its retrogression are important to give him diplomatic temperament.

Mercury—the ascendant lord and a lord of a cardinal house placed with Venus, which happens to be the lord of a trine house produces an important *Raja Yoga*. There is also an interchange between the lords of eleventh and eighth houses, which qualifies him very well for serious diplomatic assignments. Both combinations are extremely favourable in the present case. They raise the general status of the horoscope. The exaltation of Mercury in the fourth house and the occupation of Jupiter in its own sign in the tenth house produce *Bhadra* and *Hamsa Yogas* respectively which make him a very powerful personality and evolved in an extraordinary manner. The cardinal houses in the chart are fortified without any malefic aspect on them. The ascendant lord Mercury and the Sun—are free from any affliction. These combinations raised the social and financial status of the individual and in his special area of responsibilities, he is destined to scale much higher peaks. Saturn and Jupiter along with Mars create a situation, which is highly propitious for a diplomatic career and the individual is likely to take the best advantage of this combination.

8

MIKHAIL GORBACHEV

Rahu			Asc / (R) Jupiter
Sun Mercury	*2nd March 1931* (Rasi)		Moon Mars (R)
Venus			
Saturn			Ketu

Jupiter Sun		Asc	
Rahu	*(Amsa)*		
Venus			Mars Ketu
Moon Saturn	Mercury		

Mikhail Gorbachev was born on March 2, 1931 in the village Privolnoye near Stavropol in the erstwhile Soviet Socialist Republic sometime after midday. His father worked in a machine-tractor station. He was politically oriented from his early childhood. He joined the Moscow University as a Law student, where he met Raisa, a fellow student. He married her in 1954 and graduated in 1955. He began his career as an active political worker from his native place, and gradually went up in the hierarchy. The early 1980s began recognising his talents and was drawn towards the centre; he became a full member of the politburo, later the General Secretary of the Communist Party of the U.S.S.R. During the upward movement in the communist hierarchy, he never displayed any sign of radical departure from traditional Lenin-Marxist ideology, but towards the end of 1980s, important changes began to take place. The country with 'iron curtain' began to loosen its shackles. Openness and restructuring became his watch word. He began to undo what the communist regime had done to the people during the last seven decades or so. He began to introduce greater liberalism in the economy, freedom of initiative, thought and expression, less centralisation of power and better international relationship. These changes introduced during the course of a few years created an extraordinary niche for him in the world history, contributed to world peace and liberated in a democratic manner millions of intellectuals, who were made prisoners in the narrow cage of communist isolation. He made God a respectable entity in the Soviet land, the church bells rang louder and family culture began to be revived. Gradually, the east European countries were no longer tethered to the Moscow hegemony.

The first flush of freedom from state control made the people jubilant, the international society greatly relieved of ever increasing nuclear threat, and a few communist countries of the world were greatly perturbed. When the people realized that freedom brings responsibilities also, and the bread was more important than freedom, social progress and regeneration of spirit, the fundamentalists began to foment dissent.

Towards the end of 1991, Gorbachev was dethroned from the central seat of power, fortunately not annihilated for ever but stripped of all glamour, power and decision making authorities. Inquiries were set up against him, angry demonstrations were held and he was jeered and whistled by angry crowds. One does not know whether Gorbachev accepted these as a part of liberation of spirit movement, or as an expression of the ingratitude of the ignorant people, who did not know what they were doing. But the planetary delineation showed that not a leaf moved without the sanction of the Divine Will.

Mikhail Gorbachev was born with a specific mission and having completed it, he probably had to work towards his own personal unfoldment. In absence of precise astrological data, one has to resort to indirect methods of horoscopic rectification. It seems fairly plausible that Gorbachev was born under Gemini ascendant in Punarvasu asterism while Moon in Ashlesha gave him approximately 12 years of Mercury mahadasa, in balance. Jupiter in ascendant was retrograde and so was Mars which occupied its debilitation sign with *Neechabhanga Rajayoga* and in association with Moon occupying its own sign. Rahu is placed in tenth and Ketu in fourth, thus the Rahu-Ketu axis joined *Karmasthanam,* the house of profession and *Sukhasthanam,* the house of mental peace. The planets are aligned around the central position of Sun, which constitutes the main nucleus in relation with other planets trying to contribute their input. The Sun along with Mercury is placed in ninth house and Saturn aspects it from seventh house. Venus auspiciously placed twelfth from the Sun; Moon enjoys *Anapha Yoga* by the placement of Jupiter twelfth from it which leads to well-formed organs, majestic appearance, good reputation, politeness, generosity, self-respect, fondness for dress and sense pleasures. The combination leads the individual in later life to renunciation and austerity.

The Punarvasu nakshatra itself means the appearance of Sun again: the asterism is ruled by Jupiter, its presiding deity is Aditi, and it is symbolised by a house as well as a bow. Aditi being a female principle shows that the qualities of the asterism cannot fructify by themselves. In order to bear fruit, the asterism must come in contact with an external positive, or masculine force. The asterism provides the suitable soil on which healthy seeds can effectively sprout.

The positive force in the present case is provided by the Sun which along with Mercury enjoys *Buddha-Aditya Yoga* and occupies the ninth or the house of righteousness. Whether a bow is used for destroying the Gods as was done by the demons or aimed at protecting the Divine seed from perishing depends upon the person using it. The agent, who receives the impulse generated under Punarvasu determines the nature of the decision. As far as the asterism itself is concerned, it is merely the preparedness for greater action towards the concretisation of the divine will. It was for such a reason that Gorbachev became an ardent champion of communism upto a particular phase, but when the impulse for protecting the divine seed came to him, he did not hesitate in demolishing the communistic edifice thereby liberating the individual divinity to express the freshness of open sky. The disposition of Sun revealed the innate spirit for which Gorbachev appeared on this earth, while the lesson he learnt was decided by Rahu-Ketu axis.

The Sun along with ascendant lord Mercury is placed in Aquarius falling under Satabhishak nakshatra. Aquarius represents a pitcher from which water is flowing out: it stands for positive life-energy. It gives less importance to pitcher and more to the water contained within it. Gorbachev realised that communism was a social structure which existed for the free action of the human individuals who comprised the society; he saw the need for restructuring of the society. The asterism has the quality of producing ultimate harmony in spite of trials and tribulations it creates in the process. It is represented by a thousand petalled flower which represents hundreds of stars constituting the constellation. The presiding deity of the asterism is Varuna—the bestower of wisdom.

In the present context, it is also significant to note that *Pracheta*—a synonym for the asterism refers to Manu, Daksha, and Valmiki representing the mighty progenitors of the human race. Satabhishak provides the impulse for the blossoming of our inner potential. In order to achieve this objective, there must be the blending of the individual consciousness with the univeral one. It leads to the experiencing of Infinite, the illimitable. Such achievement necessarily entails immense psychological expansion, sacrifice and pain. The experiences that Gorbachev underwent during post-1990 period reflect the terrible psychological strain to enable others to experience the delight of the 'Illimitable, the Infinite'. This indeed had been his mission in life.

For his personal unfoldment, Gorbachev is under the influence of Rahu, which is placed in his tenth house. Rahu leads one to material achievement but such attainments contain within itself the seed for spiritualisation of the matter. The individual having attained wordly position and status, in a mysterious way, which differs from individual to individual, learns his spiritual lesson through it. Rahu in the present case, occupies *Revati* nakshatra. It has been mentioned that:

> Considered as female, the passivity and receptivity of Revati makes an individual very sensitive to external conditions. The creative faculties—both at the physical and psychological levels are considerably energized. Categorised as an outcast, upon whom the social organisation depended for support, Revati enables its beneficiaries to do great service for the fellow beings without expecting much in return. A sense of psychological disappointment and feelings of inferiority result under its impact. As a species, Revati is an elephant—arouses a sense of grandeur, awe, while at the personal level there is little awareness of the honour bestowed on it. The psychological transformation, which gives rise to such mental attitudes is highlighted by the asterism possessing a godly temperament.[1]

The personality of Mikhail Gorbachev underwent a radical transformation after the rebellion, which led to the emergence of Yeltsin and various disturbances, inquiries and charges of treason and so on. Gorbachev was stripped of his power and position, yet remained very much a positive personality concerned with himself and the society at large. He still belongs to many intellectual societies of the world.

Astrologically, the horoscope of Gorbachev shows extraordinary placement of planets, which clearly indicated a momentous birth from the soul's standpoint. The planets in cardinal houses have acquired malefic disposition from the material standpoint: Saturn in seventh, Rahu in tenth and Ketu in fourth and Jupiter in ascendant in retrogression could never assure a peaceful, gradual rise in political field.

Furthermore, debilitated Mars afflicts Moon, which is joined by Saturn in navamsa chart. The Sun is seriously weakened by its placement in Aquarius—a sign owned by Saturn, which aspects it.

1. *Myths and Symbols of Vedic Astrology*., op.cit., p. 253

Sun is also aspected by debilitated Mars. The lord of tenth house where Rahu is retrograde in ascendant thus acquiring certain qualities of its occupancy of twelfth house. The mahadasas of Mars and Rahu are the most crucial in his life. All other planets only prepared him for this catastrophic period which had been calamitous from worldly consideration, yet his soul had to undergo these ordeals to uncover his own latent spirituality.

He began his life in Mercury main period, which ended towards the beginning of 1943. Ketu's main period was devoted to his schooling, thoughtful observation of social and family events; he completed his basic education and went to the University during this period. During the twenty years of Venus, Gorbachev was very creative in expressing his talents. Venus is vargottam, so it was capable of sending him to very high status in the society. He married his wife during the early part of this period. By the end of this period, he had become a full member of the politburo.

The Sun mahadasa could not be considered spectacular, but Moon main period brought him in limelight. At the time when Andropov, Chernenkov, Gromyko and others were at the helm of affairs, Gorbachev made steady progress in political hierarchy and when Moon-Mars began, he was catapulted along the Soviet leadership ladder. By the end of the Moon mahadasa, he had become the General Secretary of the Communist party and came to the helm of the affairs. Moon in its own sign, importantly placed in the second house and aspected by vargottam Venus gave him immense political success. International recognition in several ways began pouring to him. He made friends with Russia's arch enemy—the United States. He introduced the concept of freedom, restructuring of the society, economic liberalism and religious revival. His programme was still taking off, when the fiery Mars, retrograde and debilitated, lord of the sixth house (the house of impediments and difficulties) and associated with Moon and aspecting Venus, began creating difficulties for him. There is basic discordance between Mars and the ascendant lord Mercury, and they also form sixth-eighth relationship between them. Mars could never be expected to be congenial to Gorbachev. In spite of several saving features, Mars on the whole was inauspicious for Gorbachev: its beginning mahadasa began to arouse internal dissensions against him. The sub-periods of Rahu and Jupiter were crucial, but the simmering discontents among the communist hardliners and material minded self-seekers however, remained underground waiting for the sub-period of Mercury to begin when the explosion could take place. Rahu initiated the task of teaching him a personal lesson and Jupiter showed the results of retrogression, by which it had to produce the results of affinity with the twelfth house and destroy the fruits of his lifelong good work. Jupiter also placed twelfth from the lord of the main planetary period Mars, did not hesitate in striking its decisive blow though the results had to surface only during the sub-periods of Mercury and Ketu. During these periods, Gorbachev lost all political power, but was luckily saved of his life. Since then, Gorbachev remained a highly concentrated individual taking stock of his life's experiences.

Rahu in the tenth house occupying Revati asterism owned by Mercury, presided over by Pushan—a name given to the Sun for measuring the sky—is bound to bring a cataclysmic change in Gorbachev's personal life. Revati leads to the expansion of awareness. It moves us to the cosmic expanse, boundless duration, and preserves the seed of future growth and splendour in the infinite sea of quietude and beatitude. Revati refers to the involvement of the soul in self-preservative activities, which extend from Kalpa to Kalpa, from one eternity to another.

Even the disposition of Rahu is significantly in great affinity with this disposition of the asterism in which it is placed. Rahu itself represents the great cyclical law related to the rejuvenating and regenerating process. It relates the present restrictions and opportunities of the individual with his past actions. Acting as the 'messenger' of the great cyclic law of manifestation, Rahu works under the direction of a still higher law, a mission in which it functions ruthlessly but with the assistance and cooperation of many cosmic forces. The important point to note is that this shadowy planet functions as an agent of a higher law of manifestation according to which all other planets and many finer forces of Nature work.

During the current mahadasa of Rahu, naturally one does not expect Gorbachev to retrieve his lost glory and political power and status, yet this is going to be the most important phase of his life. There is bound to be a radical transformation in his psychic life: he will become much detached from material forms of existence and directly experience the spiritual reality of cosmic cyclic law. What he earns during this phase of life would be more concerned with his future growth and expansion of consciousness. The disposition of Rahu suggests that experiences for Gorbachev had been preparatory for a radically new type of life which awaited him.

9

CARL GUSTAV JUNG

Rahu	Moon		Mercury Venus
Saturn (R)	*26th July 1875* (Rasi)		Sun
Asc.			
	Mars	Jupiter	Ketu

Mars	Asc. Mercury	Venus	Moon Ketu
	(Amsa)		
Rahu		Saturn Sun Jupiter	

The pioneer of the psychoanalytic school who differed with Sigmund Freud on the contents of the unconscious and severed his association with him to set up his own Viennese School of Psychoanalysis, Carl G. Jung was an outstanding scientist of the modern age. He was deeply religious and a great exponent of astrological efficacy. He turned the Freudian tide of psychoanalytical school and laid the foundation of spiritual guidance in tackling mental disorders of modern man.

When he was born, the rapid advance of physical sciences was relegating human psyche and religious values to backwaters of human learning. Man was getting deeply involved in material riches, carnal satisfaction, and hedonistic philosophy. These were becoming his guidelines for his everyday life, specially under the impact of Darwinianism engendered by the Mercantilist way of life followed by the Industrial Revolution. Competition had become the hallmark of success under the new way of life and the changing thought currents. Under the rising crest of materialism, it was thought that all was well with the world and God was in his heaven.

Outwardly, the human individual was conceived as a self-sufficient unit and his horizon of personal relationship did not extend beyond his immediate family circle. If he could establish a satisfactory, sexually pleasing and professionally balanced relationship with his wife, children and his society; he could be held as a perfectly balanced person who need not look to the infinite expansion of the universe, nor was he expected to respect ethical values of traditional religious philosophy. God was considered a superstition; racial mythology was an indicator of one's backwardness; interest in occultism was a symptom of mental disorder; and astrology was stigmatised as revealing lack of one's intelligence.

It was the relentless efforts of Carl Jung that astrology and spiritualism were accepted in scientific circles in the west as respectable pursuits of human endeavours and God—a desirable goal of mankind. If the anxiety neurosis, disappointment from life, especially during the later phase of one's life, and the realities of the super-physical world had to be rightly understood by the modern man, he needed a reorientation of his approach to human psyche and its primary motivations. One may or may not agree with the contribution of Carl Jung in reviving sanity in the western human society, but his horoscope does show that an outstanding personality is always born with an outstanding constellation of stars.

Carl C. Jung himself ardently believed in astrology and its possible use even in identifying mental disorders in human individuals. His interest in the subject began when he was in his early twenties and not yet aware of the international destiny awaiting for him. This interest continued with him till the last days of his life. Even in his medical practice, often when personal symptoms of patients did not throw much light on the ailment, he would get the horoscope of the patient prepared for his examination. He is on record to state that, "I must say, I very often found that the astrology is of particular interest to the psychologists, since it contains a sort of psychological experience which we call 'Projects'—this means that we find the psychological facts as it were in the constellations". This deep-rooted conviction in the constellations throws considerable light on the supremacy and importance of astrology in modern age. Professor Jung's understanding of the hidden mysteries of the human psyche and the laws of nature is eminently carved out in the constellations under which he himself was born.

The sixth house in a horoscope is very relevant from a psychologist's standpoint. It stands for one's latent faculties and the process by which it is externalized in human individuals. The various difficulties with which exoteric astrology associates this house is merely a superficial indicator of external events and karmic forces interacting with one's inner being in arousing his real nature, his faculties lying buried at different levels of his personality. In the natal chart of Carl Jung, the significance of this house, which is concerned with psi-function of the individual is great specially, because Mercury and Venus both are posited in it with full aspect of Mars: the two planets occupy Gemini the sign ruled by Mercury, and Mars is aspecting them from its own mysterious sign Scorpio. Jupiter which occupies the tenth house in Libra—a sign owned by Venus aspects Venus and Mercury. Such a combination enabled Jung to establish an intimate relationship between religious propensities of the individual, externalisation process under which latent faculties come to surface, and the libidinous, intellectual and psychic forces operating on him. Even Ketu, Jupiter and Mars above the visible horizon are effectively controlling those aspects of his life, which are governed by the planets situated below the horizon. His Saturn, the lord of the ascendant occupying its own sign and aspected by Jupiter from the tenth house enjoys mutual exchange of aspects with Mars. Saturn also aspects Moon. Jupiter aspects Saturn and Moon both. Such interrelationships of planets have tremendous significance in this chart: they produce deep interest in occultism, psychic development and other spiritual subjects: Jung emphasised on collective psyche always pushing the individual towards a universal goal, and his approach to past tribal experiences, traditional mythologies and everyday reactions and behaviour patterns of the individual are to a great extent the result of Saturn's position along with these planets.

Professor Carl C. Jung was born on July 26, 1875 at 7.35 p.m. at a small Swiss village named Thurgen. He was born when the constellation of *Shravana,* the 22nd asterism ruled by the psychic planet Moon, was rising on the eastern horizon; his M.C. was in *Anuradha,* the 17th asterism ruled by the occult Saturn, while Moon was in Ashwini, the first nakshatra concerned with rejuvenation and healing art. Sun setting in the western sky was situated in *Pushya,* ruled by Saturn, presided over by the Vedic deity Brihaspati and radiating the primary impulse of spiritual magnetism. There was nothing spectacular on the external plane when he was born in his family, though in the planetary hierarchy considerable missionary impulses were being directed to this incarnating ego. The mission took some time for its expression and fruition. As a child, Carl Jung lived in the world of his own solitude, played his own games alone, and lived in an exclusive self-centred world. From a superficial study, his horoscope does not seem to contain much to prognosticate the eminence which Carl Jung later attained in his life.

Capricorn is not taken as a sign of happiness and comfortable life. The affluence with which most of the people are fascinated is not necessarily an indicator of the maturity of an ego; for it—one has to look for some other base. When Carl Jung later became eminent in his profession, he demonstrated on the basis of his clinical pragmatism that many successful persons having acquired much money, fame, eminence and having lived a balanced family life suffered from neurotic symptoms, because they lacked that which stabilised human emotions and gave direction to life's unfoldment. Whatever may be the metaphysical approach to Capricorn ascendant, on a superficial examination of his chart Jung is likely to be considered greedy, coveting other person's wealth, extremely miser, unoriginal and plodder in life radiating an aura of selfishness, prejudice, self-centredness and depression often verging on suicidal tendencies and unsociability. The tenth house lord with the lord of the sixth house occupying the sixth house itself aspected by a malefic planet

Mars does not give much hope for the eminence and successful career of a person. The Sun in the seventh house should make the person extremely unadjusting and unhappy in his marriage relationship. Ketu in the ninth house is not good for father, Saturn aspecting Moon produces depressive psychology of the person. The lord of the fifth house is in sixth which is not conducive to creative activities. But, these prognostications do not apply in the case of Carl Jung; the lives of matured egos require special rules for deciphering the role of planets in their life.

The common astrological approach does not hold good in the present case, because the ego took its birth for an extraordinary purpose and so it did not interact in the ordinary manner on the physical plane. Jung was born with a purpose which was signified by the disposition of Saturn around which all other planets moved in an interesting manner. The flanking of Jung's tenth house by Mars and Ketu on either side of it revealed that the Jovian impulse aroused by its placement in the house of Karma or profession and flowing through him in his interactions with the people and society at large was greatly conditioned by the highly occult and deeply abstract (philosophical) Ketu, and the grossly material and basically physical planet Mars. Jung's entire working life in a way was concerned with externalisation (Mars) of the deeply occult unconscious mind (Ketu) for humanitarian purpose, in which activity his own role was projected as the learned and old traditional wiseman (of the east) symbolised by Jupiter in the tenth house.

Unless the question relating to the purpose of one's life in any specific incarnation is satisfactorily examined, the assessment of various planetary impulses on any individual cannot be realistic. Only on the right determination of the destiny of the individual for the fulfilment of which he is born—his *karma* in a comprehensive sense, can one understand the nature of his profession and the various conditions likely to be bestowed to him and the innate qualities and faculties that can be aroused in him. Only in this way, one can assess his opportunities and the latent faculties he himself can develop. In such an examination, the nature of tenth house as well as the cusp of the tenth house—both are very important.

In the present case, though the zodiacal sign Libra occupies the tenth house, the M.C. lies in Scorpio in *Anuradha* asterism. Libra is a balance. But it produces more than merely a placid uneventful well-harmonised life between material achievements and spiritual aspirations making the individual efficient as a man of the world. It is a sign where the universal evolutionary impulse gets its upward direction; materialism gets weakened and spiritualism begins to take a stronger hold on the person. It is a sign which signifies Nature's bestowal of special power of growth and development. It contains within itself all the powers of septenary principles, which enable life to grow in its multi-dimensional extension in a meaningful manner. It gives power to the seven force-centres, the *Chakras* of which the yogis speak and which when aroused yield enormous power over the finer forces in Nature. It is also the sign of great objectivity and detachment. The point of M.C. which if we like may call the central direction in any one's life lies in Scorpio in the case of Carl Jung at 6° 28' in the star *Anuradha,* which is symbolised by a lotus which is a flower representing growth of the soul and fecundity in human beings.

Taken together, one gets the perception of the unseen forces hovering around Jung's destiny. His karma did not lie in the usual humdrum passage of worldly existence. He had to be concerned with giving direction to his own life and to the life of others. He was to develop either his own yogic powers or he had to lead others of unravel their own inner faculties. The planet to provide the active impetus to it, to ignite the fire, so to say, is Jupiter. It is located in the tenth house suggesting Jung's immense suitability as a teacher, counsellor, sympathiser, beneficent influence to the society where he lived; his impact on the persons around him was in directing them to their upward evolutionary journey. Jupiter is aspected by Moon from fourth house with Aries occupying it and from the star *Ashwini.* The fourth house represents human emotion, capacity for empathy, heart, the great inner depth (*Bythos*), and it is linked with the very source from which the spark of one's *Jivatma* has been reeled off. Jupiter and the Moon are in mutual aspect resulting in *Gaja Kesari Yoga,* which produces lasting reputation even long after one's death.

The reflection of Jupiter on Moon when neither of them has been sullied by any other planet, either by association or aspect except Saturn, which has special significance in the horoscope, points to the fact that the God's adviser Jupiter will find his revelations from the great depth of human psyche represented by Moon, of which Jung talked in terms of collective psyche. The innermost secrets will be laid before Jung by the Jovian impulse working through him. Born in *Ashwini* nakshatra (the Moon sign), the revelations to Jung would be like new pearls, new aspects of human life. All these symbolic and suggestive indications of the planetary influences are very appropriately reflected in the life and work of Carl Jung.

Carl Jung had been concerned with analytical psychology as a psychopathic aid to his patients in restoring their mental health and to lay bare to them their potential and the psychological impediments obstructing their fuller expression. In doing so, he took their consciousness back to millions of years of racial memory, and through the language hidden in religious mythologies, dreams and symbols entirely personal to the individual concerned, he aroused, unravelled and released their latent faculties so that they could function freely without any impediment. He made his patients aware of their past relationships and revealed to them their future destiny. In order to identify the inner convictions of his patients and make them aware of their 'individuation' process, Carl Jung did not transgress their religious sensibilities and beliefs; he did not transgress their reverence for family ties and personal responsibilities; he however instilled in each of them enduring values and understanding of the glory of God and how the Supreme cared for every individual soul. Jung discovered a pattern of growth in the human psyche, he could lay his finger on the universal design specific to each individual. In his own conviction and in fulfilling his own destiny, he asserted himself confidently.

Jung differed with Sigmund Freud, who was once considered the final authority on matters relating to psycho-analysis and with whom Jung worked for very many years. But Freud was emphasizing too much on the Venusian sensuality in human mind. Even God, to Freud was a phallic symbol and all religious performances substitutes for sex act. Such follies were challenged by Jung and when appropriate occasion arose, he differed with humility to his mentor and with due regard to the vanity and emotional feelings of his former collaborator and guide, he founded an entirely new school of psychology, where there was place for God and for traditional scriptures and occult sciences. He revived religious susceptibilities by establishing appropriate importance of the Tibetan mandals, gave the justified importance to astrology and revealed the psychological principles of transformation in the hidden (esoteric) symbols of alchemy. It was not without significance that once he wrote that theosophy and astrology could provide much needed security and guidance to the modern man. He tried to restore the religious balance in the modern scientific and technological age when religion and human values were being discounted. That was his destiny revealed by the pattern of planets established around the central Saturn, which happened to be retrograde desirous to occupy his ascendant .

And what were his resources for fulfilling his destiny? Unless the stars apportioned sufficient strength and appropriate faculties to fulfil one's aspirations, the destiny would remain merely a dream and the desire cannot materialize making the individual a frustrated person. For inherent strength of a person one has to examine the ascendant and the planets connected with it. In the present case, the ascendant is occupied by Capricorn—a strong sign with much significance. A person born in this sign is generally a type by himself. He is ascetic in his disposition. He has singleness of purpose, which enables him to harness all his energy for the fulfilment of his desired objective. He is well coordinated with all his faculties and entire personality is integrated for achievement of the goal: he is one-pointed and well integrated. No amount of sacrifice for the fulfilment of his mission is too dear for him. He melts like snow in the warmth of friendship and thirsts for the goodness of the spirit.

Jung was born in *Shravana* asterism, which is a lunar mansion representing an ear or an arrow, presided over by the Vedic deity Vishnu, who is the god preserving the universe as one of the Hindu-triad. The lord of the sign—Saturn is said to be Lord Shiva himself in his aspect representing Eternity contained in Aquarius, its own sign featuring great many humanitarian activities. Saturn is placed in the star *Dhanistha* symbolised by a musical drum presided over by Vasus, who are eight in number nourishing and sustaining the cosmic evolution. The ascendant lord is aspected by Jupiter occupying the tenth house, which also happens to have the zodiacal sign where the ascendant lord is exalted. Mars the lord of the fourth house representing emotion and the eleventh house, representing income, aspected by Saturn from a powerful position, it also aspects Saturn providing enough courage and initiative in its pursuits. The ascendant lord Saturn aspects the fourth house and acquires special relationship with matters pertaining to human psychology. As Saturn is retrograde, it acquires certain features which arise due to ascendant lord occupying that house, while it abandons some (malefic) qualities which would have accrued due to its position in the ascendant; at the same time, it enjoys certain advantages as a result of its occupancy of the second house, yet it does not do so fully; by virtue of its retrogression Saturn possessed hind-sight, whereby it does not only aspects the fourth house, but does so also to twelfth house.

These features of the ascendant lord Saturn in the present case enable the individual to attain great heights. *Shravana,* the asterism of the ascendancy is in harmony with the Great Silence, the *Bythos,* lying at the very base of manifestation as well as at the root of microcosm. It sends the impulse of meditational attention. Even in ordinary individuals, it could endow the capacity of obedience. *Dhanistha,* where Saturn is located represents the radiation of life-force and it leads the individual to great occult attainments though in ordinary individuals it may lead them to depravation of material conveniences.

Placed seventh from the ascendant, Sun powerfully aspects it from *Pushya* nakshatra—the eighth asterism, which is symbolised by a flower, a circle or an arrow, all of which are deeply mystical symbols. The asterism is presided over by the Vedic deity Brahmanspati—the lord of wisdom, as a result of which the star is capable of bestowing abundant spiritual magnetism giving to the individual a tranquil mind. Jung's mind represented by Moon is aspected by Saturn, which in weaker egos may lead to mental instability and emotional imbalance. In the present case, the situation is different, because the aspect of Mars on Saturn is from the sign Scorpio representing spiritual powers and hidden mysteries of the universe, while *Jyestha,* the asterism in which Mars is placed is symbolised by an earring or an umbrella—both of which refer to great recognition of one's merit and receipt of much reward and honour. *Jyestha* is presided over by Indra, who is the supreme god of gods; the *Kundalini* or the Serpent Fire, is the special domain of this star bestowing divine benediction, which to an ordinary individual may produce arrogance. Jupiter's aspect on Saturn—the ascendant lord, from the tenth house itself forms an important planetary combination establishing a relationship between tenth and second houses. Jupiter's aspect on the Moon forms *Guru Chandra Yoga* which strengthens the quality of Jung as a teacher. Jupiter is in *Chitta* nakshatra symbolised by pearl, presided over by Tvastra—the celestial architect, represents the great cosmic dimension of space, or the dance of Shiva and provides the creative impulse generating new thoughts in the world binding the world together in great harmony. Under such a constellations, one could very well expect the ego, the *Jivatma*, to have direct affinity with higher creative intelligences. The person born under such constellation should have a mind capable of delving deep in the hidden mysteries of life and creation. He would certainly be an exceptional person endowed with extraordinary insight in hidden mysteries of the universe and in the inner recesses of man.

In actual life, Carl Jung very appropriately reflected the features of the constellation in which he was born. The various characteristics of the ascendant and the ascendant lord mentioned above corroborate the many-coloured splendour of Carl Jung. His feeling of loneliness and the desire for solitude could be well explained by his stars. He was well aware of his innate nature. "As a child I played alone and in my own way", he once wrote. On another occasion, he talked of his delight in solitude and said that he "had a secret world" of his own. About his interest in occult powers, he wrote that he practised yoga exercises, when he found that his feelings were getting out of hand. About the deeply spiritual urges of his being, especially exemplified by the aspect of Jupiter on Saturn and both of these aspecting his Moon, one could have a feeling of their impact on Jung from his several observances made on different occasions indicating how he aligned himself on the side of God and felt an intimacy with Him: "Often I felt that in all decisive matters I was no longer alone among men, but was alone with God. And when I was there, I was no longer alone. I was outside time. I belonged to the centuries."

The duality in him caused by a strong Saturn and a strong Jupiter affected his psyche (Moon) so much that he once wrote that he had a family, he had a job, a medical diploma from a Swiss University, and had a wife and five children (Jupiter), but somewhere in him he felt that he was a very different person, an old sage (Saturn). "Somewhere deep in the background", he wrote, "I always knew I was two persons. One as the son of my parents who went to school, the other one grown up, old, in fact remote from the world of ours but close to nature, and above all to dreams and to do whatever God worked directly through him". Like this, one can get many utterances of Carl Jung signifying that his whole approach to human problems, to his own self, and to the civilisation as a whole was directly the result of the constellation under which he was born.

One of the clues to his ever present involvement in creative activities which were always balanced and bringing to the surface the profundity of his approach to every aspect of life with which he was concerned lies in the fifth-ninth relationship of the various planets in his horoscope. Mercury and Venus, one of which is the lord of the tenth house occupies ninth house from its Libra sign (sixth house) along with the lord of the ninth house (Mercury) which is placed in fifth house from the sign occupied by the ascendant lord Saturn. Mercury and Venus together also constitute a powerful *Raja Yoga,* as they are lords of cardinal and trine houses. They formed another auspicious combination namely *Laxmi Yoga* formed by the association of lords of ninth and tenth houses, which bestowed immense honour, wisdom and prosperity. Saturn and Jupiter—the two powerful planets in the chart also formed a similar relationship: they are placed ninth and fifth from each other. It ensured much creative power directed for useful purposes.

Such combinations made Carl Jung a chalice for receiving useful creative divine beneficence for its distribution to every aspect of his own life as well as to other individuals who came in various relationships with him. The individual planets, at times, produced many irritating situations in Jung's everyday life, but cardinal signs occupying cardinal houses and powerful planets occupying them gave him much strength to overcome them without much difficulties. The horoscope of Carl Gustav Jung is an example of stellar composition, which makes the individual live more for the society, and the people with whom the individual is born than for his own self.

10

RANABIR RAJ KAPOOR

Mars			
	14th December 1924 (Rasi)		Asc / Moon Rahu
Ketu			
Jupiter Mercury	Sun	Saturn Venus	

Saturn Sun		Jupiter	Venus
Rahu	*(Amsa)*		
			Moon Ketu Mars
			Asc. / Mercury

Raj Kapoor was such a cine celebrity of India that his parallel is yet to be born. He was the eldest son of Prithviraj Kapoor, who was an outstanding movie producer and an acting genius famous for his idealistic and historical movies. The junior Raj Kapoor rose to the most respected and admired position in the profession, but he was much different from his father. His pictures were different and so was his personality. Ranabir Raj Kapoor was a happily married man, which was a rare achievement for men in his profession. He had three sons and a daughter—all of whom adored him with great affection and respect. His wife was not an actress. His sons joined him with credit to the film profession. His only daughter however followed the calling of her mother and became a housewife. Raj Kapoor was not much educated, but he soared very high in his imagination and was greatly successful in capturing the moods and feelings of others which he effectively portrayed on the silver screen. His acting, direction and the capacity to make heroines out of the raw stuff made him a household name in many countries. He won the *Grand Prix* at an early age of 32 years and was awarded India's most prestigious *Baba Saheb Phalke* award before he could complete his 61st year of age. His popularity transcended the national frontier. His songs and films became a craze in the former U.S.S.R., China and many African countries. The secret of his popularity was his capacity to establish instantaneous empathy with those with whom he came in contact. He had no enemies, not even among his professional rivals. He had friends all over the world in all walks of life. Raj Kapoor was a universally liked person.

Raj Kapoor was born on December 14, 1924 at Peshawar, now in Pakistan. He migrated to India during Partition. Eversince he came to this country, the invisible hands of destiny pushed him from one situation to another till he attained the highest peak of his popularity. His heart from the very beginning of his life was in cine industry and till his very end, he was planning and contemplating new innovations and ideas to be introduced. He left his studies in Law to enter the film industry. His father was already one of the pioneers of Indian film industry, where he had reached the pinnacle and established a moral standard for Indian films in which he depicted ancient Indian cultural heritage with extreme dexterity. It was an easy access for Raj Kapoor, but he did not desire to be a replica of his father and thereby lose his individual uniqueness. Raj Kapoor was different. He wanted to explore and depict finer psychological susceptibilities of human beings at large. He was himself full of human passions; it was however so much restrained that it became a kind of universal love. He knew how to love and be loved. This quality of empathy was so much evident when he moved to All India Institute of Medical Sciences in New Delhi for treatment of his last illness that the topmost medical doctors and members of the medical fraternity thronged at the Institute to be present around him, more out of their love and respect for him than what their professional duty required. Between May 2 and June 2, 1988, when he played the last drama of his life and death, the All India Institute of Medical Sciences became the hub of the city, where almost everybody who mattered was present. The entire hierachy of the Indian Government was in attendance, besides the rickshaw pullers, street coolies and students from local colleges. Boys and girls eagerly awaited the latest information about his struggle on the mortal plane.

When the doyen of the Indian movies breathed his last at 9.20 p.m. on June 2, 1988, the news was received even by western cinephiles with a sense of great personal loss. The touching farewell was given to him not only from the rich industrialized consumeristic western countries, but also from the Soviet Russia and the Communist China. Pakistan and Middle East countries joined in expressing the universal sorrow. Heartfelt condolences and personalised messages were received in abundance from Muslims, Christians and other religionists. Raj Kapoor had transcended the barriers of religion, class, caste, politics and nations. His goodwill and friendliness overflowed much beyond all narrow boundaries.

The secret of Raj Kapoor's popularity and his disposition was enshrined in his stellar composition. He had extraordinary planetary combinations which combined together powerful contradictory impulses such as Moon in (its own sign) Cancer occupying ascendant but in association with malefic Rahu; sensuous Venus in its own sign Libra occupying the fourth house (the house of emotion) posited there along with austere Saturn in its exaltation sign; Jupiter—the planet of religiosity situated in its own sign placed in sixth house along with inimical planet Mercury ruling over intellect and acting; Sun in his horoscope was in highly occult sign namely, Scorpio and the fiery Mars occupied the watery Pisces.

Planets formed very auspicious pattern among themselves suggesting an extraordinary birth. Moon owned its own sign and occupied the ascendant making Raj Kapoor extremely emotional which had tremendous impact on his social relationships. Exalted Saturn along with Venus occupying own sign in fourth house formed the two most important Panch Maha Purusha Yogas namely, *Sasa* and *Malavya.* Sun in the mystical Scorpio situated in the fifth house from ascendant as well as the Moon identified him with universal consciousness for which his heart yearned. Jupiter, the planet of popular esteem, occupied its own sign Sagittarius along with Mercury, the planet which carried the divine messages to the humanity at large, which was also a planet of acting and verbal communication: they occupied tenth position from the lord of the tenth house, Mars (which was placed in Jupiter's sign Pisces), and these two planets namely, Jupiter and Mercury, occupied ninth position from the tenth house which bestowed upon Raj Kapoor extraordinary gift for his brilliance in cine industry.

These planets also occupied cardinal houses in relation with their own signs which further added to their auspicious nature. Mars occupied creative fifth house relationship with its own sign Scorpio and it occupied ninth position from the ascendant, which bestowed to Raj Kapoor much fruitful initiative and beneficence from his past *Sanchita Karmas.*

In navamsa chart, Mercury occupied its exaltation sign, Venus was in Mercury's sign Gemini, Saturn and Sun were in Jupiter's sign Pisces and all these were in cardinal houses in relation with Ascendant's navamsa Virgo. Jupiter occupied the navamsa of Venus, which assured him tremendous popularity. Jupiter was associated with Mercury in natal chart and it aspected Mercury in navamsa chart. These planetary placements made the horoscope extraordinary, specially for a person in the cine industry, directing planetary impulses to provide him with much creative power.

An important feature of Raj Kapoor's horoscope emerges from various planets, which hinged around Saturn-Venus combination. In fact, these are the two planets which form the basic core of this horoscope; a careful delineation of these two planets reveals much of the inner forces working through the life of Raj Kapoor. Saturn aspected the ascendant, but as the planet was exalted and formed an exceptional yoga it does not cast so much of its restrictive influence as its extraordinary beneficence making his life of enduring value. As Saturn aspects Jupiter, the tenth house, Moon as well as ascendant, it bestows to Raj Kapoor the great quality of objectivity, akin to spiritual detachment. Saturn is associated with the lord of eleventh house which assures abundance of monetary inflow. Saturn is aspected by Mars, a *yoga karaka* planet in the chart, which owned the tenth house as well as the fifth house, which imparted much innovative genius to him, which could raise him to dizzy heights in his profession. Ketu placed in Saturn's sign Capricorn aspected Moon from the seventh house, while Moon was also aspected by exalted Saturn. These combinations made Raj Kapoor greatly detached in life though making him greatly sympathetic towards the people at large; they enabled him to establish closer affinity with the masses. They gave him deep insight in the working of life. They also enabled him to act different roles in movies with complete identification with his *dramatis personae.* Saturn-Venus togetherness operating as the fulcrum of Raj Kapoor's natal chart around which all other planets established special relationships contained within it the secret of his life's success and popularity.

There are three planets in their own signs, which make Raj Kapoor a powerful personality. Saturn is in its exaltation sign along with Venus in its own sign posited in a cardinal house—thus producing two powerful *Panch Maha Purusha Yogas* which are exceptional: this combination makes an individual unique in many ways. It reveals the maturity of soul in certain respect. The placement of Jupiter in sixth house from Moon forms *Sakata Yoga,* which stands for periodic indigence and misfortune, but its intensity is greatly reduced by both of them occupying their own signs, while one of them is in a cardinal house. The possibility of arousing much hostility against Raj Kapoor and various kinds of legal difficulties is greatly marginalised by the restrictive aspect of Saturn on the sixth house which otherwise could have been much accentuated due to its occupancy by benefic Jupiter and Mercury. The occupation of a trine (ninth house) by Mars, the lord of a quadrant (tenth house), produces a *Raja Yoga*; Mars is also the lord of the house of creativity (fifth house) with deep acting Scorpio in it, which is occupied by Sun; this special stellar relationship leads Raj Kapoor to draw upon secret sources of energy which make him much impulsive, courageous and extremely popular. Saturn and Venus combination in the fourth house with Libra sign makes him down-to-earth in many creative enterprises, but with a streak of sorrow and limitation which account for much of his eminence as a cine producer, both as an actor and director.

Saturn in exaltation is the most important base in the horoscope. It makes the person famous, head of a clan, chief man in the town, commander of a force or headman of the village in which he dwelt; he is destined to be wealthy. Saturn and Venus occupying the same sign enables the individual to obtain wealth through young women. Such individuals, are said to be skilled in writing and painting. These planets enabled Raj Kapoor to collect beauties around him, write his own plays and direct them effectively. Saturn is in *Swati* nakshatra, which provides strong passionate impulses and urge to seek pleasure; Venus in *Vishakha* symbolised by potter's wheel pours forth psychism and leads to purification, austerities, but it also makes the individual experience restrictions. These qualities made his pictures highly emotional portraying depth of feelings very realistically.

The association of Venus with Saturn made the latter outward-turned. The sensitivity produced by Venus was so intense that the viewers could instantaneously establish rapport with the *dramatis personae.* That is why Raj Kapoor is reported to have once stated that the heroines of his films saw their images in his eyes. His ego was so much universalised under Saturn that his individual idiosyncracies were completely ironed out. His Venus gave him so much adaptability that one of his critics once wrote that "Wherever he went, he was at home. He was quite at ease at disco, at a jubilee jamboree, at a film festival in Trivandrum or at Tashkant. You saw he could live out of suite-cases." The combination of Saturn and Venus did not only give him versatility in dramatisation of everyday event, it made those incidents so lifelike and so full of pathos and compassion that they aroused immediate empathy from his audience. The Saturnian influence was so great in the selection of his themes that they transcended nationalistic considerations and became so much universalised that they became extremely popular without becoming vulgar. The Venusian touch always brought the females in his pictures as the main attractions with mass appeal for them.

The quality of Saturn in its concretisation aspect is very important in the present case. When a sculptor concretises his abstract ideas in stones, he expresses the impulses received from Saturn; or when the poet or the artist puts his ideas in language or dance sequence or even in colour or in musical notes, these are made possible as a result of the concretisation efforts of Saturn. Whatever the outer expression of such Saturnian impulses, psychologically, it will never make a person feel "liberated", it will make him feel small, specially if Saturn aspects Moon as in the present case. Raj Kapoor is on record to state that "we are all sentenced to solitary confinement inside our skins". It expresses the typical Saturnian feelings of being caged and confined.

Sun in Scorpio posited in the fifth house from Moon gave Raj Kapoor immense productivity and an unending flow of creative ideas. [The Sun in the fifth house is extremely active and productive on the mental rather than on the physical plane.] Till the last amount of life-force ebbed out of him, he thought of new lines of production and themes for his movies. He never thought of retiring from the profession. He was never in want of new ideas and directions in his creative activities. That is why he was always considered a pace-setter for others.

But Saturn's aspect on the tenth house from the ascendant as well as from the Moon-sign made the actor-director taste the bitter fruit of failures as well. When his picture *Mera Naam Joker* to which he had given much thought and care did not lift, he received serious setback to his spirit. This gave him an understanding that he could not assume his right to succeed as a matter of course. Saturn gives failures under such a situation atleast once in life. It makes the person realize his smallness. It happened even in the emotional life of Raj Kapoor. When his relationship with heroine Nargis did not materialise in marriage and she married another actor Sunil Dutt, Raj Kapoor felt extremely depressed. Saturn makes its imprint on the psyche of the person very seriously and very deeply. Whether it was success or failure, a powerful Saturn makes its impact effective and enduring, often changing the course of one's life. It was true even in the case of Raj Kapoor. After the Nargis affair, Raj Kapoor was never the same earlier self, he matured much more emotionally. He became much more sensitive and perceptive to the feelings and happiness of others.

Out of the several combinations in the horoscope, one would like to emphasise the significance of *Sakata Yoga* and *Adhi Yoga*, which in an important manner affect material welfare or its deprivation. The former is produced by sixth-eighth house relationship between Moon and Jupiter, whereas the latter is formed by the occupancy of sixth, seventh and eighth houses from the Moon by benefics. Both these yogas are formed in this horoscope due to the placement of Jupiter though for the latter yoga, Mercury also occupied the sixth house from Moon, so the combined effect of these yogas have given extraordinary effect. Sakat Yoga made Raj Kapoor happy and unhappy both; gaining unusual eminence and status and experiencing frustration, failures and loss, both features in his life. Sakat yoga presents life-events like the wheel of a chariot under which one loses all and retrieves his lost position once again freshly.

Thus, the wheel of fortune shows its course of wide fluctuations. As a result of such experiences, one gets a realisation of the transitoriness of various situations. Detachment attained as a result of it is very much like the one produced by Saturn's aspect on Moon and ascendant. There is however a subtle difference between the two. *Sakat Yoga* produces detachment as a result of wide fluctuations of one's fortune, while Saturn produces it by intensive deprivation and psychological frustration. *Adhi Yoga* is a combination for fortune and in the present case, it is partially formed by Mercury and Jupiter occupying one of the three houses stipulated under the yoga. This planetary combination enables the individual to attain the height of popularity and affluence, happiness and pleasures, it also helps the individual to overcome his foes and live for a long life. Raj Kapoor did not live for long, but he received all that a person could legitimately aspire to secure in life: plenty of respect, pleasure, wealth and prosperity. He had a happy family life where he could retire after a hard day's work for rest and relaxation; he received highest recognition and respectability inside the country and abroad. It is for these yogas that R. Venkatraman, the President of the Republic of India left his podium and went to his seat to decorate him with *Baba Saheb Phalke Award,* the highest award in his profession, and when Raj Kapoor breathed his last the entire humanity was stirred at the loss.

11

JIDDU KRISHNAMURTI

	Sun	Mercury	Venus Jupiter Mars
Rahu	*11-12, May 1895*		
Asc.	*(Rasi)*		Ketu
Moon		Saturn (R)	

Mars		Rahu	
Mercury	*(Amsa)*		
Jupiter Saturn			
Sun	Venus Ketu	Moon	Asc.

J. Krishnamurti, whom his friends called Krishna and his admirers Krishnaji had been the most controversial philosopher of the twentieth century. He was born on May 11, 1895 at midnight in a small village of south India with adverse living conditions in the highest Brahmin community, who followed orthodox religious practices but Krishnamurti taught the futility of thought processes, religious observances and efforts for acquiring religious merits. But what he taught remained an engima even to highly disciplined intellectuals in spite of his incessant lecturing for more than five decades from place to place at different parts of the civilised world. His early upbringing had no relationship with what happened to him later in life. His childhood was heavily afflicted with bad nutrition, malarial fever and poor schooling.

At the age of 14 years, while he was playing at the adjoining sea-beach near the Theosophical Society, Madras where his father worked at the headquarters, C.W. Leadbeater who was a clairvoyant at the Theosophical Society spotted him as a person with very powerful spiritual aura around him. It was a turning point in his career. He was taken away from his traditional family members and members of his orthodox community, brought up under the guardianship of Annie Besant and such other eminent persons, and preparations were made to enable him join the Oxford University in England. At home, the orthodox Brahmin community and even his father at the instance of vested groups revolted against the arrangement and sued Annie Besant in order to resume guardianship over him. The case went upto Privy Council by which time Krishnamurti had become an adult. So he could exercise his option and remained with Annie Besant.

Krishnamurti had joined the Theosophical Society at an early age, and he was acclaimed as a likely vehicle for the advent of the new messiah for which mission Krishnamurti was expected to purify his various *koshas*, the sheaths of the body (of which Sankaracharya has spoken in great detail in his *Viveka Cudamani*). For this new advent, an organizations called *Order of the Star of the East* under his direction was founded which had its branches all over the world. Over a number of years, the belief in his new mission intensified greatly. Many a time, it was said that the "Higher Beings" spoke through him to give out their messages; he was even stated to have visited in 'his astral body' the abode of these mystic beings. The *Order of the Star of the East* of which he was the head—swelled in membership and it even acquired enormous property. But, again, there occurred a radical revolution in the life of J. Krishnamurti: in 1929, he dissolved the *Order*, returned the property, and even resigned from the membership of the Theosophical Society, and even seemed to question the veracity of the belief in Mighty Beings, whom the Theosophical literature described as the *Masters of the Wisdom*. J. Krishnamurti even claimed that he had completely purged his past thoughts and he did not remember any thing of the past, and no one seems to know what Krishnamurti meant by it. His discourses which he continued till his death on February 17, 1986 greatly emphasised the need for constant alertness of the thought process; in his comprehension there was no place for any organized religious institution. Even the concept of God and the questions relating to *life after death* seemed irrelevant in the so called 'teachings' of Krishnamurti, though he did not like his talks and discourses to be categorised as 'teachings'. This metamorphosis by which the larva became a chrysalis and finally flew to the open sky eludes the historical process of human transformation, yet the planetary disposition at the time of his birth seems to reveal much of the spiritual mission for which Krishnamurti was sent to this earth.

Krishnamurti was born at 12.30 a.m. on May 11/12, 1895 at Madanpalli in Tamil Nadu, about 250 kms. north of Madras, now in Andhra Pradesh. Sanjeevamma, the mother who ultimately gave birth to 11 children, at the time of her eighth delivery was confined to her pooja room, the place specially earmarked for observances and rituals to be exclusively used for religious purposes, and to violate this practice was an unorthodox decision for the delivery of an offspring. It was done so on the basis of certain indications that this child was going to be a very unusual one. But, the child birth was seemingly the most ordinary one. The father, Narayaniah, belonged to a family of eminent, orthodox and educated Sanskrit scholars, who for several generations had held high positions in Administration. The usual expectation of an august incarnation as expected did not seem to fructify at the time of the delivery of the child and the matter was taken as closed, and the child birth was considered as the most common event of the family.

Jiddu's great grand father was an eminent Sanskrit scholar. He held responsible position under the *East India Company*. His grand father was a learned scholar and a civil servant. His father was a graduate of the Madras University, as an official in the Revenue Department in the State, he was qualified to become a District Magistrate, a very coveted status. This great ancestry was not reflected in Krishnamurti's early life. He was born a weakling. He always suffered from bouts of fever, malaria, bronchitis and several other such ailments. Many a time, the parents thought that he was gone mad. But the astrologer Kumar Shrowtulu who had cast his horoscope on the second day of his birth always affirmed that the child was going to be a great man. The more the father complained of the uselessness and ill-health of the child, the more the astrologer assured him of Jiddu Krishnamurti's greatness.

A few months before completing his 91 years of age, Krishnamurti died at Pine cottage, California at ten minutes past midnight leaving behind him, one of the most abstruse philosophy of everyday life denouncing all scriptures and upsetting everyone who wished to enquire deeply into the mysteries of living and everyday life. Personally, he was a lonely man in spite of the fact that a large number of persons surrounded and wanted him to guide and relieve their sorrow. Krishnamurti himself was always dogged by ill-health, misunderstanding and confrontation. He was declared as messiah by Dr Annie Besant, who adopted him as her son and provided all the facilities and opportunities necessary for his growth and unfoldment. Both parted company in the end though without any ill-will and always having reverence and deep-rooted affection far each other. A few weeks before his final ending of his mortal life, he is supposed to have told Pupul Jayakar that he knew the date of his death, but would not reveal it to others. He always made cryptic comments about astrology, but occasionally even explained the rationale of predicting, rather of seeing the future with clarity.

J. Krishnamurti suffered acutely and had to suffer many kinds of physical ailments till his very end, yet he maintained his original teeth and did not need reading-glasses for his eyes. He possessed at one time in his life millions of rupees, but towards the end he dissolved all his property; even with regard to his personal income from royalty of his books and speeches, he had to face many kinds of problems, legal disputes and misunderstandings. He died penniless and subsisted more or less on the kindness of his friends and associates. It is stated that he could dismantle an automobile and reassemble it easily; he could repair the most complicated watches and cameras (a trait common with Dalai Lama and J.R.D. Tata) but at one stage, he is reported to have completely washed away his memory and would not remember any event of his past. He could read people's thought as clearly as on open page, but he considered it unethical similar to reading anyone's private letters. He was adept in spiritual healing till his very end: he had practised it successfully on many persons including the world famous Aldous Huxley, but was very reticent in making use of the same. He had great psychic powers and could force the dice in casinos to fall the way he wanted. But such miraculous powers possessed by him never came between him and his activities in his everyday life. He never made use of any such powers for his personal use and never displayed them for any gain whatsoever. These were mere parts of his personality structure, which he possessed without considering them exceptional assets of any kind. Such was the life of J. Krishnamurti. He was turned out of the Theosophical Society, where he was brought up and which gave him his international status; he was not even permitted to enter the compound for a long time. Towards the end of his life, an understanding grew between him and the society, specially when he was actively engaged in his educational programmes, and he began to frequent the Theosophical Society on his way to the sea-beach for his evening walk whenever he happened to be in Madras during the last phase of his life.

J. Krishnamurti was born under extremely important astrological combinations. His ascendant fell under Dhanistha asterism symbolised by a drum which is used on auspicious occasions to invite angelic beings, and to announce sometimes when the kings achieved any remarkable victory over his enemies, or even to make some important proclamations. The birth in *Dhanistha* was a kind of proclamation of the victory over anti-spiritual forces, or a kind announcement that the 'king has promulgated a new order'. Krishnamurti was indeed a new beginning; one will have to accept it, even if one did not believe in his role as a messiah. In his natal chart, the ascendant lord Saturn placed in exaltation in the tenth house under the star *Uttara Phalguni* symbolised by the four legs of a cot indicated the prime object of his birth was to provide the resting ground for some special energy to fructify in the universe. *Uttara Phalguni* ruled by Sun, and Capricorn as the ascendant ruled by Saturn were all very powerful and they were even placed in a very powerful manner.

The Sun in exaltation is placed in the fourth house tenanted by

Krittika, a fiery, destructive star but which had the responsibility of assisting the divine incarnation when it occurred directly opposed Saturn, Sun and Saturn both were strong in the chart. The father represented by the Sun and son by Saturn in opposition were both amicably supportive of each other. The Sun in the fourth house linked the newly born child with the innermost centre of the great deep, *Hiranyagarbha,* as a result of which the heart of the person, his central core of the physical being was moved by a deep centre of Atmic forces represented by the Sun and the materialistic, restrictive energy represented by Saturn. As a result of Sun in the fourth house and Saturn in the tenth house, a mystic relationship is established between the two; the Sun activates the eternal past, the *Hiranyagarbha,* where lie buried all the seeds and potentials for their fructification in time under the pull of future destiny, the tenth house, where Saturn is posited in the present case. Both planets—the Sun and Saturn are impersonal, they do not let personal considerations last for long. Both have different methods of destroying the personality: the Sun leads to enlightenment, irradiating inner wisdom whereby the individual perceives the unreality of the form-side of existence and thus makes the individual realise the inner indwelling spirit in all forms of manifestation, which shows the eternal nature of the inner energy, the spirit, the spark of the eternal radiance.

The method adopted by Saturn is through the destruction of matter, worldly relationship, accumulation of wealth and later its loss, attainment of worldly status and later its denial and so on. Saturn produces sorrow as a result of the loss of material acquisitions. In the tenth house, when it is retrograde trying to occupy the ninth house which pertains to philosophical attitude and religious disposition while posited in the sign of Libra it has attained its exaltation, Saturn would not have any morbidity of temperament rather it would arouse that disillusionment which arises when one realises that there is nothing permanent, nothing real. It only occurs when the inner being of the individual has reached the stage of *Maha-Sunya,* the primeval nothingness, of which the Vedas have spoken in its *Nasadiya Sukta* (the Doubting Mind) when it exclaimed: "The non-existent was not then, nor the existent; the Earth was not, nor the firmament, nor that which is beyond. When there was nothing then what could cover what, and where and in whose care? Did the waters and the bottomless deep then exist?"

Such being the impulse of Saturn, when it attempts to retrieve the seeds of future, the destiny of the individual necessarily becomes extra-ordinarily mystical, his understanding of the law of life extremely abstruse, and personal life full of sorrow. The Sun-Saturn axis provides an important pointer to the destiny of J. Krishnamurti.

Mars the lord of the Dhanistha asterism in which lies the ascendant of Krishnamurti occupies the sixth house along with Jupiter and Venus; has exchanged signs with Mercury (the owner of the sixth house, Mercury, occupies the fifth house while the lord of the fifth house which has Taurus in it is Venus, which is located in the sixth house). This exchange produced an extra-ordinary mind, an extremely sharp intellect, while his creative impulses were related with arousal of latent faculties or release of innate happiness: that explained why the highest as well as the lowest went to Krishnamurti to get their tears wiped out and sorrow removed. He himself however failed to qualify for admission to the Oxford University even after repeated efforts which is a common (exoteric) result of the placement of the lord of fifth house in the sixth house. Apart from Mars' association with Venus, it is also associated with Jupiter in the sixth house but Jupiter is lord of twelfth house or the house of life beyond death.

This combination of Mars, Venus and Jupiter presents an interesting feature. Mars is friendly with Jupiter but not so with Venus. Jupiter and Venus are counsellors of opposite camps: Venus is the preceptor of *Asuras*, the demons so to say, while Jupiter, is that of *Devas*, the gods, Thus they can be considered together as counterpart of each other. These planets directly aspect Moon, which is placed in the twelfth house owned by Jupiter. Moon governs psychic faculties and emotional expressions. Saturn also from the tenth house aspects Moon.

The twelfth house represents the Sea of Dissolution and in esoteric astrology it is related with awakening from sleep, liberation, entry into heaven, and renouncing one's couch. In the twelfth house, all individual forms of existence merge with the eternal stream of the life-force. Exoterically, it is related with death, the cessation of all activities, expenditure, the end of the journey, voyages oversea, the pleasures of bed and signifies the cessation of all mundane activities, but dream experience and psychic phenomena are also prognosticated by this house. In the background of this house flows the eternal life-force which is at play behind the individual; everything ultimately returns to the shoreless ocean of immutability and this house shows the process of return at different levels of existence. The relationship of this house with five planets in the chart of Krishnamurti very intimately reveals in his life the extraordinary importance of super-physical realm of existence, which extends beyond our physical senses of perception. Mars standing importantly in this combination in the sixth house aspects the ninth house as well as the ascendant besides the Moon.

We have been told about Krishnamurti's early experiences with the Masters of the Wisdom dwelling beyond the Himalayas where he used to go astrally during his early years of life, where he was taught and prepared for his future mission. He himself has recorded how he used to see persons, who were no longer in their physical body, which he thought would be a common experience with every one. His biographers have mentioned of "the process" under which he experienced terrible pain but psychically used to be transported into a different realm; he had asked his companions not to touch and disturb him during such "processes", which had been quite frequent till his last years. He had also shown to many of his companions the presence of mighty powers around him. Evidently, J.Krishnamurti imbibed the planetary impulses transmitted to him through the psychic Moon. While establishing the centre of his life in the innermost depth of the Great Deep, J. Krishnamurti had the immense potential for forming direct contact with powers beyond the realm of the physical level existence, and in his actions and march towards the fulfilment of his destiny he could proceed ruthlessly and undauntedly.

In all his actions however, the Venusian touch affected his external behavior. He could almost be captivating in his relationships; he possessed great mesmeric powers. Moon has an extraordinary placement in the present chart; it is posited in the twelfth house which by itself is an integral component of the eternal, the everlasting pre-cosmic existence, death, or life-beyond is but a very feeble expression of it. Moreover, the Moon is placed in *Moola* asterism, which is the asterism in which Ravana, the demon king who challenged the great Lord Rama, the divine incarnation, was born, which act in fact paved the way for the beginning of a new era. The word Moola means the trunk, the base, the foundation. The Moon's placement in this asterism heralded the beginning of a new way of life, a new relationship, a new society, which could be ushered as a result of Krishnamurti's thought and teachings, his mental efforts.

It would not be an exaggeration to say that Krishnamurti challenged the modern concept of God, as it is prevalent among the masses and paved the way for the beginning of a new intellectually satisfying society, a divine era. This rebellion against the superstitious Godhood, or the physical incarnation of God has become differently coloured in relation with Krishnamurti as his Moon is aspected by Venus—the planet of sensitivity and social harmony, by Jupiter, the planet of Divine Wisdom and wise counsel, and by Mars, the planet of extreme degree of (sexual) purity and fearless activity.

In his pursuit of bringing to the surface, the realities with regard to superstitions and false gods, Krishnamurti did not use even foul language or undertake anti-social destructive activities, but he fearlessly proceeded according to age-old wise counsel of ancient seers with due caution and strict moral discipline. The Moon in his chart was also aspected by Saturn, which happened to be exalted and the ascendant lord. As a result, keeping in line with its natural proclivities, Saturn kept Krishnamurti's crusade against all gods and religious worships within reasonable rational limits with great objectivity and detachment.

Another important feature of the chart is the exchange of the lords of the fifth and sixth houses to which allusion has already been made. Usually to expect that the children of the native would not give him happiness, which is the common interpretation of this combination does not hold good in this case, as there was no possibility of any marriage for him or deviation from the strict vow of chastity.

J. Krishnamurti did not take such a vow as is known to the world but he always desired, specially under the advice of Annie Besant to remain a celibate, so as to maintain the purity of his 'aura' which was essential for the special role he was expected to play in the world for its religious and spiritual renaissance. His chastity was born out of his desire for austerity. Resulting from this abstinence, his mind had become so clear of personal emotional involvements and enlightened by the inner glow that every thing—concrete as well as ethereal—could reflect itself in his inner mind without any illusion or distortion, thereby leaving no sediments of any emotional attachment on his psyche. His association with female sex was not therefore impelled by any sexual impulse, and as such there was no question of any marriage for him. This fact is well indicated by the seventh lord Moon placed in the twelfth house; the lord of the seventh and the seventh house both are aspected by Saturn; and Mars also aspects the lord of the seventh house.

Jupiter, the planet of family life and happiness is placed in sixth house, which is considered inauspicious for such purposes. Jupiter's aspect on Moon gave him respectability and genuine austerity which made him a true modern yogi, celibate and chaste in mind and body without doning any ochre robe. The exchange between the fifth and the sixth lords produced in him a kind of austerity which made him completely physically as well as emotionally self-reliant; he needed no female companion for his emotional fulfilment.

It was probably under the same impact by which his creativity, the fifth house, and the eleventh house, the house of income, got related in the sixth house that his intellectual pursuits such as his writings, poems and books were neither a source of income for him, nor a means of self glorification. His language and the spoken words were mesmeric, yet they were no source of income or any means of personal satisfaction for him (which common people ordinarily derive from their offspring).

We have often emphasized that the Rahu-Ketu axis in every horoscope plays an important role; it is the fulcrum around which all important events of one's personal growth revolve. Their placement in the horoscope of Krishnamurti had been very powerful. In navamsa kundali, Rahu is exalted and otherwise also, if its nature is assumed to be akin to Saturn, then also it would be reckoned very significant. Rahu also has half aspect on the third house from itself: Sun being placed third from Rahu receives its half aspect. Rahu occupies *Poorva Bhadrapada,* which is ruled by Jupiter and is symbolised by a sword. As this shadowy planet is placed in the second house, the house of family relations, Krishnamurti is expected to have no family life of his own, but for a person who does not care for his own personal glorification, such a shadowy planet would bestow a sense of complete indifference to his personal family relations, which would make him a kith and kin of the world as a whole.

His speech can be very pungent, but under severe discipline it could be a source for arousing the solar influences directed to make the other person search for the essential core of things and relationships. Krishnamurti's dialogues with various individuals showed this faculty very clearly. It is his Ketu, which almost destroyed him on the physical plane, but made him extremely active on the psychic plane. The story prevails among his people that as a child he was considered a dunce, while he was dreaming of another world and watching the fairies, angels and dead persons. He saw his own mother quite frequently during those early days and he was fully aware of the realities of clairvoyance. *Uttara Phalguni* asterism in which Ketu is located is considered quite auspicious: Lord Shiva is said to have started for his marriage under this star. Krishnamurti also began his earthly journey in this birth in Ketu's main planetary period of rulership, which paved the way for his future glory (or suffering?) whatever it could be considered.

Saturn and Rahu, which are the two important planets for any one, who traverses the path of renunciation and enlightenment, are placed in a special relationship. Saturn is posited in an exalted position in the tenth house from which Rahu is in the fifth position. Saturn and Sun demarcate the range of Krishnamurti's activities: Saturn is at the zenith, while Sun is at the nadir point. The three powerful planets namely, Venus, Jupiter and Mars are ninth from Saturn and fifth from Rahu. The four vacant houses are ascendant, and the seventh, besides ninth and third houses. He had nothing personal (ascendant), nor had the necessity of any special field or of a woman for the expression of his personality (the seventh house); he did not come to this earth specially under the compulsion of his past karmas (the ninth house); he did not have any special impediment in his mission so to say, and he had no coequal of his, even Nitya was more a collaborator in his work rather than a sibling (the third house). The nine planets formed a kind of six-pointed* star with Mercury as an exception, which happened to be the lord of the ninth house placed in the fifth house which signified that his main area of creativity was through his intellect and delivering the messages of gods for humanity at large, while he himself personally operated as the mouth-piece or the representative symbolised by the six-pointed star of the divine power.

The announcement that J. Krishnamurti was destined to be the future messiah deserves some detailed examination. He was born in Ketu main period with a balance of 5 years 9 months and 22 days. His early infancy was full of physical illnesses, often with bouts of malaria, hay fever and nose bleeding. It was often believed that his end was

---

* Sun, Moon and Ketu formed three angles of a triangle and Saturn, Rahu and (Jupiter, Venus and Mars) three angles of another.

near. Ketu in eighth house could not be otherwise. An important event of his life occurred during Ketu-Mercury sub-period, when he was formally given the sacred-thread and permitted to begin his studies as was the tradition with the Brahmins. Mercury in the fifth house justifies his formal educational career during its rulership.

The real unfoldment of Krishnamurti's personality began with Venus main period of planetary rulership. During Venus-Venus sub-period, his eldest sister died at the age of twenty years and she was cremated in his presence, who however continued to see her apparition vividly as if in life though he was aware that she had died and was cremated. This feeling often made him fearful and nervous, but he got the first hand experience of the reality of life and death. His clairvoyance began to be unfolded at the advent of Venus main period itself. It is to be noted that Venus is a planet of sensitivity and its placement in the present case in the sixth house accentuated the effect. Moon represents mother, so during Venus-Moon sub-period, Krishnamurti lost his mother: the placement of Moon in the twelfth house with full aspect of Saturn and Mars, the two major malefics made him lose his mother. During Venus-Moon sub-period, he started going to school and was declared a 'dunce', which so happened because his mind was, during that period, mainly hovering over the super-physical realms.

Rahu, as it has been emphasised even earlier, is very important in the horoscope. So it is logical to expect important developments to take place during this period. Venus-Rahu sub-period began in May 1908 and on January 23, 1909, Krishnamurti moved to the Theosophical estate at Adyar, in Madras which became his future abode for many years to come. Under Venus-Rahu sub-period, the two planets linked with foreigners and sophistication, J. Krishnamurti, a shy boy came in contact with Rev. C.W. Leadbeater, who noticed J. Krishnamurti's aura as very bright and sought his father's permission to take him under his care. Krishnamurti's father as well as Annie Besant, were agreeable to the proposal and Krishnamurti began to blossom luxuriantly under his new environment and the new tutelage. Not only his spiritual growth began to take place rapidly, he also learnt the sophistication of putting on shoes, riding a bicycle, and also to read and write English effectively.

On the spiritual side, he is said to have been "put on probation" and "taken as a disciple" by occult teachers, and finally, "Initiated" into the Mystery School of the East and included in the outer ring of "the Occult Hierachy". His monumental book *At the Feet of the Master* still selling extensively was penned by him during this period. Rahu is indeed very important in his chart giving him much courage, piercing intellect and powerful speech. Placed fifth from his ascendant lord, much of Krishnamurti's physical and psychic activities began during the rulership of this planet. It was during this dasa, sub-rulership, that he went abroad, began to enjoy going to theatres, watching cricket matches, and also preparing for the entrance examination for admission to Oxford University in which he however failed to qualify.

Venus-Jupiter sub-period took Krishnamurti to Paris, where he visited casinos, exercised his mind to control the balls to win in the gambling and felt elated at the prospect of successfully doing that kind of control of external substances by the exercise of his mind-force. He even realised the possibility of making much money that way. During this period, his spiritual contact with the *Great Ones* continued but on the negative side, there arose some litigation over Annie Besant's guardianship over him. The litigation had adverse effect on his physical and psychic energy. As the lord of the third and twelfth houses, Jupiter was in sixth house in the sign of its enemy Mercury; Jupiter was bound to create troubles of various kinds, including court of law cases. Venus' association with Jupiter produced disquieting vibrations. The litigation relating to the guardian issue was a reflection of the disharmony existing between Jupiter, which represented natural father and guardian of Krishnamurti, while Venus represented Annie Besant, the foreign (legal) guardian.

But Venus being the lord of the tenth house signifying its intimate relationship with Krishnamurti's destiny made everything turn in his favour. In 1912, he once wrote to Mrs. Annie Besant, "Even if all the world turns against you, there is one who will never abandon his beloved mother". It shows the impact of Venus-Jupiter on the mind of young Krishnamurti who had began to show the signs of early adulthood. During this period, Krishnamurti conducted some kind of spiritual training classes for his close friends: one could note that Jupiter was the lord of third house, extending its influence on close co-equals of the native. Krishnamurti's interest in educational system also intensified under Jovian impulse: he wrote his famous *Education As Service* during this period. He also came under the spell of heavy downpour of influences from the outer world, which reflected the impact of Jupiter, which was the lord of twelfth house (supra-physical worlds) representing the life-beyond and the realm of the higher beings, and was placed in the sixth house representing the latent faculties, the *siddhis* in the individual. During this period, one day like many other days, he recorded, "Something will happen tonight. I am sure of it. I feel so excited". One may note the touch of Venus and Jupiter in such writings and expressions.

During Venus-Mercury sub-period Krishnamurti had another devastating experience which seemed to completely destroy his personal self. What happened is not precisely known, but Krishnamurti felt so much impersonal about himself that he wrote: "Personality will be knocked out, and it is by that way alone, I am positively certain, that one can really serve the Lord". That was a reflection on some deeply inner experience during Venus-Mercury sub-period, the two planets owning fifth and sixth houses and exchanging their places. None of the personal achievements and creativity of Krishnamurti was of any avail to him personally. It is during the same period that Krishnamurti received some setbacks in his Matriculation and other examinations, which finally closed any possibility of his having formal schooling.

One of the most exceptional period in Krishnamurti's life was Venus-Ketu sub-period. From indirect sources one leans that this was the period of intense personal upheaval in Krishnamurti's life. Many things which ought to have remained secret happened to him and got publicised. Firstly, on the physical plane, he started having overtures from persons of the opposite sex. On February 12, 1920, a woman smiled and followed him at a casino which Krishnamurti had gone to visit. A week later, another lady invited him at her suite in the hotel under the pretence of having some philosophical discussion with him, where though she was married she embraced and embarrassed him. Mars and Venus association sometimes expressed its result in such a way. In the chart of Krishnamurti, Venus and Ketu have flanked his seventh house, so one could expect such aberrations to happen. Ketu placed in the eighth house had to produce something bizarre and secret.

Ketu having some semblance with Mars had to produce some sudden and impulsive situations. During this period, Krishnamurti also felt some kind of craving in his heart, which was difficult to label or to describe. In spite of the adulation that he had received, he felt a little lost, he wanted to have some kind of love relationship, some companionship for sharing his thoughts and feelings. The nature of this relationship was extremely complex and non-descript; it was very much mixed up. During this period, he would often say or write, "I am seriously in love with...", or "all day I have been very dreamy...". He even wrote, "I must find myself and then only can help others," He became intensely attracted towards Lord Buddha and Nietzche's book *Thus Spake Zarathustra.* Abstract philosophy began to take a hold of his psyche. At the same time, the planets in sixth and eighth houses, Venus and Ketu began to affect his physical health very adversely. He contracted towards the end of this period sinus infection, fell ill, which turned out as serious bronchitis; he also had high temperature which often made him delirious.

During the main planetary rulership of Sun, Krishnamurti reached his pinnacle of glory. The Sun in exaltation drawing the life-force from the very source of its existence in order to reveal the hidden and inner potentialities of Krishnamurti's personality came to fruition by producing its destined results during its own period of planetary rulership. Now, Krishnamurti began to lecture publicly and face big audiences very confidently; he began to assume the role of a leader. But Saturn's opposition to Sun gave Krishnamurti certain unpleasant experiences. He had to be examined in the United States by a detective of the Police department in order to ascertain the purpose of his long lonely walks in woods around his Ojai Cottage. He also felt that his 'mental body was not well developed enough' and that he wanted to study quietly and uninterruptedly. While he was trying to attend to his mental and physical side of development, he also suffered from slight cancerous growth in his intestines and left lung and several such other ailments, which could astrologically be related with the fourth house. In spite of such physical problems, he began his meditation very seriously and regularly. He began to experience special type of feelings and almost became 'God Intoxicated'. The Sun in its exalltation sign could help him raise his emotional nature to great heights.

During Sun-Rahu sub-period, he had an experience which gave him the possibility of unifying his consciousness with the entire universe. He recorded his experience on August 19, 1922, as follows:

> There was a man mending the road: the man was myself, the pick-axe he held was myself; the very stone which he was breaking up was a part of me; the tender blade of grass was my

> being, and the tree beside the man was myself. I almost could feel. The birds, the dust, and the very noise was a part of me. Just then there was a car passing at some distance: I was the driver, the engine, and the tyres: as the car went further away from me I was going away from myself. I was everything, or rather everything was in me, inanimate and animate, the hill, the worm, and all breathing things. All day long, I remained in this happy condition.

This uniqueness of experience studied in relation with the special features of Rahu and Saturn in this horoscope would indicate that the fifth position of Rahu from the ascendant lord Saturn, while the eighth lord in the fourth house is exalted would very appropriately produce this state of psychological loftiness and identification of individual consciousness with every form of manifestation existing around oneself. The Jovian aspect on Rahu which gave Krishnamurti a sublime experience of universalisation of the self is better described in the following narration, which also formed a part of Krishnamurti's own record of the state of his being which pertained to the same period:

> Like the lake, I felt physical body, with its mind and emotion, could be ruffled on the surface but nothing could disturb the calmness of my soul. The presence of the *mighty beings* was with me for some time and then they were gone. I was supemely happy, for I had seen.

In the same recording, Krishnamurti continued which showed that Rahu in eleventh house from the Sun and fifth from Saturn which was the ascendant lord must during its planetary rulership, whether in its primary or in its secondary rulership, produce something extraordinary for him. One such experience is recorded as follows:

> I have not been what is called "happy" for many years: everything I touched brought me discontentment: my mental condition, as you know, my dearest brother, has been deplorable. I did not know, what I wanted to do nor did I care to do much: everything bored me in a very short time and in fact I did not find myself. After August 20th (the incident in the above description occurred on August 19, 1922), I know what I want to do and what lies before me—nothing but to serve the Masters and the Lord.

Krishnamurti further indicated his state of the being as a result of this transforming experience as "much more sensitive and slightly clairvoyant.... such a thing had not happened to me for over seven years. In fact, for the last seven years I had been spiritually blind". These descriptions showed that the period of Sun-Rahu sub-period, opened a new phase of experiences for Krishnamurti, which radically altered his subjective state of the being and his inner nature. Rahu invariably affects the psychological state of the individual: if it operates as a malefic, it leads to depravation while the beneficence of this shadowy planet spiritualises the individual making him more attuned to the world of psychic forces.

The astrological factors which vitally affected Krishnamurti can be followed systematically till the end of his life, but the above very clearly, to a great extent, emphasised the fact that a link exists between the disposition of the stars and the life of an individual in the subtlest possible manner. It also becomes apparent that these influences are not restricted merely to the external conditions of life, but they impinge on various level of one's existence importantly. An example of such relationship can be cited for the period of Sun-Mercury sub-period. Mercury had been the ruler of the sixth sign from the ascendant as well as of the ninth sign which should have given him very adverse as well as very enlightening experiences.

During this period, Krishnamurti lost his dearest brother Nityanand which happened in October 1925. But he also experienced unification with his brother on the "eternal plane, where there was no birth or death"; Krishnamurti also composed poems which later showed a very important phase in his life. He even declared himself at the Golden Jubilee Convention of the Theosophical Society that "I come to create and not to destroy" which asserted his identification with higher powers which guide the destiny of mankind. This was an expression as many persons, who were present at the lecture, where he affirmed so which included even Annie Besant and such others felt, Krishnamurti's identification with higher beings, whose vehicle of expression and action in the outer world he was expected to become he had become. It was very surprising that Mercury awaited for the main period of Sun to produce its natural result of making Krishnamurti—a messenger for gods for the mankind. But it is to be noted that the main planetary period of Mercury was not likely to be present in Krishnamurti's life and Ketu and Venu were not powerful enough to provide strong foundation for such an onerous task. Mercury owns the ninth house, and it occupies the fifth house situated second from Sun. Mercury placed second from the Sun produces the auspicious *Vesi Yoga* strengthening the power of the luminary to bestow its benediction effectively. Moreover, Mercury occupies the navamsa of Krittika which is ruled by Sun and its presiding deity is Agni, which makes evertything pure and dissolves them to ther ultimate essence. Krittika born are always ready to assist the seers and gods by carrying out the most difficult assignment for them. Mercury took the first opportunity during the main period of Sun's planetary rulership to produce the most auspicious result in the life of Krishnamurti.

It was during Sun-Mercury sub-period that Krishnamurti for the first time effectively and powerfully discharged the responsibility of carrying the messages of the higher beings to the world at large. The identification during this period was so electrifying that those who heard the lecture thought that at the time of delivering those sentences not only Krishnamurti's face and demeanour changed but his whole psychological being was so much transformed into universal consciousness that everyone present felt a kind of magnetic current passing through them. That was also the period when J. Krishnamurti was composing the verses contained in his book *Kingdom of Happiness* and his mind was almost completely saturated with the thoughts of the Divine.

Many a time Krishnamurti gave several inspired (and even possessed) talks when his visage is believed to have taken the form of his mentor which he himself had been desirous to know (see) how it looked, but never was the experience so thrilling as the first powerful one in December 1925. Mercury's nature as the lord of the sixth house (the storehouse of latent possibilities) sandwiched between Sun and Venus could naturally extol a person to such a superb height of beneficence. This fulfilment of the promise synchronised with utter desolation experienced at the death of his beloved brother Nityanand (brothers associated with Mercury which had some inauspicious traits too).

After this glorious event, Krishnamurti's life took a radically different turn. He primarily became a peripatetic teacher, periegrinating from one country to another delivering his spiritual message, discussing personal problems with innumerable individuals and wiping tears of sorrow and getting engaged in a new kind of educational programme. He also had problems with his co-worker, housekeeper and even editor of his several publications Rajagopalan, which persisted for some time and his health had never been very sturdy, there were always some or the other kind of physical ailments. These could be very well explained by changes in planetary periods, but there was one incident, which happened soon after the end of Sun main period which ought to be mentioned here.

During the Moon period which lasted from May 1927 to May 1937, Krishnamurti renounced his membership with the Theosophical Society, disbanded the Order of the Star of the East, renounced his position as the chosen messenger of God, and returned all property gifted to him. It was during the same period that Annie Besant and C.W. Leadbeater, two of his greatest supporters passd away with whom he was greatly attached and for whom he had the greatest veneration. These changes in the life of Krishnamurti greatly upset several thousands of his followers, who had accepted him as the new Messiah; even Annie Besant was quite perturbed over these events. But Moon, the lord of seventh house placed in twelfth house aspected by his ascendant lord Saturn and fourth lord Mars, made J. Krishnamurti a complete recluse, without any property to support him; no friend and no security in life! That was a desolate state J. Krishnamurti was put in during Moon main period. Yet, Moon placed ninth from exalted Sun and third from his ascendant lord Saturn provided enough courage and sustenance from his idealism and went ahead in life to meet his destiny alone.

During Rahu main period, there were many psychological transformations including his experimentation to live without any support or relationship with the world at large. For a few years, he isolated himself from all human relationships; he grew his own corn, milked himself from the cow, cooked his own meals and answered no communication from the world at large. Rahu taught him the lesson to stand alone and face his problems without any outside assistance.

The end of Krishnamurti came on February 17, 1986 at midnight. At that night, he was running Saturn-Venus sub-period. On the psychological and the psychic planes what was happening to Krishnamurti was difficult for anyone to know or to describe. The outer expressions as reflected in his relationships with various people were undergoing important changes. He had become extremely irritable, but at the same time superbly tranquil. In fact, this contradictory state of his being was a matter of experience, which any one with the slightest sensitivity could feel during those days even during his public talks. An unprecedented event happened during the last few talks of his life which so far has remained enigmatic. Never in his public talks, he insisted anyone to leave the hall or the pandal, but on this occasion he asked one among the audience to leave his seat and refused to address unless the person left the congregation or moved elsewhere. Such things had never happened before. During the last talk, there was another mystical episode. Krishnamurti asked his audience to be quiet for a few minutes and not to move immediately after the end of the talk. There was complete silence after the talk: everyone present had a strange feeling of elation, an experience of enormous energy descending on them.

Astrologically, such occurrences could be explained by the fact that Saturn and Venus formed a mysterious combination. On the physical plane, they generally produce a kind of jarring effect, but psychically, Venus makes a person sensitive and responsive to the people. In the present case, Venus has enormous power to produce psychic vibrations, but Saturn is 'heartless'. Combined together, Krishnamurti had to bear tremendous strain on his body of both these influences. On the physical plane, his body was finding it dificult to cope with them. He suffered from many undiagnosed diseases. Even during the course of the last series of his talks, he had to announce that the possibility of the next talk depended upon the doctors certifying his ability to undertake the strain and asked the audience to wait to know the doctor's decision. In spite of complete exhaustion after an hour long talk, which often stretched upto an hour and thirty to forty minutes, he unflichingly persisted with the audience which often wanted to hear more unmindful of the exhaustion experienced by the speaker. That was the tenacity which only Saturn could impart and that sympathy for the people, Venus.

Malignancy of the pancreas with secondaries in the liver were diagnosed decisively on January 29, 1986 and on February 16, 1986 retaining his full consciousness he went to sleep on Sunday, the day of the Sun, and the same night after midnight, ten past twelve, when February 17 began, Krishnamurti left his physical body "with utter repose with a lingering smile on his lips, a picture of beatific beauty", as his biographer Pupul Jayakar described it. A few days before his end, Krishnamurti talked about his own death: "I am ninety years and that is good enough for me. I have lived with death and life together all the time, all my life". Indeed, Saturn-Venus sub-period, during which period, life and death brought the supreme exaltation of J. Krishnamurti whereby his physical body old and age-old, though he did not use glasses, and his natural teeth continued till the end of his life, was fully used up, worn out and needed rest and it was given so. That is the life and the end of J. Krishnamurti, born with Ketu mahadasa and ending with Saturn.

What is most important in Krishnamurti's horoscope is the supreme importance of his ascendant sign, which stood for universalisation of the individual self, and the ascendant lord Saturn in the tenth house in exaltation and retrogression, which stood for redemption from bondage. J. Krishnamurti in his entire life fulfilled one mission gloriously, he set his own self free from all material bondage for which he suffered all kinds of troubles—physical, psychological and yogic, and finally showed to the world the path of redemption, which he very rightly called *First and the Last Freedom.* With Saturn radiating its primary impulse, and Venus the secondary, Krishnamurti completed his pre-set task and gave up his mortal coil, which he kept scrupulously clean and wanted to be given to fire after his death in that very pristine purity. Or, was it that he wanted his mortal coil to be given back to Saturn, the *Yama*, and his spirit to Venus, the pure sensitivity? Saturn always remains an enigma, and nobody could decipher its mysteries or the mystical ways of its operation.

12

NELSON ROLIHLAHLA MANDELA

		Ketu Venus	Jupiter
	15th July 1918 (Rasi)		Sun Mercury Saturn
			Asc.
	Rahu	Moon	Mars

Rahu		Moon	Mars Venus
Saturn	*(Amsa)*		Sun
Mercury			
Jupiter		Asc.	Ketu

Nelson Rolihlahla Mandela, whose middle name Rolihlahla means 'stirring up trouble', indeed has lived a tempestuous life eversince his birth. He showed from the very beginning the spirit of adventure and dauntless courage, which could not be tamed by any amount of torture or seduced by the greatest allurement. He knows his mind firmly, he takes up a course of action after much contemplation, and once begun the journey he must come to its logical end—no matter how much difficulties he has to encounter for the same. The exact epoch of his birth is not known, but at the age of 76 years, a tall, sturdy, and a leonine gait of trained boxer with his confident and self-assured look suggest the underlying characteristics of Leo ascendant; his tempestuous life for more than seven decades reveals the dominance of his planetary deities in controlling, regulating and directing his life.

Nelson Mandela was born on July 18, 1918 at Qunu near Umtata, the capital village of the Transkei 'reserve' (31°50' South; 28°47' East) in an affluent family: his father Henry Mgadla Mandela was a chief councillor to their relatives and the paramount chief of Thambu, and his four wives bore him about a dozen offspring among whom Nelson was the only male child. Nelson was very attached with his sisters, but he spent his time mostly with the elder members of the family. His mother, Nonquaphi, commonly known as Nosekeni was a person of strong character and dignity. As a child, Nelson herded the cattle, tended the sheep and helped in the ploughing but he loved most the adventurous stories which he listened with great attention and fascination from the bearded old men, who gathered around a huge open fire. They talked of good old days before the arrival of the white men. Nelson's imagination was fired by these early stories of the age old tradition, when his country was independent and his people free to take up whatever avocation they wished to follow.

Nelson Mandela was born in the Jupiter main period with a balance of a little over 10 years during which period he was groomed for respectability, status and sheltered living. He cherished the old values of life. Nelson Mandela was initially anticommunist, not only because of his strongly traditional background, but because of his religious upbringing which taught him that the communists were anti-Christ. The fifth-ninth house relationship between Moon and Jupiter without any malefic influence on them gave his life the strong foundation of morality, humanitarian aspiration and the great sensitivity, which during the latter phase of his career made him a unique personality even when he was agitating against the State and was being charged for treason, or kept in solitary confinement. The Jovian grace and balance of mind never left him even when he became the head of the State after spending a period of 27 years in gaol. It has given him the rare quality of making friends even of his most deadly foes. Leonine grace and Jovian amiability combined together enabled Mandela while serving his life sentence in prison to earn the respect of prison officials. One of his fellow inmates when released from the prison reminisced about him by stating that "he was known to fellow prisoners by his clan name, 'Madhiba.' Warders called him Mandela though most inmates were simply referred to by their prison numbers." He further stated, "I remember one sergeant in particular even calling him 'Mr. Mandela' - unheard of on Robben Island".

Even on the occasion of Presidential inauguration at the Hill-top union buildings in Pretoria, Mandela was magnanimous to invite his old prison warder James Gregory, who developed a strong friendship with the African National Congress' leader during his 24 years on 'the notorious Robben Island prison off Cape Town'. In fact, whenever, Moon is aspected by Jupiter, it produces nobility of heart, but in the case of Nelson Mandela, Jupiter in its own sign in navamsa aspects seventh house enhancing his sociability and amiability, especially when neither Jupiter nor the seventh house gets afflicted by any malefic influence. The quality of righteousness, generosity and transparency of motives became ingrained in his character from the very early childhood in his life.

A great change occurred in the life of Nelson Mandela, when the main period of Saturn began and his father died. Saturn has the inherent attribute of dissolving all materialistic proclivities in the fire of one's trials and tribulations so that the essential qualities of one's personality come to the surface: Saturn abhors non-essentials and to eliminate them so that the primeval self-assurance, confidence and the direction of one's destiny are unveiled, Saturn adopts a method radically different from that of Jupiter. It adopts the surgical methods: cuts away the damaged portion and removes the cancerous growth of ignorance from its very base.

In the twelfth house, Saturn accentuated its forces in a special manner. It brings to the surface those intimations from the eternal past, which urge the individual onto the path of spiritual unfoldment. The native is persistent in getting whatever he wants; his opinions are very important to him. Sometimes, there may be deep-rooted spiritual intonations in those ideas, but the native is primarily activated by the fact that these are his own ideas, and for that alone will he work. But in instilling such ideas and laying the foundation for this kind of self-unfoldment, Saturn works perseveringly in spite of waywardness of the individual. Such a situation arose in the case of Nelson Mandela, when he was about 11 years of age. At the age of 12, his father died but he transferred the guardianship over Nelson Mandela to the paramount chief with such poignant sentiments, which revealed his deep-rooted affection for his only son from his four wives. He said:

> "I am giving you this servant, Rolihlahla. This is my only son. I can say from the way he spoke to his sisters and friends that his inclination is to help the nation. I want you to make him what you would like him to be; give him education, he will follow your example".

Nelson Mandela was a brilliant student; his mind is extraordinarily sharp. Saturn's malefic nature in the present case is illusory: as the result of its affliction to Sun and Mercury, they have been considerably affected by its nature, but Saturn by itself has gained much from their association. Moreover, Saturn in the sign of Moon greatly influenced its mental capacities; its association with Mercury sharpened his intellect; and under the influence of ascendant lord Sun, received the aspiration towards lordly status. In navamsa, Saturn occupies its own sign, but in rasi chart, it occupies *Ashlesha* nakshatra presided over by the Nagas and the asterism is ruled by Mercury which is associated with it.

Undoubtedly, Nelson Mandela's extraordinary quality of his mind is the gift of planetary deities, but so are his impetuosity, uncommon approach to the problems of life, will-power making him unyielding and adopt terrorist tactics following communist philosophy, sometimes overlooking his basic Jovian background. Because of his sharp intellect, when he joined the Methodist School and appeared for his Matriculation examination he secured a first class with special scholarship for higher studies, but political predilections during the period of his studentship attracted the attention of the authorities and he was often reprimanded for such 'digressions'.

Nelson Mandela has Ketu associated with Venus occupying its own sign, while in navamsa, it is associated with Mars. Obviously, Mandela does not believe in celibacy, nor does he want to be bound by orthodox sexual morality; even his tribal upbringing had been quite permissive in this regard. At the age of 16 years, during the period of Saturn-Ketu sub-period, Nelson Mandela had the elaborate rituals at the time of his circumcision which initiated him into manhood. At this time, Nelson Mandela spent several weeks in the mountains with young men of his age group. Their faces were painted white, their bodies were grass-skirted, and the tribal elders led them through the initiation rituals, schooling them to prepare them for manhood and for participation in tribal councils. Ketu in tenth house occupying eleventh house from the main ruling planet had to initiate him in a position of authority.

An important change which radically altered the course of Mandela'a life occurred at the age of 21 years. Usually the period of Saturn-Venus sub-period, is quite upsetting, though both of these planets are friendly to each other; the nature of this psychological disturbance is very difficult to decipher. The period of Saturn sub-period within the main period of Venus is worse, but Venus in the sub-period within Saturn main period is also not less disturbing. In both cases, there is something which the people at large would feel as something pleasant happening, but the individual concerned feels disturbed, his life's plan is given a jolt. It was a similar situation even with Mandela. He reported that "My guardian felt it was time for me to get married. He loved me very much and looked after me as diligently as my father had. But he was no democrat and did not think it worth while to consult me about a wife. He selected a girl, fat and dignified; *Labola*, the symbol of bride-wealth was paid and arrangements were made for the wedding." This was the critical situation: Mandela the democrat wanted his freedom, and not the servitude of traditional tribal life with wives bringing up a large number of children and moving with his tribal folk. The unknown destiny was haunting him. So Mandela decided to run away from the family and scan the wide horizon even if it meant penury, hard work and sacrifice of the family comforts and affection.

Mandela was an athlete and was confident that he would be able to eke out a living for himself. This journey into the unknown began during Saturn-Sun sub-period. Sun was the ascendant lord but occupying twelfth from its own sign, it could not leave Mandela in comfort. He had to stand on his own. Away from home without any support, except his own inner determination, where could he find a job to maintain himself? In his escape from his family, he could not be sure that his guardian would leave him to do whatever he liked and not trace him and bridle him. He went to a small mining town near Johannesburg, where he could get the work of a security guard at a gold mine. He was 'armed with *knobkerrie*, a heavy, knobbed stick and a whistle'. He guarded the gate of the compound in which black miners were housed. But soon, the paramount chief, his guardian, located him and he was again on the run. By the time Moon sub-period started, the fugitive life gradually became more secure and many factors of far-reaching consequences began to exert themselves. Moon obtains the auspicious aspect of Jupiter. Saturn is tenth from Moon. Moon is situated in the sign of Venus which occupies the tenth house which was going to play a decisive role in his life.

So, one finds that Nelson Mandela got a room in Alexandra, a sprawling township on the north-eastern edge of Johannesburg. It was at this place that Mandela met Walter Sisulu and life-long bond of intimate friendship was forged between them. Sisulu influenced Mandela to do law and he became a part-time student at the University of Witwatersrand, which was also a gold mining place in the district of Transval. While a student he met Evelyn Ntoko, a pretty, soft-spoken nurse at the City Deep Mine hospital and married her. She generously contributed towards his university fees and other expenditure. They set up home in Orlando, one of the expanding towns interspersed with uniform match-box type houses, about 10 miles north-west of Johannesburg, which was later named Soneto. Evelyn Ntoko Mase bore him two sons and a daughter (one of the sons died in a car-crash in 1970). These were the result of Saturn-Mars sub period, the latter aspected by Saturn made Mandela restricted to the four-walls of domestic life having his wings clipped to a great extent. Mars even owned the fourth house, but its ownership of the ninth house and placement in the second house gave much strength and respectability, though Nelson Mandela's inner restlessness was being aroused and he was looking for a suitable outlet as soon as an opportunity came. The urge to do something great and impersonal—inherent as an essential feature of Mars was inwardly making Mandela dissatisfied with his married life.

During Rahu and Jupiter sub-periods, his interest in national politics became intense. J.N. Singh and Ismail Meer, who were fellow students at the Witwatersand University were leading activists of the Transval National Congress. Mandela was friendly with Ismail Meer and he used to frequent at his house. There he met J.N. Singh and the three friends frequently discussed politics and even chalked out their political strategy and programmes. In 1945, the African National Congress celebrated a Victory March, which brought the three friends much in limelight. Jupiter has the special impulse of making a person widely known, give him eminence and turn him towards altruistic involvements, irrespective of the motivating cause which impels him to do so.

In the life of Mandela, Moon and Jupiter have special significance. Saturn-Jupiter sub-period made him participate in political activities with much enthusiasm and zeal. In 1946, their agitation became more pronounced. The Smut's Ghetto Bill was designed to restrict the Indians permanently to certain restricted areas. It became recognised that the government was not only oppressing the Africans, but the Indians were also its target, it seemed a discrimination against the coloured people giving special privileges to the whites only. It was injustice. Mandela was extremely sensitive to individual's dignity and it was important for his leonine disposition to register his protest. The three friends organised a passive resistance to the *Ghetto Bill.* The democratic disposition of Saturn greatly helped Nelson Mandela in whole-heartedly working for such a cause. The resolve changed the life of Nelson Mandela for all times to come.

Soon after the beginning of the Ketu sub-period in Mercury main, the African National Congress gave a call of national strike. Mandela by now had become a political leader and he could not avoid the government's wrath: the government wanted to arrest and immobilise by imprisoning him, while he wanted to avoid it to address the masses and arouse their participation in the popular movement. In June 1950, as soon as Mercury-Ketu sub-period began, he was jailed for the first time. In his horoscope, Mercury enjoys the company of Saturn and Sun on its both sides, and Sun being more than 20° away from it, there is no question of its combustion, yet the flanking of the planet by two malefics could not leave it unaffected. Ketu's position with Venus in the tenth house is also very inauspicious, making it capable of arousing the displeasure of the State.

A new development in the country in which anti-establishment views were being propagated was the joining hands of the Communist Party and the South African Congress, especially its students and the youth league. Nelson Mandela was a leading figure in this movement. The combined impact of these groups in the compaign against the *Pass Laws,* which stipulated the natives to always carry their identification documents and restrict their movement to certain specified areas was so powerful that Mandela became the popular leader, a position which he never abdicated.

Mercury associated with Sun, the ascendant lord and itself the ruler of the eleventh house in which Jupiter was situated and of the second house in which the fiery Mars was located, was bound to make a serious impact on the mind and career of Mandela, but Ketu's position in the tenth house occupying the navamsa sign of Mercury made the period a kind of launching pad for the future national leader always to be showered with public acclaim and governmental wrath.

In December, 1950 he was elected the President of the Transval African National Congress while he remained the leader of the youth group for coordinating various programmes. During this period, Mandela was exposed to many kinds of people, some social elites representing Venus, some anti-establishment persons representing Ketu and many important individuals intellectually very advanced. During Mercury-Venus sub-period in December 1952, when Albert Lutuli was elected President-General of the African National Congress, he was elected his Deputy. During his early phase of political career, the Mercurian intelligence and Venusian sensitivity made Mandela a champion of passive resistance following the footsteps of Mahatma Gandhi, while his friend and mentor Sisulu argued for militancy. During this period, he also wrote to the Prime Minister for the grant of constitutional rights to his people. The government was becoming much concerned with the activities of Nelson Mandela and put several restrictions over his movements and activities.

Mercury-Venus sub-period was important for Nelson in several other ways also. During this period, Mandela qualified to practise as an attorney and in 1952 itself he set up his office in partnership with Tambo near the Magistrate's court in Johannesburg. The association of Venus with Ketu could not leave Mandela worry-free and without some disturbing allegations. He was charged under Suppression of Communist Act: what was known as Defiance Campaign under which disciminatory laws were generally disobeyed and Mandela was held as a leader of these campaigns. He was prosecuted and jailed for nine months in June 1952. Even afterwards his life did not remain peaceful and he could not find any time for his wife and family members.

Saturn had moved in transit to Virgo in September 1950—thus afflicting his Moon, which had to continue for the next seven and a half years upto 1958. It was the most disturbing period in Mandela's life. He was being put to so many vicissitudes that very little interval occurred between one problem and another. In September 1953, he was ordered not to attend or address any public gathering. For six months, he was confined to Johannesburg. But Mandela did not remain idle during this period. Venus owned the third house with Moon in it having full aspect of Jupiter from the Mercurian sign of Gemini: Mandela began to organise community schools. He felt that mass movements against powerful political adversary cannot succeed without general enlightenment for which education was essential. He wanted to work for grassroot organisation so that public awareness could be aroused. It was the same kind of understanding under which Mahatma Gandhi started his Basic Education Programme for the Indian masses.

Mandela now was no longer a believer in passive disobedience: he was now very active and true to his leonine ascendant, he was actively pursuing his objectives. In 1953, he went even underground so as to elude government clutches and restrictions over his activities. But it did not last for long. Now came the turn of his colleagues in creating troubles for him. In 1954, during the period of Mercury-Sun sub-period, the Transval Law Society petitioned the Supreme Court to have the name of Nelson Mandela struck off the roll of legal practitioners for "having been convicted as a leader of the Defiance Campaign activity which did not conform to the standards of conduct expected from members of an honorable profession. Sun in the case of Nelson Mandela is vargottam and powerful enough to ward off any such difficulties: the Supreme Court did not agree with the allegations made by Mandela's colleagues and gave judgement in favour of Mandela and instructed the Law Society to pay the costs to him. However as his movement was curtailed and restrictions were imposed on his movement outside Johannesburg and addressing public gatherings, Mandela during the sub-periods of Venus, Sun and Moon found time for his family members. He was generally with his wife during this period and he and his wife, Evelyn Ntoko Mase got three children, two sons and a daughter. Mercury in the twelfth house dogged Nelson Mandela throughout its main period, and the short palliatives received during the sub-periods of various planets were not very enduring. Even during the Moon sub-period, which otherwise should have been tolerably comfortable did not leave his mind unperturbed. The third house Moon is not generally peaceful, it had the Jupiter's fifth aspect, which should have been supportive but it was not so effective. As soon as the first order of restrictions on his movement and addressing of public gatherings came to an end, new orders were imposed immediately afterwards extending the restriction for another five years. Even the family life seemingly peaceful for the last three years or so began to show cracks with the beginning of Mars sub-period and the fissure became pronounced. Mars was a yoga-karaka planet, had the function of making the individual extremely active and important which in their turn brought much renown as a result of its ninth house lordship, but the Saturn's aspect on it from the twelfth house began to threaten imprisonment.

Two important events during this period had been the formal separation from his wife Evelyn Mase leading finally to divorce and the treason charges against him towards the end of 1956. The political activities distanced Mandela and Evelyn. The latter was away in Natal studying midwifery and Mandela caring his own life and his political involvements, though he managed to see as much as he could of the children. Meanwhile, Mandela's friendship with Winnie Nomzama, who became his wife for the next three and a half decade and supported him during his political activities took place. As a matter of fact, both the events—treason charge and engagement with Winnie showed the typical nature of Martian impulses. Winnie was a social worker, 16 years younger to Mandela, and their meeting was sudden with Mandela inviting her on the following day for a lunch at an Indian restaurant, where he entertained her with Indian curry. Their attraction was instantaneous which materialised a year later in marriage and Winnie giving birth to two daughters and supporting the entire family including Nelson Mandela during his political involvements. In the same way, instantaneous was his arrest which finally resulted in his acquittal but it changed his life-style. On 5th December 1956, there was a knock at his door at dawn and Mandela was taken from his house in Orlando, just as 155 others including thirteen women were similarly roused in different parts of the country. They were all arrested and charged with high treason.

Nelson Mandela met Winnie Nomzamo Madikizela in 1957 soon after he was charged with treason and she was terribly 'overawed by this commanding man' and in June 1958 when Mandela had begun Rahu sub-period they got married. Rahu usually leads to marriage specially during *sade-sati*, its affliction of 7½ years of Moon. Mandela was granted four days leave from the orders restricting him to Johannesburg for the marriage. On August 1, 1958, the trial concerning the treason charge proper opened in Pretoria. Mandela spent much time preparing his defence for the trial. The trial continued for a long time and on March 29, 1961 he was acquitted of the treason charge. On March 21, 1960, there was massacre at Sharpeville and 69 unarmed Africans were shot dead. Mandela was implicated, but he firmly denied any association with such brutal murder: he stated that 'violence will not come from us'. The judges found him not guilty and discharged him.

Now that Mandela was identified as a topmost African leader, the government was looking for an opportunity to remove him from his position, while his friends were of the view that Mandela could lead the country to its ultimate destiny so he should be protected and enabled to project the South African case to international fora and different heads of States. In 1961, Saturn and Jupiter were for a long time together in Capricorn, Mandela's sixth house in the natal chart and fourth from Moon sign, while Jupiter sub-period in Mercury main dasa had the weakness of being placed twelfth from Mercury. During this period, Mandela went abroad, having been smuggled out of the country.

Jupiter is the ruler of the eighth house also, which stands for hidden aspects of life. The African National Congress now no longer believed in peaceful non-cooperation agitation, to regain its independence after a foreign dominance of nearly four centuries. Mandela was now keen to have military training. It was about the same time that the first African National Congress bomb exploded. One does not know whether Mandela during this period came in contact with Subhash Chandra Bose's philosophy, but his thinking showed much of the same traits as those of Bose and distinct departure from that of Mahatma Gandhi.

Mercury-Saturn sub-period was the most momentous period in Mandela's life. He jumped in the fray at the peril of his life. Saturn rules the sixth house; it was inevitable that it brought out various faculties of the individual, even if it meant serious difficulties for him.

During the seventeen months period ending 5th August 1962, covering portions of Jupiter and Saturn sub-periods, Nelson Mandela did the most perilous business for his country. He made extensive tour of various countries in Africa and even went to the United Kingdom. His flight took him to Ethiopia where he met Emperor Haile Selassie and attended the Pan-African Conference. He was enthusiastically received by the delegates from East, Central, and Southern Africa. During this very period, he flew with Tambo to London and met Hugh Gaitskell and Jo Grimond, leaders of the Labour and the Liberal parties. On his way back, he met Colonel Boumedienne, Commander-in-Chief of the Algerian Army. While away from his country, Mandela met Julius Nyerere, future President of Tanzania, Kenneth Kaunda, President of Zambia, and Ogina Odinga, the opposition leader of Kenya. These experiences helped Mandela in working out his strategy for his political programmes; they also gave him the first hand knowledge of the likely reactions of world leaders. These experiences gave him tremendous confidence in his own powers and strategy; he was now an international leader, whom it would be difficult to ignore. Mercury associated with the ascendant lord and Saturn and the latter occupying an important place in navamsa chart raised the status of Nelson Mandela. Mercury-Saturn sub-period made him a great international leader, but sowed seeds of serious hardships for him.

On Sunday 17th June 1962, Mandela was feeling very light and relaxed: he spent a day off in London and went sight seeing around Westminister, but in less than two months time, on

August 5, 1962 he was arrested in Natal along with Walter Sisulu and six others. It ended his period of foreign escapade for mobilizing international opinion against the apartheid. Now his trial began: the lord of the sixth house in the twelfth produces a kind of Raja Yoga, but it is not completely absolved of the maleficence of sixth house ownership. Nelson Mandela was now charged with inciting people to strike and leaving the country without a valid passport. He conducted his own defence. But the facts were that these charges in the eyes of law were punishable and they could not be denied; Mandela was sentenced on November 7, 1962 to five years of imprisonment with hard labour.

In Pretoria Central prison, a turreted red-brick remnant of colonial times, Mandela began serving his sentence, wearing garments of baggy shorts and tunic with sandals. The small cement-floored cell was furnished with felt mat, sanitary pail, enamel dish and mug. Woken before dawn by alarm bells and commands shouted in Afrikanas, he followed his usual strict routine of exercise and the basic food *mealiepap,* some kind of liquid gruel prepared out of maize corn with lunch at 10 a.m. and supper at 3 p.m. His days were spent sewing mail-bags. Thus passed Nelson Mandela the remaining portion of his Saturn sub-period. Twelfth house Saturn in Cancer sign makes the individual indigent, shabbily dressed, penurious in habit, and unhealthy in general attitude. He even suffers from many physical ailments.

True to its basic disposition, Saturn during its sub-period completely stripped Mandela of his regal leonine might and main. These physical conditions however differed from what was occurring on his inner mental plane. In the prison, he never behaved in any undignified manner: in ordinary circumstances, students under the influence of Saturn aspiring after occult accomplishments often assumed such rigorous discipline voluntarily. The sixth house is also the house of enormous latent natural forces which when controlled and harmonised with one's own supra-physical vehicles produce many yogic Siddhis. In the present case, the close association of Saturn with Mercury and Sun enabled Mandela during the Saturn sub-period to chew the cud of his past experiences and get out of them many valuable lessons, which ordinarily elude common people.

The troubles of Nelson Mandela did not end with the five years of imprisonment which, the political lion accepted as a part of the inevitable component of such a task of national importance that he has undertaken. Saturn grinds very finely and produces its impressions very deeply. It was therefore not very surprising that fresh accusations were made against Mandela, even while he was serving five year period of gaol. The government seized during its various raids at different establishments connected with African National Congress and the places from where Mandela conducted his political activities, some documents which implicated him in high-treason conspiracy.

The four allegations made the previous allegations, for which he was already sentenced—very minor and insignificant. These charges included sabotage, mass rebellion, use of fire arms and lethal weapons and overthrow of already established government. These charges made him a deadly criminal. He was moved in July 1963 to maximum security prison on Robben Island. He had already obtained permission to study and appear for law degree of the University of London; even in this he had to encounter many difficulties of different kinds which however were finally resolved. After a trial of about 11 months, when the court assembled on Thursday, June 11, 1964, only a few days after he wrote from the jail itself his papers for the London examination, the important verdict was delivered. Nelson Mandela was found guilty on all four counts.

On the following day instead of death which was the usual punishment for such criminal acts, Mandela was awarded only life imprisonment which closed him from the rest of the world.

Towards the end of 1964, when Ketu main period began, all his mundane activities—political as well as personal ceased except occasional meetings with his very close relatives and a very limited number of duly censored letters permitted to him. The seven years of Ketu were very distressing for him, though during the period he passed his London examination. The strong determination which he displayed during the time of Rivonia trial in 1963-64, never left him: at that time he had boldly declared:

> A time comes in the life of any nation where there remain only two choices—submit or fight. That time has now come to South Africa. We shall not submit and we have no choice but to hit back by all the means in our power in defence of our people, our future, our freedom.

This spirit of defiance never left him. During Jupiter and Saturn sub-periods during Ketu mahadasa he experienced some of the most distressing experiences of his life. During this period, his eldest son died in a road accident; he himself suffered high blood pressure, but his deep-rooted desire that his patriotism and sacrifice for his motherland could be an object lesson for the coming generation so that they could carry further the struggle did not abandon him. Ketu in its real disposition stands for idealism which was displayed throughout its main period in Mandela's life.

With the beginning of Venus main period, a new impulse of life-wave making Nelson Mandela more eminent and more hopeful with better international response to his cause was received. Venus occupies the most auspicious position: it is a yoga-karaka planet in this case owning the tenth house as well as the Moon sign. Its weakness lies in its association with Ketu, situated eights from the Moon, and being an enemy of the ascendant lord. In spite of these weaknesses, the overall impact of Venus as in the present case generally enhanced the stature of the individual. We have stated elsewhere that Taurus in the tenth house enables the individual "to produce a harmonious impact on the world around him. The difficulties arising from his proud temperament, combined with the true empathy he feels for his fellow beings, create a contradictory situation which sometimes destabilises his personal relationships. While he remains isolated, engaged in an enterprise in which he does not come into contact with other equally strong personalities, his repute is very high and his relationships with his subordinates and dependents very amiable, but the moment he encounters anyone who does not accept his supremacy—either implicitly or explicitly, he is driven into a frenzy."[1]

When Venus occupies this position in Taurus sign, it becomes "very powerful and bestows special merits on the individual. His abilities, sociability, and demeanour are so captivating that he will be a natural leader in society. Such a person is born into a particular family or society for some special purpose, and in the discharge of that task he enjoys easy success and enormous support from the people".[2]

1. *Planets in Signs and Houses,* Bepin Behari, Passage Press, Utah, pp. 201-2.
2. *Ibid.*, p. 202.

These results are evident in abundance in the case of Nelson Mandela. Probably, it is the unique case in world history that so much international honour was showered on a person extending over a period of two decades, while he was in imprisonment. During the period of his imprisonment, he was given the freedom of the cities of Rome, Glasgow, Olympia, and Aberdeen. In Grenbole (France), a place was named after him; in London's Camden Town, a street was called the Mandela Street. His 65th birthday was observed in the German Democratic Republic by the presentation of the Star of International Friendship. Honorary Doctorates of Law were conferred on him by universities as far apart as Lesotho, Stratchlyde, and New York. In 1976, there was a Release Mandela compaign.

Mandela's 60th birthday was an occasion for international celebration. On this occassion, *The New York Times* said, he would probably head a black government in South Africa. In the House of Commons, in London, a meeting honoured him and since Mandela himself was not allowed to receive the mass of greetings card from all parts of the world, they were addressed to No. 802, the location—Drandsfort, where the family gathered to pray for all political prisoners.

During Venus-Rahu sub-period, Mandela suffered from right heel trouble and consulted an orthopaedic surgeon for treatment. During the same period, the authorities relaxed conditions of hard labour: the days of hard labour were now over and he was even allowed to buy his own groceries and such articles of daily requirements. In August 1980, the Nehru award for International Understanding was bestowed on him. In March 1981, he thought of competing with Princess Anne and Jack Jones for the chancellorship of the University of London and won 7,199 votes. Near about the same time, he also suffered from enlarged prostate gland. Rahu and Venus aspect each other; the former has the great capacity of producing over-due karmic fruits, good as well as bad. Rahu is renowned for producing diseases which are often serious and elusive. (But the enlargement of prostate was detected during Venus-Saturn sub-period: Saturn specialises in old men's diseases.)

With the beginning of Jupiter sub-period, there occurred marked changes in Mandela's immediate physical conditions; while international honour continued to be showered, local authorities were becoming more lenient. In Venezuela, he was honoured with Simon Boliver award along with Juan Carlos, the King of Spain, for contributing to freedom and democracy. Several times, the world's highest body of the United Nations sponsored his cause and honored him on different occasions. He was moved to another prison at Victor Verster, nearer to Cape Town on the main land itself. He was allowed to continue with his studies for higher degrees. On May 22, 1984, Mandela was permitted to embrace his wife for the first time in 22 years though on earlier occasions he was not allowed even to participate at bereavements of family members or even at the death of his mother. In fact, the attitude of the government considerably softened during the Jupiter sub-period.

In January 1985, President Botha offered to release Mandela if he renounced violence as a means of attaining political objectives. In 1985 itself, he was honoured with Doctorate of Law from the Strathclyde University in Scotland. This happened during Saturn sub-period within the main period of Venus. Venus provided a favourable milieu, Saturn as the lord of sixth house showed him the possibilities of victory but its placement in twelfth could not produce decisive fruit. He had a meeting with South African cabinet ministers, but the final day of deliverance was yet far away.

During Venus-Mercury sub-period, Mandela succeeded in obtaining his advance degree in law for which he was permitted to study in 1982 while at Pollsmoor prison in a white suburb of native Cape Town. It was only on February 11, 1990, still during Mercury sub-period, that Nelson Mandela was released from prison after 27 years and addressed a rally of more than 50,000 people. On March 2, 1990 he was named Deputy President of the African National Congress. The Mercury sub-period also produced another significant result. Mercury has a special conciliatory role: it does not like terrorism, guerilla warfare or any kind of militancy. It is basically a planet of understanding and adjustment. In association with Sun, its negotiating and diplomatic skill is greatly heightened. Quite in consonance with its nature, on August 6, 1990 Nelson Mandela who was virtually the head of African National Congress due to ill-health and old age of President Oliver Tambo, declared the suspension of armed struggle against the White Government. At that time Mandela was astrologically in a very strong position to do so. Mars was well dignified in transit occupying the ninth house having its own sign Aries, while Saturn in transit occupied Sagittarius aspected by the natal Jupiter and itself was auspiciously placed third from the Moon sign and there from aspected the natal Mars. These conditions indicated that Mandela was not in a weak position but he was not inclined to assert his military strength. This announcement was a good gesture.

Ketu always brought glorification to Mandela, and true to its nature during its sub-period in Venus main, it once more brought some elevation to Mandela. He became the President of the African National Congress on July 7, 1991. It was a prestigious post with respectable status but power over the people and responsibilities were still awaited. Only with the beginning of Sun main period, Nelson Mandela began to possess greater and greater administrative control and centralisation of political power. He arrived at the helm of national affairs with much international goodwill during Sun-Rahu period on May 9, 1994, when he was elected the first Black President of South Africa and the ruling President F.W. de Klerk as his Deputy. But before coming to this position, Mandela had to pass through a series of steps: Sun does not bring suddenness of change, it unveils the inner grandeur gradually till the full glory begins to shine. So it was almost after its half way through that Mandela reached at this place.

The advent of Sun's main period began to unfold a radically different aspect of Mandela's personality. A vargottam planet invariably produces unexpectedly very auspicious results. In Mandela's horoscope, Sun occupies twelfth house along with the rulers of sixth and second house, which are related with the *Mysterious Depth.* The twelfth is the house of dissolution connected with "awakening from sleep, Liberation, renouncing one's couch and entry into heaven". The second house is related with creativity, sensitivity, living power, wealth, diamonds, and death"; the sixth house represents the Churning of the Ocean, the process which involves joint efforts of the Devas and the demons for obtaining the gems hidden in the infinite ocean and the ultimate drink of immortality, the nectar. The sixth house with which Saturn in the present horoscope is linked represents *inter alia,* "fighting in combat, obstacles, enemy's satisfaction, and Great Illusion." The Sun itself is a royal planet, concerned with the highest in man, but Mercury is a messenger who brings to earth the messages from gods and as the planet connected with *vishuddhi chakra* transmits the essential experiences of worldly events to one's highest nature, and Saturn is the planet which concretises the Divine Will in physical nature and finally dissolves the same back to its essential nature; it is also related with *Muladhara chakra,* which if properly aroused might enable the latent Kundalini or the serpent fire active in one's life. All the three planets are placed in the Moon's sign which is the planet of pure intelligence.

During the period of Sun's rulership, Nelson Mandela is certain to receive enormous power from the unknown sources enabling him to express some extremely useful results, but in the process he has to go through the inevitable process of the churning of the ocean. He certainly obtained the nectar of immortality, *Amrita,* in the form of liberation for the South Africa, which had been under bondage for approximately half a millenium. But the struggle was not an easy one. It involved much hard efforts at different levels and much personal sacrifice. A new dimension of Mandela's personality certainly began to unfold with the beginning of Sun's main period from the early months of 1992. So far he had been stirring up as his middle name Rolihlahla indicated troubles, creating problems for his guardians, straining the life of his wife and children as a result of his political preoccupations, and rebelling against established rule of foreign white settlers whom the common people had almost accepted as irremovable destiny, which created storm in the national life of South Africa. In consequence of these irrepressible urges, Mandela accepted solitary imprisonment with hard labour, denied himself the pleasures of married companionship and comforts of family life and tribal chieftainship, and bore complacently the bereavement of his mother's death without even the permission of attending the funeral.

In spite of these hardships and the inner turmoil undergoing in his inner self, the magnanimity of his disposition can be gauged by his enunciation of the role of his oppressor in the independent South Africa or by his preoccupation, while in jail helping fellow prisoners tackle all sorts of legal issues and emotional problems. He was so concerned with the fact that prisoner's children were only allowed to see their parents through a glass window (How can a child grow up without ever touching his father?'' he would say) that he campaigned to get the rule changed and succeeded in his efforts. In 1985, he had stated, even while he was struggling to wrest power from the white rulers, that "unlike white people anywhere else in Africa, whites in South Africa belong here - this is their home. We want them to live here with us and to share power with us". This attitude remained the same even after his release from a little less than three decades of jail-life: he was no more stirring up troubles.

There was a qualitative change in his disposition with the beginning of Sun's major period. He was more assured, more radiant with power and benevolence, more constructive and reconciliatory. When he was released from the jail, and addressed a rally of 50,000 Africans on February 11, 1990, he was still concerned with securing independence for South Africa, but once the all white referendum votes were cast and political reform was overwhelmingly approved in March 1992, the qualities of solar impulses began to manifest and Mandela began to show his statesmanship and administrative qualities. Now the end of the white rule was decided: it was a matter of overcoming the transitional impediments. The far-sightedness of F.W. de Klerk in mobilising public opinion among the white settlers for sharing power democratically paved the way for a transformation in the life of Mandela from Rolihlahla—'stirring up troubles' to that of 'search of reconciliation and accommodation'.

The Sun being the soul of the universe, it has the potential to absorb everything in it; every thing manifest in the universe moves and lives in the solar aura and finally merges in it. In expressing the qualities of Sun, one does not become divisive, one becomes unificatory. This is what happened to Mandela now. Together with F.W. de Klerk, he began to forge unity among the diverse groups so that a smooth transition could emerge. The attention of the comity of nations was drawn to the dramatic changes emerging in South Africa: and they were requested in September 1993 to lift the various sanctions imposed on the Pretoria government. The response of the international community was so appreciative that the 1993 Nobel Peace Prize was awarded jointly to F.W. de Klerk and Nelson Mandela. It happened in October 1993 when Mandela was undergoing the period of Sun-Rahu sub-period.

The relationship between Sun and Rahu, generally trying had been very extraordinary in the case of Mandela. Rahu in Scorpio is debilitated in the horoscope of Nelson Mandela, but it is placed fifth from the sign occupied by Sun whose main period Mandela was having. It directly aspected the tenth house and *swagrihi* Venus reciprocated the aspect. The lord of the sign occupied by Rahu is a yoga-karaka in this horoscope having the lordship of ninth, a trine house, and fourth, a cardinal house, and it occupies a sign, whose lord is associated with the ascendant lord the Sun, whose main period was running. Rahu-Ketu axis in every horoscope provides the fulcrum around which all the major events of one's life revolve, and in the present case there is also Kala Sarpa Yoga, which makes Rahu important. If Rahu were exalted with such benefic combinations, it would have produced much spiritual (and occult) impulses, but in the present case it had to be restricted to mundane activities by making the world's most prestigious award possible for Nelson Mandela.

There were many problems to tackle before the actual transfer of power. There were many who believed that the Black majority rule in South Africa would usher an anarchy and mayhem, with Blacks illegally seizing white's property. There were dissensions even among the Black Africans. The King Goodwill Zwelithini, the slow-spoken hereditary monarch to South Africa's nine million Zulus thrived under tribal passion of Zulu nationalism; he had to be pacified, reconciled and merged into the national mainstream for a peaceful transition. Zulu nationalism as a separate identity fostered by Inkatha Freedom party and its chief Mongosuthu Buthelezi depended to a great extent on the support of King Goodwill Zwelithini. The Inkatha was a serious rival of African National Congress and without their cooperation, Mandela could not lead a united nation. If this was not achieved, there could be a civil war. It needed special diplomacy (Mercury) of Nelson Mandela to overcome this hurdle. He spent much time trying to woo King Goodwill for he was Inkatha's biggest political asset, the key to unlocking the support of millions of traditional Zulus.

Nelson Mandela tried to strike separate peace with the King as well as forge closer alliance with chief Buthelezi. The chief had persisted with boycott in the general election and had threatened with a civil war, which Nelson Mandela and everyone else feared. The breakthrough came along with the efforts of President F.W. de Klerk and Nelson Mandela: special status was recognized for the Zulu King and strong regional power in the Zulu heartland of Kwazulu-Natal, home to one-quarter of South Africa's population. It was a remarkable diplomatic victory of Mandela. Buthelezi announced participation in the national and provincial elections, and King Goodwill Zwelithini called on his subjects to renounce violence and vote. Inkatha was a major stumbling block, but there were other political parties and groups which had to be welded together for an effective governance of the country.

The National Party founded in 1914 which captured power in 1948 was primarily a party of the white people advocating racial separation. The three sections of South African population, such as the 'Pure Black', 'the colored race' and the 'white population', had different approaches to the political governance, and they thrived on mutual distrust and suspicion. Winnie Mandela, the estranged wife of Nelson Mandela told a group of coloured supporters of her in 1991 that "you are called coloured because not long after the Europeans landed here in 1652, these despicable people raped our grandmothers". Such comments reveal the intensity of hatred on which the different groups subsisted in the country. The National Party accentuated this kind of difference: during their election compaign, their party agents spread rumours that blacks would occupy the homes of the white people after election, and distributed a comic book claiming that an African National Congress slogan was "Kill the Farmers! Kill the Coloureds!" The Communist Party of South Africa was allied with African National Congress with many of its members filling many top positions in the latter, but its ideological radicalism alienating itself from the bulk of population and several other political parties. Pan African Congress was founded in 1959 when an African faction left the African National Congress and advocated radical economic reforms including redistribution of land which were likely to produce explosive situation in a newly formed State. The Conservative Party founded in 1982 was similar to the National Party which did not favour racial amalgamation; they intended boycotting the forthcoming election. The Conservative Party strongly believed in apartheid. The Freedom Front was another group of army officers formed in 1993—specially meant for the white settlers and were bitterly opposed to transition. The Liberal Democratic Party founded in 1989 having historical links with the Progressive Federal Party aimed at working for a homogenous unity with different groups and evolving a national joyous living. The Indian community which had participated in the economic prosperity of the country as well as political awakening were the distrusted lot whom neither the Africans accepted as friends nor the white settlers recognised as equal.

Thus Nelson Mandela and F.W. de Klerk both faced the stupendous task of welding together the Zulu nationalism, *Afrikaner Volkstaat* or the homeland for the white people, the Black Africans, the coloureds or the mixed race and the Indians so as to have a smooth passage. It was at this stage that special skill in dealing with human individuals which comes with coolness of mind and diplomatic handling of the situation, could lead to success and Mandela was amply favoured by Moon and Mercury so as to emerge successful in the mission. Moreover, he had the auspicious influence of Jupiter sub-period from the beginning of 1994 which made the astrologers optimistic. On January 2, 1994, a 26-party negotiation team set April 27, 1994 as the election date. The task ahead now was of organisational expertise.

One of the outstanding features of Jupiter is its great organisational ability: it produces enormous *yajnas* with millions of people participating in it. It provides the impulse for religious rituals. The essential quality of these impulses is that they bring forth the sociability of the participants, orderliness in the common observances and raising the participants to a higher level of (spiritual) consciousness. With such support provided to Sun, it produced *Vasi Yoga* which is formed by planets other than Moon occupying the twelfth house from Sun which resulted in making the individual happy, prosperous, liberal and favourite of the ruling classes—Jupiter provided the most favorable *milieu* for electoral success. Nelson Mandela was faced with the task of organising fair and peaceful election. Recent demographic surveys suggested that there were 22.5 million eligible voters in the 41 million population, but there was no electoral rolls. It was also expected that every South African who was 18 years old or above could vote *anywhere* in the country for whom about 10,000 polling booths were arranged. The voters had to show their identification documents, vote not for any individual but for the parties contesting election, and have the indelible ink on the finger at the polling booths. As the black Africans had never voted before in any democratic election, they had to be taught and instructed in the process. A massive voter education programme was undertaken for the four months.

It was a much publicised election and around 1,200 journalists, television crews and photographers witnessed Nelson Mandela casting his vote in the Zulu heartland in the dusty township of Inanda, north of Durban (Natal), not very far from the Phoenix settlement of Mahatma Gandhi which was razed to the ground by hooligans in August 1985, though Nelson Mandela was usually a resident of Transval near Johannesburg. During the voting, tension prevailed in the country and those who were opposed to the peaceful transition did create trouble.

The election process was marred by numerous bomb blasts allegedly planted by white right-wingers and aimed at distrupting the election. In a 24-hour period, ten bombs blasted off in the province of Transval, where most right-wingers were based, and they resulted in loss of lives, injuries and substantial damage to the property. A bomb blasted the Jan Smuts international airport at Johannesburg minutes after Mandela cast his vote. The blast injured 18 people, two seriously. The blast was so powerful that it was felt about 30 kilometers away. Yet the fears that apathy and security problems would keep the voters away from the polls proved groundless.

As a result of the election, Mandela's party got 62.65 per cent of votes giving it 252 seats, 15 short of a two-third majority. The National Party of F.W. de Klerk finished second with 20.39 per cent votes entitling it 82 seats. Inkatha Freedom Party representing Zulu nationalism won 20.39 per cent votes securing for it 43 seats. Finishing fourth in the overall vote with 2.17 per cent and nine seats in parliament was the pro-apartheid Freedom Front, and the fifth was the White Liberal Democratic Party with 1.7 percent votes and seven seats. Two other parties won seven seats. This ensured Mandela a majority of seats in the parliament, but according to the interim constitution it could neither have unrestricted absolute power in the forthcoming Constituent Assembly, nor could it give him absolute freedom to form the government. He had to keep representatives from other parties in proportion to their votes received in the political governance of the country.

In May 1994, Sun-Jupiter sub-period, with Jupiter in Punarvasu asterism, made Mandela almost identified with the new birth of a new nation.

With *Punarvasu,* the radiation of the Sun changes the divine warmth condensed to give wetness under the previous asterism into water vapours or physical life-particles. At this stage, the creative agents are imparted fresh impetus for the performance of their arduous work primarily on a mental level. The asterism provides the impulse under which abstract ideas are concretised. It provides a resting place for the downward flow of divine energy with a view to enabling it to function with increased energy.[1]

It was under this impulse that Nelson Mandela brought to fruition the results of his hard work for more than four decades. On May 3, 1994 to celebrate Nelson Mandela's victory, millions of South African Blacks chanting "Free at last, free at last" exploded into jubilation. Staging their biggest party to victory, they poured onto streets in towns and cities across the nation to toast the win by Mandela, South Africa's most famous prisoner who was to take over power next week as its first Black President.

In Soweto, Johannesburg's teeming township and cradle of Black resistance to apartheid, hundreds of thousands flocked to Mandela's old house there. People of all ages thronged the house, some coming on foot, some on bicycles and others in cars. Cars blocked roads and honked their horns in an unprecendented carnival atmosphere (true to the spirit of Jupiterian rejoicing). World leaders hailed South Africans for exorcising the demons of racial supremacy in an election that ended apartheid and gave the country its first Black President, Nelson Rolihlahla Mandela. He was elected as such on May 9, 1994.

But soon the constructive, materialising influence took sway; the jubilation had to be only a passing phase. The nation needs reconstruction: that which was destroyed over centuries had to be rebuilt. This was the task ahead of Nelson Mandela during his Sun-Saturn sub-period. Unemployment among the blacks which stood at 40 per cent was an acute problem staring at the new government. The election manifesto of the African National Congress promised to provide work to 2.5 million over the next ten years, a million houses within five years, electrification of 2.5 million rural and urban houses and a programme that would create jobs by focussing on the provisions of water, health clinics,

1. *Myths and Symbols of Vedic Astrology,* Bepin Behari, Passage Press, Utah, USA pp. 191-3

electricity and roads. These constructive programmes required much of Mandela's energy and administrative skill.

But, in all these moments of jubilation and concern for the future betterment and welfare of the society, Mandela did not lose his sensitivity and magnanimity. The leonine people are graceful in their behaviour, in defeat as well as in victory. It was amply evident at the very beginning of Mandela's governance of the country. The victory of the Black majority and the formation of Mandela's government made many white people nervous and they began thinking of migrating to other white settlements. But Nelson Mandela soon assured them and announced:

> Defenders of apartheid would be pardoned for crimes. Anxious ethnic minorities would retain their jobs and cultures. Big business would play an influential role in shaping economic policy. The departing President Mr. Frederick W. de Klerk, and other holdovers from the white government would be trusted partners in the cabinet.
>
> From the racist outlaws of the Afrikaner Resistance Movement, whose members have been accused by the police in spate of pre-election bombings aimed at sabotaging the transition, would not be banned but invited to the bargaining table.
>
> There could be no dismantling of monuments or symbols cherished by whites, no renaming of streets and cities, without "very intense, patient, serious discussions".

I the Sun main period has made Nelson Mandela unfold his life's mission, but he has yet to go very far. The Sun is the lord of his ascendant; its rulership period will be momentous in his career. The Sun however is placed in the twelfth position from its own sign: it is also placed in the twelfth house of the chart. Saturn as lord of the sixth house afflicts it in an important manner. The Sun however is vargottam and in navamsa chart occupies the tenth house. The effect of Sun will therefore be the effective implementation of his plans and programmes but it could not be assumed to be a smooth sailing. There would be plenty of difficulties and ordeals. Nelson Mandela would gradually realise restrictions of the real world in which one has to function.

During the sub-periods of Ketu and Venus, Mandela would experience fruits of some of his hard efforts and would rejoice the success of his achievements. The Moon period, commencing in the middle of 1997 would provide much relief to his physical body and Mandela would have to prepare himself for the journey's end. Moon is very closely and in many different ways related with Venus which is the lord of his tenth house. During the Moon main period, great monuments will be erected for him; eulogising him to greater heights!

13

KAPILDEV NIKHANJA

Ketu	Mars		
	6th January 1959 (Rasi)		
Venus			
Sun Saturn Mercury	Asc. Moon Jupiter		Rahu

Asc. Ketu Venus	*(Amsa)*		Jupiter
			Rahu
	Mercury Mars	Sun	Moon Saturn

Kapildev, a legend of his life-time and one of the topmost Indian test cricket all-rounder, who surpassed the earlier record of wicket taking by Sir Richard Hadlee of Auckland, New Zealand is popularly known as *Haryana Hurricane.* On his taking 432 wickets—a new world record, the President Dr. Shankar Dayal Sharma wished him many more laurels while Prime Minister P.V. Narasimha Rao stated that the country was proud of his feat. Some lawyers even sent a memorandum to the President and the Prime Minister, requesting them to honor Kapildev with *Bharat Ratna,* the highest civilian award in India. By November 2, 1994, Kapildev had played 131 Test matches, taken 434 wickets, made 5,248 runs, 8 centuries, twenty-seven 50's and 23 times taken five wickets in an Inning, which placed him on the eve of his retirement from first class international matches on the top of the cricket world.

Yet, Kapildev was never considered a steady player. Once when India was already on the mat for 17 for 5, Kapildev rescinded India from defeat with an amazing knock of 175 not out and held the World Cup aloft at Lords, England, after defeating West Indies by 43 runs. On another occasion, he smashed Eddie Hemmings record of four sixes in a row and thus equalled the world record of scoring maximum runs of 24 runs in a six-ball over in test cricket. Often Kapildev had been a miserable failure and the Cricket Board had to think differently on him. He was made Indian skipper twice, but his performances as captain had not been so bright. Once Mankand very correctly described him as "a perfomer, not as a thinker".

It is also observed that Kapil is known to take challenges with gusto, probably on ordinary occasions his inner self remains dormant! With the advent of 1980s, Kapil's batting which was based more on instinct than training was ordinarily relegated as tail-ender, received a serious provocative remark by Sunil Gavaskar who said that Kapil would never make even one 50 in test cricket. This goaded Kapil so much that he soon became even a successful player adding runs to his cricket; his final tally of 5,248 runs is by itself a record.

There are two traits in the character of Kapildev which make him very special. He has very sensitive by emotional nature. Any remark, any action, or any good turn to him is not easily wiped out of his memory. The loss of his first-time captaincy supposedly caused by manoeuvres of Sunil Gavaskar was never excused by Kapildev. The various actions of the Cricket Control Board deeply affected his psyche that even after his attainment of supreme position in several directions, he never exonerated the members of the Board for their supposed conscientious discharge of responsibilities. Kapildev keeps the feeling of hurt for ever.

Kapildev comes from a region known for hard work, great vigour and closed family unit. Yet, his concentration or his self-centredness is extra-ordinary. He is not selfish, but self-centered. He is loving, benevolent, friendly, considerate and even generous, but in all these responses to social interactions he is never oblivious of his own interests, his own conveniences and his own pleasures. It is usually said that "his self admitted desire for material pleasures makes him out as a true post-nationalist 'puppie'. First class air travel, an amazing range of watches and shoes, a BMW and Mercedes and two Dobermans are all symbols of upward mobility." His urge for money earning is so insatiable that he is already established as an important businessman with range of undertakings from hotels to exports; he is proficient in promotional media appearances. Such activities have earned him so much money that he is probably Indian cricket's first millionaire. And true to this new taste and inflow of riches along with exposure to international culture, the Haryana Hurricane has lost touch with indigenous *lassi* and has imbibed the culture of liquor and wine.

Such a personality who lost his father at the age of 16 years, three years before he made his first test debut at Faisalabad glided in international cricketing almost fortuitously. In 1976, when selection was being made for the state under–19 side for the national championship, Kapildev was not included in it, but two years later at the insistence of Bishen Bedi, then an influential voice in Indian cricket—he was included among the players for the Pakistan tour which completely changed his career. To a student of astrology, the life-story of his emergence, subsequent glorification and final retirement—all seem to be enshrined in the stars.

Kapildev was born on 6th January 1959 in Chandigarh in a Jat family, which had been very traditional. Even now his mother Mrs. Lajwanti Nikhanja is so much religious minded that on hearing the latest achievement of Kapil, she said, "I am grateful to the

Almighty for bestowing His blessings on my son to enable him to bring name and fame to the country and inscribe his name in the history of world cricket in letters of gold"; even Kapil on making his world record attributed the credit to his parents. Such a relationship between the mother and the son is clearly reflected in the disposition of Moon.

Kapil was born early in the morning, a little before the sunrise: Moon as a lord of the ninth house was placed in ascendant along with the lord of the second and fifth houses, Jupiter, while Sun along with Saturn occupied the second house occupied by Sagittarius. The proximity of Sun to Moon weakens the power of Moon and so is the case of it even due to its debilitation. The quality of Moon in the present case is very mundane, but it does not lessen the attachment between the mother and the son.

As far as Kapildev is concerned, the ascendant has become very significant. The aspect of Mars greatly energises those planets situated in the ascendant and the ascendant itself acquires much strength. Physical strength necessary for a sportsman arises from Martian influence, and in this regard Scorpio as ascendant is preferable to Aries. Physically, a Scorpio ascendant is usually beautiful and attractive with rounded legs and thighs. Vindictive by nature and sensitive to criticism, he can be very alert and quarrelsome. Ordinarily, he is lucky in marriage. He is ignorant of his own long-term interests: immediate gratification is more important to him than permanent benefit. Moon in Scorpio as ascendant bestows honour from the state and cooperation from his colleagues, but the trial of his life never ends. Greatest help for Scorpio ascendants comes from Jupiter, Mars and Moon. It is also found that close association of Moon and Sun gives good results. Tranquillity of mind as indicated by a good and benefic Moon along with controlled mind shown by a powerful Sun often gives the best results for Scorpio ascendants. These general results of Scorpio ascendants in the case of Kapildev are well applicable to him specially, because the combination of Jupiter and Moon in ascendant produces powerful *Gaja-Kesari Yoga* leading to much protection from untoward consequences, and influx of affluent conditions. This combination also leads to fame and auspicious rewards. Furthermore, the aspect of ascendant lord Mars to the ascendant and to planets situated in the same greatly adds to them physical strength and material prosperity.

The most important factor which made Kapildev a great sportsman is the occupation of ascendant lord Mars in its own sign Aries occupying the sixth house. Mars in this position makes the individual very enterprising. Engaged in sports, the individual draws upon immense inner strength and often externalises them in such a way that people feel that he is putting his heart into his play. The sudden influx of tremendous force he puts in his balls while bowling at fast speed or in his batting, when he secures big runs or large number of 4s or 6s several times in the same over, comes from his inner source represented by the sixth house. The aspect of Mars on ninth house, the sign owned by Moon which occupies the ascendant and on the ascendant itself are all plus points for making Kapildev a successful, renowned and extra-ordinary scorer of runs as well as wickets: once his psyche is aroused, there could be no lack of strength for scoring victory. Only when the challenge was lukewarm, or when Kapil is playing the game in a routine manner that his performance could be average or even less than average, not otherwise.

Kapildev is fabulously rich for a sportsman. His horoscope portends the inflow of much wealth. The most important combinations for wealth are formed by relationships between the ninth, tenth, and eleventh houses and ascendant and second house. Even one relationship of this kind is sufficient to make a person wealthy. In the case of Kapildev, the lord of ninth house is in ascendant, while the lords of tenth and eleventh houses are in the second house. The lord of second in the ascendant aspected by the lord of it also increases affluence of the person. The association of Moon and Jupiter in ascendant is a great positive factor for wealth. The second house which is primarily related with one's financial assets is well fortified and sufficiently strengthened by benefics on its both sides: Jupiter and Moon on its twelfth and Venus on second. It is significant that these planets will have their sway over the cricketer almost for four decades following his retirement from active sports career. Freedom from financial worry is therefore assured for him for his entire life.

A very special combination is present in the birth chart which is liable to give misleading impression. Saturn and Sun, both of which are inimical to each other are placed in the second house. One is superficially likely to conclude that there may be problems regarding his wealth. On the physical plane, these planets will certainly be adverse for father because of affliction of Sun; his speech cannot be diplomatic because of the special disposition of Mercury. He will be deeply entrenched in materialism and much concerned about money matters because of Saturn, the lord of the fourth house situated in the second house. But transcending these considerations, the combination of Sun and Saturn in this horoscope has another significance. Saturn is the lord of fourth house. The fourth house represents the *Hiranyagarbha,* the *bythos,* in which all possibilities in the seed form are stored: it is the storehouse of all past karmic forces, bio-psychological nature, general prosperity, etc. Saturn as a ruler of this house will enable the individual to take selective seeds out of it.

The auspicious nature of malefic planets owning cardinal houses specially when they are not situated in cardinal houses has much more deeper implications than ordinarily realized. The present is an example of such cases, where Saturn has the potential of concretising the past karmic forces and bringing them to fruition. This proclivity of Saturn is further accentuated by its association with Sun. The tenth house represents the future archetype towards which the ego is constantly pushing and pulling the personality during the course of every life. It is known as the house of the father, glory, royal patronage, profession and karma of the present incarnation. What is however important is its esoteric implication. From this standpoint, the tenth house is the externalising of the fourth house, which is the container of that primeval seed that blossoms forth during the course of one's various incarnations. The fourth and tenth houses in a horoscope are innately connected with the Moon and the Sun respectively—the Moon being the reflection of the Sun which for each individual had the similar reflection of the divine on earth. In that sense, the Sun represents the Divine Will for the individual. The tenth house connected with the Sun draws the individual towards his future, whereas the Moon reveals the past. Success in life is determined on the basis of the tenth house. The avenues through which past forces lead the individual toward the future are presented here. This externalisation process occurs when the individual involves himself in mundane activities that bring him into contact with the world at large. For most people, it comes through their profession. The union between the two, the fourth and the tenth houses signifies the past forces contributing significantly towards the future archetype willed for the individual.

Saturn is known for concretisation, materialisation, and it dissolves all forms and activities almost to super-physical level. That is why when Saturn dissolves all worldly attainments and physical affections, the individual is completely broken, he feels utterly in despair and weeps and laments his heart out, but in all these expressions there is an under current of understanding that human efforts and human will against destiny, by whatever name it is known are totally powerless. The past potentialities and karmas can be dissolved only when they are externalized and transmuted into divine will. In pure mundane terms, it implies the urge to bring forth inner impulses in some extra-ordinary manner. The Sun, the lord of tenth house in the present case, inspired Kapildev to attain excellence, not to be contented with the average; he wanted to be at the top of the cricket-world. Both planets were not only united together, they were put in a fiery sign Sagittarius owned by Jupiter which is associated with Moon in ascendant. The inspiration to attain the topmost position was supported by fire, the divine energy (Sun and Mars) and Jupiter's association with Moon made Kapil tremendously attached with his urge towards perfection. Jupiter's placement in ascendant also enabled him to put his whole personality (ascendant) in making whole-hearted efforts for making his fire of inspiration active, positive. The second house also represents creative potential as well as material possessions. Saturn and Sun together in that house as lords of fourth and tenth houses enabled Kapildev to apply himself towards the inspired direction and from these efforts also to receive much material returns.

The most important question in the life of Kapildev arises with regard to his cricket career. The pattern of planetary placements gives a clue to it. The Rahu-Ketu axis in the present case lies between eleventh and fifth houses. Rahu is in Virgo, the sign owned by Mercury, while Ketu occupies fifth house with Pisces owned by Jupiter. In the life of Kapildev, Mercury and Jupiter will evidently play special role. Furthermore, Rahu being in the eleventh house, many of the problems in life would arise from his socialization, social interactions, and the way he acquires money. Ketu being in Jupiter's house and with Jupiter's aspect on it (from a friendly house), it is through his creative activities that he will learn his lessons of life. These are the general principles which will determine the effects of planetary impulses, but this Rahu-Ketu axis divides the planets in two groups, on one side there are six planets namely Jupiter, Moon, Mercury, Saturn, Sun and Venus, while Mars falls alone on the other side. Whenever the Rahu-Ketu axis isolates a single planet in this way, the significance of this planet greatly increases in the life of the person concerned.* As such, Mars assumes a karmic role in the life of Kapildev.

Mars occupies its own sign in the natal chart and does it so even in navamsa chart, but in the former it occupies Aries while in the latter it occupies Scorpio, his ascendant sign. In the sixth house, Mars externalizes inner potentials in the man. Kapildev is not an intellectual. His Mercury is (almost) on the borderline of two signs, thus greatly nullifying its basic trait under which one becomes intellectual and his mind principle is activated. It is for this reason that Kapil is said to be a performer, neither a thinker nor a strategist. Sun which gives insight into the inner principles activating any action is beseized with restrictive Saturn, so the intuitive understanding which is intelligence going beyond the realm of mind is also greatly fettered in the case of Kapildev.

But Mars, which is purely a physical plane impulse for taking out the inner energy (or anything contained inside such as child in the womb, blood in the veins, and past deeds, meritorious or otherwise, lying inside the karmic store, *Prarabdha*), in the sixth house will become fruitful in creating its impact. Mars is placed fifth from the central planets namely, Saturn, Sun and Mercury forming the nucleus for his physical activities, thus the material life of Kapil will find its expression through Mars.

Mars inspires sportsmen and Kapil has not restricted his sportsmanship only to cricket. He plays golf, squash, tennis and even soccer though he synthesizes all his sports in a way that his efficiency in cricket is increased. It is again his sportsmanship, expressed by Mars (and Saturn) that his physical ailments arise. The various surgical operations he had to undergo arose due to his sportsmanship. The sixth house also represents diseases and illness and Mars naturally externalises them. From the sixth house, one also predicts litigations and legal conflicts, and Kapildev's legal fights have so far been primarily related to his cricketing. Evidently, Mars guides his karmic activities.

---

* See the biography of J. Krishnamurti (*Supra*, p. 217).

Kapildev was born in the early hours of 6th January 1959 at about 5.30 A.M. at Chandigarh with a balance of approximately 11 years 7 months of Saturn main period. It ended in August 1970 and the main planetary period of Mercury began and along with it began his cricket career. He began his training at the age of 15 years, but in his early days of practice he was not considered very bright. Mercury-Venus sub-period extending from the end of 1973 to the end of October 1976 was not a good period for Kapil: his father died in 1975. In 1976, though Haryana state fans acknowledged him as a bright cricketer in the making, yet when a team under-19 years was being finalised for the national championship, he was left out. Venus rules over the twelfth and seventh houses which are death-inflicting houses.

Only in 1978, during Mercury-Moon sub-period, Kapil was taken on Pakistan tour mainly as a result of the efforts made by Bishen Bedi who at that time was an influential person with Indian Cricket Board. Kapil's performance on his first tour was not spectacular except showing flashes of aggression in batting. It was reported that Kapil "forced his first Test victim, Sadiq Mohammed, to call for a helmet seeing the young newcomer firing away on all cylinders on his Test debut in 1978 at Faisalabad; Kapil was never a terror in terms of pace". But his skipper opined that "Kapil bowled his heart out on that tour". During the same period, Gavaskar is reported to have made some uncomplimentary remarks by stating that Arif Iqbal's Pakistani team would make a pulp of them, by which Kapil's natural talents were aroused to meet the challenge. Kapil became a terror for the visiting Pakistanis. Zaheer Abbas, who came with an enviable reputation to India was reduced to a nervous wreck midway through the tour due to a well thought out plan by the captain and Kapil, the bowler. Having realised the leg-side weakness of Abbas, Kapil consciously changed his line for Pakistan's master batsman which paid him good dividends. It established Kapil as an ace bowler of the Indian side.

During Mercury-Mars sub-period between 1978 and 1980, Kapil came to be recognized as an extraordinary cricketer. Mars requires a challenge and provocation for showing its best. On 31st January 1980, during a cricket career of 1 year 105 days, Kapil captured his 100 wickets by dismissing Pakistan's Tasleem Arif, who according to Gavaskar was expected to make a pulp of Indian players. Two days later on February 2, 1980, Kapil became the youngest player to achieve "the double", 100 wickets and 1,000 runs in a record time of 1 year and 107 days of cricket career at the age of 21 years and 25 days. It was during this period that Gavaskar had stated that Kapil would never make even one 50 in a Test cricket.

Kapil achieved greater heights during Mercury-Jupiter sub-period. It was during this period that he was made to captain the Indian cricket team. He went to the toughest team of the Caribbeans as the captain and the West Indies under Clive Lloyd is said to have made a "mincemeat of Kapil's Indians". This disastrous tour however challenged Kapil's spirit so much that he determined to defeat the West Indies team sooner. For the first time since the limited overs version of the game began, India beat the West Indies at Lords, which laid the foundation for the golden summer in 1983 in England.

It was still the planetary period of Mercury-Jupiter sub-period, when Kapil's greatest moment of cricket career came at which India won the Prudential World Cup in 1983, beating the hot favourites West Indians at Lords in England. Kapil had single-handedly inspired the Indian team, which entered the tournament as non-starter to the pinnacle of one-day cricket's top-most tournament. In another match against Zimbabwe in the World Cup 1983, when India was literally on the mat with 17 runs for 5 wickets, he scored 175 runs and remained not out. So the entire nation went berserk a few days later when the Indian team under his captaincy lifted the World Cup. His extremely well-judged catch to send Viv Richards back to the pavilion is even today a part of every cricket fan's happy memory. The picture of Kapil sprinting away to catch Viv Richards and to steal the triumph became a part of cricketing folkore. But soon the aura around him began to fade.

During Mercury-Saturn sub-period, he was even dropped from Calcutta test. As usual with Saturn, it made Kapil taste the frustration, and he became aware that achievements and efficiency are not always the basis for public recognition and grant of prestigious position. Having given the taste, Mercury-Saturn sub-period was strong enough to make him the captain again in March 1985 and during the same period, he became the youngest cricketer ever to achieve the distinction of scoring 3,000 runs and taking 300 wickets. In 1987, he again lost the captaincy for ever. With the beginning of Ketu main period in 1987, the unfoldment of cricketing career reached its maturity and Kapil began to receive bouquets and brickbats equally.

Ketu stands fifth from the ascendant receiving full aspect of Jupiter. Ketu brings honour provided the supporting planets exercise their influence, otherwise it makes the individual introspective. One way to do so is to make him much criticised, involve him in unnecessary scandal, litigation and such mentally depressive situations. Immediately after the beginning of Ketu, the board began to question Kapil's ability for captaincy. The public began to feel that he was unsteady and his ability to score was declining. During Ketu-Sun sub-period, such questions began to be raised and during Ketu-Moon sub-period, it became serious. Only during Ketu-Mars sub-period, he once again showed his remarkable ability in batting and bowling both. He smashed Eddie Hemming's record for four sixes in a row to help India avoid a follow on at Lords in 1990. He equalled by this achievement the world record of scoring maximum 24 runs in a six-bowl-over in Test cricket.

During Ketu-Jupiter sub-period, he took his tally of wickets to 400 when he dismissed Mark Taylor at Perth. He became the only all-rounder to have 400 wickets and 4,000 runs in his tally.

But soon during Ketu-Saturn sub-period, hints were dropped that he should retire. But his goal was set at achieving the highest wicket-taker position. He wanted to achieve this position before retirement, while the Indian Cricket Board was becoming increasingly critical of his performance. His past performances however made the Board reluctant to take any adverse decision. It was only during Ketu-Mercury sub-period, that he achieved his target: on February 8, 1994, at the Sardar Patel Gujarat Stadium he dismissed Sri Lanka's Hashan Tillekaratna and claimed his 432 wicket, one more than the record established by Sir Richard Hadlee, who held it for about five years. The whole nation celebrated the jubilation. Kapil's mother said, Kapil's Tapasya paid off; Prime Minister Narasimha Rao acclaimed him as his hero too. President Dr. Shankar Dayal Sharma felicitated him, and the whole country went jubilant.

Under the fiery enthusiasm, the disillusionment that arises from Ketu's impulses was rapidly approaching. Within a month of his world record, the talk of his retirement became louder. But Kapil wanted to continue for some time. Within a month, in March 1994, he played his last Test match in Hamilton, New Zealand where he claimed Hartland as his 433 Test victim. But in April 1994, he was dropped from the team which went to Sharjah. There was much resentment against this decision and the Board argued that Kapildev himself wanted to rest. The real story seemed something else. In October 1994, when Kapildev had finished his Ketu mahadasa, and was in the early years of Venus main period, West Indies players came to India and One-Day International match was played at Faridabad in Kapil's own home state. Venus was not Mars, it was neither Mercury nor Ketu: Venus as the lord of death-inflicting houses, *Marakasthan,* placed in third house did not support Kapil. He was booed by his fans. Shortly afterwards on November 2, 1994, he announced his retirement from first class cricket matches and took up his posting with Doordarshan as Indian commentator on Test matches.

The cricketing phase, as represented by Mars is over. The coming years under Venus and other planets will unfold the materiality in the Cricket Hero and his life will probably move on the usual humdrum manner with greater involvement in family affairs, and finally fading in the oblivion like many legends of the human history.

14

SRINIVASA RAMANUJAN

Moon			Asc.
	22nd December 1887 (Rasi)		Saturn(R) Rahu
Ketu			
Sun	Jupiter Mercury	Venus	Mars

	Venus	Mars	Sun Ketu
	(Amsa)		
Mercury			Jupiter
Rahu		Asc. Moon Saturn	

During the last few centuries, there has not been any one like Ramanujan in the mathematical world. He was unassuming in his personal life; godly by temperament; simple in food habits; greatly handicapped in family relationships; yet in the realm of mathematics, especially in the field of the Theory of Numbers, there was no one his equal. He needed support from the western world. He showed a few samplings of his mathematical scribbling to mathematical stalwarts of the time, who became extremely fascinated by his work. They provided the financial support for his research, enabled him to get admitted in appropriate institution where his genius could effectively flower, and bestowed the honour which recognized the supernal spark in him. However, all the medicare and best possible intellectual support could not make him live for long. He died early. His wife was not permitted even to be at his bed-side to nurse. Superstitious beliefs haunted his family members. He himself believed that he was merely a mouthpiece of divine energy. He even predicted deaths of his friends and interpreted their dreams. Even his own stars revealed that his life moved according to a divine pattern. He was a miracle, but a miracle patterned in the divine scheme of things and events.

Srinivasa Ramanujan was born in a poor, unhealthy, traditional, Hindu family in an obscure village of the southern part of India. He could not receive any satisfactory schooling in India. At the age of 22 years, when he was not in a position to secure even two square meals for himself literally; he was married to a girl of nine years of age, whom to support became an additional burden to him. With sympathetic support from the father of one of his childhood friends, he was somehow appointed as an accounts clerk, a very ordinary post at Madras Port Trust. While passing through such uncongenial environs, he continued amusing himself with mathematical equations written either on a slate or small bits of paper, which none could understand or comprehend and they regarded them doodlings of an eccentric. These insights into higher realms of the *Theory of Numbers* were however soon sent back to the oblivion either erased from the wooden slate or the scraps of paper destroyed to make room for fresh visitors from the realm of the unknown.

By a stroke of luck, or by inner impulsion, or (who knows?) by divine inspiration he wrote to Professor Hardy of the Cambridge University in England enclosing a few of his mathematical outbursts. This was a turning point in his career.

Hardy tried for his admission at Cambridge, arranged for his financial support, removed academic hurdles arising from his lack of requisite qualification and put him on the road of fame. He was invited to Cambridge; without a qualifying degree he was admitted to the University, and at an age younger than even that of Sir Isaac Newton, he was elected Fellow of the Royal Society. Even then, neither his health problem could be satisfactorily attended to in spite of best medical and sanatorium facilities, nor could he be financially secure to discharge his personal and family responsibilities effectively. His health deteriorated, he came back to India, got embroiled in family troubles, yet in such trying conditions he continued preparing and sending to Professor Hardy original pieces of mathematical papers till he finally breathed his last. Even before his mathematical work could be properly recognized and its significance assessed, he died of tuberculosis at the age of 32 years 4 months. Since then, the world has been much concerned with every bit of scrap on which he wrote. Presently, universities from all over the world are spending millions of dollar to salvage everything concerning Ramanujan that could be possible. Such is the story of this mathematical genius who was born in penury, lived a miserable life and died forlorn in indigent conditions. It is interesting, even illuminating to find out how much of these were circumstantial and to what extent were they incribed in the planetary disposition at his birth.

Srinivasa Ramanujan was born on December 22, 1887 at Erode in Tamil Nadu. He was the eldest son of Pandit K. Srinivasa Aiyangar and Shrimati Komalata ammal, both were devout but extremely poor. They were traditional Brahmins with several generations observing religious rites which had much attuned their psychological and psychic constitution to higher vibrations so that they became very suitable vehicle for the birth of an exceptional ego with special mission in life. Affluence often draws the family towards material involvements which are detrimental for establishing a bridge between the physical and the spiritual realms. Pandit Srinivasa Aiyangar's family was so much rapt in penury and religious observances that they could neither think of breaking away from the traditional bondage nor could they obtain succour from any material profession. They had to be completely dependent upon their inner faith to keep their body and soul together as long as this could be maintained.

The father earned rupees twenty at a textile merchant's shop at Kumbakonam, a neighbouring town. It was very inadequate to maintain the family, but their faith in their religion was so firm and their acceptance of destiny so deep-rooted that they never swerved from the path of spirituality. But such a faith does not provide food. So many a time, the infant Ramanujan had even to go to sleep without any food in his tummy. The child was also so much influenced by the Brahmanical tradition and faith in spirituality that poverty and hardships of life experienced during the early years of his mundane existence did not destroy his innate mathematical genius or his conscious control of his psychic potentialities. He was born in *Gemini* lagna in *Mrigashirsa* nakshatra while his Moon in tenth house was in *Pisces* in *Uttara Bhadrapada* nakshatra.

Gemini as ascendant sign and Mrigashirsha as the asterism rising at the time of birth both were very significant. Gemini is related with cosmic intelligence, the first and the guiding principle in Nature. It stands for the great principle from which the other principles, the *tattwas*, or the essential constituents of manifestation originated. Gemini represented the impulse which enabled cosmic intelligence to manifest and through which further differentiation took place. It is not far fetched to consider the *Theory of Numbers* as related with the reflection of the basic principles of differentiation, which occurred at the stage where noumenon began to concretise and express itself in variegated forms.

In retrospect, we are aware that Srinivasa Ramanujan was not particularly interested in sexual relationship, and even his marriage was more of a traditional formality than an outlet for natural biological instinct. His mind was however fertile and creative but on expansive cosmic plane, as it is evident from his instantaneous intuition of various abstruse mathematical and numerical relationships which any conscious man working out the same would take enormous time. His mind soared above the limitations of time and space.

Indicating the basic feature of Gemini impulse, it has been indicated that this stage of manifestation does not only express polarised attraction of the male for female. It is in fact, characterized by much activity on the mental plane. Its great attraction for the opposite sex is not produced primarily on the physical plane. It is important to note that this impulse is at primeval stage asexual. This stage of cosmogenesis is described in Hindu scriptures in terms of certain Prajapatis, the mighty cosmic beings who refused to do their assigned task of generative creation because they considered it impure. Astrologically also, Gemini is not considered conducive to human fecundity. The preference for meditative practices by the Prajapatis at this level finds its reflection in Gemini types, who are more adjusted to intellectual harmony than the physical relationship. On the cosmic plane, it is signified by the development of the mind principle and expressed as the recognition of space and time, which are the result of thought. Time and Space are abstract principles that do not have any objective existence of their own. They are produced by the mind of the person.[1]

These features of the ascendant were, in fact, so much deeply rooted in Ramanujan that one could even cosider his entire life a mere unfoldment of these qualities. If his mother would have known the primeval energy enveloping Ramanujan, she would probably not have tortured her daughter-in-law for not begetting a child like Ramanujan. His teachers and associates would not have considered him a student seeking to learn mathematics instead of being a cosmic agency revealing certain basic principles of the theory of numbers latent in the cosmic principle of manifestation.

Similarly, the asterism rising at the time of his birth, namely Mrigashirsha heralded the advent of a great cosmic energy. It is an asterism which is extremely active on superphysical plane making the individual attuned to complete freedom from all kinds of physical limitations. For this asterism, every dross of materiality is an impediment for its expression and a source of dissatisfaction. The asterism is ruled by Mars, though first half of it lies in Taurus and the second half in Gemini. Its primary motivation is *moksha,* liberation, while its basic attribute is *rajasic* activity. The presiding deity of the asterism is Soma, the God of mystic nectar that imparts great sensitivity and gives enlightenment. It is the asterism with

1. *Myths and Symbols of Vedic Astrology,* Bepin Behari, Passage Press, U.S.A. pp. 129-31

which Lord Krishna is also identified. The birth of Lord Shiva's consort, Uma took place under Mrigashirsa asterism, and they were also married under the same asterism. Kali Yuga also began under the same asterism. In some occult literature, mention is made of the shift of the earth's poles from North to South and vice versa. The last shift of the poles, which caused important geological changes as well as the influx of new evolutionary impulses was said to have occurred under this asterism.

All these phenomena relate to the revival of life on a global scale. The birth of Ramanujan under this asterism was also indicative of a new influx of intellectual revelations. It was under this influx that Ramanujan was born in order to impart something rather to take something from the contemporary world. It is in this context that the various remarks made by the mathematical stalwarts to the effect that Ramanujan was born a few centuries before his time can be better understood and appreciated. Mrigashirsa stands for a search—either inward or outward under which the spirit penetrates the outer crust of materiality with a veiw to revealing its own reality and the illusory nature of matter. Evidently, this spirit of search is amply revealed in the life of Ramanujan: but this search was of a unique kind so it was necessary to give a special body to the searcher and make him explore a radically different terrain. This divine purpose behind the birth of Ramanujan takes us to an area, which requires certain understanding of occult principles of human birth.

Mrigashirsa birth reveals a missionary birth, a divine purpose behind the birth, but the incarnating energy (the soul) requires appropriate medium through which it has to function. Ramanujan had to reveal highly subtle divine principles of cosmic manifestation. These principles had at first to be reflected on a sensitive mind. This sensitivity of the mind could be acquired only if the body in which it has to function is provided by parents who have lived a pure life, had been abstinent, emotionally god-ward turned, and free from the attractions of materiality.(*) Only in such families egos which could freely vibrate at higher realms of intelligence, the *Mahat* principle, can take birth purposefully. Gen-

(*) Kindly note the antecedent conditions in the life of J. Krishnamurti and Rukmini Devi Arundale, and also the birth condition of Dr. Vashishta Narayan Singh who got into difficulties due to impurities of his various 'sheaths'.

erally such families are poor, religious and orthodox as in traditional Brahmanical families, where several generations have purified their physical life and attained a sensitive astromental "aura". For this reason, Ramanujan was born in the indigent, traditional Brahmanical family too much devoted to supernatural beings. But the mission of unveiling certain principles which could be comprehended meaningfully lay abroad.

Ramanujan's most fruitful years were at Cambridge; even presently, mainly the foreign universities have funded resources for collecting and preserving every scrap of papers connected with the work of Ramanujan, whether comprehended or not by the contemporary scholars. This juxtaposition of a traditional Brahmin body with a highly sensitive mathematical intellect had been the basic feature of Ramanujan's life: when the strain of the latter could not be sustained by the former, Ramanujan became seriously ill and finally died.

Two things in this connection are important to note: Ramanujan directed all his energies to bring down the higher laws of mathematics which he did till the last drop of energy was present in him; secondly, (many modern intellectuals may feel with this uncomfortable) Ramanujan did not corrupt his "aura" by mixing it with any female, not even with his wife. In the divine plan, his case of tuberculosis, keeping his wife away even when his physical self had (often) desired her company were all intended with the purpose of keeping his astro-mental body pure. Occultism teaches us that there is nothing meaningless in life; as the individual develops, and his ego (soul) matures, every single event in his life is directed towards preparing him for the attainment of his archetype, and such a situation is revealed by special patterns of planetary disposition appearing in such horoscopes. Ramanujan's life comes in one such category in which it is necessary to understand the role of planets in the wider context of occultism.

Moon, the cosmic reflective medium which for a messenger like Ramanujan had to be exceptionally sensitive occupies Pisces ruled by Jupiter and Uttara Bhadrapada, which is ruled by Saturn. Moon in navamsa chart occupies Libra and is associated there with Saturn. Saturn in the natal chart is retrograde which makes it very powerful, and it occupies the sign of Moon. Saturn is aspected by Jupiter which occupies Scorpio, a mystical sign owned by Mars which in turn aspects Moon; Jupiter is also associated with

Mercury the ascendant lord. The three planets namely, Jupiter, Saturn and Mars are very important for understanding the disposition of Moon in this horoscope. Pisces is the last sign of the zodiac. By the time the individual attains this level of evolution, he has to resolve that "Not my, but Thy will be done" and he feels almost one with manifestation: his sorrows and frustrations do not vanish at this stage, he certainly registers their existence, but considers them as parts of existence and his inner quietitude is not unduly disturbed. Often one perceives that Pisces is full of storm and stress—inwardly as well as outwardly, but the inner nature of the person is so poised with one universal life that his mind is capable of reflecting the true nature of the inner or the superphysical world.

For a scientist or a seer, it is essential to possess such a tranquil mind. Moon's position in Uttara Bhadrapada intensifies this quality of the zodiac. This asterism is presided over by the Vedic deity Ahir Budhanya, the dragon of the deep sea. It is said that this deity is of the nature of Soma—the Moon, which is associated with water and has the quality of passivity. The passivity of darkness* with which Ahir Budhanya is associated is the mysterious source from which all forms of creation have arisen and this kind of passivity predominates at the asterism, it is for this reason that the asterism is considered female by sex. Uttara Bhadrapada becomes powerful and effective only when it is associated with a planet. Its singular feature is its complete passivity, non-action; it is without motion unless another force impinges on it. It is of the quality of clear, untarnished mirror which shows its quality only when an image is reflected on it.

Ramanujan's mind, his consciousness was so passive, equipoised, that any image cast on it could be reflected without any distortion which proved immensely powerful in articulating the latent relationships of the cosmos as a part of mathematical laws. In his case, the positions of Jupiter, Saturn and Mars are important, but other planets also greatly supportive. Mars occupies Virgo, a sign in which Mercury is exalted. It aspects Moon from the fourth house. This house represents all the karmic forces so far generated by the individual; it is the storehouse of all the cosmic laws and

---

* Kindly refer to the meditational pratice of Dalai Lama and his efforts to reach the stage of *Mahashunya*. (*Supra* pp. 108-10)

energies which under favourable impetus sprout forth so as to ultimately make the goal represented by the tenth house possible. Mars in this house helps in externalizing the forces and energies latent in this house. Mars is in *Hastha* asterism, which is ruled by Moon; the deity presiding over this asterism is Savitar, the Sun god, particularly as the reservoir of all generative energy in the universe. Mars in this position is engaged in externalizing the manner in which this cosmic energy represented by Savitar, the Sun god, is expressed through various forms and relationships. Reflecting itself on the Moon by its seventh aspect, it activates, and the mind in Ramanujan becomes active. But Mars by itself is impulsive; left to itself it could not produce well directed lunar quality. Saturn aspects Mars, which has the main effect of restraining the Martian impulsiveness. The externalisation process induced by Mars on the mind of Ramanujan could therefore be well regulated, controlled but not necessarily in an orderly, methodical manner. It was for this reason that Ramanujan was not a researcher of the usual type, he depended on inspiration (Mars) for his output. As far as Moon is concerned, it is not aspected by Saturn in this horoscope, but Jupiter associated with Mercury, the ascendant lord, aspects it with its fifth auspicious aspect. The sixth house is *inter alia* related with hidden *siddhis,* the various perfections and psychic powers obtained as a result of yogic practices. Jupiter's occupancy of this house, specially in Scorpio sign shows its affinity with nature's hidden powers.

Jupiter is in *Anuradha* nakshatra, which is symbolised by a lotus flower and presided over by the Vedic deity Mitra. The *Atharva Veda* states that Mitra uncovers in the morning what Varuna conceals during the night. The power which brings to light what is attained during the night is found under Anuradha. All the efforts of men done in order to cultivate their natural powers, or to wrest them from the hidden recess of Mother-Earth are watched over by Mitra. It is through the benevolent influence of Mitra that our efforts succeed and the secret powers begin to open out. Mitra is the light of the day that heralds the dawn, the beginning of new possibilities. Anuradha strives to rend the veil of ignorance and uncover our central core to show what is hidden within us, or within the manifest universe. Mitra's uncovering in the morning (the intimations of our divine heritage) what is concealed by Varuna in the night (the ignorance under the influence of Maya) indicates the impulse to arouse us to the ultimate truth.

So Jupiter along with Mercury (intelligence, capacity to articulate and comprehend the divine message) strengthens and protects the mind principle to uncover the covered laws of the universe. In working to reveal this quality of cosmos, the orderliness of it, Moon has been assigned a special portfolio, which is indicated by the position of the Sun in tenth from it. The Sun occupies *Mula* nakshatra, it occupies Sagittarius sign, and occupies the seventh house. The profession of an individual is deciphered by the tenth house in a horoscope, but according to the rule of *Bhavatbhavam,* seventh house being tenth from the tenth house is important in deciding the profession, or the goal in life of the person concerned. For this reason, the position and disposition of the Sun is important with regard to the special secret or the cosmic principles that Moon is activated to externalise or unveil.

Sagittarius is the sign which looks heavenward. It transmutes the animal or horse into an aspiring human being, thus the physical energy is transmuted into divine principles.

Mula nakshatra contains within it the root-matter, the very word *Mula* means the root. The asterism takes its energy from the primordial nature of everything. The Sun sustained in this horoscope on the strength and quality of Sagittarius, and Mula occupying the tenth position from Moon; it has its own disposition which would be the sphere of action of Moon. The Sun is described as the soul of the Universe. It represents the life-force that vivifies, animates and enlivens the solar system. The Sun operates from the inner depths, illuminating the mind and soul, arousing spirituality and making the personality glow with its radiance. It is concerned with the principle which animates the universe. For this reason, it is associated with Vedantic philosophy which dissolves everything in the final analysis to Supreme Will, the Absolute All. In association with Mercury, it has the tremendous power to make a person a great logician, rationalist or a mathematician.

The basic quality of Sun is to destroy, or to uncover the external trappings and present the inner core of the object in its bare essential quality. The Sun by itself may be considered to produce the philosophy of mathematics, but because it is Moon in the present case which decides the goal of life, it has to reflect, and not to interpret. The philosophy of mathematics would be verbalisation, interpetation, and amplification of the mathematical principles revealed, as distinguished from enunciated statement by Ramanujan. The planets in his case were not much concerned with verbalisation (Mercury). The entire life of Ramanujan, even when he was predicting deaths of his friends and other future events, he was not interpreting planetary disposition in different cases as the astrologers usually do, but he was just reflecting, bringing to the physical level what he perceived at higher, super-physical or psychic plane.

It is interesting to see that all the planets which we have considered so far and even Venus which produced *Adhi Yoga* by occupying one of the sixth, seventh, or eighth house from Moon, all have occupied such positions whereby they support the special disposition of Moon. Srinivasa Ramanujan was born with a message and a mission enshrined in the planet occupying his tenth house namely, Moon: he was born with the mission to give out, unveil or articulate and reflect some of the hidden laws of nature expressed as various mathematical principles, that could be enlightening for the coming humanity during the course of the next few centuries.

Each individual, whether messiah, avatara or an ordinary individual, whosoever takes birth and assumes a human form has to obey necessarily the Law of Karma under which all manifestation operates. This law is represented in individual horoscopes by the Rahu-Ketu axis. In the horoscope of Ramanujan, Rahu occupies Cancer in second house along with retrograde Saturn, while Ketu is placed in the eighth house. The second house represents the family relations, finances and creative potential. It is also related with death. The eighth house related with hidden aspects of life is chiefly represented as the house of psychic experiences, diseases and past lives. The Rahu-end of the two poles generally represents the material or the physical causes and the Ketu-end, the psychological impact of experiences or the repercussions of these physical causes. In determining the nature of physical impulses generated by Rahu, it will be necessary to relate the shadowy planet Rahu with Ashlesha—the asterism in which it is placed and Saturn the planet with which it is associated. Ashlesha is ruled by Mercury but Naga, the Serpent deity is its presiding power.

Ashlesha is an intense energy capable of great spiritual attainments as well as deep material immersion. The Naga symbol and the Naga deity are recurrent themes in Indian philosophical system and intense study in their esoteric aspects reveals one of the secrets of the nature of divine wisdom, which is always dual in character like the forked tongue of a serpent. People under the influence of this asterism are deeply philosophical, thoughful, austere, self-reliant and reclusive, but they can on occasion behave in the most ordinary and crude manner—harsh, selfish and venomous. Ashlesha is the asterism, which imparts intellectual and mental development, enabling its beneficiaries to change their perception of life. The placement of Rahu in the second house leads Ramanujan to individuals and family relations who are often very crude and materialistic in their approach; in short, very ordinary. But his creative faculties arise on the spiritual plane from which all wisdom arises. The second is also a constitutent of the *Mysterious Depth* and represents that portion which produces the results of the churning of the ocean: from it one prognosticates creativity, sensitivity, determination, morality and scholarship.

The presence of Saturn in the second house is a great restrictive power. So one expects the life of Ramanujan to be the churning ground, where he would be surrounded by very ordinary individuals with their material and physical requirements and demands. His own inner urge for the quest of wisdom and to un-veil Saturnian restrictions obstructing the fruition of his inner urges would lead to deprivations of material needs of his family relations and would impinge on his own expressions of his creativity. The pole represented by Rahu would always haunt Ramanujan. As a result of such hardships, he learns or attains, as if it were the efflorescence of austerities, his psychic experiences, and the benedictions of the unseen represented by the eighth house tenanted by Ketu.

The lower part of the shadowy planet which digests all the poisonous inputs received (produced) by the upper part of the serpent Rahu, which swallows all the filth of the world, the materiality of life, and dissolves them into nutritive wisdom, is in the present chart of Srinivasa Ramanujan situated in *Shravana* nakshatra. This asterism is assigned the symbol of an ear as well as of an arrow: such characterisations are intended to emphasise the profound nature of the impulse flowing through it to equip the individual to listen to the cosmic music, the harmony prevailing all around him in spite of all the squalor and disorder around him. The primary *Sattwic* attribute enveloping the asterism indicates that every impact under it must arouse a deep perception of the harmony that prevails around oneself. Describing the basic characteristics of Shravana nakshatra, it has been stated that

> The essential feature of Shravana is the great silence, upon which subsists the entire scheme of manifestation. The asterism leads one to meditation. If someone is still on a materialistic path and in need of considerable experience to equip himself for a spiritual orientation, he will develop those qualities under Shravana.
>
> Shravana means "listening", the necessary quality which leads to alertness. Only after subjugating personal emotions and thoughts can one listen to that cosmic music which reveals the beauty and harmony of the universe and purifies the inner nature of man. Shravana can enable one to attune himself to *Naada*, the cosmic ideational sound which leads to one-pointedness.[1]

Ketu's placement in Shravana refers to the quality in this horoscope of trasmuting one's personal, financial and family limitations into a quality and opportunity to attune oneself to the cosmic order and perceive the divine harmony surrounding the individual, or pervading around him. Ramanujan's sojourn to Cambridge and to almost seclude himself from all and sundry were aimed at probably to this harmonising process with the Infinite. His mathematical achievements were the efflorescence of this digestive and dissolving function of the lower shadowy planet. The situation in the eighth house further intensified this process. What is important to realise is that the fruition of this attunement with the Mysterious Depth, where the dissolution of Time and Space is complete and its perception is possible only with superphysical consciousness, is possible only under serious austerities. In the present case, Rahu's placement in the second house along with Saturn could make the necessary austerity possible. With these two poles of physical hardships and psychic development, all the major events of Ramanujan's life are intimately related. This is the extraordinary features of the horoscope, which

1. *The Fundamentals of Vedic Astrology*, Bepin Behari, Passage Press, Utah, USA, p. 78

is central to all other individual prognostications.

At the time of his birth, Ramanujan had the planetary rulership or mahadasa of Saturn with about nine years in balance. Saturn's position in the second house, which represents financial position of the individual produced acute poverty, hunger and neglect; he remained introvert during this period. Ramanujan was very fond of his mother, warm internally but unmindful of what the world thought of him. Along with his mother, he went to temples, listened to discourses on religious scriptures, worshiped the goddess of Nammakkal, the local goddess, who often appeared in his dreams. Poverty, psychism, and deep religious attachment resulted from the special disposition of Saturn, which was posited in Cancer whose lord Moon was in Pisces in the tenth house. Saturn in retrogression aspected the fourth house, where Mars the lord of the sixth house, the house of psychic perfections, *siddhis,* and of eleventh house was posited. This unspectacular period of life could not reveal the future greatness and recognition that were awaiting him. Associated with Rahu, these two malefics primarily operated to wash out his much accumulated karmic indigence. As the second house is related with finances and family, these hardships were natural for him to experience.

Life began to unfold for Ramanujan with the advent of the main period of the ascendant lord Mercury. The beginning of Mercury main period began to show the stuff Ramanujan was made of. At the Primary School examination organised by the Thanjavur authorities which covered unusually a very large area, Ramanujan topped the list.

At the age of 17 years, when he joined the Junior First in Arts class in the Government College at Kumbakonam, he was awarded the prestigious Subramanyan scholarship, which was generally offered for proficiency in English and Mathematics. This was the period when he was running Mercury-Moon sub-period. At the age of 22 years, under Mercury-Jupiter, he was married to a girl of nine years of age, and the pressing demand of family responsibilities having made him miserable, Ramanujan was almost driven to accept the post of accounts clerkship at the Madras Port Trust and that also due to the good offices of a large number of well-wishers and helpers. Mercury-Saturn sub-period gave him low paid job, where he could earn only rupees thirty per month. Mercury related to accounts and Saturn connected with foreigners, while the latter was the lord of ninth house (as well as of the eighth house) occupying the second house, did only that much. The foreigners were helpful to him at various stages of his life, but the future was still veiled.

The period of Ketu, the planet of psychic visions, abstract thinking, and unmindfulness of the existence on the physical plane was the most creative and spectacular one in the life history of Srinivasa Ramanujan. Ketu, as we have already indicated, always played an important role in his life.

Saturn in retrogression is the lord of eighth and ninth houses. It is placed in the second house along with Rahu, a fact which has to be noted almost with every aspect of his life. Furthermore, in navamsa, it is with Moon. Cancer is the sign of the zodiac which is intimately linked with the fourth house of *Kala Purusha*, the Cosmic Man. Saturn is also related with *Pushya* nakshatra which represents fruition of efforts. It is presided over by the Vedic deity Brahmanspati, who energises the planet Jupiter and personifies it. The asterism is symbolised by a flower which stands for fruition and expression of one's innate beauty and harmony. Its basic motivation is *Dharma*, righteousness; its primary attribute is *Rajasic*, activity—secondary attribute *Sattwic*, harmony, and tertiary *Tamasic*—inertia. These attributes make Saturn produce its results, which could be depressive (*tamasic*), induce the individual to take initiative (*rajasic*) and keep the mind attuned to higher spirituality (*sattwic*). The guradianship of Brahmanaspati over the asterism imparted to Saturn some protective power as well as incentive to achieve one's desired goal. The asterism under which the planet is situated is helpful, but the very nature of Saturn which is depressive, restrictive and other-worldliness could not be completely wiped out. As Rahu is associated with it, Saturn's period of rulership, whether its own main period or its sub-periods under main periods of other planets had to be very significant in making Ramanujan proceed towards the attainment of his goal in life.

We have already seen that Ramanujan had an extremely difficult childhood often sleeping without any meal. Only when Mercury main period started that Ramanujan began his educational career, but during the sub-period of Saturn, an important change occurred in his career. Saturn always brought depressive feelings and a feeling of tremendous frustration for which reason during its main period, Ramanujan even tried to commit suicide once. But during Mercury-Saturn sub-period, he struggled to earn and to pursue his intellectual interest. As a matter of fact, as long as he was under the main period of Saturn's rulership, he had not even seen any book on mathematics dealing with higher mathematics. With the beginning of Mercury-Saturn sub-period, Ramanujan became anxious to help his family financially for which a job was essential. On March 1, 1912, about a year after the beginning of the sub-period of Saturn, Ramanujan succeeded in his efforts and joined the accounts section of Mạdras Port Trust as Class III employee in its Grade IV earning a monthly salary of Rs 30. The job did not absorb him completely: while working as a clerk in the Madras Port Trust, he secretly jotted down his original mathematical ideas in a note book. He was very little interested in his physical appearance, which is a special characteristic of Saturn, but with his frayed notebook he would approach anybody whom he thought could help in his mathematical equations. Dewan Bahadur R. Ramachandra Rao, District Collector of Nellore, and P.V. Seshu Iyer of the Kumbakonam College, who taught Mathematics took interest in this unusual person with a short uncouth figure but with shining eyes though they did not understand the worth of his efforts. However, Gilbert T. Walker, Director General of Observations of the Madras Port Trust recommended to the Madras University that Ramanujan be sanctioned a special scholarship of Rs 75 per month for carrying out his mathematical research at the university; he was also granted two years leave from the Port Trust to work as the university research scholar.

Meanwhile, his professor of Mathematics P.V. Seshu Iyer and others persuaded him to approach Professor Hardy of the Cambridge University to accord him better guidance and some financial assistance for the pursuit of his mathematical studies. Ramanujan wrote to Professor Hardy enclosing a few of his theorems, and he also wrote that "to preserve my brains, I want food". The few theorems that Ramanujan had sent to Hardy impressed him so much that he made financial provisons of Ramanujan's stay at Cambridge and wanted him to join Hardy at the earliest. But Ramanujan was reluctant to leave India. Hardy made another attempt to persuade Ramanujan to go to Cambridge: he asked E.H. Neville to personally exert influence on Ramanujan to join

Hardy at Cambridge. After a lot of persuasion and cajoling Ramanujan was made to agree to leave the shores of India (and to go to the land of Mlechhas) in his pursuit of learning. His mother, the main stumbling block was also made to give her consent, but finally the matter rested on the local deity Managiri who was the patron goddess of the family. Many of the mathematical solutions to Ramanujan were shown to him in dream by her; she also appeared to the family in dream and encouraged Ramanujan to proceed to Cambridge.

The period of Mercury mahadasa and Saturn antar-dasa showed the result by sending Ramanujan to a foreign land (Saturn) for intellectual evolution which was his life's mission (Mercury). A lot of difficulties arose between Ramanujan's decision to proceed for Cambridge and his actual departure. Saturn's capacity to create difficulties is enormous in almost every case and in every situation, even if it is going to bestow its blessings it does so after producing a lot of frustration. Ramanujan had to wait for the period of Ketu, another pole of the Rahu-Ketu axis, for the fruition of his Cambridge trip. Ketu's main period started towards the end of December 1913 and on March 14, 1914 Ramanujan left for the United Kingdom. On his arrival at London, when the boat was to reach Southamption, Hardy had sent Professor Neville of Cambridge to receive Ramanujan at the dock. So much care and consideration was shown to Ramanujan despite the fact that Ketu was in his eighth house. As indicated earlier, Ketu was destined to bestow the great honour to him which however did not assure a comfortable and anxiety-free life.

Ramanujan's stay at Cambridge itself was an extra-ordinary experience. The entire stay was during the main period of Ketu. The primary characteristic of Ketu is to withdraw the individual from the humdrum mundane life, make him introspective, intensify psychic sensitivity, arouse tremendous attraction for the ethereal world and turn the fruits of success on the physical plane into dust. It is a planet of the philosophers. In Ramanujan's life, as we have emphasised before, Ketu played an extra-ordinary role. Almost immediately after taking sway over the life of Ramanujan, it took him to the modern seat of higher mathematical and philosophical learning.

At the Cambridge University, Ramanujan had almost become circumscribed by his own self. He hardly mixed with others; he had few friends and visited only a couple of Indians at that place. Professor Mahalanobis, the great statistician associated with Pandit Jawaharlal Nehru, whom he assisted in formulating the early models of Indian economic planning, was a contemporary of Ramanujan at Cambridge. They were known to each other, and Mahalanobis mentioned that Ramanujan would derive his (physical) nutrition from South Indian vegetarian self-prepared food with a liberal sprinkling of Indian pickles, but on the intellectual plane remained soaring on higher spiritual mathematics. Ramanujan often spoke to him of 'zero' as the symbol of Absolute, that is the Nirguna Brahma of Advaita or monism. He also enunciated the abstract philosophy of cosmic ideation by stating that the product of zero and infinity would supply the whole set of finite numbers. An equation had no meaning to Ramanujan, unless it expressed a thought of God. Ramanujan was greatly interested in Samkhya philosophy of which mathematics was only a branch. Such abstraction of physical reality arose from the spiritual impulses of Ketu.

Ramanujan did not possess the initial academic qualification for admission to the Cambridge University, and his contribution to mathematics transcended all academic curricula; he dwelt at a level which was several centuries ahead of the contemporary scholars; he often produced the final solution without stating the intermediate stages for which at a later stage he would adduce several routes to arrive at the conclusions. Professor Hardy realised the genius hidden under the unsophisticated, uncouth visage of the Indian native. Hardy had an unparalleled status so he exerted his influence in overcoming the formalities of common university career and Ramanujan was made a regular student scholar at Cambridge pursuing the subject of his own liking.

The strain of an alien atmosphere, inhospitable society, lack of physical nutrition and tremendous preoccupation at higher mental plane sapped his energy and he became impoverished: during Ketu-Rahu sub-period, it was discovered that he had contracted tuberculosis. Saturn's aspect on the fourth house with Mars in it sapped his life-energy and physically Ramanujan became famished: it was found out that his health would soon deteriorate seriously. He was shifted to a sanatorium, but in none of these nursing homes he received the warmth of the tropical sun. His Indian vegetarianism further aggravated the malady. He pined for the affectionate nursing hands of his wife, but the traditional mother would not allow this to happen. Physically, Ramanujan gradually became too weak. Professor Hardy apprehended the worst: Ketu-Rahu sub-period confirmed that Ramanujan had tuberculosis and the medical assistance was not adequately available to a satisfactory level. But Ramanujan's mind was as alert as ever.

It is said that on one of these days of his illness, when he was quite depressed, Hardy went to see him at the nursing home in London at Putney. He went in a taxi with its number as 1729. To divert Ramanujan's mind from his illness and to cheer him up at the same time impelled by his premonitions, Professor Hardy commenting on this number 1729, said: "I came by taxi cab No. 1729. It seems to me rather a dull number. I hope it is not a bad omen". Ramanujan's genius and alert mind immediately flashed back, "No, it is an interesting number: it is the smallest number especially resulting as a sum of two cubes in two different ways, such as $1729 = 12^3 + 1^3 = 10^3 + 9^3$." This showed the alertness and the level at which Ramanujan's mind worked even during the period of his illness.

Professor Hardy was keen that Ramanujan was made a Fellow of the Royal Society in spite of his ebbing life-force: he thought Ramanujan's contribution was considerable to be elected to this status. Generally, it is a prestigious position which is not accorded at the very first proposal, but Hardy was earnest about Ramanujan's fellowship and argued Ramanujan's nomination with great determination. Finally, he succeeded and Ramanujan was elected Fellow of the Royal Society. The great register was taken to him at the nursing home for his admission signature. He became the first F.R.S. in India. He was accorded this status at an age younger than that of Sir Isaac Newton, when he was similarly honoured.

Having suffered for about two years with this emaciating disease in England, Ramanujan returned to India in March 1919, during the planetary rulership of Ketu-Saturn sub-period. But Saturn sub-period did not destroy the physical sheath of Ramanujan. Much care was taken of him in India, but the lord of ascendant, Mercury could not provide much physical sustenance to Ramanujan. Mercury is situated in the sixth house, which is one of those houses, where impulses coming from the super-physical plane arouse much super-physical perfections, *Siddhis,* but on the physical plane it produced difficulties and diseases.

Under such an impulse from Mercury during its sub-period in Ketu main planetary rulership, on April 26, 1920 Ramanujan withdrew his mortal coil and went to the abode of his goddess Namakkal, who had been the guardian angel throughout life inspiring him with formulae in his dreams which he would note down on becoming awake and surprise the world with his discoveries which in fact he did as an agent of the goddess who inspired him to do so, and who had even accorded her permission and given her blessings before he had set sail to the highest seat of mathematical learning in the contemporary world. And there, in spite of all physical hardships, he attained the highest award and remained for a long time the youngest man to be thus honoured. With the scholarship money that he received as a result of his attainment, he was almost obsessed with the idea of spending that on his family's welfare. On the basis of his own astrological predictive capacity and others' predictions, he was aware that he would die young in years. Even on his death-bed, he worked incessantly on mathematical problems: he sent his contribution on *Mock-Theta Function* to Professor Hardy from his death-bed. Such was the life story of one of the greatest genius that India, nay the world, had produced with some divine mission.

The divine mission in the birth of Srinivasa Ramanujan can be easily deciphered from the planetary disposition in which he was born. It is an esoteric rule of astrology that the maturity of ego and special mission in one's birth can be traced to special alignment of the planets at the time of birth. This planetary interrelationships is deciphered by the patterns which emerge in horoscopes of truly great men and women.

Vargottam planets reveal the possibility of attaining high social status and conditions of material affluence, but the special patterns reveal the uniqueness of the soul and the divine forces poured on him for the completion of special task assigned by the spiritual hierarchy. This honour however, is not a bed of roses. Of course, with the consent of the incarnating ego and mutual agreement wiith the Lords of Karma, the individual agrees to complete the divine mission though it is almost always accompanied by serious physical and psychological sufferings. Such examples even in modern times are available as in the cases of J. Krishnamurti, Ramana Maharshi, Sri Aurobindo, Rukminidevi Arundale, Dalai Lama, Mikhail Gorbachev and others.

Life is a strange phenomenon. Many things happen to us without our being consciously aware of it on the physical plane and during our waking life. Astrologically, the mission assigned to a person who is not concerned with one's own personal advantage and gain can be deciphered to a great extent by discovering special planetary pattern in a horoscope. In doing so, one does not have to ignore or overlook the rules of exoteric astrology, but one has to weave together the exoteric and higher astrological principles to have an insight in the super-physical dimensions of the individual. In this connection, apart from *lagna*, the importance of tenth house is well recognised. It is specially so in relation with the contribution that the individual is destined to make during the course of his life-period. The relationships of the tenth house with several other linkages of the planets in any horoscope intensify the significance of those linkages from the standpoint of his worldly contributions.

In the natal chart of Ramanujan, mention has already been made of his tenth house in order to show the interaction of his self with the external world and mention has also been made of the importance of his ascendant and of Moon, Sun and Mercury. These planets are intimately related with different levels of one's being.

In the present case, Moon occupied the tenth house, Mars in fourth and the Sun in seventh house, all of these being cardinal houses have special roles to play. Their positions are very meaningful in relationship to one another. The Moon, which represents one's intelligence, the nature of one's psyche and the capacity to reflect the solar radiance that is the capacity to comprehend the divine law and its message is located in tenth house. It implies that the present life of Ramanujan was meant to understand the divine law and to disseminate it to the world through his interaction with his society. The planet situated tenth from Moon is the Sun, which represents the Supreme Self itself. The goal of Ramanujan's efforts (of his tenth house) is to glorify the Sun, the Supreme Self which is the all pervading Law in the cosmos. Ramanujan had often stated that an equation had no meaning unless it expressed a thought of God. His tremendous interest in Samkhya philosophy was also an aspect of the same involvement.

Mars is situated tenth from Sun and it is in the fourth house.

The position of Mars in this position in exoteric astrology could indicate weaknesses of the heart region which in this case was expressed in the form of Ramanujan's suffering from tuberculosis as well as in the strange behaviour of his mother, but esoterically, it revealed his great initiative and courage in plunging deep down the nadir which the house represents and to retrieve from this mysterious depth the precious jewels that the world would ever witness: Mars is courage, initiative, sacrifice, self annihilation for a noble cause and such deeds specially as in the unprecendented explorations. In order to fulfil the mission assigned to him by Sun, Ramanujan was accorded adequate Martian energy to carry out the assigned task. Thus a unique feature of the horoscope is that the Moon is occupying the tenth position from ascendant, the planet tenth from Moon is Sun and from this planet (Sun), Mars occupies the tenth position. This inter-relationship shows the externalisation process or the operation of the personality of Ramanujan which was directed primary towards the activities of the mind, intelligence and the development and expression of psychic faculties.

These faculties are directed towards unravelling the mysteries of the unity lying behind the cosmos, abstract principles of mathematics where all forms of concretisation are completely eschewed and basic principles realised. In this operation, Venus also contributes significantly its own influence by occupying its own sign Libra in the fifth house of the horoscope though it has certain other functions as well. Ramanujan felt his affinity with the life-universal pervading around him, which was the basic foundation for his creative impulses. This unity he perceived in nature expressed in the form of the Theory of Numbers, his fundamental contribution, and the externalisation of the abstract idea was influenced by Mars and Jupiter flanking Venus on both sides, while Jupiter itself was associated with Mercury, the ascendant lord and the planet concerned with intellect and mathematics (with support from Sun). The direction towards cosmic perception was to a great extent given by Mars which aspected the Sun with its fourth aspect and was placed tenth from it.

Mars played the active role in externalising the Venusian sensitivity of the abstract principle of universal unity (Sun). In the absence of Mars in this place where it exchanges the signs with Mercury, the ascendant lord, there is a possibility that Ramanujan would have probably become merely a mystic philosopher (which in any way he was) perceiving the underlying unity of the universe without being able to articulate it in Theory of Numbers. In that case, Ramanujan could have seen the mystic unity, enjoyed the divine bliss of identification with it, and remained personally absorbed in it *without revealing the underlying Truth for the humanity at large.* In that case, Ramanujan would not have functioned as the messenger of God and discharged the special mission with which Mercury is associated at higher levels of manifestation; without this special externalisation (Mars, the planet for the same, aspecting Sun which is tenth from Moon placed in the tenth house), Ramanujan would have remained in that case a very ordinary person wasting his life (Mercury) by getting embroiled in mundane involvements and difficulties (sixth house). In his present horoscope, the tenth house relationships between the major planets gave Ramanujan great capability and conditions for working in the special area of mathematical specialisation.

Another interesting feature of the horoscope is deciphered in a different pattern. Like the tenth house, the eighth house and the interplanetary eighth relationships also are very revealing. The eighth house relationship relates the individual with secret domain of nature's manifestation. In esoteric astrology, the eighth *bhava* represents awakening of Buddhi. This house refers to the Vishnu aspect of creation, Vishnu implying expansion. The eighth house is thus the storehouse of expansive energy latent in the microcosm. In essence, the eighth house signifies all things hidden and symbolises the powers in Nature embodied as the *kundalini shakti.* All these spring from the Great Deep, the *Bythos* which exists forever. Any relationship with the eighth *bhava* establishes the relationship with this Mystic Depth. Ramanujan had the unique power to tap some of these mystic powers, intuitively and understand the nature of this supra-cosmic or hidden plane; this uniqueness of Srinivasa Ramanujan becomes evident by the placement of various planets in the eighth position in relation to his major planets namely the Sun, Moon and Mars. Ketu occupies the eighth house in the natal chart. From Moon, the eighth position is occupied by Venus in strength, unaspected by any malefic or benefic except by Saturn (by its hind-sight due to its retrogression) which itself is the lord of the eighth house from the ascendant. As Venus occupies a trine house in the natal chart, its inauspicious tendencies accruing due to its ownership of the twelfth house are greatly reduced. Venus gave Ramanujan intuitive insight and penetrative mind into the hidden laws of nature and reflected the same through the Moon. The eighth house from the Sun is occupied by Saturn and Rahu, the two planets which are custodians of nature's secrets. The eighth house in relation with the Cosmic Man, *Kala Purusha,* namely Scorpio contains within the undiscovered laws of the unknown realms of the cosmos. It encompasses the *bhava* concerned with latent powers in man and occult laws in nature which if properly comprehended and harnessed could bestow to man enormous power over nature. The ascendant lord Mercury in association with Jupiter, the two planets which together controlled all the four quadrants in the horoscope are posited in Scorpio. They themselves occupy the sixth house, which linked the individual with the possibilities of acquirinig *siddhis,* occult attainments. These relationships with the houses representing nature's secret powers bestowed upon Ramanujan many special gifts, besides his mathematical genius, such as foretelling the future events. He often predicted deaths from the reading of omens in the dreams of some of his friends. These were results of powerful eighth bhava relationships among the planets.

These planetary inter-relationships producing special patterns among them show extraordinary stellar concern with regard to externalisation of hidden knowledge of Nature in which mission the ascendant lord Mercury and the tenth lord Jupiter were ever ready to lend the support. The special contribution of the two planets in supporting, preserving and nurturing other planetary impulses made Ramanujan's contributions to the world very special otherwise they would have remained merely potentialities, not actualities and effective. If the externalisation was not achieved, Ramanujan might not have succeeded in revealing the mathematical mysteries. The intuitive flights and the intellectual understanding of the cosmic laws would have remained within his own self; they would have remained in that case, unknown, unsung and lost to the posterity.

Can we consider such a horoscope as a lucky one? Or, should we treat Ramanujan as one of the unfortunate persons born in uncongenial circumstances? Should we give significance to various planetary combinations producing indigence, ill health and misunderstandings, which are present in abundance in the present chart, or should they be considered inevitable conditions for the downpour of exceptional spiritual benediction to lead humanity to new heights? These may appear ethical and metaphysical questions with which astrologers may not be concerned, but the common individuals cannot afford to ignore such questions. If properly analysed and intelligently explained to the individual who has to bear such heavy burdens of karma, specially for the sake of humanity, often unknown to him, it may provide much encouragement and solace to him.

Many a time individuals suffer for the sake of others, and do not receive any compensation for it in the physical world. Sometimes, it is the inevitable Law of Karma which they themselves have invoked to work out their past personal debts. A knowledge of these supra-astrological knowledge imparted on the basis of astrological metaphysics might perhaps provide to these individuals psychological stability and sufficient strength to bear the various vicissitudes confronting them in their everyday life. It may even show them the direction of their egoic evolution as well as the direction of their natural efforts that required attention in order to attain their specific goals. Without any inkling of the onerous responsibilities with which many persons are born, their misfortunes could appear extremely burdensome often producing unnecessary depression and disheartenment.

These are some of the problems for astrologers to ponder. As far ar Ramanujan was concerned, we should accept that his birth as well as his vicissitudes contributed enormously to the pool of world scientific knowledge, though on his part for making his contribution, he had to carry his cross which however did not make him embittered. It is evident from his several letters and memoirs that he had a premonition of his missionary assignment, which made him realistic about his family members, the society in which he lived and the world around him. He remained till his last breath, a deeply God fearing individual, experiencing the hand of the Supreme in everything around him. He radiated special spiritual aura, which even after his death encouraged many pilgrims on their intellectual and Divine pursuits. That is what a powerful horoscope shows: the effect of the ego on the world around him even when his physical self is no more present on the physical plane.

15

THIRUNILAYI NARAYANAIYER SESHAN

			Moon
Rahu	*15th December 1932* (Rasi)		
Asc. / Saturn			Jupiter Mars Ketu
	Sun Mercury	Venus	

Saturn Rahu		Moon	Venus
	(*Amsa*)		Sun
			Asc.
Jupiter	Ketu Mars Mercury		

Thirunilayi Narayanaiyer Seshan, popularly known as T.N. Seshan, is a unique phenomenon in the present day politico-administrative framework of India. He is not a commodity to be sold; he cannot be tempted, seduced or bullied; he is an extremely rude, rough and discourteous person if superficially considered. Yet when slightly scratched externally to find out the inner Seshan, he reveals his emotional nature ready to respond like a child. Malavika Sanghvi, a columnist in a prestigious national daily very rightly called him a Holy Terror. In fact, he has put the fear of God in every politician's heart—every political party and even the highest echelon of Indian judiciary, which at some time or the other had been critical of his action, yet everybody thinks that he is a man of integrity, a no-nonsense authority and will not be persuaded or cajoled to shift once he has taken a stand. He does not take any decision without much serious deliberation, but once he has arrived at his conclusion like a mathematical law, there is no possibility of any adjustment under any temporary change of conditions.

It is said that Seshan's forehead has that particular look that begs for sacred ash to be smeared across, yet he is one of those civil servants in the country who reached the highest status possible simply by his one-pointed devotion to his duty, he was not one to flinch from duty, no matter how unpleasant it was. He never identified himself with any status, but he functioned objectively at every position no matter how high or low it was without compromising his own conscience. He is utterly transparent without the slightest duplicity of diplomacy.

It is often felt that such an individual is born once in a century for certain social or humanitarian work. Such souls are born as ascetics, who suffer personal deprivations, yet they live in this world to carry the task assigned to them by the Supreme. It is difficult to classify T.N. Seshan in any known category. Such a person was born in a little village Tiruvillakad in the state of Kerala in a devout Tamil Brahmin family on December 15, 1932 shortly before mid-day.* From the very beginning, he was unusual. He always showed a will of his own, but he was very rev-

(*) T.N. Seshan himself gave this birth date though some astrologers give May 15, 1933 as his birth day. Many of them believe that he was born a little before midnight. Seshan is himself a great astrologer, but has been reluctant to give his exact birth time. Here his birth time is assumed a little before midday.

erential to traditional values. He religiously followed the family practices more as a mark of respect for elders and others than as a blind superstitious follower.

T.N. Seshan has by now lived for more than six decades and his personality pattern has to a considerable extent matured. Whatever the planetary disposition at his birth, one can by now be fairly certain about the main motivational impulses at the centre of his being; one also knows the professional and social status attained by him. The plant has by now fully grown, we have only to watch the profusion of its fruition. Planetary position however abudantly shows the essential character of Seshan.

Born with Saturn and Venus in their own signs forming two of the Panch Mahapurush Yogas, Mercury and Sun together in eleventh house producing Budha-Aditya Yoga, five planets occupying the houses representing the Mysterious Depths, Jupiter's unique relationship with Mars and Ketu on one hand and with Saturn on another, Rahu-Ketu axis joining the second and the eighth houses, and special disposition of Moon, T.N. Seshan is probably one of those rare egos, who are shadowed by higher influences not so much for their self-evolution, though it inevitably comes their way, but to carry forth certain divine plan. They are very powerful egos; they cannot be restrained by any amount of physical force. They are like funnels through which higher forces almost always pour down. It is for this reason that T.N. Seshan has been little understood by his contemporaries, by his (officially) superiors or by the politicians. The saints and seers very well understand and appreciate his values.

Seshan knows that people greatly admire him, but he is also aware of loud condemnations he receives. He is known for his forthright decisions, fearless disposition, transparency in his personal life, and integrity of character untouched by any corruptive temptations. But he is attributed even unprintable appellations: to say the least, he is said to be a megalomaniac, publicity crazy, vindictive and inflexible. Former Chief Justice of India M.N. Venkatachaliah on one occasion even while complimenting him for his excellent efforts to clean the electoral scene in India, reprimanded the Chief Election Commissioner T.N. Seshan for using 'atrocious language'. On another occasion, hearing a petition in connection with the security needs of Tamil Nadu Chief Minister Ms Jayalalitha, the Chief Justice of the Supreme Court told Seshan's Counsel as follows: "Your client seems to think that he is the judge of everyone's security. There should be some limit to this. You seem to be deciding the whole thing for the world. You do such excellent work and even have the appreciation of this court. No one doubts your motivations, but somewhere along the line you do something to spoil the image". One of the prestigious national weekly once very aptly described the contradictions in Seshan's character. It stated, "Seshan is a big man. He clearly loves playing the bully. He is deeply convinced of his duty before God and the country. Somewhere beneath burly exterior is a heart that goes bit-pat for the plight of the nation". On one occasion, Seshan himself clarified his approach to various problems and persons when he stated: "I have no special reason to target anyone. I am committed to setting right what is wrong in the electoral system and if you feel there are hidden motives behind this, I can't help it, Can I?"

Underneath such remarks, there are certainly candid observations which reveal contradictions, complete dedication to the task assigned, and the highest degree of impersonal approach to the various problems of life. The central being working through T.N. Seshan seems unperturbed in the stormy journey of this physical plane; Seshan is often (rather very frequently) angry, shouting, gesticulating, yet deep within himself he is deeply religious, he would spend his hard earned lakhs of rupees just to be present at the last Samadhi of a Sankaracharya so as to regulate the swarming crowd pouring in to pay their last homage, or he would flatly prostrate before a Sankaracharya in the presence of multitude of people quite oblivious of his rank or status.

Seshan does not care for public opinion; he does not care of any one's opinion howsoever high he may be in the official hierarchy excepting that of the Supreme, the call of his duty. One does not know whether he is a bureaucrat, ascetic, or a highly emotional and impulsive person. In the Bhagwadgita, Lord Krishna once stated that "the higher Self of him who is self-controlled and peaceful is uniform in cold and heat, pleasure and pain, as well as in honour and dishonour." He also stated, "he that performeth such action as his duty, independently of the fruit of action, he is an ascetic, he is a yogi, not he that is without fire, and without rites".

It is said that an ascetic lights no sacrificial fire and performs no sacrifices nor ceremonies, but merely to omit these, without true renunciation, is not to be a real ascetic. Seshan is often accused of assuming such a supreme authority almost above (even) the highest political executive in the country only when he became Chief Election Commissioner, but was a very conforming civilian, accepting the orders of his 'bosses'. But this very characteristic of Seshan reveals his basic nature, the primary motivation of his life: the renunciation. He is neither attached to himself, his personal welfare and preferment, nor to official hierarchy or political power; his primary concern is obedience to his Higher-Self without any regard to praise or condemnation. This order of spirituality is evident in the planetary disposition that heralded the birth of T.N. Seshan. Seshan is not a past-master in the game of duplicity. There is much revelation about Seshan's inner life and motivation in Capricorn as the ascendant and in the relationship of its lord Saturn with other planets than in superficial psychological studies of this mystical being.

T.N. Seshan was born with a very powerful ascendant: Capricorn sign, Dhanistha asterism and Saturn occupying Uttarasadha last quarter. One of the classical texts stated that persons born under Capricorn ascendant indulge in mean activities, have many offspring, are greedy, lazy, afflicted in many ways and always struggling in their life. Such characteristics of Capricorn sign do not correctly indicate the basic nature of T.N. Seshan. It should be borne in mind that Capricorn is certainly owned by Saturn, the most dreaded planet, yet the persons born under this sign are not necessarily poor, anti-social and engaged in nefarious activities. In its basic nature, the sign is said to be the most blessed one. It is specially for those who are striving after perfection and usefulness. Discussing the esoteric nature of the sign, T. Subba Rao related it to divine effulgence which leads the individual to 'discipleship'. He stated that "Makaram is the tenth sign and the term 'Dasadisa' is generally used by Sanskrit writers to denote the faces or sides of the universe. The sign in question is intended to represent the faces of the universe and indicates that the figure of the universe is bounded by Pentagons... Makaram may be taken to represent simultaneously both the microcosm and the macrocosm, as external objects of perception"[1]. It shows that the sign

1. *The Esoteric Writings*, T. Subba Rao, TPH, Madras, pp. 10-11.

is not connected with crocodile, but with the vast universe as an expression of the divine noumenon in the process of manifestation with which humankind is completely identified.

The esoteric astrology describes the nature of Capricorn impulse elaborately. It stated that "the creative water of life—the very essence of energy—has been circumscribed by *Kara*—the hands, the vehicles of action—ten, when both the sets of vehicles working on the levels of action and understanding are taken into account. Thus when Capricorn represents the involvement of the highest spirit in the grossest matter and when that imprisoned splendour has been struggling to liberate itself from the shackles of matter, the Capricorn individuals must experience in some measure this imprisonment. Obviously, therefore the Makara ascendants, whatever their nature, spiritual or materialistic, must feel imprisoned, constricted, gaoled, fettered, whose wings have been clipped. The white dove of freedom has been caged within the dark hours of limitation. No wonder Makara persons are full of energy, enthusiasm, idealism but they find themselves helpless in expressing their talents."[1]

The mysterious nature of Capricorn sign was discussed by H.P. Blavatsky by relating this sign with occult hierarchy. She stated that "Makara is related to a mysterious order of beings known as Dhyanis."[2] These Dhyanis, according to her, were connected with the crocodile, and their abode is in Capricorn. She further revealed that these (the *Dhyanis*) were convertible terms in Indian Astrology, 'for the tenth sign of the Zodiac, which is called Makara', is loosely translated 'crocodile'. The word itself is occultly interpreted in various ways. In Egypt, the Defunct, whose symbol is the pentagram or the five-pointed star, the points of which represent the limbs of a man—was shown emblematically transformed into a crocodile. Sebekh or Sevekh (or Seventh)...is a dragon in reality, not a crocodile. He is the Dragon of Wisdom, or Manas, the Human Soul, Mind, the Intelligent Principle.[3] From this it may be concluded that the tenth zodiac sign named Makara, meaning crocodile is not actually the reptile, but the Universal Intelli-

1. *An Introduction of Esoteric Astrology*, Bepin Behari & Madhuri Behari, Sagar, Delhi, pp. 143-4.
2. *The Secret Doctrine*, H.P. Balvatsky, T.P.H., Madras, Vol. I. p. 266.
3. *Ibid.*

gence, the Dhyanis, represented as pentagram (as numerically indicated by the word) whose abode is in Capricorn.

These suggestions relating to the esoteric nature of the tenth zodiacal sign become very difficult to apply in everyday astrology. The primeval impulse of this sign becomes pronounced only under favourable spiritual milieu when the individual is prepared to dedicate his life to his Higher-Self, as indicated by Lord Krishna when he described the true psychology of an ascetic. In fact, the basic impulse of this sign, which with its proper adaptations can be applied at all levels, was very suggestively discussed in *A Study in Astrological Occultism.* There it was mentioned that the esoteric symbol of this sign stands for the individual personality of the human being, when it begins disintegrating and merging into the universal consciousness, and the individual cries, *Not mine, but Thy Will be done.* It is an attitude of great renunciation, and laying aside one's personality for the transcendental spirit to flow through it. It is a sign of Discipleship under which the individual ego may pass through personal sorrow but not of 'deeper' sorrow. One accepts the Inevitable, the Everlasting, and is prepared to abandon the transient for the sake of the Eternal. It was elaborated and stated that:

> Under the impact of Capricornus, the tenth sign, the individual joins the occult hierarchy and becomes a mysterious being. When the divine downpour takes place, the past karmas are churned violently. While being stormed by the highly activated forces of the past actions, the individual is also attracted by the irresistible future glory awaiting him. The tenth house in a natal chart stands for avocation, the vital efforts which determines the course of one's life. The fundamental aim of the heavenly man, his avocation, is manifestation; the subject becomes object under this sign. Under its impulse, the outer vehicle of consciousness is so changed as to make it an appropriate medium for the expression of the inner—the psychological and the psychic being. The Capricornus personality is often moved by the inertia of *Kama-Manas,* mind and heart, though the voice of intuition - Buddhi-Manas - has begun to be faintly audible.[1]

1. *A Study in Astrological Occultism,* Bepin Behari, IBH Bangalore, pp. 39, 55.

From the various description about the interaction of T.N. Seshan with his conditions of work and interpersonal relationships, there is obviously much significance in the opinion that his forehead begs for sacred ash to be smeared across it. The people fail to appreciate the inner urge working through the outer Seshan. T.N. Seshan is not only spiritual rigorously subjecting his life under strict regulation and discipline verging almost on austerity, but psychologically he has so much transmuted his Kama-Manas, desire-mind to Buddhi-Manas, intuitive-mind that the presence of the Higher-Self or the divine governance of the universe is almost a reality to him. Since he tries to live a life guided by this central spiritual core of his being, he does not have to fear anyone, he therefore cares little for any status as such in life, howsoever high or mass appealing it may be. He has even repeated this several times publicly.

A large number of people are skeptical about this affirmation of his attitude, but there are evidences to indicate that Seshan has actually declined many such offers. This kind of introversion centralising the motivating impulses of his life in the divine consciousness, also known as Higher-self, results from his ascendant occupying Dhanistha asterism, first quarter. It is an asterism which provides deeply spiritual impulse. It is ruled by Mars, the planet which stands for valour as well as complete devotion; its impulsiveness arises from its intuitive inspiration. The asterism is primarily influenced by *Sattwa guna*, the radiation of harmony and is presided over by the Vedic deities known as the Vasus, who personify the cosmic energy. Those who have seen Seshan's involvement in the task assigned to him would testify not only his great zeal, enthusiasm and devotion, but also the tremendous energy beaming through him in all that he does. The asterism has been assigned the symbol of a drum called *mridangam*, a musical instrument, and it radiates the motivational impulse of *Dharma*, righteousness.

One often feels that T.N.Seshan is a text book picture of Dhanistha asterism. When one analyses the significance of *mridangam*, the symbol assigned to the asterism, the inner attitude of Seshan becomes clearer. Explaining the significance of this symbol, it has been stated that "the word Dhanistha means a bamboo-cane flute as well as a drum. Both these musical instruments are hollow inside. They resound and reverberate the tune played by the musician. Depending upon the touch on the drum or the blowing of the flute music comes forth. The instruments are merely links between the music and the musician. Similarly, under Dhanistha, the basic impulse is to purge the soul from whatever it considers its own so that the Divine Plan for it can be unfolded smoothly. The individual must come to function like a reed through which the divine music is played uninterruptedly and without distortion."[1]

Seshan often states that his role is that of a referee, to blow the whistle whenever anyone disobeys the rule of the game. This reference however reveals that Seshan does not wish to impose his personality on what he does: the parameter is decided by the Constitution or the authority entrusting him with the responsibility of carrying out any specific task, but for his integrity of judgement he depends upon the Higher-Self who plays the drum, which in the present case is the inner Seshan himself.

The ascendant lord's disposition greatly helps in articulating the basic impulses provided by the sign and the asterism. They produce the *milieu*, the necessary background or the potential which may fail to fructify unless the active planetary force is present. Saturn in the horoscope of T.N. Seshan presents a very significant result. In the present case, the usual negative characteristics of this most dreaded malefic have been transmuted into highly spiritual influence. Saturn occupies the asterism of Uttarasadha, which is ruled by Sun while its presiding Vedic deity is Vishwadeva(s). Occupying the apex of the spiritual triangle in its own sign, it forms *Sasa Yoga*, one of the *Panch Mahapurusha Yogas*. It is unaspected by any planet. Moon is placed sixth from it in the sixth house, while Jupiter, Mars and Ketu are situated in the eighth house. Rahu is second from it and occupies its own trine sign. Saturn aspects the tenth house, the house of avocation tenanted by Venus in its own sign constituting *Malavya Yoga*, which is also one of the *Panch Maha Purusha Yogas*. Sun with Mercury forming *Budha-Aditya Yoga* occupies eleventh position from Saturn. Thus Saturn becomes the guiding planet in this chart. Rahu-Ketu which is the fulcrum around which all the important events in Seshan's life would revolve is very close to Saturn. The distance between

1. *Myths and Symbols of Vedic Astrology*, Bepin Behari, passage Press, Utah, U.S.A. p. 238.

Saturn and Rahu is less than 10°, though there is a difference in their signs. This conjuncture of planetary relationships enables T.N. Seshan to draw cosmic energy in abundance to disseminate it for some impersonal universal purpose. It would be interesting to go into a little greater depth in this aspect of the horoscope as it reveals the tremendous downpour received by Seshan, which makes him almost invincible attributing to him the appellation of "the Holy Terror".

The Vedic deity Vishwadeva(s) who presides over Uttarasadha is one of those divine forces whose nature has been difficult to decipher. While discussing the characteristics of this deity, even Sri Aurobindo confessed his inability to decide for certain whether these Vishwadevas formed a class by themselves or are simply the gods in their generality. He believed the term to mean "the universal collectivity of the divine powers". As a result of this feature of the presiding deity over this asterism, the impulses flowing through it become "fosterers and increasers of man and upholders of his labour and effort in the work, the sacrifice". In practice, Vishwadeva(s) enables the individuals under its influence to possess tremendous influx of divine energy and in disseminating the same to sacrifice their personal comforts, conveniences and all ideas of personal glorification. Those born in Uttarasadha perceive the problems of life in a different light. Saturn in this asterism would make its impact perceived differently: the necessary deprivations accompanying Saturn is perceived as a gift of god to be borne with pefect equanimity. T.N. Seshan does not always enjoy even basic conveniences of life, yet he never grumbles about them. He has an approach to life which is radically different from that of others; he perceives life differently. If any one tries to analyse the attitude of Seshan to various situations confronting him about which he often quotes scriptures, he would find that Seshan has an inner understanding of the process of life's unfoldment, whereby he weaves a pattern of life in which the universal rather than the individual, social rather than personal considerations are more important.

Saturn forms *Sasa Yoga,* which is formed by Saturn in exaltation or in its own sign in strength occupying a cardinal house. It is a rare combination. It can occur only during seven years or so of its thirty year sojourn around the zodiac; on such occasions also only those births which take place with the signs occupied by four sensitive points in a horoscope namely dawn, midday, dusk or midnight, qualify for this yoga. On such occasions, it produces a kind of psychological transformation which makes the individual immune to personal sorrow, frustration and deprivations usually accompanied with the results of Saturn. It is such a powerful combination that the exoteric astrology often gives elusive results of this yoga. But we have elsewhere mentioned some of the characteristics of this combination which reveals the primary nature of T.N. Seshan very well. We stated:

> The individual has the disposition of a leader, and though physically he is not beautiful, he likes sex in its various expressions. He does not treat sex merely as an act for satisfying carnal passions, but rather as a means for establishing rapport with the inner core of the other person. Any expression of pure lust repels him, but the expression of erotic feelings as indicators of a love relationship between two persons soothes him immensely. As a result of his relationship with different types of persons, he acquires much insight into their problems and modes of expression. This gives him insight into human character. He can see the faults and weaknesses of others very easily. He is often learned. His knowledge consists of esoteric wisdom; his wanderings among forests and inaccessible places are induced by his thirst for spiritual experiences. Sasa Yoga makes the individual outwardly an ordinary person with ordinary conveniences in life, but his leadership ability is phenomenal. He leaves an imprint on the society in which he lives. He may establish a school of philosophy which contains much wisdom. He leads large numbers of people by his good advice and spiritual knowledge. Sasa Yoga does not so much operate on the external plane as on inner and subjective levels. The individual's fondness for lonely places, mountains, rivers and fortresses are expressions of his essential subjectivity, which is less favourably expressed as impatience, cruelty and an unconventional life-style. Sasa Yoga produces inner greatness through a vision of eternity and complete detachment from worldly life.[1]

1. *The Fundamentals of Vedic Astrology*, Bepin Behari, Passage Press, Utah, U.S.A., p. 238.

Saturn is related with *Muladhara chakra* whose activation releases *Kundalini*, the serpent which leads to much needed inner illumination and immense control over hidden powers of nature. In ordinary householders, it suggests physical and psychological preparedness for changing the direction of vital energy ensouling a person from pure materialistic goals of life to purification and spiritualization of one's inner self. The stimulus for this change comes in one's life according to the cardinal house in which Saturn is placed. In the present case, Saturn forms Sasa Yoga by occupying its own sign in ascendant, so the inner transformation in Seshan's life comes from his complete subjugation of his personal likes and dislikes, and mastery over his involuntary reflexes. In Seshan's horoscope, Saturn occupies the navamsa of Jupiter in the sign of Pisces, along with Rahu. The special relationship between Saturn, Jupiter and Rahu, while Saturn forms Sasa Yoga makes the most dreaded planet extremely helpful though its basic nature of producing personal sorrow, frustration and deprivations is not eliminated.

The real nature of Saturn is annihilation of material/physical proclivities and release of spiritual/universal principle. Saturn is known as the God of Death, Yama: but he is also the son of Aditya, the Sun, the source of eternal life-force. Yama presides over death so as to release the soul from its physical bondage and experience its eternal existence, assimilation in the cosmic totality.

The whole life of T.N. Seshan including his official career had been an exercise in this process of assimilation with the cosmic totality, an ideal towards perfection, and transcendance over personal calculations. From his early childhood, he always behaved without any fear, functioning within the parameter of the duties assigned to him. There has been no fear in him; he is aware of his limitations, tradition, religion, civil service rules, constitution, but refuses to be cowed down by extra-constitutional authorities for he is identified with Yama, the final arbitrator from whom he takes his marching orders. He is so bold and self-reliant, because he is identified with his true-self, with the ideal of universal consciousness which in the ordinary language is called spirituality. But in astrological analysis, this attitude springs from the special impulse produced by Saturn in his chart.

One of the qualities of Yama is that he is nobody's friend or nobody's foe; he is a part of the divine justice and dispenser of the karmic law. It has been reported at Seshan's own admission that he often simulates anger only to instil some fear in the other person. Even otherwise, his life shows great deal of real spirituality: he can spend *his* own vast sum of money on what he considers his religious desire or duty; he can mingle with the most questionable personalities, if that enables him to gain some inner enlightenment. And he does not conceal his spiritual and religious aspirations and observances under the garb of pretensions. He often quotes religious scriptures not to display his erudition in Sanskrit language, but to reveal that his everyday life and relationships aim towards identification with the law of nature. In his personal associations, he expresses his amiability, but in his official dealings he is ruthless, incisive, strictly according to the rule-book and goal oriented. His official position is not a status symbol, but merly a condition to execute certain task. Yama also has his personal feelings completely put in abeyance while enforcing the law of karma or like a surgeon carrying out the operation to eliminate the malady without yielding to the cries of the patient. It is for such reasons that Seshan is dreaded by a large number of people, who have official dealings with him.

In determining the life-pattern of Seshan, the disposition of Saturn is important in another way: it is in sixth-eighth house-relationship with Moon and it powerfully aspects Venus which is situated in tenth house, the house of avocation and which occupying its own sign forms *Malavya Yoga.* Commonly understood the sixth-eighth house-relationship is considered inauspicious and productive of difficulties as well as negation of helpful influence of the planets concerned. But such expectations in exoteric astrology are based on superficial consideration of the interrelationship. From a deeper standpoint, the sixth as well as the eighth house represent portions of the Mysterious Depth, which radiate influences to the individual from the shoreless ocean of eternity beyond time and space; they link the individual with the primeval ray of manifestation. In their expression on the physical plane of existence, they assume diverse forms. Describing the deeper import of these houses, it has been mentioned:

> The sixth house is the third corner of the Chaos. It signified *Maya,* the creative illusion, as well as the potential energy, *Sakti* or *Mahamaya,* which ultimately grows into a limitless splendour. The potency of growth arises only after the

> Universal Womb has been impregnated by the Male Creative Principle, the *Purusha.* Then only the seed will sprout forth to unfold its hidden splendour. The power contained within this primeval seed of creation will gather around the *Prakriti, Akasa,* or the Root Matter, to mould it in the desired form. The three houses, namely, the twelfth, second and the sixth taken together represent the Universal Life existing in nature. The fourth corner—that is, the eighth house is a veil. The reference here is to the Serpent Fire concealed in *Muladhara Chakra.* It is the creative fire described in the Upanishads as an Ultimate without which creation is not possible. The purpose of this latent fire is to make subsequent levels of manifestation possible so that the individual could merge himself in the Universal Entity. The four houses connected with the Great Depth, the Bythos, always intimately endeavour to arouse conditions favourable for the return of the individual to the Universal Life Principle.[1]

These principles applied in actual analysis of astrological forces operative on an individual reveal the troubles and tribulations met by the individual in order to uncover his latent faculties and to dissolve the karmic impediments coming to him from his past; they also show the manner in which manifestative process takes place which is shown by the planets concerned with these houses. In Seshan's horoscope, Moon and Saturn are in sixth-eighth house relationship, so are Jupiter, Mars and Ketu with Saturn. Moon represents mind, higher intelligence. Saturn placed eighth from it implies that the latter will work upon the former so as to manifest the divine mission earmarked for him. Moon reflects the rays of the Sun representing the highest nature in man; Saturn will eliminate vacillations of the mind so that the pure light could shine on his psyche. Moon is exalted in navamsa and Saturn is in the navamsa of Jupiter (Pisces) along with Rahu which show the spiritual disposition of Saturn. Saturn will lead to deprivations, difficulties, tremendous psychological pressure so as to arouse essential spirituality in life.

The extraordinary imperturbability of mind and the special disposition of Moon (situated in Mercury's sign Gemini, exalted

1. *A Study in Astrological Occultism,* Bepin Behari, IBH, Bangalore, p. 78.

in navamsa), besides *Budha-Aditya Yoga* formed in sixth house from Moon has made T.N. Seshan one of the finest astrologers in the country who did not only predict the impending danger to Rajeev Gandhi's life eleven days prior to its actual occurrence, forewarned Rajiv Gandhi to desist from participating in the fateful celebration, but after the episode he took everything very philosophically.

The quality of Saturn's influence is greatly affected by the planets in the eighth house. Mars by nature is impulsive, ever ready to explode, bring the inner vibrations to the surface (externalisation is the most important attribute of Mars) and always impatient with slow moving actions, but it is always transparent in its dealings and goal oriented activities. Along with Jupiter, which is friendly to it, its strength is greatly increased. In navamsa also, Mars is situated eighth from Saturn. Jupiter is the lord of the twelfth house as well as of the third, Ketu is also there in the eighth house. As a result of these associations, Mars has obtained tremendous power to direct the activities of Saturn in such a manner that it produces suitable circumstances for the unveiling of latent powers in the individual. As Jupiter is related with twelfth house, related with expenditure and with third house connected with enthusiasm, courage and initiative, the Martian initiative might induce Seshan to spend money which from common or popular standpoint might be considered wasteful expenditure, but to Seshan himself that would give him immense emotional satisfaction (Mars also owns the fourth house related with emotional satisfaction).

A typical result of these planetary dispositions was evident from Seshan's reaction to the situation at the time of the death of the former Sankaracharya of Kanchi. T.N. Seshan went to Kanchipuram spending about rupees one lakh of his hard earned money just to control the crowd gathered at the last rites of elder Sankaracharya which Seshan did simply because the *acharya* had asked him to go there immediately and regulate the crowd assembled there to witness the seer attain the eternal Samadhi. In fact, there is no religious duty which is too mean for T.N. Seshan, and no amount of expenditure is too much for him for doing what he thinks right.

It is very significant to observe that the personal life of Seshan is very austere in spite of his being so lavish in his expenditure: in his drawing room, there is no ostentatious furnishing. Only a few chairs and a writing desk serving his basic needs. He is not unwilling to perform even the menial work as sweeping his floor, or washing his own utensils when such needs arise. There is great transparency in his behaviour, social relationships and personal life: he does not wish to hide what he is, what his emotions and intentions are, and he does not shut himself off from the society. He does not have a child of his own, but he has great number of children friends, who very freely swarm around him oblivious of the fact that to a large number of people he is even a 'terror'. He has a large number of friends, who have deep attachment with him. There is hardly any saint or seer of eminence, who is not on intimate terms with him. The secret of this complexity of character and contradictions in his nature lies in the relationship between Saturn, which forms *Sasa Yoga* and Venus in the tenth house forming *Malavya Yoga* and aspecting the fourth house directly which also receives the auspicious ninth aspect of Jupiter.

In a treatise on Vedic Astrology, it is indicated that an individual with Saturn rising in Capricorn is exceptionally evolved, but his uniqueness is not revealed in terms of Martian courage or victory over his enemies, rather it is expressed in matured dispassion and enlightenment leading to liberation. Such a person is certainly wealthy and possesses conveniences of life, but he is not concerned with outer expressions or the way he looks, instead he is very particular about the quality of his thinking and the impressions he makes upon the society in which he resides. He has an intuitive understanding of the iniquitous psychology of unrighteous people which gives him great courage in dealing with them. He becomes a leader of some sort in the society. Yet when such Saturn aspects Venus as in this chart, it produces extraordinary results which does not manifest on expected lines.

Astrologically, Venus and Saturn are friendly planets but when both of them are powerful, their mutual association of any kind creates cataclysmic changes in the individual's life either in their own main or sub-periods. This is so because, when they are in their power, their physical nature is transformed to their spiritual attributes which impart special quality to them. Both planets acquire much spiritual nature, but their physical influences are not eliminated, rather they become the means, whatever they are whether deprivations (Saturn) or abundance (Venus) of physical conveniences, for the spiritualization of the person.

Describing the results of *Malavya Yoga*, Varahamihira stated that "the one belonging to this combination becomes a monarch of cultured mind, rules over the Malwa, Broach, Saurastra, Lata (which is identified with central and southern parts of Gujarat, Ptolemy is also said to have referred to Larika, which included Broach and Ujjain, and Alberuni mentioned it as Lardesh), Sindhu region, and over the areas of Pariyatra mountains (supposed to be identical with the western part of the Vindhya range west of Bhopal including the Aravali mountains) having amassed wealth by his prowess. He lives for 70 years and shuffles off his mortal coils in a sacred place through yoga and penance." These results cannot be taken literally true as these great seers have often veiled the basic planetary influences in symbolic language and one should take these *slokas* merely as hints and suggestions for penetrating the inner meanings of the planetary situations.

From the sloka however it is clear that the *Malavya Yoga* makes a person highly cultured, prosperous, rich and religious and his end is spiritually glorious. But these attributes by themselves do not reveal the rationale of including the combination as one of the rare yogas of human greatness (*Mahapurusha*). The clue for it lies in deciphering the significance of the activation of *Anahata Chakra* in spiritual development of a person with which Venus in *Malavya Yoga* is closely related. This energy-centre has the primary impact on opening the portals of one's affection and sympathies for other beings; it blends the individual consciousness with that of the world at large. When the heart-chakra known as Anahata chakra in Yogic literature is activated, the seer can succeed in raising his personal consciousness to that level wherefrom divine consciousness without any central core of personality descends on all. At this level one completely blends one's consciousness with the world around him. His heart pulsates with every movement of the universal life around him. He does not feel any difference between himself, other human beings, animals, birds, trees and in fact with any form of manifestation. It is a glorious experience when this blending takes place.

In modern times J. Krishnamurti has described* this state of universalisation and opening of the portals of one's heart when

(*) See biography of J. Krishnamurti and his experiences during Sun-Rahu period, *supra*; pp 221-2.

he indicated how he felt one with the distant worker labouring at the roadside mending the road, how Krishnamurti felt one with the worker as well as with his axe, with the road boulders and pebbles, how he could simultaneously vibrate the life-wave pulsating with the ant, flies, birds and the distant horizon, yet he was fully aware of himself but without any 'I-ness' in this experience. Such an experience often lasts only for a few limited moments but with activation of Anahata chakra it leads to the possibility of its being a permanent feature. The activation of Anahata chakra establishes immediate symbiotic relationship with all forms of manifestation and the one-ness of life begins to flow between them. The intensity and degree of rapport depends upon the energy radiated from this yogic centre, which is directly related with the strength of *Malavya Yoga* present even in this horoscope.

The blossoming of this *chakra* can be visually perceived only by clairvoyants. One can however understand the status of this unfoldment by studying the social relationships of the person and his interpersonal linkages in the energy-field. Seshan does not allow his emotional outbursts take a sway of his outer mode of social behaviour (because of strong Saturn's aspect on Venus) nonetheless he claims that there are at least 50 young people in Delhi alone who hold him in deep affection. When he attends public functions and address the people, specially the young-folks, the response he receives shows the intensity of immediate rapport between him and his audience.

Seshan himself experiences tremendous influx of energy from his responsive audience and feels tremendous responsibility to convert this radiation of energy into concrete social regeneration (or creative) force. This is precisely the result of *Malavya Yoga* reinforced by *Sasa Yoga* (specially formed by the Ascendant lord). Seshan's eminence is so remarkable that the highest in the land, though generally afraid of him because of his extreme uprighteousness had been thirsting for his sympathy, friendliness and consideration. The younger generation (the result of Venus) is so much fascinated by him that they adore him.

Seshan is forthright in his demeanour, but he is renowned for his spoken words too. His spoken words get him applause as well as admonitions from the highest quarters. Astrologically, Mercury is connected with speech, but it is also the planet through which the messages from the highest spirit is received on the physical plane and at the same time only Mercury has the power to transmute the experiences of everyday life into pure understanding. Much of the articulations of Seshan's spirituality in his personal life, as well as his insights into the inner motives and the manipulative techniques of different individuals which are responsible for much of the jarring impact he creates on politicians are due to the special disposition of his Mercury. In his chart, Mercury occupies Scorpio in Anuradha asterism; it is associated with Sun in the eleventh house, and in navamsa it occupies Libra (the sign ruled by Venus) along with Mars (the planet of fiery element with outgoing energy) and Ketu (which is extremely thoughtful unveiling before the individual the central core of every act of human behaviour and every form of divine manifestation). Moon, which is a planet of pure understanding, occupies the sign of Mercury (Gemini) and is placed in the sixth house related with innate faculties of the individual. Mars which is the lord of the sign in which Mercury is placed, is in Leo whose lord, the Sun, is in eleventh house, and there is mutual exchange between the lords of eleventh and eighth houses. These planetary combinations enable Moon (imagination) to faultlessly express itself through spoken words. His speech is fiery (Mars), full of enthusiasm and inspiration for constructive activities, vibrant with idealism which explain tremendous fascination and great trust of young generation in the leadership of T.N. Seshan; his words are also highly illuminating and instructive (Jupiter) and full of deep thought though not at all times couched in polished words (Ketu). Eleventh house also represents one's popularity, socialisation and gain. In analysing the personality of Seshan, it is significant to note that the various factors such as his status, family relations, austerity in living and integrity of character are the general background on which his 'mind' plays the most important role, it is the most effective instrument in the armoury of his personality.

Mercury is linked with *Visuddhi chakra* which primarily transmutes mundane experiences to resolve them in their spiritual essence and transmit the same to one's eternal storehouse of knowledge, ultimately leading the individual to enlightenment. It is also the channel through which the divine vibrations are intoned to make the subjective voice powerful in one's everyday life. Anuradha, the asterism in which Mercury is placed, breathes hot and cold at the same time. Its presiding deity is Mitra, who is the deity of friendliness and cooperation among men. Mitra as the light of the day is worshipped along with Varuna, the light of the night. The power which brings to light what is veiled during the night is found under Anuradha. Mitra is the light of the day that heralds the dawn, the beginning of new possibilities. At the dawn of the new life, the fruits of past labour yield their result.

Seshan's words, howsoever humourous and light-heartedly spoken are full of constructive suggestions and deeply felt truths of life. The directness of his expressions (Mars) is sometimes so disturbing that Seshan is much misunderstood and has to bear wrath of many high authorities. He was even asked by the Supreme Court to restrain himself. The Supreme Court Judges were once so visibly upset over Seshan's remarks on some matter that no sooner the court reassembled it asked the counsel for Seshan to "advise your client that he is talking too much and behaving in a manner unbecoming of a high constitutional functionary that he is". One of the Judges even remarked that "This person seems to have lost his balance". Such situations arise when Mercury and Moon are situated in sixth-eighth houses from each other, when the lord of the sign in which Mercury is placed occupies the eighth house along with Ketu (the planet of humiliation).

One also finds in the present case that the Rahu-Ketu axis lies between second and eighth houses. The latter represents the hidden, mysterious and the unknown depth while the former represents the beginning of the primeval creative impulse. Rahu in the present chart is situated fourth from Mercury, and Ketu, tenth: the most important aspect of Seshan's life from his early childhood has been the expression of his deeply felt emotions, convictions and impulses irrespective of the consequences likely to result from these. In all these important poles of his life, his idealism (Ketu), inspiration and devotion (Mars) and vision of divine immanence (Jupiter) resulting from the urge of discipleship (Aquarius) and creativity of the primeval energy (*Vacha*, speech) are pivotal.

There is a mission in Seshan's life: it is immaterial whether T.N. Seshan is fully aware of it or not, but the fire of idealism directing him towards helping the 'orphan humanity' in a special manner is an indication of the special mission entrusted to his 'soul'. This aspect of his inner life is revealed through special planetary pattern formed in his chart. In horoscopes of all such persons, who are assigned special mission to carry forth, the planets are aligned in a special manner.

In the case of T.N. Seshan, five planets namely, Moon, Jupiter, Mars, Ketu and Rahu are placed in those houses which are known as the *Mysterious Depth* (the second, sixth, eighth and twelfth houses represent the Mysterious Depth in every horoscopy). The fourth corner represented by the twelfth house is concerned with future life, while the other three houses are related with the eternal storehouse of the potential already acquired and earmarked to be developed during the course of any specific birth. The five planets situated in these houses are always receiving intonations from the past to work out in the present birth. Yet they cannot be accepted to be always pleasure producing: the impact of these planets would depend upon the benefic or malefic nature of past forces generated by the ego. They include not only the impulses generated by physical actions of hurthful or helpful kind, but also by interpersonal emotional relations as well as aspirations of serving the humanity thus becoming a channel of divine outpouring.

Secondly, three planets namely, Venus, Mercury and Sun, besides Saturn are in action houses (first, fifth, tenth and eleventh are action house, which determine the type of *karma* generated in the present birth). The planets in these houses guide the individual towards his predestined goal of his present birth. In determining the impact of planets on any one's enduring life, the life eternal, the planets situated in these houses are very important. It is from this standpoint that they are significant for determining the avocation of a person.

Thirdly, all the planets in this chart, excepting Saturn, Sun and Mars which have special significance in Seshan's chart are situated either sixth or twelfth from its own sign. Mercury is sixth from Gemini, Venus is sixth from Taurus, Jupiter is sixth from Pisces, and Moon is twelfth from Cancer. The sixth impulse represents divine expression in the realm of manifestation arousing reaction from the same as a result of this act of Divinity penetrating matter. Disease in this sense is considered as the inability of the body to respond to divine influx due to impurities of the physical constitution of the human personality; when these material impurities (which include impurities of the astral sheath as well) are sufficiently purified, their reaction results in unravelling various innate *siddhis*, perfections of the being. The twelfth or the final impulse is that of dissolution where material casement of the being is completely merged in after-death non-physical realm. The eighth impulse leads to unveiling of latent powers. These houses represent what in occult literature is described as the "trial of the neophyte" under which the person is tested and prepared for the confirment of the "Initiatory Rites".

Under the influence of planets in these houses, the individual undergoes various deprivations and ordeals which prepare as well as test the degree of psychological detachment attained by the disciple. These are very importat houses for those who are spiritualizing themselves. In Seshan's chart, Moon by its placement in the twelfth house from its own sign, while it is occupying the sixth house in the natal chart gets dissolved in universal Truth-Consciousness, which is identical with cosmic reality and as a result much inner satisfaction is experienced though there could be considerable amount of personal disenchantment (which in an ordinary human being would imply sorrow or frustration). Mercury, Venus and Jupiter in their respective fields of operation enable Seshan to penetrate in mundane grossness with his inner life-force to create a different kind of situation in consonance with cosmic consciousness or divine plan and in this process he develops extraordinary faculties, uncommon for a common-man but extremely important for those who are being prepared for some special divine misssion (especially in some future life).

The position of Ketu, Jupiter and Mars in Leo occupying the eighth house, indeed a very mysterious house, makes T.N. Seshan a deeply mystic person, who does not carry his occult greatness for displaying before the common public. It is under such planetary influences, that an individual acquires high order of Tantric perfection. There is every likelihood that T.N. Seshan has attained control over certain order of nature's subtler powers and is in close relationship with highly evolved Mahatmas, who are controlling and guiding human destiny. Generally, such persons are denied the pleasure of having offspring of their own, they are given material wealth which they cannot enjoy personally, their marital life is also beset with difficulties.

Yet they are inspired, often given visions of the future and they attain proficiency in several occult sciences. It is difficult to verify these conditions, because of their extremely personal nature. It seems plausible that Seshan would be devoting considerable time and energy in spiritualizing and developing his latent faculties and harmonizing himself with the super-physical world of nature's subtler forces of which he does not let the world know. His deep knowledge of astrology is just a very minor evidence of his occult powers. Accurate fore-vision of Rajiv Gandhi's assassination and Seshan's warning to Rajiv Gandhi of it about eleven days before its actual occurrence reveal only a little of his occult visions. It is on the support from the unseen world that Seshan is boldly trying to light a small candle in the realm of socio-political sphere to ward off corruption from modern India.

T.N. Seshan is a powerful personality born with a mission. The planetary disposition at the time of his birth has guided him to put the fear of God even among his bosses. He has been described as a strange man. Marching to the beat of some divine drum, willing to rattle swords with Manmohan Singh, the most powerful Finance Minister since independence of India and sup with Chandraswamy who had been the most controversial spiritual leader and Tantric of modern times, T.N. Seshan has proved his integrity and spirituality to such an order that even his enemies honour him with candid transparency. The chief motivating impulse in Seshan's life arose from the planetary combinations at his birth, but they also arranged effectively the gradual unfoldment of Seshan's personality according to their pre-arranged periodic rulership. The planetary rulership at different phases of his career effectively directed the journey of his life.

Seshan was born under Jupiter main period, which continued for about eleven years. The necessary ethical grounding was done during this period. The main period of Saturn started early in 1944 which continued for the next nineteen years to develop his personality. It gave him the job which could ultimately enable him to discharge his life's mission. Saturn is Seshan's ascendant lord, unaspected by any planet and enjoying the freedom of tenanting its own sign. It instilled enough confidence in Seshan early in his life. Being the ascendant lord, it also gave him the job he wanted. He was at first selected for Indian Police Service, but he wanted to join the administrative cadre. He got into the Indian Administrative Service as Venus being the lord of the tenth house had to provide him with a job in which he did not have to incur so much of physical hardships as required in the police service.

Saturn and Venus both conferring important yogas bestowed

their blessings to young Seshan early in his life. Within a decade of his serving in the administrative cadre, he drew the attention of Prime Minister of India and came close to Prime Minister Jawaharlal Nehru. During the sub-periods of Rahu as well as of Jupiter, he had to prove his mettle. During this period, T.N. Seshan was assigned a trying but the onerous task of censoring the mail to Sheikh Abdullah who had been a former prime minister of Kashmir and was incarcerated at Yercaud in Tamil Nadu. Sheikh Abdullah was not only a powerful political figure in his own rights, he was also very close to the Nehru family and thus enjoyed a special status and power even when put under restrictions. He had thought that T.N. Seshan was the usual young bureaucrat, who would like to be on the right side of political masters, both of the present and the future times. As a young officer in charge of the VIP prisoner Seshan went along the task of censoring the letters of Abdullah. Seshan was ususual; he was not the one to flinch from duty, no matter how unpleasant. This was not liked by the 'Lion of Kashmir'. He called Seshan and began admonishing him. "Young man, are you opening my letters. I won't have them", he said. "Sorry sir," Seshan replied, "I have my orders." It was too much for Sheikh Abdullah to swallow. The two glanced at each other for a while 'in a spine-chilling eyeball to eyeball contest', but Seshan emerged the winner. He continued to steam open the letters of Shere-Kashmir Prime Minister Sheikh Abdullah.

During the last phase of Mercury main period, usually known as Dasa-Kshidra, Seshan had difference with P. Kolandaivelu who at that time was a Cabinet Minister under M.G. Ramachandran in Tamil Nadu. In fact, Seshan's whole period as long as he was in Tamil Nadu is full of stories concerning his integrity and differences with ministers in the state. It was after Rajiv Gandhi came to power that there was a change in the official career of T.N. Seshan.

The beginning of Venus period brought him to the central government. He came to the Centre as Environment Secretary, stayed on to be Defence Secretary, and finally, attained highest position available for a civil servant by becoming the Cabinet Secretary. It was the influence of *Malavya Yoga* and his arrival in Delhi that a new chapter began in his life's mission. He came very close to Prime Minister Rajiv Gandhi and they developed extraordinary affinity between themselves. Seshan's term as Cabinet Secretary was very short, it lasted only between March 1989 and December 1989 but during such a short period he impressd everybody with his organizing capacity and integrity, and display of foresight. These qualities drew the attention of several political leaders, who wanted his support and to enlist him on their side. As Special Secretary to Prime Minister in-charge of his security, it was known that Seshan was a person of extraordinary quality and his services should not be dispensed with. So when he retired after his posting as Cabinet Secretary, Rajiv Gandhi had already lost power but V.P. Singh who became the next Prime Minister wanted Seshan to join the Planning Commission as one of its Members.

Much of the Venus-Sun sub-period, Seshan spent as a Member of the Planning Commission which was not very eventful. But V.P. Singh's government did not last for long. When Chandrashekhar became the Prime Minister, it is reported that Subramaniam Swamy who had been Seshan's professor at the Harvard University, U.S.A. from which Seshan had taken a degree in Mathematics, advised him to appoint T.N. Seshan as the Chief Election Commissioner. It happened in December 1990, but Seshan was not very agreeable to this proposal. It happened during Venus-Sun sub-period, and Sun being almost on the borderline between Libra and Scorpio did not enable him to make up his mind. Among the six persons whom he consulted on the subject, the advice given by Rajiv Gandhi tilted the balance. On this occasion, Rajiv Gandhi had a very good appreciation of the general disposition of Seshan and he also knew the dirty tricks of modern politicians played during the election. The Sankaracharya of Kanchipuram was held in great esteem by T.N. Seshan and when approached he advised Seshan to accept it as there seemed to be a hand of destiny in that. It all happened during Sun sub-period and the task before Seshan was enormous.

Seshan's very first year as Chief Election Commissioner was a period of great turmoil for the country. The government of Chandrashekhar fell, a fresh election had to be conducted and the Congress party was in shambles. Rajiv's assassination made Seshan very sorrowful: it was a personal loss to him. The election however continued and was completed, but the Congress government under P.V. Narasimha Rao could not take the Chief Election

Commissioner for granted. During several bye-elections that followed soon, Seshan was running Moon sub-period under Venus main period, and Moon is ninth from Venus, so it had to be a highly productive and creative period. The lord of the Moon-sign being Mercury in association with Sun and placed in second house from the ruling planet supported the initiative taken by Seshan in identifying some of the electoral irregularities and in plugging the loopholes.

In some cases, Seshan's forthright decisions even embarrassed the Government as it happened in the case of Pranab Mukherjee; it even provoked some of the contestants as it happened in the case of I.K. Gujral and others. Moon in the sixth house could not draw applause for his efforts, but the whole episode passed off as a minor irritant. The real nature of Seshan was yet to be unveiled. The sudden cancellation of Punjab election, only a few days prior to voting was the first major clarion call, which alerted the different political parties. Even the ruling party could not assume complete compliance or its absolute independence in deciding matters of such vital importance. But the militants were still at large in Punjab, and all the assurances of the central and state governments did not convince the Chief Election Commissioner about the total safety of the voters. There was grave apprehension that the wrist or the fingers of the voters would be chipped off by the militants and the security forces could remain helpless spectators. Seshan did not want it to happen even to a few voters as it could vitiate the entire election process. The decision got mixed reception: the opposition thought it was done at the behest of the Congress party which they thought had developed weak knee and had advised the Chief Election Commissioner to postpone it at the last moment, while the Congress considered the decision very unconventional and began contemplating ways and means to restrain the freedom and independent initiative of the Chief Election Commissioner.

An important confrontation occurred during Venus-Mars sub-period. As we have indicated above, Mars acquired extraordinary strength in this horoscope and it has exchanged signs with Sun. Mars is also placed in the eleventh house from the main ruling planet. Seshan could not be tamed during this period. The inflow of super-physical power had begun increasing and Seshan had begun carrying his mission like a completely dedicated and valiant warrior.

On October 1, 1993 according to some existing provision, the Government appointed M.S. Gill and G.V.G. Krishnamurthy making the Election Commission a multi-member organization and it sipulated that the decisions in the Commission would, as in the case of the Supreme Court, be decided on majority opinion. But T.N. Seshan would not have it: he was the Chief, his decision had to prevail, he was not even obliged to consult these Election Commissioners on every matter, and Seshan was a Constitutional functionary who cannot be removed without impeachment. The matter went upto the Supreme Court and the position of T.N. Seshan was initially upheld. Seshan did not fight for his personal glorification. (Mars was associated with Jupiter and Ketu) His success was certain. He soon earned much public applause when in November 1993 he succeeded in conducting a much incident free election in Uttar Pradesh. People at large and even the political parties began to feel that T.N. Seshan has taken upon himself the onerous task of cleaning the Augean stables of electoral politics and he has the capability of doing the same. Mars fortified as in the present case can never fail in any work of public interest in which the selfish considerations are absent.

People began to think over the fact that the election could be conducted in November 1993 without violence and booth-capturing in a state like Uttar Pradesh is evidence enough of Seshan's remarkable achievement. For most people, the main apprehension was not that Seshan acted in a whimsical manner, calling politicians and bureaucrats names and suspending elections at the drop of a hat, but that the system may relapse into the old corrupt ways after his retirenment. The situation was very critical for the country at large. For the mission that Seshan had undertaken, it was necessary to evolve a system from which corruption could be completely eradicated while the political parties wanted to perpetuate the electrol malpractices which could help them to manipulate the votes the way they wanted. The people at large were increasingly becoming disillusioned with the democratic system and were eager to stop the 'dictatorship of parliamentary democracy' and to regain the freedom of their individual choice. Seshan saw the "174 ways in which elections could be damaged". Seshan vowed to crusade to root out corruption from the country's electoral system.

Commenting upon Seshan's ways of functioning, one of the

national dailies editorially wrote the following:

> ...secure in the knowledge that he is irremovable except by impeachment, he embarked on a confrontationist course with the very bureaucracy of which he was an important member until recently. There is no denying the veracity of some of his remarks about the needs to stem the rot in the system brought about by the combination of cash, criminality and corruption—the three C's which he identified as the root of all evils. There is also no denying that public esteem for politicians is at its lowest ever. It is the yearning on the part of the ordinary people for someone, who could be fiercely critical of the vested interests and could speak without fear about the need to restore morality and integrity in public life that has been tapped so effectively by Mr. Seshan.

This articulation of the popular desire gave Seshan tremendous courage in fulfilling the mission of his life. Rahu is situated fifth from Venus, the ruling planet during this phase of 'Seshan's life's unfolding'; the sub-period of Rahu starting from early months of 1994 churned the life of Seshan fiercely and it brought about a stormy situation in nation's political history. The people wanted to fight the prevailing rot in the body politic, Seshan was prepared to spearhead the movement, and the young generation was receptive to his ideas. Seshan began to insist on strict compliance of the Code of Conduct during elections, strict control of poll violence and booth-capturing, and severe measure against 'bogus voting'. His insistence on Identity Cards for every voter after the end of 1994 began to upset the politicians. He began to take steps so that no candidate spent more than it was constitutionally permitted for his electioneering. Unless something was done against the Seshan's power, political manoeuvrings would not be possible.

So to chain the crusader Chief Election Commissioner, the Government introduced on June 14, 1994 the Electoral Reforms Bill, 1994 by which it hoped to provide immense power to the two additional Election Commissioners and to clip the wings of Seshan. A four days session of the Parliament was specially called to pass this constitutional amendment. The Bharatiya Janata Party president L.K. Advani stated that the Electrol Reforms Bill aimed at "cutting the chief election commissioner to size, would be a scar on the Constitution if passed by Parliament" and demanded that it should be withdrawn. When the Bill was discussed in Parliament, the Government was adamant that the Bill should be enacted in Parliament during the same special session. The four days session for the purpose which began on June 13, 1994 however failed to evolve any consensus on the issue and the failure to muster the necessary two-third majority forced the Government to drop the electoral bill and the House was adjourned *sine die.* Never before in the country's parliamentary history had the Government faced such a humiliation as on this occasion. The Government sheepishly moved a motion seeking leave of the House to withdraw the Bill on the ground that it could not get the support of sufficient numbers in either House to ensure its smooth passage.

As a result of this official setback, the entire opposition demanded the resignation of the Government for having called the four day special session of Parliament to enact the law and failing to ensure its adoption. The former Prime Minister Chandrashekhar said that if the Government had any sense of honour it should quit. The leader of the Opposition—Atal Behari Vajpayee said that he had been a member of Parliament since 1957, but never before had the Government conducted itself in such an 'incompetent' manner. He said, "It was not a question of the Chief Election Commissioner Mr. T.N. Seshan. We are not agreeable to many of the things he says. But he has certainly put the fear of God in the minds of even ministers, when they tour their constituencies". What he said later is more important, for it indicated the significance of what Seshan had been doing for purifying the democratic system in India in order to ensure real freedom to the masses by eliminating corruptive electoral practices. Vajpayee stated that "He (Seshan) would retire in a couple of years. What happens later? The Government ought to have viewed the question in broader perspective. Having raised expectations from this session and now pleading its helplessness to do anything about electoral reforms, the Government ought to resign". Leaders of Janata Dal as well as of the Communist Party of India also indicted the Government.

Rahu is a planet which gives some kind of mental worry in whatever one does, but it is also capable of bestowing immense wealth, renown and victory provided the individual has earned them in his past lives. Seshan was fighting a social cause and he had earned them in his past, as evident from the disposition of Venus as well as Rahu—so his success was a natural consequence. The outcome at the Parliament session made Seshan vow that he would continue his crusade to root out corruption from the country's electoral system. It was a task in many ways more significant than winning independence from a foreign power.

Venus-Rahu sub-period would last till the beginning of March 1997; Seshan would retire from the present position during this period. He is also aware of the possibility of relapse of the system after he retires. He is trying to ensure that a system could be evolved so as to deter the possibility of adopting corrupt electoral practice even later. Identy Card for the voters, model code of conduct for the contestants, strict reinforcement of the ceiling on electoral expenditure, video filming of the voting, mixing together of the votes cast so as to confuse the voting pattern and sufficient security arrangements are some of the measures being introduced by Seshan so that even after his retirement, the chances of corrupt practices are reduced to the minimum. Another set of measure relates with arousing the conscience of the people. He is urging the young generation to be watchful of those who are usurping their basic rights; he urged the youth "to get up and fight" Seshan's method of putting across his message is abrasive (Rahu), but the message makes a deep impact.

While addressing the Bharatiya Nritya Kala Mandir at the invitation of the Lok Swaraj Andolan at Patna, he exhorted his audience by saying "A member of Parliament misbehaves with an air-hostess in the plane 30,000 feet above the sky and I did not like it at all. But did you protest? If you did not, what is the difference between this MP and you?" Such exhortations have telling impact. (One should note Mercury, the planet of speech in the sign of Mars, and Rahu aspected by Mars and Jupiter. Such dispositions of planets would enable the speaker to make pungent, abrasive, emotional, and deep acting, though indirect and elusive, exhortations.) He wanted the students to rise to the occasion and uphold the banner of democracy. He urged them to step in to emphasise the fundamental values ingrained in the Indian consciousness. He urged the industrialists to refrain from funding electioneering expenditure of different parties.

The action of Rahu is deeply felt and it is *always* enduring, and during Venus-Rahu sub-period Seshan is trying to arouse enduring impulses. On August 15, 1994, he launched an awareness compaign for voters and called upon them to "awake, arise and fight". He emphasized that people without conscience have no right to expect a clean government. In order to arouse this awareness, the Election Commission will fund the National Voter Awareness Campaign and the programme will be implemented by non-governmental organizations. They will use handouts, cinema slides, audio-tapes and documentaries to educate voters about their rights, duties and responsibilities. Jurists and electioneering experts will speak in universities and colleges countrywide as a part of this programme. A 'training kit' including the gist of various acts and rules will also be provided. The central thrust of this programme will be to make every voter aware of his right to franchise and the importance of exercising it.

The two-pronged attack on electoral malpractices will reduce the malady to a great extent. Astrologically speaking, the results of the effect of Rahu cannot be avoided by any palliative; Rahu must eradicate the malady completely. Rahu is a karmic planet; it activates the past karmic propensities in the individual so that he could eradicate the same and learn the desirable lessons of life. Rahu can be propitiated by understanding its impulses and make necessary reorientation in one's attitude so that fresh karmic impulses do not have ingredients for future unhappy results. That is precisely what Seshan have presently been doing. He is holding the mirror of electoral practices before the nation and is almost forcing the different constituents of the nation to see for themselves the process by which they are augmenting and intensifying the national corruption at different levels and precipitating miseries of different kinds.

Even the biography of Seshan published by Konark Publishing House under the title *Seshan: An Intimate Story* by K. Govindan Kutty is Seshan's attempt to hold mirror before the various personalities, who came in relationship with the Chief Election Commissioner at different stages of his life's unfoldment. In fact, Seshan's life itself represents 'holding mirror of Divine Will'; the occult symbol of Capricorn, the ascendant sign in Seshan's horoscope, represents the impulse which emphasises '*Not mine, but the Will of God be done*'. And Seshan throughout his life has been struggling to reflect the Divine Will for the welfare of Indian society. Venus-Rahu sub-period has also been a period of serious setback for Seshan. Saturn's transit on Rahu, and Jupiter's transit on scorpio, sixth from Moon, made Seshan taste humiliation resulting from Supreme Court's decision equating Chief Election Commissioner with the other two Eelection Commissioners. But Seshan took it in his stride, believing that to be the God's dispensation. After his retirement, when Jupiter's sub-period begins to rule over his life, he would have earned enough spiritual merit and might devote much of his time in developing his latent faculties as Jupiter is placed in his eighth house, the house of secret mysteries and initiation in higher spirituality.

16

JEHANGIR RATANJI DADABHOY TATA

	Jupiter		Asc. Mars
Moon Ketu	*29th July 1904* (Rasi)		Sun Venus
Saturn (R)			Merucry Rahu

	Mercury	Mars	Asc. Ketu Jupiter
	(Amsa)		
			Venus Saturn
Rahu	Moon	Sun	

Popularly known as J.R.D. Tata, Jehangir Ratanji Dadabhoy Tata was hardly addressed by his full name: he was either JRD to the world or Jeh to his friends. In 1992, he was awarded *Bharat Ratna*, the highest civic award by the Government of India for exceptional contribution to nation building activities. On November 29, 1993, he passed away in Geneva at 7.30 A.M. (IST) at the age of 89 years and was cremated at his family mausoleum at Pere la Chaise in Paris, where JRD's parents, Ratanji Tata and his French wife Suzanne, renamed Sooni (probably due to her long golden hair) were cremated. The ashes of two of his brothers are also there. The mausoleum where JRD rests is also the resting place of famous personalities such as Oscar Wilde, Frederic F. Chopin, Jim Morrison and others. A year later, in 1994, the Government of India issued in his honour a beautifully coloured postal stamp. Such an honour bestowed on a person who often gave lift to strangers waiting for their buses at the stand who sometimes considered Tata a sympathetic and helpful chauffeur employed to some rich Bombayites and wanted to tip him, which JRD very politely declined without revealing his real identity, was an act which the Government did to acknowledge one of its really great sons. He was so great that no words could describe his real magnitude, his activities were so multifarious that he could not be categorised under any one label, he was almost *non plus ultra* in every activity he wanted to pursue.

J.R.D. Tata belonged to the family of the richest industrial pioneers of the country, and the Tata house of industries was renowned not only for its assets and size, but also for its quality of product, business efficiency and human treatment without any trace of any kind of industrial or political corruption. He was born in Paris, he possessed no academic degrees, but he was a nationalist and a patriot: he was one of the pioneers of industrial and economic planning, who along with a few other industrialists and financiers had prepared what is popularly known as the *Bombay plan* when Indian independence was imminent, but later on when he met Jawaharlal Nehru to discuss matters relating to Indian planning and industrialisation, Nehru often looked outside the window of his room, while Tata continued speaking. JRD was the earliest pioneer of Indian aviation; the story of Indian aviation, even the birth of Air-India began on October 15, 1932 when JRD landed in a Puss Moth at Juhu airport from Karachi via Ahmedabad carrying mail. He started Tata Airways which gave birth to Air-India International on March 8, 1948; it struck a blow to him when it was nationalised on August 1, 1953, though he remained the chairman. For a man who built Air-India, it was a matter of humiliation when Morarji Desai as Prime Minister of India asked him to step down from its charimanship without any apparent cause. Yet, JRD took these in his stride.

JRD was married to his Austrian-born wife Thelma at the age of 26 years. She was the daughter of a buccaneering Parsi known as Prince Viccaji and his English wife Muriel. JRD was captivated by her, when he espied her in the flat across the window of his room in the Taj Mahal Hotel. The couple had no children and in her later life she became an invalid, bedridden and unable to move. But her hauntingly beautiful photograph always adored JRDs working table at his Bombay House office in memory of their happier days. In spite of such sharp contrast in his life, JRD was never bitter. He always thought of helping others to initiate new programmes, set up philanthropic institutions and fund the causes which helped other individuals, the country and the world at large.

He always thought ahead of his time and worked in a positive manner. His futuristic mindset was reflected in his concern for matters as diverse as scientific endeavour and population. He funded the Tata Institute of Fundamental Research and sounded the first alarm bell of demographic explosion. He initiated what could later become the International Institute of Population Studies in collaboration with the United Nations in 1956. Such a personality who was a mighty flow of energy for humanitarian, social and economic welfare could not be just a matter of "synchronicity"; they are born under powerful planetary impulses.

It is often said that there is destiny for each nation and this is linked with certain great individuals. All great men of the world working in different fields, whether political regeneration, military conquests, scientific explorations, technological achievements, or religio-philosophical renaissance, they are guided by the hand of destiny which works through planetary disposition. J.R.D. Tata has been no exception to this rule: his birth, early upbringing, training, achievements and frustrations, bouquets and brickbats were all decided before-hand and expressed through the stars. And the destiny of India was inextricably related with him.

The emergence of J.R.D. Tata, who was born in Paris where he passed his early childhood and adolescence imbibing the best culture from the free society arrived in Bombay, the commercial centre of the country at a crucial period in the Indian national development, which without his contribution would have certainly been radically different.

Jehangir Ratanji Dadabhoy Tata was born in Paris on July 28, 1904, a decade prior to the outbreak of the first world war and more than four decades before Indian independence. At the time of his birth, the European civilisation and the French way of life in their delicacy, social demeanour and culture were at their acme of splendour. Experiments in aerial flights were successfully completed, but the future prospects of these technological innovations were still uncertain.

J.R.D. Tata was born at the early hours of the day, a few hours before the sunrise. At his birth *Punarvasu*, the seventh asterism, was rising in Gemini: the former was ruled by Jupiter and the latter by Mercury. Mars was also in the same asterism, but it had not as yet come up the horizon. The ascendant lord Mercury occupied the third house, the house of courage and initiative occupied by Leo and associated with Rahu. The ascendant lord was fully aspected by Jupiter, the asterism lord in which JRD was born. The lord of the second house, Moon, occupying the ninth house, the house of meritorious deeds, located in *Satabhishak*, the 24th asterism, aspected the ascendant lord. These were some of the planetary indications that a powerful ego had taken birth whose field of operation would be enunciation of progressive thoughts and freedom of travel in the open sky. His birth in a country where freedom of thought, action and expression had acquired special significance and the aerial experiments had attained its perfection could not be a mere coincidence.

Another astrological feature which revealed the extraordinary nature of his birth was that only three planets, Jupiter, Moon and retrograde Saturn were above the horizon, while all others were invisible. These are the three planets which are very important in the realm of physical manifestation: Moon reflects what is contained inside the mind of the divine, the plan of evolution, as represented by the nature of the Sun, Saturn concretises or materialises the abstract ideas and Jupiter connected with *Prana-Shakti*, vital air, flowing from the Sun directs this power to all forms to nourish and sustain their existence. We know in retrospect that JRD was not a theoretician, he was not a philosopher, he was not even a politician to manoeuvre, manipulate and mobilise public opinion in favour of his own programmes. He was certainly a visionary but he was one of those dreamers, who worked for concretising their dreams, put them in actual operation by providing life-blood to them.

JRD was primarily an engineer, he was primarily a planner who put his resources to the best possible use and achieved profitable returns; his mind soared in the sky and for this purpose he learnt aviation, organised air companies and flew the aircrafts. When any machine went wrong, he did not believe in instructing others as how to set it right, he changed himself to his *lungi* and overall, dismantled the machine and reassembled them. He was a practical person under the influence of these three planets, which made him a builder of the highest quality. His ascendant was *Vargottam* which implied that the individual was certainly destined to attain a high social status. The occupancy of the second house lord, Moon, in the ninth house leads to the same results. Such combinations proclaim births of important personalities, whose every turn in life would be intimately related with his destiny, *karma*, and his impact on the society would continue long after him.

The planets in JRD's horoscope are polarised in an important manner around the Sun on the one side and the Moon on the another. Such inner planets like Mercury and Venus along with Mars and Rahu form one cluster around the Sun; Saturn which represents the physical aspect of one's personality, and Ketu which is a shadowy planet imbibing the psychological experiences aroused by one's material attainments and conditions are polarised around the Moon. Even Jupiter is nearer to Moon than to the Sun. In the latter group, Jupiter and Saturn are in mutual *kendras*, cardinal houses; Ketu and Moon are together in Saturn's zodiacal sign, Aquarius. Moon is aspected by Mercury, the lord of the ascendent, and of the fourth house, the house of emotion. Saturn is aspected by Mars, the lord of eleventh and sixth houses. Saturn is also aspected by Sun and Venus. Jupiter, the lord of the seventh and tenth houses aspects Mercury, the lord of the ascendant which give much strength to JRD's intellectual contribution. The two groups of planets polarised around the Sun and the Moon are significantly related with each other. These relationships suggest that the meritorious deeds of the past reflected as the destiny of the individual, represented by the ninth house, where the lunar nucleus is located, powerfully supported the individual's prowess, initiative, innate capacities and natural proclivities. (The Sun around which another cluster is formed owns the third house).

As a result of these conditions, the mind of JRD—which he has inherited from his past is unique with intense adaptability, imagination and practical acumen (Mercury in association with Rahu is situated next to the Sun and produces *Vesi Yoga.*) There would be natural philanthropy in his disposition, absence of false sense of vanity in his nature and wisdom as well as aristocratic sense of aloofness in his demeanour. (Jupiter aspects the ascendant lord Mercury.) The polarisation around the Sun in which the ascendant lord and the eleventh and sixth lord participate in an important manner has also Venus, the lord of twelfth and the fifth houses, and Rahu one of the karmic planets. These planets mainly act on one's subjective nature, Mars however works as a link between the subjective and the objective sides of the life. As it is posited in the ascendant, it externalises karmic Mercurial impulses (Rahu is associated with Mercury) throughout his life in different realms of his activities with great gusto and enthusiasm.

The integrated influence of these planets which makes J.R.D. Tata not a visionary dwelling only in the imaginary world of ideas, theories and Utopias; every one of his dreams he wanted to concretise, externalise and establish on the objective plane so that their significance could be properly evaluated, weakness removed and the quality perfected. This approach to his various programmes made J.R.D. Tata one of the topmost industrial managers of the world. The five planets in the solar cluster have many other special features. The lord of the fifth house and that of the third house, Sun and Venus occupying the second house aspected by Saturn, the lord of the ninth house in a cardinal position in relation with Jupiter, the lord of the tenth house made JRD very extraordinary, sociable, rich, highly placed in social status and they provided him with enormous force to his speeches and excellence to his managerial skill.

The cluster of planets containing the ascendant lord, Mercury aspected by Jupiter, the lord of the tenth house, and also by Moon, the lord of the second house made his ascendant very extraordinary. No malefic or weak planet aspects Mercury, but it is significantly associated with the karmic shadowy planet Rahu. Obviously, J.R.D. Tata was born with some overwhelming karmic mission. As a result of the polarisation of planets around Moon and the Sun, Tata inherited the unique quality of detaching his thoughts, status, abilities and relationships with various persons from his personal emotions, duties and austerity needed in the performance of his different responsibilities. This detachment was essential for him, otherwise the conditions of the society in which he was born and lived were such as to sweep him away from his destined goal. The quality of detachment, objectivity, and psychological conviction were necessary for the fulfilment of his destiny.

J.R.D. Tata came to India after the formative years of his life were over. India, with all its problems and socio-economic backwardness was the country where he had to pass his working life and fulfil his mission. The success of his mission depended upon the bondage of affinity he could feel and establish with the country of his destiny. India is considered to have Virgo as its ascendant, the sign is not related with the country formed after the independence attained in 1947, but Virgo is assumed as the ascendant of the ancient India of which the post-1947 landmass is just a poor leftover. J.R.D. Tata as we have seen above was a Gemini ascendant and Gemini is the tenth sign from Virgo. The emergence and flowering of the personality of JRD had close affinity with the natural efflorescence of the Indian culture and tradition. JRD represented all that is truly traditional and asistocratic about the Indian spiritual heritage. On the other hand, Virgo being fourth from Gemini shows his emotional relationship and deep commitment and an intense sense of belonging to the country.

In the Independence chart of India, Taurus is considered as the ascendant. The ascendant of JRD is second from the Indian ascendant from its independence chart. Such a relationship made J.R.D. Tata a valuable asset for the country. He was expected to provide much creative outlet, wealth, ideas and constructive suggestions for the growth and development of the country. This impulsion in the life of Tata shows how natural it was for him to feel thrilled at the prospect of India attaining independence (without any partition) and to collect together way back in 1944 for the preparation of a blueprint—*A Plan for the Economic and Industrial Reconstruction and Development for India*—important industrialists and financial experts such as G.D. Birla, Kasturbhai Lalbhai, Purushottamdas Thakurdas, Sir Ardeshar Dala, and others. It was known as the *Bombay Plan,* and showed the foresight, devotion and commitment on the part of J.R.D. Tata. It was the first exercise on development planning of the kind attempted anywhere in the world, except in the Soviet Russia in a rough way, and on a much smaller scale. Even the Indian nationalists who later on, after the Indian Partition and Independence were concerned with the welfare of the masses had not, at such an early stage, realised the significance of planned economic and industrial development and the place of public participlation in the stupendous task ahead of the country. But JRD's vision for the welfare of an independent India extended much beyond the immediate time-horizon.

The ascendant in the horoscope of Independent India being Taurus which was the twelfth sign from that of J.R.D. Tata, it was unhelpful to him. Much of the post-independence political and economic programmes of India had been extremely loaded against the interest of all that J.R.D. Tata represented. He is on record saying that his suggestions and promises of assistance offered to the highest executive in the country, Prime Minister Jawaharlal Nehru were often met by the latter looking across the window and changing the topic of the conversation. The various programmes designed under the soical objectives of the country under the socialistic pattern of the society demonstrated this antipathy between the two. Astrologically, it has been the story of one-sided love, which is borne out by facts of the historical development of the country during the first fortyfive years of its development planning. The two did not have the harmonious rapport between them though JRD would be pouring his whole life-force (Sun) for the welfare of his motherland. The association of karmic shadowy planets with ascendant lord Mercury, and with Moon which owns the sign in which Sun, the lord of the sign in which the ascendant lord is posited, and the aspect of Saturn on Sun, besides the polarisaion of planets around the second and the ninth houses in the natal chart of J.R.D. Tata leads one to believe that the overwhelming appreciation for his contribution could be received only decades after his death, when he will not be there to justify his actions or to refute the charges labelled against him.

Gemini is the ascendant of J.R.D. Tata and the ascendant is

Vargottam which by itself is an extraordinary feature of his horoscope. The ascendant lies in the asterism *Punarvasu* and the ascendant lord Mercury occupies *Makha*, the tenth asterism. The dispostion of the ascendant goes to the root of JRD's personality. Punarvasu is categorised as female—implying thereby that the basic impulse energising JRD would be receptive rather than aggressive. It greatly enhanced his sensitivity of disposition; this quality is also accentuated by the aspect of Moon on ascendant lord Mercury. These factors make JRD intuitive of the various forces impinging on him and around him. It is a trait of his character intensified further by the polarisation of Saturn, Ketu and Jupiter around Moon. The symbol of *Punarvasu* is a bow or a house, while the presiding deity of it is Aditi, "the visible infinity". They make the person not concerned merely with his immediate gain, rather he would look to the distant future and long-range repercussion of his actions and programmes. He will be a practical idealist. *Makha*, the asterism in which his ascendant lord is placed, complements the qualities imparted by Punarvasu. At Makha, the human individual is bestowed with divine capabilities. The soul is informed of its divine mission and is stationed at the place wherefrom it can make its onward journey.

At this stage, the individual has to make up his mind, take decisions and direct the faculties toward the destined goal—the human soul has reached a situation, where the natural impulses guiding his progress cease and he is required to take a stock of his resources and regulate his own actions. At this stage, the soul in its individualised form begins to manifest outwardly its archetype. The transformation of ideas into forms induces the spirit to long for freedom lost in the process of manifestation. This craving for its lost original nature is expressed as ambition, and through restlessness, the arousal of the urge to recapture the lost paradise characterises this asterism. The combined effect of Punarvasu and Makha made J.R.D. Tata highly sensitive, intuitive and sympathetic to the needs of the people and the society around him, while Makha made him energetic, restless, ambitious, and zealous to mobilise all the resources at his command for the redressal of shortcomings around him and thereby fulfill his own destiny, the archetype towards which his own life was leading him.

While J.R.D. Tata was a visionary capable of taking a long-term and very extensive view of the problems and situations, he remained extremely practical and down to the earth. All his programmes and projects were well founded, viable, and able to succeed without any special impediment. As a result of such qualities, he succeeded well in managing his affairs so well that he became the undisputed leader of Indian industrialists, and the Government could not even ignore his ideas and opinions. The asterism *Punarvasu* means again the Sun, which suggested that the impulse for revitalisation of the manifestative process has been released once more. The ascendant at birth rising under this asterism implied that the individual born under the constellation would be very dynamic, positively constructive, innovative and sustaining the system. *Punarvasu* is very purposive, so J.R.D. Tata could feel that his life was with a mission. The concept of 'visible infinity' pointing to a kind of contradiction in meaning has reference to self-imposed austerities which the individual under its impulse would assume for the fulfilment of his mission in life. This explains self-imposed austerities, accepted by JRD in accordance with his views on his own purpose of life: he was extremely successful even in coordinating his ideals and actions. He was never lukewarm in sacrificing his personal pleasures and rights for the fulfilment of his ideals. He involved himself fully in whatever he did; he never accepted even membership of any committee or any position, which was merely ornamental: when he associated himself with any cause or any organisation, he did so in order to contribute his mite to it.

As *Punarvasu* means the birth of the Sun again, those who are born under this star have very special mission to carry out, as the Sun has a special mission to carry out in the solar system. Presently, it is merely an hypothetic question as to what would have happened if Tata was not born at the time when India was struggling to be independent and establish itself industrially: nonetheless, one could very emphatically affirm that in his absence the path for economic and industrial reconstruction and development that India took during the last five decades, if not more, would have certainly been radically different.

Mars is the planet of courage, bold initiative and tremendous strength and vigour at its command. Its placement in Gemini, the sign ruled by the ascendant lord in the present context, while Mars is also the lord of eleventh and sixth houses, shows that J.R.D. Tata was provided with much latent powers (sixth house) for undertaking extra-ordinary initiative with much enthusiasm (Mars) and much insight and vision (Mercury) which were very productive and highly profitable (eleventh house). These qualities made his actions very systematic in unfolding his plans and programmes whenever any new idea or suggestion was submitted to him. The Bombay Plan itself is an example of his detailed, constructive and futuristic thinking. Another example of this kind had been his creation of the personnel department in 1943 at Jamshedpur, where his main steel factory is located, when no statesman or any industrialist in India thought of such an organisation in such a great detail. As a result of the various schemes of the kind, which J.R.D. Tata initiated in his several concerns, at least 15 years prior to any labour strike in his organisation, one could confidently lay down that JRD was ever contemplating the mechanism, whereby the system could be self-regulatory and develop in a harmonious order.

Mercury is very important for J.R.D. Tata: it is the winged messenger of gods who carries their messages to human beings and those of human beings to gods. He is a swift messenger. He is so swift as to be related with thought and intelligence. Every creative effort requiring intellect, reasoning, flight of imagination and application of mind owes its basis in Mercury. Poetry is an aspect of this planet but more so with Venus: Venus provides the sensitivity and feeling while Mercury provides the vehicle of their expression, the language. Tata loved poetry but that was the result of Venus, the lord of fifth house in second.

Tata loved aviation, fast driving, skiing, all of these indicate the importance of Mercury in his life. He was the pioneer in organising air transportation in India. He was very meticulous about his literary expressions; he was never satisfied with his first draft and unless he corrected it several times, he would not like the same to be issued. These are the results of Mercury, but his Jupiter aspected it from the eleventh house and it happened to be the lord of the tenth house. The Jovian impact on Tata's literary efforts made him want to use his words as effective as possible for helping and guiding others. Even in his private conversation, he was more concerned with helpfulness rather than mere display of witticism, though he was very absorbing and witty in his conversations.

J.R.D. Tata was born under Mars main period of planetary

rulership lasting for about a year and a half. Mars as lord of eleventh house occupied the ascendant itself which bestowed on him good patrimony. He was born into wealth and culture: he was the first son of Ratanji, a cousin of the legendary industrialist Jamshedji Nasarwanji Tata. He was a child of the mixed marriage but was brought up in the Parsi tradition. He was born in Paris, which exposed him to a radically different environment and culture from what prevailed in India in early twentieth century.

Soon after his infancy, he came under the planetary rulership of Rahu which provided him the necessary foundation for his future mission. Rahu-Ketu axis always plays important role in every individual's life history and JRD was no exception. He was exposed under the mahadasa of Rahu to various experiences which created deep imprint on his psyche and conditioned his future life in an important manner. An important feature of Rahu is that it makes its impressions on the mind of the person and thereby alters the individual's attitude to other individuals and the society around him. Rahu in the horoscope of J.R.D. Tata is associated with his ascendant lord, but it is placed far away as not to overpower it by its affliction. So Rahu aroused such inner urges, which inspired him throughout his life for the fulfilment of certain innate desires and fructification of his innate capacities. While doing so, it influenced his approach to life and psychological frame of mind in such a way that he could never be spoilt by the abundance of money and wealth that came in his way.

Rahu associated with Mercury and aspected by Jupiter, aroused deep interest in aerial travel and respectability; Rahu's own nature made him isolated from his immediate environment making him feel that he did not belong to the place where he was at the moment; its natural feeling of loneliness, self-consciousness and the psychological limitations due to external conditions which characterised JRD as his basic nature were instilled in him during the planetary rulership of Rahu itself. As a child when he joined the school in France as well as in England, he was not accepted as one of their fellow students; he was made to feel that he was different. His teachers in Paris dubbed him L'Egyptien, and his British school chums called him 'Frenchy', because of the Gallic roll of his syllables.

Tata's craze for flying and aviation started when he was hardly four years of age and it became intensified by the time he was ten years old. During this period, the sub-periods of Rahu, Jupiter and Mercury greatly accentuated his intense attraction for aeroplanes and flying. The neighbourhood in Normandy, where JRD lived during his childhood helped in sharpening this interest because of the presence of an illustrious aviator Louis Bleriot, who had constructed a hanger on the beach near the beach, and was the first person to fly across the English channel. Whenever the flying machine of Bleriot landed on the beach, JRD's heart leapt up and he was thrilled to the core: his desire to take himself up to flying could never be substituted by any other passion in life. When the first world war occurred, JRD was already flying aeroplanes. His formal exposure to it took place under an English teacher E.D. Cummings, and on January 22, 1919 he received his first pilot's log book. This important event took place during Rahu-Venus sub-period.

Rahu's association with intellectual planet Mercury and aspected by imaginative planet Moon saved him from being drafted for military service and be enrolled for the officers' training course: Saturn and Mars did not have any aspect on the ascendant lord which saved him from such an eventuality. It saved Tata's life, because the squadron to which he was attached was marked for fight in Morocco, where it had to subdue the rebel chief Abdel Karim and where every one of the group was slaughtered to the last man in the ambush except JRD, for his father had objected to Tata joining the officers' training course.

The academic career of J.R.D. Tata had been very bleak for the reason Rahu itself is a planet of academic obstructions, but Jupiter aspected fifth house so there was some hope but Saturn's aspect on fifth house as well as on the lord of the fifth house made his academic career bleak. He was all set to go up to Cambridge but his joining the French military service thwarted the programme, and the refusal of his father to let him enrol in the officers' training course foreclosed the higher military training.

Towards the end of Rahu mahadasa, J.R.D. Tata was brought to India where his father initiated him in his business, for which he did not think even an engineering degree, a subject which greatly fascinated J.R.D. Tata, as of much use. Thus, on the eve of Jupiter's planetary rulership, JRD had come to India with his craze for aviation, fascination for mechanical instruments, and fondness for poetry and creative arts. He had come also with complete detachment from personal material advancement: he had imbibed the value of taking life in its stride as it unfolds itself.

The main period of Jovian rulership covered approximately the twenties and thirties from 1923 to 1939. Jupiter occupies eleventh house, rules tenth and seventh houses, aspects the ascendant lord Mercury and fifth and seventh houses. No planet aspects it, but retrogression of Saturn enables it to be influenced by its tenth hind-sight, which somewhat reduces its beneficence. During the main period of Jupiter, JRD got established in his profession; his personality grew in fullness and he got married. JRD's father was strict disciplinarian: he did not desire that his eldest son should be a spoilt child. He wanted the young master to be well equipped for the task ahead so that he could discharge his responsibilities with understanding and independence. Saturn's aspect on Sun and tenth house was a valuable asset in this regard. Before JRD was entrusted with the Tata empire, he was at first made an unpaid apprentice in early twenties. Later, John Peterson, who headed the Tata Iron and Steel Company (TISCO) handed over its charge to J.R.D. Tata. During Saturn's sub-period, he became the director of the Tata holding company, the Tata Sons Ltd, in 1926.

The sub-period of Mercury in Jupiter's main period of planetary rulership was very momentous for JRD. During this period which extended from 1927 to 1930, he met his future wife Thelma and married her; in February 1929, he did his first solo flight in a Gipsy Moth and a few days later on February 19, he did a 45-minute solo flight which earned him an aviator's certificate from the *Federation Aeronautique Internationale,* on behalf of the Royal club of India and Burma, which was signed by Sir Victor Sassoon in his capacity as chairman of the Bombay Flying Club, which made J.R.D. Tata the first pilot to qualify in India, holding Private Licence No. 1 from March 1929. Jupiter and Mercury are both extremely supportive to J.R.D. Tata: apart from helpful situation in the natal chart, even in navamsa, Jupiter occupies the Gemini sign, and Mercury occupies Aries, the sign occupied by Jupiter in the natal chart, (while Mars in the natal chart was in Gemini).

JRD was so thrilled about his achievement of aviator's certificate that he stated, "No document has ever given me a greater thrill. Added to the joy of having an aviator's certificate was the knowledge that I was the first pilot to have qualified in India with the very first flying licence". He was so excited about the aviator's certificate that when the *Flight* magazine of November 22, 1929, announced "the Agha Khan prize" of £ 500 for the first flight from the United Kingdom to India and vice-versa by an Indian, the 25 year old J.R.D. Tata entered the race for the sheer joy of participation in an air-race, the prize money being of no consequence to already the Director of the Tata Sons Ltd. When the race actually began, it was Ketu's sub-period and Ketu situated with Moon or even otherwise, never bestows any untainted material reward or honour, so his aircraft strayed off course by as much as 100 miles on account of a small fault in its compass.

During Jupiter-Venus sub-period, Tata's innovative genius and business initiative showing his foresight mingled with emotional involvement led him to found the Tata Airlines as the Aviation Department of Tata Sons Ltd. It was the beginning of an important enterprise even when India was under the British rule but proved to be of great significance when India became independent fifteen years later. On October 15, 1932, J.R.D. Tata landed in a Puss Moth at Juhu airport from Karachi via Ahmedabad carrying mail, which heralded the real story of Indian aviation and even the birth of Air-India, which in times to come became one of the most luxuriant air services in the world: it happened so because of JRD's special care and patronage accorded to its development. Towards the end of Jupiter's main period by 1938, J.R.D. Tata took over as the chairman of Tata Sons when there were fourteen companies in the group, which made him one of the richest industrialists with the most efficient managerial system.

The mahadasa of Saturn—true to its basic nature began to test JRD's mettle and moral fibre and began to slowly precipitate troubles and tribulations for him. Often, he suffered deep mental anguish, but one cannot say that he belittled himself on any occasion. There were chances when the highest executive in the country did not appreciate his contribution to the nation or his sacrifices for its economic and industrial reconstruction, but JRD never lost his faith in the nation, was never negative in his approach, and never humiliated himself. Slowly and surely, the gold in him began revealing itself whose realisation continued even after his death. Saturn's placement in the eighth house had to exhume his inner, hidden qualities, which could happen only when those items which he loved intensely were taken away and his heart bled. Saturn however happened to be the ruler of the ninth house as well, which bestowed some recognition of his contribution to welfare activities.

It was during the sub-period of Mercury in Saturn mahadasa that J.R.D. Tata presented in collaboration with G.D. Birla, Kasturbhai Lalbhai, Purushottamdas Thakurdass, Lala Shri Ram and others, a model of Indian planning known as Bombay plan, which showed that his interests transcended his personal business preoccupation: it proved his patriotism and displayed the sharp intellect he possessed. Saturn helped concretisation, gave concrete shape to his insight and ideas of national possibilities; the Bombay Plan was an intellectual exercise with business acumen and organisational requirements for the national socio-economic welfare which had to be faced soon after attaining independence. It was an exercise carried out at a time which neither the politicians nor the enonomists of the country thought of at that early time. During Saturn-Venus sub-period, he became the Chairman of Air-India Ltd (in 1946) and also of Air India International, when the Tata Airlines launched it soon after Indian independence, on March 8, 1948.

Saturn-Rahu period lasting for about 2 years and 10 months beginning towards the end of 1952 was quite disturbing for him. On August 1, 1953, the Nehruvian passion for socialisation executed a serious blow to J.R.D. Tata, and the Indian avitation which he had nurtured since its inception was nationalised. It came as a blow to JRD, but his passion for aviation remained unaffected. He still was the chairman of the air company on behalf of the Government. It was during the same period that he was made a nominated officer of the Legion of Honour by the French Government in Paris.

He funded the Tata Institute of Fundamental Research during Saturn-Jupiter, and sounded the first alarm bells of a demographic explosion. He also initiated what later became the International Institute of Population Studies in collaboration with the United Nations in 1956. During the nineteen years period of Saturn, J.R.D. Tata learnt much of life, he matured enough to survive in the chiaroscuro of changing political scenario, his wife's health aroused much concern and he became more outward turned as far as his social contribution was concerned.

The main period of Mercury's planetary rulership lasted from early 1958 to early 1975. Mercury as a lord of ascendant and fourth house was important, but its placement in the third house and the lordship of benefics not occupying cardinal houses tainted it a little. The political climate during this period was quite disturbing; the Government was initiating many regulatory devices to curb the power and initiative of private enterprises, specially of large business houses. J.R.D. Tata could not remain completely untouched by this political *tour de force,* yet it was the period when national and international honours were showered on him profusely. In 1958, he was elected the President of the International Air Transport Association (IATA). During 1963, he was made the Honorary Member of the Iron and Steel Institute, London. During Mercury-Sun sub-period, J.R.D. Tata was accorded special honour, when His Holiness Pope Paul VI on the occasion of his visit to India in December 1964 made him the Knight Commander of the Order of St. Gregory the Great.

Mars is situated in his ascendant and is eleventh from his ascendant lord Mercury; by itself, it rules over the sign in which the most powerful benefic planet Jupiter is placed. During the sub-period of Mars in Mercury main period, J.R.D. Tata was made the Honorary Air Commodore of the Indian Air Force.

Special honours were bestowed on him during Rahu's sub-period in Mercury mahadasa: both these planets are situated together receiving powerful aspect of Jupiter and Moon. During this period, Tata was made the Honorary Fellow of the Tata Insititute of Fundamental Research in November 1968, Honorary Fellow of the Indian Institute of Science in January 1969 and Honorary Member of the Rotary Club of Bombay. During December 1969, he was accorded the Madras Management Association Business Leadership Award; it is interesting to note that all these honours reflected the influence of Mercury and Jupiter. In fact, Rahu and Jupiter are so important for JRD that their periods witnessed abundant recognition of his contribution. Apart from being made the Honorary Fellow of the Aero-Medical Society of India, he was also awarded the prestigious Durga Prasad Khaitan Memorial Gold medal during this period. During Saturn's sub-period, in 1974, JRD was made the Honorary Air Vice-Marshal of the Indian Air Force.

During the seven year period of Ketu's planetary rulership, his equation with Government was very much scaled down: what happened to him during this period could have been considered serious setback and humiliation in the life-history of an ordinary individual. But J.R.D. Tata had by now become emotionally much matured and strong enough to bear severance of the last emotional link with Indian aviation, which he had nurtured from its very beginning. In 1978, when Morarjibhai Desai was the Prime Minister of India, he desired J.R.D. Tata to step down from the chairmanship of Air-India unceremoniously without citing any reason. For a man who built this organisation from its inception, such a treatment was very humiliating but JRD had to learn his bitter lesson of detachment: Ketu-Rahu period could have been the most disturbing for any individual psychologically and J.R.D. Tata was no exception. In his case, however, there was a redeeming feature that Ketu in the navamsa chart was placed in Gemini along with Jupiter, so the emotional setback was also accompanied with some palliative. In August 1978, he was awarded Knight Commander's Cross of the Order of Merit of the Federal Republic of Germany, and Tony Jannus Award from Florida, U.S.A.

J.R.D. Tata began his Venus main period in May 1982 when psychologically inauspicious period of Ketu ended. He began to take active interest in social activities. The Government of France, where he was born, promoted him to the rank of Commander of the Legion of Honour in January 1983. In 1982, on October 15, he commemorated the Golden Jubilee of Indian Civil Aviation by flying in Leopard Moth from Karachi to Bombay. The Federation Aeronautique Internationale which had granted him India's first aviator's certificate more than 55 years ago awarded him its Gold Air Medal in 1985. During Sun's sub-period, in 1986, he received Edward Warner award from the International Civil Aviation Organization.

After more than half a century's leadership of the Tatas, probably the longest reign in the corporate history of such a large industrial empire—the House of Tatas controlled more than fourteen companies, whose group sales had reportedly crossed Rs 10,000 crore, JRD now considered it appropriate to step down from the stewardship. On March 25, 1991, during Venus-Rahu sub-period, he passed on the mantle to Ratan Tata, his nephew. During the sub-period of Jupiter, J.R.D. Tata received the United Nation's award and the Government of India honoured him by Bharat Ratna, the Jewel of India, the highest civic award.

On 29th November 1993, he breathed his last in the shadow of the Alps. He died in sleep while he was vacationing in Geneva, where he suffered a kidney infection. He was ailing for two weeks and he wanted to return to Bombay. The Swiss doctors advised him against the travel, and his personal physicians could not reach him in time. By the time he passed away, the sun had risen in Bombay, but in Geneva it was still dark. When he died he was 89 years 4 month. JRD had desired that in case of his death abroad, his body should not be brought back to India.

J.R.D. Tata was born of foreign mother, he was born on a foreign soil, he married a foreign wife, he died in a foreign country, he was cremated abroad and the ashes of his mortal remains were cremated along with his parents and two brother in a Paris mausoleum, yet the most valuable part of his life was spent in India and for the Indians. He was indeed a *Bharat Ratna,* a Jewel of India, yet he was a Divine Messenger sent to this earth for putting India on the industrial map of the world. The association of Rahu with his ascendant lord with Jupiter's fifth aspect on them to a great extent provided a clue to his life's secret.

17

VASHISHTA NARAYAN SINGH

Asc. / Sun Moon Mercury	Venus		Saturn Mars Rahu
	2nd April 1946 (Rasi)		
Ketu		Jupiter (R)	

	Ketu	Venus Mars	Saturn
	(Amsa)		
			Asc.
Sun Mercury	Moon	Rahu Jupiter	

During recent years India produced a mathematical genius among the simple villagers for whom the universities changed their rules and regulations, and constituted a special board of examiners to test his calibre to find out whether a degree could be conferred on him at the very first year of his joining the college and without his undergoing the study of prescribed course over the stipulated period. He was, however, in spite of having completed the test successfully and having won several laurels throughout the world for his outstanding mathematical achievements, found recently begging at a wayside railway station in a remote village in a demented state of mind. After much difficulties, when the government agreed to look into the matter and help, the assistance provided proved so inadequate that he had to leave the mental hospital without successfully completing the treatment. When the last reports came in, he was still in a schizophrenic condition without much social interest or concern about his recovery and mental health. This is the story of Dr. Vashista Narayan Singh, who deserved special attention and recognition.

Born in a remote village in Arrah district of Bihar, Dr Vashishta was admitted as a special student at Berkley University in the United States, where he was conferred M.Sc. and Ph.D. degrees in a record period of eighteen month. His professor in the United States rated him as one of the most outstanding mathematicians of all ages, unique in many ways. Yet his patriotism and love for his family and people did not allow him to have his fruitful career abroad and he returned home after spending only six years in the United States.

After his return to India in 1971, Dr. Vashishta did not only experience a radical change in his life-style, he also underwent serious turmoil and catastrophies, which drove him to the lunatic asylum. On his return to India, he was given some posting at the Indian Institute of Technology at Kanpur from which he had to move out soon. He got a position at the Indian Statistical Institute at Calcutta and other prestigious institutions, but merely at a monthly salary of about Rs 1,200 or so. He married a girl from a rich family. His wife was educated and pretty. Yet within a few years of marriage, the couple were divorced. Dr. Singh was shunted from one mental hospital to another at times, even being kept a captive for want of full payments for the treatment rendered, till finally he disappeared in August 1986 from a railway train *en route* to the Military Mental Hospital near Bombay. He was discovered only in February next year in very bad mental health. He was then sent after much efforts with the government of Bihar to financially assist in his treatment to the National Institute of Mental Health and Neuro Sciences at Bangalore. Even by the end of 1994, Dr Singh did not seem to have been rehabilitated. He was reported to be without any institutional support and no sign of mental normalcy. The usual tendency of the people under such conditions is to blame government, society or marital incompatibility. But there are many other dimensions of the problems which are deeply metaphysical. For successful and effective tackling of them, one cannot assume an ostrich-like approach. The importance of astrological prediction, as it could be evident from an analysis of Dr. Singh's case lies in identifying such non-physical forces impinging upon the individual as well as upon the society in which one lives, though we shall not study the latter here. Even in the former, we shall be greatly handicapped due to absence of detailed personal history and precise astrological date. Our primary concern in this case study is to explore super-physical or planetary causation of various difficulties, which have arisen in the life of Vashishta Narayan Singh.

The exact birth particulars of Vashishta Narayan have been difficult to obtain. However on the assumption that some meaningful conclusions based on *Chandra Kundali*, the Moon-sign horoscopic delineation is possible, the following attempt has been made to examine a few principles of occult astrological principles. The general readers may like to know that there are many aspects of one's life, which can be realistically studied by Moon-sign as well as Sun-sign horoscopes besides the usual birth-time ascendant.

Dr. Vashishta Narayan was born on 2nd April 1946 at Basantpur village near Arrah in Bihar. On the basis of various photographs of his appearing in different reports and on the basis of his past life-history, I am personally inclined to presume that he was born under Pisces ascendant and his birth-time could be sometimes during the morning. As these are mere tentative assumptions, no attempt will be made to draw precise conclusions on their basis.

A rough tallying of directions that is of *dasa* and *bhukti* with actual events points to a balance of Saturn main period of a year and half. It roughly shows that with the advent to Ketu dasa in 1964 September he entered his spectacular career by joining the Patna Science College and he was given a seat in its Faraday Hostel, a very prestigious hostel for promising students. It was then that he was picked by Dr. T. Nath, who became instrumental in his subsequent placement at Berkley University and introduction to Dr. Kelley, the world famed mathematician. It enabled the simple village student to blossom into an internationally famous mathematician.

The importance of Ketu in Singh's career cannot be overlooked. The shadowy planet Ketu in the tenth house fully aspected by Saturn, Mars and Rahu from Gemini ruled by Mercury may be considered special in his case. This placement of Ketu under favourable support could possibly raise an individual to great mystic heights, but it is not so in the present case. The greatest benefic Jupiter located in an inimical sign and posited in the eighth house aspects Saturn, Mars and Rahu placed in the house of intelligence and emotional stability. Jupiter is itself denied of any favourable influence on it and is incapable of imparting any auspicious influence to ascendant. By its aspect on the fourth house, it intensifies materiality of the planets located there. It wipes out any spirituality possible from the planets located there. The aspect of Jupiter on these planets energises them to concretise abstract principles and impress them very strongly on mental plane. The strong material impact on tenth house Ketu capable of vibration on higher mental plane therefore arouses a kind of tension in Dr. Singh's mind, which destabilises his emotional body and makes his personality schizophrenic.

Furthermore, the sixth-eighth house-relationship between Jupiter and Sun generally shows considerable possibility of spiritual growth resulting in strengthening of higher nature in the individual, but it was not so in the present case. Mercury, the ruler of the fourth house representing emotional stability is debilitated in ascendant; it is not combust under the solar rays because of its considerable distance from it, but the proximity between the Sun and Moon is not a favourable situation. The tenth aspect of Saturn falls on this house. So one could expect that Dr. Singh could be experiencing tremendous restrictions on various aspects of his personality and the lack of psycho-mental stability caused by the weaknesses of the luminaries and non-coordination of mental activities and reactions could make him a depressive maniac and unfit for any organised mental avocation.

There are many forces which obstruct the intellectual absorption of higher radiance on Moon and make it difficult to reflect the same on lower material plane, often expressed as understanding of higher mathematical principles, nor could they uplift the mind (Mercury) to the opening of divine magnetic attractions. Dr. Singh therefore failed to have divine insight which was possible in the case of Ramanujan. Dr. Singh's mental plane of abstract thinking vibrated in consonance with the nature of Ketu in imparting to it abstract intellect so it made him a great mathematician but he was not qualified for higher mysteries of nature. His concentration and receptivity at this realm of asbtract intelligence enabled him to work out innumerable solutions to tricky mathematical problems which made him world renowned, but his inability to tap the higher spiritual forces disintegrated his brain.

Astrologers have been skeptic about the results of Ketu in the tenth house. Dr. B.V. Raman saw the possibility of religious merits and worldly renown during Ketu dasa if it was in the tenth house, but he was hesitant in granting it a strain-free life. Saturn's aspect could make the person even a scavenger, he thought.

These are some of the exoteric results of Ketu. Dr. Raman was here addressing very general readers and was not considering deeper significance of shadowy planets which becomes effective in extra-ordinary individuals. In the present case, one will have to go beyond the superficial understanding of Ketu and approach the problem from the inner or the standpoint of the evolving ego.

Describing the special features of Ketu, it has been stated that the process by which the soul's liberation from its mortal coil is achieved is signified by this shadowy planet. Ancient scriptures, besides several others gave it the name of *Adrishtaroopas,* that is the form which is invisible, and *Sankaram,* the God of Liberation. The way Ketu operates is actually invisible in the sense that one cannot know the process of its operation, but the effect is certainly is unmistaken and sure. It is stated that the planet assumes special significance when the ego is ready for psychological mutation. It makes the individual suffer for the actions of his past life. He endures much hardships, he has to work harder than the rest of his fellows, but he does not receive commensurate rewards by way of worldly positions and status. Such persons often work for an ideal and even die for an ideal.[1]

Discussing the nature of Ketu in tenth house, it has been indicated that Ketu is our critical faculty, seeking self-knowledge and self-importance in exchange for which it receives humiliation in the short run, followed by enduring recognition and respectability. In the tenth house its impulse often causes the individual to be maladjusted to society. However, his respect for others depends upon the real worth of a person based upon his inherent qualities. Since society in general favours the external forms of behaviour and the recognition of traditional values—despite spiritual contradictions between the hidden and the visible—an individual under the influence of Ketu will find most social interactions based upon hypocrisy. Much animosity and resentment will be levelled against the person. He will, however be considered quite intelligent with a very fertile brain having original ideas on almost all subjects with which he deals; he will be religious in the true spiritual sense of the term. His knowledge of scriptures will be profound and authentic, and his understanding of their esoteric implications and meanings will be extraordinary. Placed in Sigittrarius, Ketu shapes a native in a significant way even if he is quite disorganised but mentally very sharp. He will say and do things which his peers will fail to understand or appreciate.[2]

Based on these features of Ketu, if the life-story of Dr. Singh is examined, there will be no doubt that the shadowy planets indeed provided the fulcrum around which his whole life has been revolving. The immense mental unrest, the extra-ordinary powers of his brain, uncoordinated nature of his inner and external nature, thinking and behaviour, his marital and social incompatibility, his professional tribulaions as well as his brilliant academic performances, all arise from the special disposition of Ketu in his horoscope.

One has to recognise that Ketu is an intellectual planet and in a fiery sign, Sagittarius with its ruler Jupiter placed in eighth house it could be very enigmatic. Under retrogression, Jupiter acquires special mental power which has the potential of precipitating devastating consequences, if the vehicle of the individual

1. *Solve Your Problems Astrologically*, Bepin Behari, IBH, Bangalore, pp. 337-8, 343
2. *Planets in the Signs & Houses*, op. cit., pp. 119, 210.

and the society in which he operates do not vibrate harmoniously. It is for this reason that Dr Singh flowered beautifully and luxuriantly as long as he worked in the United States, but no sooner he arrived in India with his flowering mind, it began to wilt and finally died out.

In fact, Ketu bestows too much of intellect which makes the individual precocious and flower too soon. It relates the individual psyche with life beyond the phenomenal existence. This often makes the individual function in a manner with non-traditional ideal or approach. For such an intellect, it is necessary to have his physical brain strong, balanced and developed enough to absorb the vibrations radiating from beyond the realm of perception. If the brain is not adequately prepared, the planet leads to imbalance, aberrations and even insanity. *The Fundamentals of Vedic Astrology* mentions that Ketu creates turmoil and impels the mind towards deep thinking which finally induces enlightening results. It assimilates experiences and activates intellect, leads the individual to contemplation. Ketu's influence is more pronounced, when it is placed in sensitive houses. If functions on the mental plane.[1] In the tenth house, the role of Ketu is much pronounced, because it is the *Karmasthanà,* the house of one's interaction with the realm outside oneself, which is the object of one's specific birth. In this house, Ketu's impulse produces persons of great merit, devotion and religious susceptibilities. If Sagittarius happens to occupy this house, Ketu makes the individual quite disorganised though he is mentally very sharp. He will say and do things which his peers will fail to understand or appreciate.

It is significant to note that the fame of Dr. Singh began to shoot up with the beginning of Ketu mahadasa and it went out like a meteor at the conclusion of this planetary influence. It was in 1963-64 that Vashishta Narayan completed his Higher Secondary Examination obtaining first position in Bihar and was gracefully admitted to the Science College, Patna, where Dr. T. Nath took exceptional interest in him when Vashishta Narayan showed him more than eight ways of solving a problem while only two ways of solving the same were recognised by mathematicians all over the world.

1. *The Fundamentals of Vedic Astrology*, op. cit., pp. 108-110.

In Ketu-Venus sub-period, (Venus is in the fifth position from Ketu and directly aspected by Jupiter, the lord of his ascendant as well as the ruler of his tenth house, and Jupiter also happens to be in the sign of Venus), Vashishta Narayan left for the United States. He received his Ph.D. in Ketu-Mars sub-period, (Mars directly aspects Ketu and it owns a trine house as well). During Ketu-Mercury sub-period, he returned to India. (It was *Dasa-Chidra*, the concluding sub-period of Mercury in Ketu main-period; Mercury was also the lord of the fourth, the house of one's paternal home and one's family life and it was posited in the ascendant associated with luminaries.)

Dr. Singh's meteoric rise and extensive renown received a catastrophic setback on his return to India. With the close of the seven years of Ketu, difficult period started for him. It was so from the physical standpoint, though for the soul's growth, it was essential. Usually, Venus in the second house aspected by Jupiter produces a very pleasant phase of one's career, which was not the case with Dr. Singh. While everyone was expecting a brighter career, happy family life and comfortable home-life, Dr. Singh was confronted with marital discord, divorce proceedings, mental imbalance, non-payment of medical expenses and untold miseries at personal and family level. Venus in the present case, owned inauspicious third and eighth houses and is placed in an inimical sign. It is significant to note that the possible results of Venus in Aries occupying the second house are as follows:

> Venus, normally a very auspicious planet in the second house, loses much of its benefic impact in Aries. An individual with such a position of Venus seldom feels much gusto for undertaking new initiative; his interest in his relations is also much reduced. He begins to covet other people's wealth and marriage partners.[1]

When Venus main period began in Singh's life, he began to search for a reasonably comfortable position, he sought a respectful professional placement, but it was not what could give him satisfaction. He had to move from one place to another, from one

1. *Planets in the Signs & Houses*, op. cit., p. 37.

position to another. His salary was very meagre, several times below the expected emoluments for an academically qualified person. He got married during Venus period: his wife was certainly very pretty and sufficiently educated, yet the marital discord was so heightened that the basic love and affection of married life were denied to him which according to some opinion caused his mental imbalance, or at least it added to his mental problems. (Mars aspected the seventh house, and Saturn does so its lord Mercury). Venus-Sun sub-period, caused deterioration in the state of his mental health and he had to be hospitalised. (Sun is aspected by Saturn). Mars is associated with Saturn—its bitterest enemy, and aspecting the seventh house, it spoils the marital life and the placement of Venus in Aries adds to its malefic nature thus worsening the married life. Venus-Mars sub-period was very critical in Dr. Singh's life and the divorce was granted during this period. During Venus-Rahu sub-period, the Government which was contributing towards his medical expenses withdrew support. He was discharged from the hospital and during Venus-Saturn sub-period, he came back to his house looking for some effective treatment elsewhere. But his domestic condition was not comfortable and financial expense for his treatment was difficult to arrange. It was during this period that he eluded his escort to the military hospital from the railway compartment and got lost. He went into oblivion for the rest of the Venus mahadasa.

From this brief review of the various results of the Venus main period in Dr. Singh's life, it is apparent that the effect of this planet was somewhat manageable only during the first period of Venus bhukti, while the rest of it was only turmoil—both mentally and physically. Financially, his position was very precarious. It shows that the commonly expected results of Venus in the second house needed revision and much deeper understanding of the planet's radiation could only reveal its impact in exceptional cases which can be understood only by taking into account the various esoteric effects of other planetary impulses.

The disposition of Venus in the present case is vitiated by several factors. The following are a few important ones which deserve special mention. Jupiter posited in the eighth house being retrograde could give some results of its placement in the seventh house, but the seventh is *inter alia* a death inflicting house. The young Vashisthta Narayan had very affectionate relationship with his American professor's daughter. Their relationship was quite happy and marriage between the two was even considered a possibility. The seventh house representing married relationship and the tendency of Jupiter to occupy it indicated the impact of teacher, mental companionship and respectability. The marriage of Singh also showed all the features of Jupiter in the seventh house, namely respectability, good appearance of the wife, adverse professional career following marriage, as well as destruction of his personality.

Jupiter's actual position in the eighth house is not a very auspicious placement for it; its aspect on Venus from the eighth house, aspect of Mars on the seventh house, and the sign in which Venus was placed being that of Mars which is a malefic as far as marriage is concerned, all these contributed to marital unhappiness which finally ended in divorce. Venus in the sign of Mars and eighth from the house of marriage, while the seventh house belonged to Mercury, a eunuch planet aspected by inauspicious Saturn specially so for marital pleasure produced deep emotional strain to Dr. Singh. Virgo in the seventh house does not give normal importance to sexual relationship. The importance of sex to such a person is an expression of finer feelings in life and a means to establish a closer bond between two persons.

The native has his own individual code of behaviour and ethics. His creative faculties blossom when his urge to win the object of his love is aroused. Vashishta Narayan pined for his wife's companionship, affectionate appreciation and her assistance in his professional career and intellectual pursuits. These when denied, upset him to a large extent. Moreover, the lord of the seventh house Mercury in its depression sign Pisces did not mitigate the situation. The brittleness of the marriage could therefore easily snap the bond. To a serious astrological student, it is no surprise that the entire period of Venus had been troublesome to Dr. Singh.

It is also noteworthy that all the planets are adversely placed in relation with Venus. The Sun, Moon and Mercury are in twelfth from it, while Saturn, Mars and Rahu are in third position from it. Jupiter in retrogression occupies its inimical sign Libra and is in eighth position from the ascendant. Only when Venus dasa ended that one could hope for any change in Dr. Singh's life. But even Sun is adversely placed. Jupiter, the planet which owns the

Sun-sign is extremely unhelpful; Saturn aspects the ascendant; Sun owns the sixth house; and Moon's proximity to it reduced its power to bestow peace and satisfaction. For several years to come, there was no redemption for Dr. Vashishta Narayan Singh.

Students of esoteric astrology wish to enquire the reasons for the occurence of serious catastrophes in the life of Dr. Singh from the standpoint of his egoic growth and unfoldment. These students know that the higher trinity represented by Sun (Atma), Moon (Buddhi), and Mercury (Manas) must be in harmony and well coordinated for inner development of the person. In the present case, there is great closeness between the three. The Sun and Moon are almost conjuct, which may to a mundane astrologer give certain clues to his mental aberrations, specially when they are associated with debilitated Mercury, yet one may not forget the special results of *Budha-Aditya Yoga*, the combination of the Sun and Mercury, which makes a person highly intelligent, skilful in all works, good reputation, personal respect and surrounded by all comforts and happiness. The togetherness of Sun and Mercury is very significant for mental activity. But when the three planets are associated together, one could expect great mystic interplay of higher forces: Mystic Initiations are usually possible only under such conditions. This highly occult interplay of planetary forces is accentuated by Saturn's aspect from the fourth house which also happens to be the sign of Gemini owned by Mercury which itself is in the ascendant and associated as one of the three planets in the ascendant.

On the physical plane, Saturn in Gemini in the fourth house leads to very difficult conditions: it makes the native's mental attitude uncongenial to others. A break in education, trouble with one's elders, abandonment by one's siblings and no mental pleasure make the person unhappy in any social circle. His heart is so often broken that very little resolve is left to help him express courage and strength. Often losing his money, he may become a miser as well.

But on the higher planes, a disillusionment with existing conditions of existence, renunciation of everything material, and great abhorrence for physical existence qualify the individual to cry for divine benediction and succour for which he could seek admission at great personal and physical peril into divine mysteries. But such mental stirrings and craving for divine light can be fruitfully accomplished only when the various physical sheaths of the individual represented by lower quaternary are well organised. This is known from the disposition of Saturn, Jupiter, Mars and Venus. In the present case, these planets are very disharmoniously placed. Jupiter aspects Saturn and Mars, but these two planets are very destructively placed. Jupiter's protective power mitigates the adverse relationship between Mars and Saturn only marginally. Venus, which forms an important bridge between the physical and the inner self and whose harmony with Mercury, Moon and Sun is essential for superamental influence to penetrate the lower sheaths constructively is very adversely situated in the chart. Jupiter which absorbs Vital Air, *Prana Vayu* essential for the maintenance of physical body in the present case is greatly disturbed, because of its retrogression, its position in the eighth house, and its adverse placement with regard to ascendant to which it is not lending any significant support though it happens to own that sign.

As a result of this situation of the four planets, namely Saturn, Jupiter, Mars and Venus, the human individual becomes weak to absorb the higher divine outpourings and this weakness of the lower quaternary made the life of Dr. Singh very disorganised and incapable of producing a perfect integration between his various sheaths harmoniously with its higher triad, namely the Sun, Moon and Mercury representing Atma-Buddhi-Manas.

The symptoms of disorganisation are evident even otherwise. Most of the planets in the chart are very adversely placed. The Sun is in the eighth house from its own sign. Moon is almost conjunct with Sun. Venus is in the twelfth position from its sign Taurus. Mars is in its inimical sign. Jupiter is in eighth place from its sign Pisces. Saturn is in the sixth position from its Capricorn sign. These placements evolve a pattern of planetary conjuncture, which is very unfavourable for the individual in receiving planetary support for his self-development.

Again one finds that the horoscope hinges around Ketu and Venus. All the planets are adversely placed in relation with Venus while in relation to Ketu they are placed in an important manner. The Sun, Moon and Mercury are placed in fourth place from Ketu, Venus occupies the fifth house from it, Saturn, Mars and Rahu are in seventh position from it. Jupiter, the best benefic of the planetary system, is from Ketu either in tenth or eleventh position depending upon its position one assumes in view of its retrogression and in both the placements it provides to it helpful influence. But the highly abstract, metaphysical results of these placements can be effective and harmonious only when the brain consciousness of the individual is well harmonised and is capable of absorbing the higher impulses (due to radiation from Ketu), store them in the brain, and gradually let them flow to the physical consciousness. These conditions, as we have seen above, due to disorganised lower quaternary are not available to Dr. Singh. The inability to vibrate to higher spiritual outpourings of divine forces has in fact, led to schizophrenic symptoms in Dr. Singh which probably cannot respond effectively to any physical medication.

The task ahead for the egoic growth and progress for Vashishta Narayan Singh is to harmonise the Buddhic consciousness related to Moon. This planet is placed ninth from its sign Cancer, sixth from Jupiter and placed along with Sun. It shows the possibility of unveiling the latent powers in Dr. Singh due to Jupiterian influence, but it requires that the physical sheath ruled by Saturn is completely purified and well integrated to enable the spiritual influence to sink deep down in him.

Here comes the necessity of cultivating *Yama*, namely, non-violence, truthfulness, honesty, sexual continence, and non-possessiveness, and *Niyama* which comprised purity, contenment, austerity, study leading to self-awareness and surrender to the Supreme, which begin the purificatory practices for the various sheaths of the individual. Deep meditation for mental stability, strengthening of Moon and for securing occult advantages of Sun-Moon conjunction and absorption of Vital Air received in various forms and radiated by Jupiter will enable the individual to integrate his physical and astral sheaths by strengthening the etheric veil or the *Pranamaya Kosha*.

During the Sun main period (Sun is the lord of the sixth house representing man's latent powers) if the doctors are able to let him see the immense potential lying within, and if the ethical and spiritual values gradually dawn on him, then there is a great possibility for Vashishta Narayan's recovery and balanced life. Such an important task will probably be beyond the competence of a medical doctor, but in case the benediction of some seer and divine saint is drawn and Dr. Singh agrees to be with the seer for some time, there could be a new orientation in his life. Only a yogi could help Dr. Singh if he could surrender to him completely.

His story reveals the strong need for ethical and moral values to be inculcated in life which must go along with intellectual development. Otherwise, catastrophic development in the individual would inevitably result.

GLOSSARY

Acharya: A holy teacher, one who instructs in the Vedas.

Aditi: Free, unbound; Infinity. The mother of Adityas; the Eternal Space or the boundless whole.

Aditya(s): The Sun, a son of Aditi. Adityas were eight or twelve Suns, the sons of Aditi taken collectively.

Agni: God of fire, one of the three Vedic deities namely, Agni, Vayu (air) and Surya (Sun), who respectively preside over earth, air and sky. Agni appears in three phases—in heaven as the sun, in mid-air as lighting, on earth as ordinary fire. Agni is the source of all warmth and energy in all forms of manifestation.

Ahamkara: Egotism, selfishnes. In Vedanta, the same as ignorance, the cause of manifestation. In Sankhya, it is the third of the twenty-four *tattwas.*

Akasha: Sky, space, ether of the five elements. The primordial substance or spiritual essence which pervades all space.

Amrita: Nectar of Immortality. The elixir of life obtained finally at the 'churning of the ocean' in which gods and demons both were engaged.

Antahkaran: The heart, soul; the seat of thought and feeling, thinking faculty, mind, consciousness. Mind in general including Buddhi, Manas and Cita as the main instrument of manifestation for soul or Purusha.

Artha: Object, purpose, aim, significance, import; attainment of wordly riches; one of the four ends of human life, the other three being *kama* (Passion), *dharma* (righteousness), and *moksha* (Liberation).

Ashtakavarga: The eight sources of strength for a planet used mainly for assessing the effect of a transiting planet in different signs in a natal chart.

Atma: Divine Self, Soul, Spirit, Essence; the seventh principle in man, often translated as *Ego.*

Avatar: Incarnation of Vishnu; reappearance of the supreme spirit or gods on the earth.

Ayanamsa: Precessional distance

Bhava: House

Bhratru-karaka: Significator of brother.

Bhukti: Sub-period of a planetary rulership.

Brahma: The Creator, the first member of the Hindu triad or *Trimurti,* the other two being *Vishnu,* the preserver, and *Mahesh,* the destroyer. The supreme spirit manifested as the active creator of the universe.

Brahmin: The first of the four castes in ancient India; the sacerdotal class, the members of which were learned in sacred scriptures and lived a very pious life.

Buddhi: Comprehension, intelligence; identified with *mahat,* the second of the twentyfour *tattwas.* Also stated to be universal soul or mind, and the spiritual soul in man, the vehicle of *Atma.*

Bythos: A gnostic term meaning "depth" or the "great deep". It is equivalent to space, before anything had formed in it from the primordial atoms that exist eternally in its spatial depths.

Chakras(s): Circle, potter's wheel or wheel of a carriage. A cycle of Time. Vishnu's disc. The seven force-centres in the subtle bodies activated by the *kundalini shakti.*

Dasa: Planetary period of rulership. Its sub-periods are called *antar-dasa* or *bhukti;* synonyonous with mahadasa.

Dharma: Religious injunctions, one's moral duty, religion, ethical conduct. Righteous deeds as one of the four goals of human life.

Durga: The goddess as the saviour or rescuer from all difficulties; she rides on a lion.

Fohat: A term used to represent the active (male) potency of the *Shakti* (female reproductive power) in nature. The essence of cosmic electricity. An occult Tibetan term for *Daiviprakriti,* primordial light: and in the universe of manifestation the ever-present electrical energy and ceaseless destructive and formative power.

Guna: Quality, characteristic or property of substances. Three primary *Gunas* are *Sattwa,* harmony; *Rajas,* activity; and *Tamas,* sloth or inertia.

Hiranyagarbha: Shining , resplendent, the golden egg; the nuclear matrix from which Brahma was born. Mother nature in essence.

Jagadamba: The World Mother.

Kala Purusha: Spirit or personification of Time. In Hindu astrology, all personal predictions are made by relating the planetary positions with various impulses generated by the kala purusha.

Karma: Action, duty, fate. Consequences of actions done in former lives; the law cause and effect or ethical causation. Destiny towards which each individual is being constantly pulled. It is also known as Cosmic Man.

Karmasthana: The house-division in a natal chart from which conditions of human interaction in the present birth is predicted; the house of profession or the tenth house.

Kendra: The centre; the cardinal houses namely first,

	fourth, seventh and tenth in a horoscope.
Kosha (s) :	Sheaths. Coverings around the human body said to be like seven veils through which different consciousness producing energies such as *prana*, desire, etc circulate and give the feeling of I-ness.
Kundali:	The horoscope.
Kundalini:	The Serpent Fire; the form of the Devi or female cosmic force. It is seven layered power residing in the base of the spine. In its milder form, it is the nerve force, while its deeper aspects quicken the *chakras*, force centres. It rises and energises the seven chakras and unfolds different psychic powers, finally reaching the crown chakra at the topmost part of the head gives enlightenment.
Lagna:	Ascendant.
Lassi:	A favourite drink prepared from milk and curd, popular in Haryana and Punjab.
Lungi:	Dhoti-like dress for male; a piece of textile tied round the loin.
Mahat:	Literally, the great one, the finest principle of cosmic mind and intelligence; the second of the twentyfour tattwas of the Samkhya philosophy.
Manas:	Mind, intelligence; the thinking principle or synthesising sense, which organises and relates the sense organs with the sense objects. When unqualified, it means the Higher Self or spiritual soul in contradiction to its human reflection—*Kama Manas.*
Mandal:	A tantric ritual, symbol in which the cosmos/universe is represented in various circles and geometrical forms.
Manu:	Vedic original man or father of the human race; a cosmic progenitor.
Material Triangle:	Seventh (apex), eleventh and third houses in a natal chart.
Maya:	Illusion, enchantment, unreality. Philosophically, matter, wealth and various other objects of worldly

attachment. Another name of *Prakriti* (matter) in some philosophical system.

Moksha: Liberation, emancipation of the soul from cycle of birth and death, *Nirvana*; after-death state of rest and bliss. Liberation as the last of the four goals of human life.

Mridanga: A musical instrument.

Mrityusanjivani: Ambrosial drink which revives life of the already dead persons.

Mystic Depths: Second, sixth, eighth and twelfth houses in a natal chart.

Nakshatra(s): Twentyseven lunar asterisms or mansions of the Moon.

Navamsa Kundali: Natal chart with planets in one-ninth portion of a zodiacal sign.

Pada: One quarter.

Pitrukaraka: The significator of father.

Prajapati: Lord of creation, proprietor, governor. An epithet of Brahama, who first created seven and then ten prajapatis who superintended the creative process of the universe.

Prakriti: Prinçiple of materiality or objective existence, the passive or feminine creative principle, Mother Nature.

Prarabdha: Portion of the karmic forces allotted to be worked out in a specific birth.

Puja/Pooja: Devotional, ritualistic and reverential worship of a deity.

Purusha: A male or man; the positive generative force. The spirit or the supreme being, Atman. In Sankhya, Purusha as a soul is the inactive witness of prakriti.

Putra-karaka: Significator of offspring.

Rajas: Activity, energy, agitation; the second of the three constituent qualities of matter, very predominant in man. It gives motivation and ambition to human beings.

Retrogression: Backward orbital motion of any celestial object. Although, the planets move always in the same direction round the Sun, the apparent motion as seen from the Earth is not always in the same forward direction. They sometime *appear* (not in reality) to move also in the backward direction, which happens due to relative motion of the Earth and the planent in their orbit around the Sun.

Samsara: The mundane existence; the world.

Shakti: Divine feminine power.

Shloka: Stanzas or a complete (Vedic) *mantra.*

Siddhis: Accomplishment, fulfilment, perfection; superhuman faculties gained through yogic practices.

Spiritual Triangle: Ascendant (apex), fifth and ninth houses in a natal chart.

Sunya: Void, complete blanknes

Swarga: The heaven world.

Swayamvar: Self-selection of a husband by the bride.

Tamas: Darkness, dullness, inertia. An epithet of Rahu, the ascending node of the Moon; one of the three *gunas* of matter.

Tapas: Warmth, penance, austerity. Meditation with self-denial.

Tapasya: The act of practising tapas.

Trikona: Trine Houses in a horoscope namely, first, fifth and ninth houses; it also includes ascendant though it is also considered as a cardinal house.

Vargottam: A planet occuping the same zodiacal sign in both the natal chart as well as in *navamsa chart.*

Varuna: Vedic God of heaven and the cosmic ocean; the divine father

Vasus: A class of Vedic deities eight in number. They are grouped as eight suns.

Vedanga: Limbs of the Vedas. Vedangas are six, namely, *Siksha,* the science of pronunciation (or of teaching), *Chandas,* the science of prosody, *Vyakarana,* grammar, *Nirukta,* etymology, *Jyotish,* astrology including astronomy, and *Kalpa,* ritual.

Yama: God of the Dead; a son of Sun. In yoga literature, it refers to certain austerities meant for self purification.

Yojan: An ancient measure of distance.

Yojana: Planning.

SELECT BIBLIOGRAPHY

Behari, Bepin: *A Study in Astrological Occultism*, IBH Prakashan, Bangalore

Esoteric Principles of Vedic Astrology, Ranjan Publications, New Delhi

Solve Your Problems Astrologically, IBH Prakashan, Bangalore

Myths and Symbols of Vedic Astrology, Passage Press, Utah, U.S.A.

The Fundamentals of Vedic Astrology, Passage Press, Utah, U.S.A.

Planets in the Signs & Houses, Passage Press, Utah, U.S.A.

Behari, Madhuri and Bepin: *An Introduction to Esotoric Astrology*, Sagar Publication, New Delhi

Besant, Annie and Leadbeater, C.W. : *48 Lives of Alcyone*, TPH, Madras

Blavatsky, H.P: *Isis Unveiled*, Vols. I & II, Theosophy University Library, California

The Secret Doctrine, Vols. I-VI, TPH, Madras

Brihat Jatak (Sanskrit Text by Varaha Mihira, English translation by V. Subrahmanya Sastri) Government Press, Mysore

Brihat Parashar Hora Shastram (Sanskrit Text by Sage Parashar, Hindi translation by pandit Devachandra Jha), Chaukhambha Sanskrit Sansthan, Varanasi

Cerminara, Gina: *Many mansions*, Neville Spearman, London

Jung, Carl G. *Psychology and Alchemy*, Pantheon Books, London

Mees, G.H.: *The Revelation in the Wilderness*, Vols. I-III, Kanvashrama Trust, Tiruvannamalai, Mounalayam-606603, India

Raman, B.V.: *Notable Horoscopes*, Raman Publication, Bangalore

Hindu Predictive Astrology, Raman Publication, Bangalore

Redfield, James: *The Celestine Prophecy*, Warner Books, New York

Sankaracharya, Adi Guru, *Viveka Cudamani* (English translation by P. Sankaranarayanan), Bharatiya Vidya Bhawan. Bombay

Santhanam, R.: *Essentials of Predictive Astrology*, Sagar Publications, New Delhi

Sinha, Deokinandan: *Jyotish Ratnakar* (Hindi), Motilal Banarsidass, Delhi

Subba Row, T.: *Esoteric Writings*, T.P.H. Madras

Uttar Kalamrita (Sanskrit text by Kalidasa—English translation by V. Subrahmanya Shastri) Sadhana Press, Bangalore

Index